Recent Advances in
Fractional Calculus

Recent Advances in Fractional Calculus

Editors

Péter Kórus
Juan Eduardo Nápoles Valdés

Basel • Beijing • Wuhan • Barcelona • Belgrade • Novi Sad • Cluj • Manchester

Editors

Péter Kórus
Institute of Applied Pedagogy
Juhász Gyula Faculty
of Education
University of Szeged
Szeged
Hungary

Juan Eduardo Nápoles Valdés
Facultad de Ciencias Exactas
y Naturales y Agrimensura
Universidad Nacional
del Nordeste
Corrientes
Argentina

Editorial Office
MDPI
St. Alban-Anlage 66
4052 Basel, Switzerland

This is a reprint of articles from the Special Issue published online in the open access journal *Axioms* (ISSN 2075-1680) (available at: www.mdpi.com/journal/axioms/special_issues/Axioms_Fractional_Calculus).

For citation purposes, cite each article independently as indicated on the article page online and as indicated below:

Lastname, A.A.; Lastname, B.B. Article Title. *Journal Name* **Year**, *Volume Number*, Page Range.

ISBN 978-3-7258-1238-7 (Hbk)
ISBN 978-3-7258-1237-0 (PDF)
doi.org/10.3390/books978-3-7258-1237-0

© 2024 by the authors. Articles in this book are Open Access and distributed under the Creative Commons Attribution (CC BY) license. The book as a whole is distributed by MDPI under the terms and conditions of the Creative Commons Attribution-NonCommercial-NoDerivs (CC BY-NC-ND) license.

Contents

About the Editors vii

Péter Kórus and Juan Eduardo Nápoles Valdés
Recent Advances in Fractional Calculus
Reprinted from: *Axioms* **2024**, *13*, 310, doi:10.3390/axioms13050310 1

Ogbu F. Imaga, Samuel A. Iyase and Peter O. Ogunniyi
Existence Results for an m-Point Mixed Fractional-Order Problem at Resonance on the Half-Line
Reprinted from: *Axioms* **2022**, *11*, 630, doi:10.3390/axioms11110630 4

Sheza M. El-Deeb and Luminiţa-Ioana Cotîrlă
Basic Properties for Certain Subclasses of Meromorphic p-Valent Functions with Connected q-Analogue of Linear Differential Operator
Reprinted from: *Axioms* **2023**, *12*, 207, doi:10.3390/axioms12020207 17

Ayub Samadi, Sotiris K. Ntouyas, Bashir Ahmad and Jessada Tariboon
On a Coupled Differential System Involving (k, ψ)-Hilfer Derivative and (k, ψ)-Riemann–Liouville Integral Operators
Reprinted from: *Axioms* **2023**, *12*, 229, doi:10.3390/axioms12030229 29

Ahmed Salem and Kholoud N. Alharbi
Controllability for Fractional Evolution Equations with Infinite Time-Delay and Non-Local Conditions in Compact and Noncompact Cases
Reprinted from: *Axioms* **2023**, *12*, 264, doi:10.3390/axioms12030264 45

Isa A. Baba, Usa W. Humphries, Fathalla A. Rihan and J. E. N. Valdés
Fractional–Order Modeling and Control of COVID-19 with Shedding Effect
Reprinted from: *Axioms* **2023**, *12*, 321, doi:10.3390/axioms12040321 62

Constantin Fetecău and Costică Moroşanu
Fractional Step Scheme to Approximate a Non-Linear Second-Order Reaction–Diffusion Problem with Inhomogeneous Dynamic Boundary Conditions
Reprinted from: *Axioms* **2023**, *12*, 406, doi:10.3390/axioms12040406 84

Bahtiyar Bayraktar, Péter Kórus and Juan Eduardo Nápoles Valdés
Some New Jensen–Mercer Type Integral Inequalities via Fractional Operators
Reprinted from: *Axioms* **2023**, *12*, 517, doi:10.3390/axioms12060517 107

Mohammad Faisal Khan, Suha B. Al-Shaikh, Ahmad A. Abubaker and Khaled Matarneh
New Applications of Faber Polynomials and q-Fractional Calculus for a New Subclass of m-Fold Symmetric bi-Close-to-Convex Functions
Reprinted from: *Axioms* **2023**, *12*, 600, doi:10.3390/axioms12060600 124

Asfand Fahad, Saad Ihsaan Butt, Bahtiyar Bayraktar, Mehran Anwar and Yuanheng Wang
Some New Bullen-Type Inequalities Obtained via Fractional Integral Operators
Reprinted from: *Axioms* **2023**, *12*, 691, doi:10.3390/axioms12070691 142

Muhammad Aamir Ali, Thanin Sitthiwirattham, Elisabeth Köbis and Asma Hanif
Hermite–Hadamard–MercerInequalities Associated with Twice-Differentiable Functions with Applications
Reprinted from: *Axioms* **2024**, *13*, 114, doi:10.3390/axioms13020114 168

About the Editors

Péter Kórus

Péter Kórus received his master's degree in mathematics in 2009 from the University of Szeged, Hungary. He received his Ph.D. degree in 2012. He is currently working as an assistant professor at the Institute of Applied Pedagogy, Juhász Gyula Faculty of Education, University of Szeged. His area of interest includes real and Fourier analyses.

Juan Eduardo Nápoles Valdés

Juan Eduardo Nápoles Valdés obtained his Ph.D. degree at the Universidad de Oriente, Santiago de Cuba, in 1994. He was the president of the Cuban Society of Mathematics and Computing. He is currently a full professor at the National University of the Northeast and at the National Technological University of Argentina.

Editorial

Recent Advances in Fractional Calculus

Péter Kórus [1,*] and Juan Eduardo Nápoles Valdés [2,*]

1. Institute of Applied Pedagogy, Juhász Gyula Faculty of Education, University of Szeged, H-6725 Szeged, Hungary
2. Facultad de Ciencias Exactas y Naturales y Agrimensura, Universidad Nacional del Nordeste, Av. Libertad 5450, Corrientes 3400, Argentina
* Correspondence: korus.peter@szte.hu (P.K.); jnapoles@exa.unne.edu.ar (J.E.N.V.)

1. Introduction

This Special Issue of the scientific journal *Axioms*, entitled "Recent Advances in Fractional Calculus", is dedicated to one of the most dynamic areas of mathematical sciences today. For 50 years, the number of researchers and scientific productions dealing with this topic has been increasing day by day, which clearly demonstrates the growing interest in fractional calculus, both from a practical and a theoretical point of view.

Fractional calculus is important because it expands the scope of classical calculus, enabling the modeling and analysis of a wide range of complex phenomena in fields such as physics, engineering, biology, economics, and others. Its flexibility and explanatory power make it an invaluable tool in scientific research and practical application.

The diversity of fractional calculus, and thus of this Special Issue, is well illustrated by the various types of fractional operators considered in the published contributions, such as Caputo-type, Hilfer-type, and Riemann–Liouville-type, and the various types of inequalities presented, such as Bullen-type, Jensen–Mercer-type, and Hermite–Hadamard-type, in addition to the examined fractional-order differential equations and boundary value problems.

2. Overview of the Published Papers

This Special Issue contains 10 articles that were accepted for publication after a rigorous review process.

Ogbu F. Imaga, Samuel A. Iyase, and Peter O. Ogunniyi (Contribution 1) consider the existence of solutions for a mixed fractional-order boundary value problem at resonance on the half line, in which Caputo and Riemann–Liouville fractional derivatives appear. Conditions for the existence of solutions to the problem are given using Mawhin's coincidence degree theory when the dimensions of the kernel of the linear fractional differential operator are two. At the end of the paper, the main result is applied to an example boundary value problem.

Sheza M. El-Deeb and Luminița-Ioana Cotîrlă (Contribution 2) introduce and investigate the properties of some new subclasses of the class of meromorphic p-valent functions in the punctured open unit disk. To define these subclasses, a new linear differential operator is presented by using the combination of q-derivative and convolution. Various properties are studied, and results are given for coefficient estimation, distortion bounds, convex family, and the concept of neighborhoods and partial sums of analytic functions for the class in question.

Ayub Samadi, Sotiris K. Ntouyas, Bashir Ahmad, and Jessada Tariboon (Contribution 3) investigate a non-linear, non-local, and fully coupled boundary value problem containing a generalized Hilfer fractional derivative and generalized Riemann–Liouville fractional integral operators. Existence and uniqueness results are established by transforming the given problem into a fixed-point problem, which facilitates the application of fixed-point theorems. The main results are accompanied by three examples. The paper concludes with some new results arising from the findings as special cases.

Ahmed Salem and Kholoud N. Alharbi (Contribution 4) analyze an infinitely delaying system of Caputo fractional evolution equations with an infinitesimal generator operator. The authors examine a moderate controllability solution based on two different arguments, one using compactness technology and the other using non-compactness. The first argument is based on Krasnoselskii's theorem, while the second one is rooted in the Kuratowski measure of non-compactness and the Sadovskii fixed-point theorem. They achieve the mild solution by assuming that the generator is an infinitesimal generator of a strongly continuous cosine family of uniformly bounded linear operators. Finally, the results are illustrated with a numerical example.

Isa A. Baba, Usa W. Humphries, Fathalla A. Rihan, and Juan E. Nápoles Valdés (Contribution 5) construct a fractional-order COVID-19 model consisting of six compartments in Caputo sense. The model integrates the indirect mode of transmission of the virus, which a result of the shedding effect. The main achievement of the article is the mathematical demonstration of the fact that an uninfected population can become infected via both direct and indirect methods by the exposed or infected class. In addition to the analysis of model's mathematical properties (positivity and boundedness, computation of equilibria, basic reproduction number, existence and uniqueness analysis of the solution of the model, local stability analysis), optimal control analysis and numerical simulations are provided.

Constantin Fetecău and Costică Moroşanu (Contribution 6) address two main topics in their paper. The first topic is a rigorous qualitative study of a second-order reaction–diffusion problem with non-linear diffusion and cubic-type reactions, as well as inhomogeneous dynamic boundary conditions. They extend previously known results by enabling new mathematical models to be more suitable to describe the complexity of a wide class of different physical phenomena in life sciences, including moving interface problems, material sciences, digital image processing, and others. The second topic is the development of an iterative fractional step-type scheme which approximates the non-linear second-order reaction–diffusion problem. Convergence and error estimates are established for the proposed numerical scheme, and a conceptual numerical algorithm is formulated.

Bahtiyar Bayraktar, Péter Kórus, and Juan Eduardo Nápoles Valdés (Contribution 7) consider convex functions, general convex functions, and differentiable functions whose derivatives, in absolute value, are generally convex. They obtain various relevant Hermite–Hadamard-type fractional inequalities via non-conformable fractional integrals, using the classical Jensen–Mercer inequality and its variants for general convex functions. In addition to showing that the main results extend previously known results from the literature, their three examples illustrate the scope and strength of their results.

Mohammad Faisal Khan, Suha B. Al-Shaikh, Ahmad A. Abubaker, and Khaled Matarneh (Contribution 8), starting from the known theory of q-calculus, define a differintegral operator for m-fold symmetric functions and obtain a new class of close-to-convex bi-univalent functions. The authors estimate the general Taylor–Maclaurin coefficient bounds, the initial coefficients, and the Fekete–Szegö functional for this class of functions using the Faber polynomial expansion method. The results obtained are novel and consistent with previous research, which is highlighted by some of the obtained corollaries.

Asfand Fahad, Saad Ihsaan Butt, Bahtiyar Bayraktar, Mehran Anwar, and Yuanheng Wang (Contribution 9) establish a new fractional Bullen-type identity for twice-differentiable functions in terms of fractional integral operators. Using convexity properties, the authors obtain some generalized Bullen-type inequalities, which are supplemented with concrete examples with graphical representations. They provide an analysis of the estimates of boundaries and show that the improved Hölder and power mean inequalities give better results in the upper limit than classical inequalities. Some applications with respect to quadrature rules, modified Bessel functions, and digamma functions are provided at the end of the article.

Muhammad Aamir Ali, Thanin Sitthiwirattham, Elisabeth Köbis, and Asma Hanif (Contribution 10) present an integral identity that incorporates a twice-differentiable function. After presenting this equality, some new Hermite–Hadamard–Mercer-type inequalities are given for twice-differentiable convex functions. Furthermore, it is demonstrated that the newly introduced inequalities serve as generalizations of certain inequalities previously established in the literature. Finally, the authors provide some applications which illustrate the scope and usefulness of their results.

Acknowledgments: The Guest Editors of this Special Issue would like to thank all the authors who contributed their high-quality research papers to this publication. Furthermore, thanks are due to the reviewers and editors, who, through their tireless work, helped make this publication a success.

Conflicts of Interest: The authors declare no conflicts of interest.

List of Contributions

1. Imaga, O.; Iyase, S.; Ogunniyi, P. Existence Results for an m-Point Mixed Fractional-Order Problem at Resonance on the Half-Line. *Axioms* **2022**, *11*, 630. https://doi.org/10.3390/axioms11110630.
2. El-Deeb, S.; Cotîrlă, L. Basic Properties for Certain Subclasses of Meromorphic p-Valent Functions with Connected q-Analogue of Linear Differential Operator. *Axioms* **2023**, *12*, 207. https://doi.org/10.3390/axioms12020207.
3. Samadi, A.; Ntouyas, S.; Ahmad, B.; Tariboon, J. On a Coupled Differential System Involving (k,ψ)-Hilfer Derivative and (k,ψ)-Riemann–Liouville Integral Operators. *Axioms* **2023**, *12*, 229. https://doi.org/10.3390/axioms12030229.
4. Salem, A.; Alharbi, K. Controllability for Fractional Evolution Equations with Infinite Time-Delay and Non-Local Conditions in Compact and Noncompact Cases. *Axioms* **2023**, *12*, 264. https://doi.org/10.3390/axioms12030264.
5. Baba, I.; Humphries, U.; Rihan, F.; Valdés, J. Fractional-Order Modeling and Control of COVID-19 with Shedding Effect. *Axioms* **2023**, *12*, 321. https://doi.org/10.3390/axioms12040321.
6. Fetecău, C.; Moroşanu, C. Fractional Step Scheme to Approximate a Non-Linear Second-Order Reaction–Diffusion Problem with Inhomogeneous Dynamic Boundary Conditions. *Axioms* **2023**, *12*, 406. https://doi.org/10.3390/axioms12040406.
7. Bayraktar, B.; Kórus, P.; Nápoles Valdés, J. Some New Jensen–Mercer Type Integral Inequalities via Fractional Operators. *Axioms* **2023**, *12*, 517. https://doi.org/10.3390/axioms12060517.
8. Khan, M.; Al-Shaikh, S.; Abubaker, A.; Matarneh, K. New Applications of Faber Polynomials and q-Fractional Calculus for a New Subclass of m-Fold Symmetric bi-Close-to-Convex Functions. *Axioms* **2023**, *12*, 600. https://doi.org/10.3390/axioms12060600.
9. Fahad, A.; Butt, S.; Bayraktar, B.; Anwar, M.; Wang, Y. Some New Bullen-Type Inequalities Obtained via Fractional Integral Operators. *Axioms* **2023**, *12*, 691. https://doi.org/10.3390/axioms12070691.
10. Ali, M.; Sitthiwirattham, T.; Köbis, E.; Hanif, A. Hermite–Hadamard–Mercer Inequalities Associated with Twice-Differentiable Functions with Applications. *Axioms* **2024**, *13*, 114. https://doi.org/10.3390/axioms13020114.

Disclaimer/Publisher's Note: The statements, opinions and data contained in all publications are solely those of the individual author(s) and contributor(s) and not of MDPI and/or the editor(s). MDPI and/or the editor(s) disclaim responsibility for any injury to people or property resulting from any ideas, methods, instructions or products referred to in the content.

Article

Existence Results for an *m*-Point Mixed Fractional-Order Problem at Resonance on the Half-Line

Ogbu F. Imaga *,†, Samuel A. Iyase † and Peter O. Ogunniyi †

Department of Mathematics, College of Science and Technology, Covenant University, Ota 112212, Nigeria
* Correspondence: imaga.ogbu@covenantuniversity.edu.ng
† These authors contributed equally to this work.

Abstract: This work considers the existence of solutions for a mixed fractional-order boundary value problem at resonance on the half-line. The Mawhin's coincidence degree theory will be used to prove existence results when the dimension of the kernel of the linear fractional differential operator is equal to two. An example is given to demonstrate the main result obtained.

Keywords: coincidence degree; fractional-order; half-line; m-point; resonance

MSC: 34B40; 34B15

Citation: Imaga, O.F.; Iyase, S.A.; Ogunniyi, P.O. Existence Results for an *m*-Point Mixed Fractional-Order Problem at Resonance on the Half-Line. *Axioms* **2022**, *11*, 630. https://doi.org/10.3390/axioms11110630

Academic Editors: Péter Kórus, Juan Eduardo Nápoles Valdes and Hsien-Chung Wu

Received: 19 June 2022
Accepted: 25 July 2022
Published: 9 November 2022

Publisher's Note: MDPI stays neutral with regard to jurisdictional claims in published maps and institutional affiliations.

Copyright: © 2022 by the authors. Licensee MDPI, Basel, Switzerland. This article is an open access article distributed under the terms and conditions of the Creative Commons Attribution (CC BY) license (https://creativecommons.org/licenses/by/4.0/).

1. Introduction

Fractional calculus has become increasingly popular lately as a result of some interesting properties of the fractional derivative. For instance, the fractional derivative has a memory property that enables its future state to be determined by the current state and all the previous states. This makes fractional differential equations applicable in various fields of science and engineering [1–3].

When the corresponding homogeneous equation of a fractional boundary value problem (FBVP) has a trivial solution then the FBVP is a non-resonance problem and its solution can be obtained using fixed point theorems, see [4–7] and the references cited therein. When the homogeneous equation of a FBVP has a non-trivial solution then the problem is a resonance problem and the solution can be obtained using topological degree methods [8–15].

In [16], the authors consider a higher-order fractional boundary value problem involving mixed fractional derivatives:

$$(-1)^{m\,C}D^\alpha_{1-}D^\beta_{1+} + f(t,u(t)) = 0, \quad 0 \le t \le 1,$$

$$u(0) = u^{(i)}(0) = 0, i = 1,\ldots,m+n-2, \quad D^{\beta+m-1}_{0+}u(1) = 0,$$

where ${}^C D^\alpha_{1-}$ is the left Caputo fractional derivative of order $\alpha \in (m-1,m)$ and D^β_{1+} is the right Caputo fractional derivative of order $\beta \in (n-1,n)$, where $m, n \ge 2$ are integers.

Guezane Lakoud et al. [17] obtained existence results for a fractional boundary value problem at resonance on the half-line:

$$-{}^C D^\alpha_{0-} D^\beta_{0+} x(t) + f(t,x(t)) = 0, \quad t \in [0,1],$$

$$u(0) = u'(0) = u(1) = 0,$$

where $-{}^C D^\alpha_{0-}$ is the left Caputo fractional derivative of order $\alpha \in (0,1]$, and D^β_{0+} is the right Caputo fractional derivative of order $\beta \in (1,2]$.

Zhang and Liu [15] considered the following FBVP

$$D^\alpha_{0+} x(t) = f(t, x(t), D^{\alpha-2}_{0+} x(t), D^{\alpha-1}_{0+} x(t)), \quad t \in (0,1),$$

$$x(0) = 0, \quad D_{0+}^{\alpha-1}x(0) = \sum_{i=1}^{+\infty} \alpha_i D_{0+}^{\alpha-1}x(\xi_i), \quad D_{0+}^{\alpha-1}x(1) = \sum_{i=1}^{+\infty} \alpha_i D_{0+}^{\alpha-1}x(\gamma_i),$$

where $2 < \alpha \leq 3$, D_{0+}^{α} is the Riemann–Liouville derivative of order α, $f \in [0,1] \times \mathbb{R}^3 \to \mathbb{R}$ is a Caratheodory function, ξ_i, $\gamma_i \in (0,1)$ and $\{\xi_i\}_{i=1}^{+\infty}$, $\{\gamma_i\}_{i=1}^{+\infty}$ are two monotonic sequences with $\lim_{i \to +\infty} \xi_i = a$, $\lim_{i \to +\infty} \gamma_i = b$, $a,b \in (0,1)$, $\alpha_i, \beta_i f \in \mathbb{R}$.

Imaga et al. [18] obtained existence results for the following fractional-order boundary value problem at resonance on the half-line with integral boundary conditions:

$$D_-^a \phi_p(D_{0+}^b u(t)) + e^{-t} w(t, u(t), D_{0+}^b u(t)) = 0, \quad t \in (0, \infty), \tag{1}$$

$$I_{0+}^{1-b} u(0) = 0, \quad \phi_p(D_{0+}^b u(+\infty)) = \phi_p(D_{0+}^b u(0)), \tag{2}$$

where D_-^a is the left Caputo fractional derivative on the half line and D_{0+}^b the right Riemann–Liouville fractional derivative on the half-line, $0 < a, b \leq 1$, $1 < a+b \leq 2$, $\phi_p(r) = |r|^{p-2}$, $p > 1$, with $\phi_q = \phi_p^{-1}$ and $1/q + 1/p = 1$. $w : [0, +\infty) \times \mathbb{R}^2 \to \mathbb{R}$ is a continuous function.

Chen and Tang [9] established existence of positive solutions for a FBVP at resonance in an unbounded domain:

$$D_{0+}^{\alpha} u(t) = f(t, u(t)), \quad t \in [0, +\infty),$$

$$u(0) = u'(0) = u''(0) = 0, \quad D_{0+}^{\alpha-1} u(0) = \lim_{t \to +\infty} D_{0+}^{\alpha-1} u(t),$$

where D_{0+}^{α} is Riemann–Liouville fractional derivative, $3 < \alpha < 4$ and $f : [0, +\infty) \times \mathbb{R} \to \mathbb{R}$ is continuous.

Motivated by the results above, we will use the Mawhin coincidence degree theory [19] to study the solvability of the following mixed fractional-order m-point boundary value problem at resonance on the half-line:

$$^C D_{0+}^a D_{0+}^b u(t) = f(t, u(t), D_{0+}^{b-1} u(t), D_{0+}^b u(t)), \quad t \in [0, +\infty) \tag{3}$$

$$I_{0+}^{2-b} u(0) = 0, \quad D_{0+}^{b-1} u(0) = \sum_{j=1}^{m} \alpha_j D_{0+}^{b-1} u(\xi_j), \quad D_{0+}^b u(+\infty) = \sum_{k=1}^{n} \beta_k D_{0+}^b u(\eta_k) \tag{4}$$

where $f : [0, +\infty) \times \mathbb{R}^3 \to \mathbb{R}$ is a continuous function, $^C D_{0+}^a$ is the Caputo fractional derivative, D_{0+}^b is the Riemann–Liouville fractional derivative, $0 < a \leq 1$, $1 < b \leq 2$, $0 < a+b \leq 3$, $0 < \xi_1 < \xi_2 < \cdots < \xi_m < +\infty$, $0 < \eta_1 < \eta_2 < \cdots < \xi_m < +\infty$, $\alpha_j \in \mathbb{R}$, $j = 1, 2, \cdots, m$ and $\beta_k \in \mathbb{R}$, $k = 1, 2, \cdots, n$. The resonant conditions are $\sum_{k=1}^{n} \beta_k = \sum_{j=1}^{m} \alpha_j = 1$ and $\sum_{k=1}^{n} \beta_k \eta_k^{-1} = \sum_{j=1}^{m} \alpha_j \xi_j^{-1} = 0$.

In Section 2 of this work the required lemmas, theorem, and definitions will be given, while Section 3 is dedicated to stating and proving the main existence results. An example will be given in Section 4.

2. Materials and Methods

In this section, we will give some definitions and lemmas that will be used in this work.

Let U, Z be normed spaces, $L : dom\ L \subset U \to Z$ a Fredholm mapping of zero index and $A : U \to U$, $B : Z \to Z$ projectors that are continuous, such that:

$$Im\ A = \ker\ L, \quad \ker\ B = Im\ L, \quad U = \ker\ L \oplus \ker\ A, \quad Z = Im\ L \oplus Im\ B.$$

Then,

$$L|_{dom\ L \cap \ker\ A} : dom\ L \cap \ker\ A \to Im\ L$$

is invertible. The inverse of the mapping L will be denoted by $K_A : \text{Im } L \to \text{dom } L \cap \text{ker } A$ while the generalized inverse, $K_{A,B} : Z \to \text{dom } L \cap \text{ker } A$ is defined as $K_{A,B} = K_A(I - B)$.

Definition 1. *Let $L : \text{dom } L \subset X \to Z$ be a Fredholm mapping, E a metric space and $N : E \to Z$ a non-linear mapping. N is said to be L-compact on E if $BN : E \to Z$ and $K_{A,B}N : E \to X$ are continuous and compact on E. Additionally, N is L-completely continuous if it is L-compact on every bounded $E \subset U$.*

Theorem 1 ([19]). *Let L be a Fredholm map of index zero and let N be L-compact on $\overline{\Omega}$ where $\Omega \subset U$ is an open and bounded. Assume that the following conditions are satisfied:*
(i) $Lx \neq \lambda Nx$ for every $(x, \lambda) \in [(\text{dom } L \text{ ker } L \cap \partial \Omega] \times (0,1)$;
(ii) $Nx \notin \text{Im } L$ for every $x \in \text{ker } L \cap \partial \Omega$;
(iii) $\deg(BN|_{\ker L}, \ker L, 0) \neq 0$, where $B : Z \to Z$ is a projection with $\text{Im } L = \ker B$.

Then, the abstract equation $Lu = Nu$ has at least one solution in $\text{dom } L \cap \overline{\Omega}$.

Definition 2 ([20]). *Let $\alpha > 0$, the Caputo and Riemann–Liouville fractional integral of a function x on $(0, +\infty)$ is defined by:*

$$I_{0+}^\alpha x(t) = \frac{1}{\Gamma(\alpha)} \int_0^t \frac{x(r)}{(r-t)^{1-\alpha}} dr, \quad t \in [0,1]$$

Definition 3 ([20]). *Let $\alpha > 0$, the Caputo ($^C D_{0+}^\alpha x(t)$) and Riemann–Liouville ($D_{0+}^\alpha x(t)$) fractional derivative of a function x on $(0, +\infty)$ is defined by:*

$$^C D_{0+}^\alpha x(t) = D_{0+}^\alpha x(t) = \frac{1}{\Gamma(n-\alpha)} \frac{d^n}{dt^n} \int_0^t \frac{x(r)}{(t-r)^{\alpha-n+1}} dr, \quad t \in (0, +\infty)$$

where $n = [\alpha] + 1$.

Lemma 1 ([21]). *Let $a \in (0, +\infty)$. The general solution of the Riemman–Liouville fractional differential equation:*

$$D_{0+}^a g(t) = 0$$

is $g(t) = b_1 t^{a-1} + b_2 t^{a-2} + \cdots + b_n t^{a-n}$, where $b_j \in \mathbb{R}$, $j = 1, 2 \ldots, n$ while, the general solution of the Caputo fractional differential equation:

$$D_{0+}^a g(t) = 0$$

is $g(t) = d_0 + d_1 t + \cdots + d_n t^n$, where $d_i \in \mathbb{R}$, $i = 0, 1, \ldots, n$ and $n = [a] + 1$ is the smallest integer greater than or equal to a.

Lemma 2 ([21]). *Let $a \in (0, +\infty)$ and $i = 1, 2, \ldots, n$, $n = [a] + 1$ then*

$$(I_{0+}^a D_{0+}^a g)(t) = g(t) + d_1 t^{a-1} + d_2 t^{a-2} + \cdots + d_n t^{a-n}$$

holds almost everywhere on $[0, +\infty)$ for some $d_i \in \mathbb{R}$. Similarly,

$$(I_{0+}^a \, {}^C D_{0+}^a g)(t) = g(t) + d_0 + d_1 t^1 + d_2 t^2 + \cdots + d_n t^n$$

holds almost everywhere on $[0, +\infty)$ for some $d_i \in \mathbb{R}$, $i = 0, 1, \ldots, n$.

Lemma 3 ([21]). *Let $a > 0$, $\rho > -1$, $t > 0$, $g(t) \in C[0, +\infty)$, then:*
(i) $I_{0+}^a t^\rho = \frac{\Gamma(\rho+1)}{\Gamma(\rho+1+a)} t^{a+\rho}$;
(ii) $D_{0+}^a t^\rho = \frac{\Gamma(\rho+1)}{\Gamma(\rho+1-a)} t^{a-\rho}$, for $\rho > -1$, in particular for $D_{0+}^a t^{a-k} = 0$, $k = 1, 2, \ldots, N$, where N is the smallest integer greater than or equal to a;

(iii) $D_{0+}^a I_{0+}^a g(t) = g(t)$, $g(t) \in C[0, +\infty)$;
(iv) $I_{0+}^a I_{0+}^b g(t) = I_{0+}^{a+b} g(t)$.

Let
$$U = \left\{ u \in C[0, +\infty) : \lim_{t \to +\infty} \frac{|u(t)|}{1+t^{a+b}}, \lim_{t \to +\infty} \frac{|D_{0+}^{b-1} u(t)|}{1+t^{a+1}} \text{ and } \lim_{t \to +\infty} \frac{|D_{0+}^b u(t)|}{1+t^a} \text{ exists} \right\}$$

with the norm $\|u\|_U = \max\{\|u\|_0, \|D_{0+}^{b-1} u\|_1, \|D_{0+}^b u\|_2\}$ defined on U where:

$$\|u\|_0 = \sup_{t \in [0,+\infty]} \frac{|u(t)|}{1+t^{a+b}}, \quad \|D_{0+}^{b-1} u\|_1 = \sup_{t \in [0,+\infty]} \frac{|D_{0+}^{b-1} u(t)|}{1+t^{a+1}} \text{ and } \|D_{0+}^b u\|_2 = \sup_{t \in [0,+\infty]} \frac{|D_{0+}^b u(t)|}{1+t^a}.$$

Let $Z = \{z : C[0, +\infty) : \sup_{t \in [0,+\infty)} |z(t)| < +\infty\}$ equipped with the norm $\|z\|_Z = \sup_{t \in [0,+\infty)} |z(t)|$. The spaces $(U, \|\cdot\|_U)$ and $(Z, \|\cdot\|_Z)$ can be shown to be Banach Spaces. Additionally, define $Lu = {}^C D_{0+}^a D_{0+}^b u(t)$, with domain

$$\operatorname{dom} L = \left\{ u \in U : {}^C D_{0+}^a D_{0+}^b u(t) \in Z, \text{ boundary conditions (4) is satisfied by } u \right\},$$

and the non-linear operator $N : U \to Z$ will be defined by

$$(Nu)t = f(t, u(t), D_{0+}^{b-1} u(t), D_{0+}^b u(t)), \quad t \in [0, +\infty),$$

hence, Equations (3) and (4) may be written as

$$Lu = Nu.$$

Definition 4. *The set $Y \subset U$ is said to be relatively compact if*

$$Y_1 = \left\{ \frac{u(t)}{1+t^{a+b}} : u \in Y \right\}, \quad Y_2 = \left\{ \frac{D_{0+}^{b-1} u(t)}{1+t^{a+1}} : u \in Y \right\}, \quad Y_3 = \left\{ \frac{D_{0+}^b u(t)}{1+t^a} : u \in Y \right\}$$

are uniformly bounded; equicontinuous on any compact subinterval of $[0, +\infty)$ and equiconvergent at: $+\infty$.

Definition 5. *The set $Y \subset U$ is said to be equiconvergent at $+\infty$ if given $\epsilon > 0$ there exists a $\tau(\epsilon) > 0$, such that:*

$$\left| \frac{u(t_1)}{1+t_1^{a+b}} - \frac{u(t_2)}{1+t_2^{a+b}} \right| < \epsilon, \quad \left| \frac{D_{0+}^{b-1} u(t_1)}{1+t_1^{a+1}} - \frac{D_{0+}^{b-1} u(t_2)}{1+t_2^{a+1}} \right| < \epsilon \text{ and } \left| \frac{D_{0+}^b u(t_1)}{1+t_1^a} - \frac{D_{0+}^b u(t_2)}{1+t_2^a} \right| < \epsilon$$

where $t_1, t_2 > \tau$.

Lemma 4. $\ker L = \{c_1 t^b + c_2 t^{b-1} : c_1, c_2 \in \mathbb{R}, t \in [0, +\infty)\}$ *and* $\operatorname{Im} L = \{z \in Z : B_1 z = B_2 z = 0\}$
where $B_1 z = \sum_{k=1}^n \beta_k \int_0^{\eta_k} (\eta_k - r)^{a-1} z(r) dr$ *and* $B_2 z = \sum_{j=1}^m \alpha_j \int_0^{\xi_j} (\xi_j - r)^a z(r) dr$.

Proof. Consider ${}^C D_{0+}^a D_{0+}^b u(t) = 0$ for $u \in \ker L$, then by Lemma 1

$$u(t) = c_1 t^b + c_2 t^{b-1} + c_3 t^{b-2}, \quad c_1, c_2, c_3 \in \mathbb{R}.$$

Applying the boundary condition $I_{0+}^{2-b}u(0) = 0$, gives $c_3 = 0$. Thus, $u(t) = c_1 t^b + c_2 t^{b-1}$. Next, consider ${}^C D_{0+}^a D_{0+}^b u(t) = z(t)$ for $z(t) \in \text{Im } L$ and $u \in \text{dom } L$, then

$$u(t) = I_{0+}^{a+b} z(t) + c_1 t^b + c_2 t^{b-1} + c_3 t^{b-2}.$$

From $I_{0+}^{2-b} u(0) = 0$ we obtain $c_3 = 0$. Therefore,

$$D_{0+}^b u(t) = I_{0+}^a z(t) + c_1 + c_2 t^{-1} \tag{5}$$

By boundary condition $D_{0+}^b u(+\infty) = \sum_{k=1}^n \beta_k D_{0+}^b u(\eta_k)$ and the conditions $\sum_{k=1}^n \beta_k = 1$, $\sum_{k=1}^n \beta_k \eta_k^{-1} = 0$, (5) gives

$$B_1 z = \sum_{k=1}^n \beta_k \int_0^{\eta_k} (\eta_k - r)^{a-1} z(r) dr = 0,$$

Similarly,

$$D_{0+}^{b-1} u(t) = I_{0+}^{a+1} z(t) + c_1 t + c_2, \tag{6}$$

by boundary condition $D_{0+}^{b-1} u(0) = \sum_{j=1}^m \alpha_j D_{0+}^{b-1} u(\xi_j)$ and resonant conditions $\sum_{j=1}^m \alpha_j = 1$ and $\sum_{j=1}^m \alpha_j \xi_j^{-1} = 0$, (6) gives

$$B_2 z = \sum_{j=1}^m \alpha_j \int_0^{\xi_j} (\xi_j - r)^a z(r) dr.$$

□

Let $\Delta = (B_1 t^{b-1} e^{-t} \cdot B_2 t^b e^{-t}) - (B_2 t^{b-1} e^{-t} \cdot B_1 t^b e^{-t}) := (g_{11} \cdot g_{22}) - (g_{21} \cdot g_{12}) \neq 0$. Let the operator $B : Z \to Z$ be defined as

$$Bz = (\Delta_1 z) + (\Delta_2 z) \cdot t^b$$

where

$$\Delta_1 z = \frac{1}{\Delta}(\delta_{11} B_1 z + \delta_{12} B_2 z) e^{-t}, \quad \Delta_2 z = \frac{1}{\Delta}(\delta_{21} B_1 z + \delta_{22} B_2 z) e^{-t},$$

and δ_{ij} is the algebraic cofactor of g_{ij}.

Lemma 5. *The following holds:*
(i) $L : \text{dom } L \subset U$ *is a Fredholm operator of index zero;*
(ii) *the generalized inverse* $K_A : \text{Im } L \to \text{dom } L \cap \ker A$ *may be written as*

$$K_A z = I_{0+}^{a+b} z(t).$$

Additionally,

$$\|K_A z\| = \|z\|_Z.$$

Proof. (i) For $z \in Z$, it is easily be seen that $\Delta_1((\Delta_1 z)) = (\Delta_1 z)$, $\Delta_1((\Delta_2 z) t^b) = 0$, $\Delta_2((\Delta_1 z)) = 0$, and $\Delta_2((\Delta_2 z) t^b) = (\Delta_2 y)$. Hence, $B^2 z = Bz$, thus Bz is a projector.

We now prove that $\ker B = \text{Im } L$. Let $z \in \ker B$, since $Bz = 0$ then $z \in \text{Im } L$. Conversely, if $z \in \text{Im } L$, then by $Bz = 0$, $z \in \ker B$. Therefore, $\ker B = \text{Im } L$.

Let $z \in Z$, then $z \in \text{Im } L$ and $z \in \ker B$, hence, $Z = \text{Im } L + \ker B$. Assuming $z = c_1 t^{b-1} + c_2 t^b$, then since $z \in \text{Im } L$, then from equation

$$\begin{cases} \Delta_1 c_1 t^{b-1} e^{-t} + \Delta_2 c_2 t^{b-1} e^{-t} = 0, \\ \Delta_1 c_1 t^b e^{-t} + \Delta_2 c_2 t^b e^{-t} = 0. \end{cases} \tag{7}$$

gives $c_1 = c_2 = 0$, since $\Delta \neq 0$. Therefore $\operatorname{Im} L \cap \operatorname{Im} B = \{0\}$ and $A = \operatorname{Im} L \oplus \operatorname{Im} B$. Thus $\dim \ker L = \operatorname{codim} \operatorname{Im} L = 2$ implying L is a Fredholm mapping of index zero.
(ii) Let $A : U \to U$ a continuous projector be defined as:

$$Au(t) = \frac{D_{0+}^b u(0)}{\Gamma(b)} t^{b-1} + \frac{D_{0+}^b u(0)}{\Gamma(b+1)} t^b$$

For $z \in \operatorname{Im} L$, we have

$$(LK_A)z(t) = {}^C D_{0+}^a D_{0+}^b (K_A z) = {}^C D_{0+}^a D_{0+}^b I_{0+}^b I_{0+}^a z(t) = z(t).$$

Similarly, for $u \in \operatorname{dom} L \cap \ker A$, we have

$$\begin{aligned}(K_A L)u(t) &= (K_A) {}^C D_{0+}^a D_{0+}^b u(t) \\ &= I_{0+}^b I_{0+}^a {}^C D_{0+}^a D_{0+}^b u(t) \\ &= I_{0+}^b (D_{0+}^b u(t) + d_1) \\ &= u(t) - \frac{D_{0+}^{b-1} u(0)}{\Gamma(b)} t^{b-1} - \frac{I_{0+}^{2-b} u(0)}{\Gamma(b-1)} t^{b-2} - \frac{D_{0+}^b u(0)}{\Gamma(b+1)} t^b.\end{aligned}$$

Since $u \in \operatorname{dom} L \cap \ker A$, $Au(t) = 0$ and $I_{0+}^{2-b} u(0) = 0$, then $(K_A L)u(t) = u(t)$. Therefore, $K_A = (L|_{\operatorname{dom} L \cap \ker A})^{-1}$. Furthermore,

$$\begin{aligned}\|K_A z\|_0 &= \sup_{t \in [0,+\infty)} \frac{|I_{0+}^{a+b} z(t)|}{1 + t^{a+b}} = \sup_{t \in [0,+\infty)} \frac{1}{1 + t^{a+b}} \left| \frac{1}{\Gamma(a)\Gamma(b)} \int_0^t (t-r)^{a+b-1} z(r) dr \right| \\ &\leq \frac{1}{(a+b)\Gamma(a)\Gamma(b)} \|z\|_Z \leq \|z\|_Z,\end{aligned}$$

$$\begin{aligned}\|D_{0+}^{b-1} K_P z\|_1 &= \sup_{t \in [0,+\infty)} \frac{|I_{0+}^{a+1} z(t)|}{1 + t^{a+1}} = \sup_{t \in [0,+\infty)} \frac{1}{1 + t^{a+1}} \left| \frac{1}{\Gamma(a+1)} \int_0^t (t-r)^a z(r) dr \right| \\ &\leq \frac{1}{(a+1)\Gamma(a+1)} \|z\|_Z \leq \|z\|_Z\end{aligned}$$

and

$$\begin{aligned}\|D_{0+}^b K_A z\|_2 &= \sup_{t \in [0,+\infty)} \frac{|I_{0+}^a z(t)|}{1 + t^a} = \sup_{t \in [0,+\infty)} \frac{t^a}{1 + t^a} \frac{\|z\|_Z}{\Gamma(a+1)} \\ &\leq \frac{1}{\Gamma(a+1)} \|z\|_Z \leq \|z\|_Z.\end{aligned}$$

Thus,

$$\|K_A z\| = \max\{\|K_A z\|_0, \|D_{0+}^{b-1} K_A z\|_1, \|D_{0+}^b K_A z\|_2\} \leq \|z\|_Z.$$

Proof of Lemma 5 is complete. □

Lemma 6. *The operator N is L-compact on $\overline{\Omega}$, where $\Omega \subset U$ is open and bounded with $\operatorname{dom} L \cap \overline{\Omega} \neq \emptyset$.*

Proof. Let $u \in \overline{\Omega}$ then

$$\|Nu\|_Z = \sup_{t \in [0,+\infty)} |f(t, u(t), D_{0+}^{b-1} u(t), D_{0+}^b u(t))| < +\infty, \quad t \in [0,+\infty). \tag{8}$$

It follows that

$$|B_1 Nu| = \left| \sum_{k=1}^{n} \beta_k \int_0^{\eta_k} (\eta_k - r)^{a-1} Nu(r) dr \right| \leq \frac{\|Nu\|_Z}{a} \sum_{k=1}^{n} |\beta_k| \eta_k^a < +\infty \qquad (9)$$

and

$$|B_2 Nu| = \left| \sum_{j=1}^{m} \alpha_j \int_0^{\xi_j} (\xi_j - r)^a Nu(r) dr ds \right| \leq \frac{\|Nu\|_Z}{(a+1)} \sum_{j=1}^{m} |\alpha_j| \xi_j^{a+1} < +\infty. \qquad (10)$$

Then,

$$\|BNu\|_Z = \sup_{t \in [0,+\infty)} |(\Delta_1 Nu(t)) + (\Delta_2 Nu(t))|$$
$$\leq \frac{\|Nu\|_Z}{|\Delta|} \left[(|\delta_{11}| + |\delta_{21}|) \frac{1}{a} \sum_{k=1}^{n} |\beta_k| \eta_k^a + (|\delta_{12}| + |\delta_{22}|) \frac{1}{(a+1)} \sum_{j=1}^{m} |\alpha_j| \xi_j^{a+1} \right] < +\infty. \qquad (11)$$

Therefore, $BN(\overline{\Omega})$ is bounded. In addition, $\|Nu\|_Z + \|BNu\|_Z < +\infty$. In the following steps, we show that $K_A(I - B)N(\overline{\Omega})$ is compact. Let $u \in \overline{\Omega}$ and $m(t) = (I - B)Nu(t)$, then:

$$\frac{|K_A(I - B)Nu(t)|}{1 + t^{a+b}} = \frac{|I_{0+}^{a+b} m(t)|}{1 + t^{a+b}} \leq \sup_{t \in [0,+\infty)} \frac{t^{a+b}}{1 + t^{a+b}} \frac{\|m\|_Z}{(a+b)\Gamma(a)\Gamma(b)}$$
$$\leq \frac{1}{(a+b)\Gamma(a)\Gamma(b)} \|m\|_Z, \qquad (12)$$

$$\frac{|D_{0+}^{b-1} K_A(I - B)Nu(t)|}{1 + t^{a+1}} = \frac{|I_{0+}^{a+1} m(t)|}{1 + t^{a+1}} \leq \sup_{t \in [0,+\infty)} \frac{t^{a+1}}{1 + t^{a+1}} \frac{\|m\|_Z}{(a+1)\Gamma(a+1)}$$
$$\leq \frac{1}{\Gamma(a+2)} \|m\|_Z \qquad (13)$$

and

$$\frac{|D_{0+}^{b} K_A(I - B)Nu(t)|}{1 + t^a} = \frac{|I_{0+}^{a} m(t)|}{1 + t^a} \leq \sup_{t \in [0,+\infty)} \frac{t^a}{1 + t^a} \frac{\|m\|_Z}{\Gamma(a+1)}$$
$$\leq \frac{1}{\Gamma(a+1)} \|m\|_Z. \qquad (14)$$

From (8), (11)–(14), we see that $K_A(I - B)N(\overline{\Omega})$ is bounded. Next, the equi-continuity of $K_A(I - B)N(\overline{\Omega})$ will be proved. For $u \in \overline{\Omega}$, $t_1, t_2 \in [0, M]$ with $t_1 < t_2$ and $M \in (0, +\infty)$, then:

$$\left| \frac{K_A(I - B)Nu(t_1)}{1 + t_1^{a+b}} - \frac{K_A(I - B)Nu(t_2)}{1 + t_2^{a+b}} \right|$$
$$\leq \frac{1}{\Gamma(a+b)} \left[\left| \int_0^{t_1} \frac{(t_1 - r)^{a+b-1}}{1 + t_1^{a+b}} m(r) dr - \int_0^{t_1} \frac{(t_1 - r)^{a+b-1}}{1 + t_1^{a+b}} m(r) dr \right| \right] \qquad (15)$$
$$\leq \frac{\|m\|_Z}{\Gamma(a+b)} \left[\int_0^{t_1} \left| \frac{(t_1 - r)^{a+b-1}}{1 + t_1^{a+b}} - \frac{(t_2 - r)^{a+b-1}}{1 + t_2^{a+b}} \right| dr + \frac{1}{a+b} \frac{(t_2 - t_1)^{a+b}}{1 + t_2^{a+b}} \right]$$
$$\to 0 \text{ as } t_1 \to t_2,$$

$$\left| \frac{D_{0+}^{b-1}(K_A(I-B)Nu)(t_1)}{1+t_1^{a+1}} - \frac{D_{0+}^{b-1}(K_A(I-B)Nu)(t_2)}{1+t_2^{a+1}} \right|$$
$$\leq \frac{\|m\|_Z}{\Gamma(a+1)} \left[\int_0^{t_1} \left| \frac{(t_1-r)^a}{1+t_1^{a+1}} - \frac{(t_2-r)^a}{1+t_2^{a+1}} \right| dr + \frac{1}{a+1} \frac{(t_2-t_1)^{a+1}}{1+t_2^{a-1}} \right] \quad (16)$$
$$\to 0 \text{ as } t_1 \to t_2,$$

and

$$\left| \frac{D_{0+}^b(K_A(I-B)Nu)(t_1)}{1+t_1^a} - \frac{D_{0+}^b(K_A(I-B)Nu)(t_2)}{1+t_2^a} \right|$$
$$\leq \frac{\|m\|_Z}{\Gamma(a)} \left[\int_0^{t_1} \left| \frac{(t_1-r)^{a-1}}{1+t_1^a} - \frac{(t_2-r)^{a-1}}{1+t_2^a} \right| dr + \frac{1}{a} \frac{(t_2-t_1)^a}{1+t_2^a} \right] \to 0 \text{ as } t_1 \to t_2. \quad (17)$$

Thus, (15)–(17) shows that $K_A(I-B)Nu(\overline{\Omega})$ is equi-continuous on the compact set $[0, M]$. Finally, we show equi-convergence at $+\infty$. Let $\tau > 0$ be a constant such that

$$|g(r)| = |(I-B)Nu(r)| \leq r, \quad u \in \overline{\Omega}.$$

In addition, since $\lim_{t \to +\infty} \frac{t^{a+b-1}}{1+t^{a+b}} = \lim_{t \to +\infty} \frac{t^a}{1+t^{a+1}} = \lim_{t \to +\infty} \frac{t^{a-1}}{1+t^a} = 0$, then for same $\epsilon > 0$, there exist $M > 0$, such that for $M < t_1 < t_2$, we have

$$\left| \frac{(t_1-r)^{a+b-1}}{1+t_1^{a+b}} - \frac{(t_2-r)^{a+b-1}}{1+t_2^{a+b}} \right| \leq \frac{t_1^{a+b-1}}{1+t_1^{a+b}} - \frac{t_2^{a+b-1}}{1+t_2^{a+b}} < \epsilon,$$

$$\left| \frac{(t_1-r)^a}{1+t_1^{a+1}} - \frac{(t_2-r)^a}{1+t_2^{a+1}} \right| \leq \frac{t_1^a}{1+t_1^{a+1}} - \frac{t_2^a}{1+t_2^{a+1}} < \epsilon,$$

and

$$\left| \frac{(t_1-r)^{a-1}}{1+t_1^a} - \frac{(t_2-r)^{a-1}}{1+t_2^a} \right| \leq \frac{t_1^{a-1}}{1+t_1^a} - \frac{t_2^{a-1}}{1+t_2^a} < \epsilon,$$

Hence,

$$\left| \frac{K_A(I-B)Nu(t_1)}{1+t_1^{a+b}} - \frac{K_A(I-B)Nu(t_2)}{1+t_2^{a+b}} \right|$$
$$\leq \frac{1}{\Gamma(a)\Gamma(b)} \left[\left| \int_0^{t_1} \frac{(t_1-r)^{a+b-1}}{1+t_1^{a+b}} g(r) dr - \int_0^{t_1} \frac{(t_1-r)^{a+b-1}}{1+t_1^{a+b}} g(r) dr \right| \right] \quad (18)$$
$$\leq \frac{1}{\Gamma(a)\Gamma(b)} \int_0^M \left| \frac{(t_1-r)^{a+b-1}}{1+t_1^{a+b}} - \frac{(t_2-r)^{a+b-1}}{1+t_2^{a+b}} \right| |g(r)| dr$$
$$+ \frac{1}{\Gamma(a)\Gamma(b)} \int_M^{t_1} \frac{(t_1-r)^{a+b-1}}{1+t_1^{a+b}} |g(r)| dr + \frac{1}{\Gamma(a)\Gamma(b)} \int_M^{t_2} \frac{(t_2-r)^{a+b-1}}{1+t_2^{a+b}} |g(r)| dr$$
$$\leq \frac{M\tau\epsilon}{(a+b)\Gamma(a)\Gamma(b)} + \frac{2\tau\epsilon}{(a+b)\Gamma(a)\Gamma(b)},$$

$$\left| \frac{D_{0+}^{b-1}(K_A(I-B)Nu)(t_1)}{1+t_1^{a+1}} - \frac{D_{0+}^{b-1}(K_A(I-B)Nu)(t_2)}{1+t_2^{a+1}} \right| \quad (19)$$

$$\leq \frac{1}{\Gamma(a+1)} \left[\int_0^M \left| \frac{(t_1-r)^a}{1+t_1^{a+1}} - \frac{(t_2-r)^a}{1+t_2^{a+1}} \right| |g(r)| dr \right.$$

$$+ \frac{1}{\Gamma(a+1)} \left[\int_M^{t_1} \frac{(t_1-r)^a}{1+t_1^{a+1}} g(r) dr + \int_M^{t_2} \frac{(t_2-r)^a}{1+t_2^{a+1}} g(r) dr \right]$$

$$\leq \frac{M\tau\epsilon}{\Gamma(a+1)} + \frac{2\tau\epsilon}{\Gamma(a+2)}$$

and

$$\left| \frac{D_{0+}^{b}(K_A(I-B)Nu)(t_1)}{1+t_1^{a}} - \frac{D_{0+}^{b}(K_A(I-B)Nu)(t_2)}{1+t_2^{a}} \right| \quad (20)$$

$$\leq \frac{1}{\Gamma(a)} \left[\int_0^M \left| \frac{(t_1-r)^{a-1}}{1+t_1^{a}} - \frac{(t_2-r)^{a-1}}{1+t_2^{a}} \right| |g(r)| dr \right.$$

$$+ \frac{1}{a\Gamma(a)} \left[\int_M^{t_1} \frac{(t_1-r)^{a-1}}{1+t_1^{a}} g(r) dr + \int_M^{t_2} \frac{(t_2-r)^{a-1}}{1+t_2^{a}} g(r) dr \right]$$

$$\leq \frac{M\tau\epsilon}{\Gamma(a)} + \frac{2\tau\epsilon}{\Gamma(a+1)}.$$

Hence, $K_A(I-B)Nu(\overline{\Omega})$ is equi-convergent at $+\infty$. Therefore, by Definition 1, $K_A(I-B)Nu(\overline{\Omega})$ is compact, therefore, the non-linear operator N is L-compact on $\overline{\Omega}$. This concludes proof of Lemma 6. □

3. Results and Discussion

Here, the conditions for the existence of solutions to problem (1.1) subject to (1.2) is proved.

Theorem 2. *Let f be a continuous function. If (ϕ_1) and (ϕ_1) holds, then, the following conditions also hold:*

(H_1) *There exists functions $\rho(t)$, $\mu(t)$, $\nu(t)$, $\sigma \in C[0,+\infty)$, such that for all $(j,k,l) \in \mathbb{R}^3$ and $t \in [0,+\infty)$,*

$$|f(t, u(t), D_{0+}^{b-1}u(t), D_{0+}^{b}u(t))| \leq \rho(t) \frac{|j|}{1+t^{a+b}} + \mu(t) \frac{|k|}{1+t^{a+1}} + \nu(t) \frac{|l|}{1+t^a} + \sigma(t). \quad (21)$$

(H_2) *There exist constants $M > 0$, such that for $u \in \text{dom } L$ if $|D_{0+}^b u(t)| > M$ for $t \in [0,+\infty)$, then either*

$$B_1 Nu(t) \neq 0 \quad \text{or} \quad B_2 Nu(t) \neq 0.$$

(H_3) *There exists a constant $C > 0$, such that if $|c_1| > C$ or $|c_2| > C$, then either*

$$B_1 N(c_1 t^{b-1} + c_2 t^b) + B_2 N(c_1 t^{b-1} + c_2 t^b) < 0 \quad (22)$$

or

$$B_1 N(c_1 t^{b-1} + c_2 t^b) + B_2 N(c_1 t^{b-1} + c_2 t^b) > 0 \quad (23)$$

where $c_1, c_2 \in \mathbb{R}$ satisfying $c_1^2 + c_2^2 > 0$.

Then, the boundary value problem (3) and (4) has at least one solution provided:

$$\|\rho\|_Z + \|\mu\|_Z + \|\nu\|_Z < \frac{\Gamma(a+1)}{\Gamma(a+1)+2}.$$

Proof. The proof will be completed in four stages.

Stage 1. We will establish that $\Omega_1 = \{u \in \text{dom}\, L \setminus \ker L : u = \lambda Nu, \text{ for } \lambda \in [0,1]\}$ is bounded. Let $u \in \Omega_1$ then $u = (u - Au) + Au \in \text{dom}\, L \setminus \ker L$. This means that $(I - A)u \in \text{dom}\, L \cap \ker A$ and $Au \in \ker A$, hence, $LAu = 0$. By Lemma 5, we have

$$\|(I - A)u\| = \|K_A L(I - A)u\| \leq \|L(I - A)u\| = \|Lu\| = \|Nu\|_Z. \tag{24}$$

Since $u \in \Omega_1$, then $Lu = \lambda Nu$. Additionally, by (H_2) there exists $t_1 \in [0, +\infty)$, such that $|D_{0+}^b u(t_1)| \leq M$, therefore

$$\begin{aligned}|D_{0+}^b u(0)| &\leq |D_{0+}^b u(t_1)| + \frac{\lambda}{\Gamma(a)} \int_0^{t_1} (t_1 - r)^{a-1} |f(r, u(r), D_{0+}^{b-1} u(r), D_{0+}^b u(r))| dr \\ &\leq M + \frac{1}{\Gamma(a+1)} \|Nu\|_Z.\end{aligned} \tag{25}$$

In addition,

$$\|Au\|_0 \leq |D_{0+}^b u(0)| \left(\frac{1}{\Gamma(b)} \sup_{t \in [0,+\infty)} \frac{t^{b-1}}{1 + t^{a+b}} + \frac{1}{\Gamma(b+1)} \sup_{t \in [0,+\infty)} \frac{t^b}{1 + t^{a+b}} \right) \leq 2|D_{0+}^b u(0)|,$$

$$\|D_{0+}^{b-1} Au\|_1 \leq |D_{0+}^b u(0)| \left(\frac{1}{\Gamma(b)} \sup_{t \in [0,+\infty)} \frac{1}{1 + t^{a+1}} + \frac{1}{\Gamma(b+1)} \sup_{t \in [0,+\infty)} \frac{t}{1 + t^{a+1}} \right) \leq 2|D_{0+}^b u(0)|$$

and

$$\|D_{0+}^b Au\|_2 \leq |D_{0+}^b u(0)| \left(\frac{1}{\Gamma(b)} \sup_{t \in [0,+\infty)} \frac{t^{-1}}{1 + t^a} + \frac{1}{\Gamma(b+1)} \sup_{t \in [0,+\infty)} \frac{1}{1 + t^a} \right) \leq 2|D_{0+}^b u(0)|.$$

Therefore, from (25), we have

$$\|Au\| \leq \max\{\|u\|_0, \|D_{0+}^{b-1} u\|_1, \|D_{0+}^b u\|_2\} \leq 2|D_{0+}^b u(0)| \leq 2M + \frac{2}{\Gamma(a+1)} \|Nu\|_Z \tag{26}$$

and from (24) and (26), we have

$$\begin{aligned}\|u\|_U &\leq \|Au\|_U + \|I - A\|_U \\ &\leq 2M + \left(1 + \frac{2}{\Gamma(a+1)}\right) \|Nu\|_Z \\ &\leq 2M + \left(1 + \frac{2}{\Gamma(a+1)}\right) \|u\|_U (\|\rho\|_Z + \|\mu\|_Z + \|\nu\|_Z) + \left(1 + \frac{2}{\Gamma(a+1)}\right) \|\sigma\|_Z.\end{aligned}$$

Hence,

$$\|u\|_U \leq \frac{2M + \left(1 + \frac{2}{\Gamma(a+1)}\right) \|\sigma\|_Z}{1 - \left(1 + \frac{2}{\Gamma(a+1)}\right) \|u\|_U (\|\rho\|_Z + \|\mu\|_Z + \|\nu\|_Z)}.$$

Thus, Ω_1 is bounded.

Step 2. Let $\Omega_2 = \{u \in \ker L : Nu \in \text{Im}\, L\}$. For $u, Nu \in \Omega_2$, then $u(t) = c_1 t^{b-1} + c_2 t^b$. and $BNu = 0$. Thus, from (H_3), we have $|c_1| \leq C$ and $|c_2| \leq C$. Hence, Ω_2 is bounded.

Step 3. For $c_1, c_2 \in \mathbb{R}$, $t \in [0, +\infty)$, the isomorphism $J : \ker L \to \text{Im}\, B$ is as

$$J(c_1 t^{b-1} + c_2 t^b) = \frac{1}{\Delta} \left[(\delta_{11} c_1 + \delta_{12} c_2) + (\delta_{21} c_1 + \delta_{22} c_2) t \right] e^{-t} \tag{27}$$

Suppose (22) holds, let

$$\Omega_3 = \{u \in \ker L : \lambda Ju + (1-\lambda)BNu = 0, \lambda \in [0,1]\}.$$

Let $u \in \Omega_3$, then $u(t) = c_1 t^{b-1} + c_2 t^b$. Since $\Delta \neq 0$, then

$$\begin{cases} c_1\lambda + (1-\lambda)B_1 N(c_1 t^{b-1} + c_2 t^b) = 0, \\ c_2\lambda + (1-\lambda)B_2 N(c_1 t^{b-1} + c_2 t^b) = 0. \end{cases} \quad (28)$$

When $\lambda = 1$, we obtain $c_1 = c_2 = 0$. When $\lambda = 0$, $B_1 N(c_1 t^{b-1} + c_2 t^b) = B_2 N(c_1 t^{b-1} + c_2 t^b) = 0$, which contradicts (22) and (23). Hence, from (H_3), we obtain $|c_1| \leq C$, and $|c_2| \leq C$. For $\lambda \in (0,1)$, if $|c_1| > C$ or $|C_2| > A$ by (22) and (28), we have

$$\lambda(c_1^2 + c_2^2) = -(1-\lambda)[B_1 N(c_1 t^{b-1} + c_2 t^b) + B_2 N(c_1 t^{b-1} + c_2 t^b)] < 0,$$

which is a contradiction. Hence, Ω_3 is bounded.

Similarly, if (23) holds and $\Omega_3 = \{u \in \ker L : \lambda Ju - (I-\lambda)BNu = 0, \lambda \in [0,1]\}$, Ω_3 can be shown to be bounded by similar argument.

Step 4. Let $\Omega \supset \cup_{i=1}^3 \overline{\Omega}_i$. Finally, we will show that a solution of (3) and (4) exists in dom $L \cap \Omega$. We have shown in Steps 1 and 2 that (i) and (ii) of Theorem 1 hold. Finally, we show that (iii) also holds. Let $H(u,\lambda) = \pm\lambda Ju + (1-\lambda)BNu$, then following the arguments of Step 3, it follows that for every $(u,\lambda) \in (\ker L \cap \partial\Omega) \times [0,1]$, $H(u,\lambda) \neq 0$. Therefore, by the homotopy property of degree

$$\deg(BN|_{\ker L}, \Omega \cap \ker L, 0) = \deg(\pm J, \Omega \cap \ker L, 0)$$
$$= \pm 1 \neq 0.$$

Therefore, by Theorem 1 at least one solution of (3) and (4) exists in U. □

4. Conclusions

This work considered a mixed fractional-order boundary value problem at resonance on the half-line. The Mawhin's coincidence degree theory was used to establish existence of solutions when the dimension of the kernel of the linear fractional differential operator is two. The result obtained is new and an example was used to demonstrate the result obtained.

5. Example

Example 1. *Consider the following boundary value problem:*

$$^C D_{0^+}^{\frac{1}{2}} D_{0^+}^{\frac{3}{2}} u(t) = \frac{e^{-5t} \sin D_{0^+}^{\frac{1}{2}} u(t)}{17(1+t^2)} + \frac{e^{-t} D_{0^+}^{\frac{3}{2}} u(t)}{9(1+t^{\frac{3}{2}})} + \frac{e^{-2t}}{15(1+t^{\frac{1}{2}})}, \quad t \in [0,+\infty) \quad (29)$$

$$I_{0^+}^{\frac{1}{2}} u(0) = 0, \quad D_{0^+}^{\frac{1}{2}} u(0) = \frac{2}{3} D_{0^+}^{\frac{1}{2}} u\left(\frac{1}{4}\right) - \frac{1}{3} D_{0^+}^{\frac{1}{2}} u\left(\frac{1}{2}\right),$$
$$D_{0^+}^{\frac{3}{2}} u(+\infty) = \frac{3}{4} D_{0^+}^{\frac{1}{2}} u\left(\frac{1}{5}\right) + \frac{1}{4} D_{0^+}^{\frac{1}{2}} u\left(\frac{3}{5}\right),. \quad (30)$$

Here $a = \frac{1}{2}$, $b = \frac{3}{2}$, $\alpha_1 = \frac{2}{3}$, $\alpha_2 = \frac{5}{2}$, $\xi_1 = 4$, $\xi_2 = 2$, $\beta_1 = \frac{3}{4}$, $\beta_2 = \frac{1}{4}$, $\eta_1 = 5$, $\eta_2 = \frac{5}{3}$, $n = m = 2$. $\sum_{j=1}^2 \alpha_j \xi_j^{-1} = 0$, $\sum_{j=1}^2 \alpha_j = 1$, $\sum_{k=1}^2 \beta_k \eta_k^{-1} = 0$, $\sum_{k=1}^2 \beta_k = 1$. $\|\rho\|_Z = \frac{1}{17} \sup_{t \in [0,+\infty)} |e^{-5t}| = \frac{1}{17}$, $\|\mu\|_Z = \frac{1}{9} \sup_{t \in [0,+\infty)} |e^{-t}| = \frac{1}{9}$,

$\|v\|_Z = \frac{1}{15}\sup_{t\in[0,+\infty)}|e^{-6t}| = \frac{1}{15}$. Then, $\|\rho\|_Z + \|\mu\|_Z + \|v\|_Z = \frac{1}{17} + \frac{1}{9} + \frac{1}{15} = 0.2367$
$\Gamma(a+1) = \Gamma(\frac{1}{2}+1) = 1$. Then, $\frac{\Gamma(\frac{3}{2})}{\Gamma(\frac{3}{2})+2} = 0.3071$. Hence,

$$\|\rho\|_Z + \|\mu\|_Z + \|v\|_Z < \frac{\Gamma(a+1)}{\Gamma(a+1)+2}.$$

Finally, conditions (H_1) - (H_3) can also be shown to hold. Therefore (29) and (30) has at least one solution.

Author Contributions: Conceptualization O.F.I., methodology O.F.I., S.A.I. and P.O.O., manuscript preparation O.F.I. and P.O.O. All authors have read and agreed to the published version of the manuscript.

Funding: This research received no external funding.

Data Availability Statement: Not applicable.

Acknowledgments: The authors are grateful to Covenant University for its support.

Conflicts of Interest: The authors declare no conflicts of interest.

References

1. Ameen, I.; Novati, P. The solution of fractional order epidemic model by implicit Adams methods. *Appl. Math. Model.* **2017**, *43*, 78–84. [CrossRef]
2. Ates, I.; Zegeling, P.A. A homotopy perturbation method for fractional-order advection–diffusion–reaction boundary-value problems. *Appl. Math. Model.* **2017**, *47*, 425–441. [CrossRef]
3. Tarasov, V.E.; Tarasova, V.V. Time-dependent fractional dynamics with memory in quantum and economic physics. *Ann. Phys.* **2017**, *383*, 579–599. [CrossRef]
4. Arara, A.; Benchohra, M.; Hamidi, N.; Nieto, J.J. Fractional order differential equations on an unbounded domain. *Nonlinear Anal.* **2010**, *72*, 580–586. [CrossRef]
5. Babakhani, A.; Gejji, V.D. Existence of positive solutions of nonlinear fractional differential equations. *J. Math. Anal. Appl.* **2003**, *278*, 434–442. [CrossRef]
6. Benchohra, M.; Hamani, S.; Ntouyas, S.K. Boundary value problems for differential equations with fractional order and nonlocal conditions. *Nonlinear Anal.* **2009**, *71*, 2391–2396. [CrossRef]
7. Seemab, A.; Ur Rehman, M.; Alzabut, J.; Hamdi, A. On the existence of positive solutions for generalized fractional boundary value problems. *Bound. Value Probl.* **2019**, *2019*, 186. [CrossRef]
8. Bai, Z.; Zhang, Y. Solvability of a fractional three-point boundary value problems with nonlinear growth. *Appl. Math. Comput.* **2011**, *218*, 1719–1725. [CrossRef]
9. Chen, T.; Tang, X. Positive solutions of fractional differential equations at resonance on the half-line. *Bound. Value Probl.* **2012**, *2012*, 64. [CrossRef]
10. Djebali, S.; Aoun, A.G. Resonant fractional differential equations with multi-point boundary conditions on $(0,+\infty)$. *J. Nonlinear Funct. Anal.* **2019**, *2019*, 1–15.
11. Imaga, O.F.; Iyase, S.A. On a fractional-order p-Laplacian boundary value problem at resonance on the half-line with two dimensional kernel. *Adv. Differ. Equ.* **2021**, *2021*, 252. [CrossRef]
12. Imaga, O.F.; Oghonyon, J.G.; Ogunniyi, P.O. On the solvability of a resonant third-order integral m-point boundary value problem on the half-line. *Abstr. Appl. Anal.* **2021**, *2021*, 8870108. [CrossRef]
13. Jiang, W. The existence of solutions to boundary value problems of fractional order at resonance. *Nonlinear Anal.* **2011**, *74*, 1987–1994. [CrossRef]
14. Zhang, W.; Liu, W. Existence of solutions for fractional differential equations with infinite point boundary conditions at resonance. *Bound. Value Probl.* **2018**, *2018*, 36. [CrossRef]
15. Zhang, W.; Liu, W. Existence of solutions for fractional multi-point boundary value problems on an infinite interval at resonance. *Mathematics* **2020**, *1*, 126. [CrossRef]
16. Khaldi, R.; Guezane-Lakoud, A. Guezane-Lakoud. Higher order fractional boundary value problems for mixed type derivatives. *J. Nonlinear Funct. Anal.* **2017**, *2017*, 30.
17. Guezane-Lakoud, A.; Khaldi, R.; Kilicman, A. Existence of solutions for a mixed fractional boundary value problem. *Adv. Differ. Equ.* **2017**, *2017*, 164. [CrossRef]
18. Imaga, O.F.; Iyase, S.A.; Odekina, O.G. Resonant mixed fractional-order p-Laplacian boundary value problem on the half-line. *Nonauton. Dyn. Syst.* **2021**, *8*, 328–339. [CrossRef]
19. Mawhin, J. Topological degree methods in nonlinear boundary value problems. In *NSFCMBS*; Regional Conference Series in Mathematics; American Mathematical Society: Providence, RI, USA, 1979.

20. Samko, S.G.; Kilbas, A.A.; Marichev, O.I. *Fractional Integrals and Derivatives: Theory and Applications*; Gordon and Breach: Philadelphia, PA, USA, 1993.
21. Kilbas, A.A.; Srivastava, H.M.; Truuillo, J.J. *Theory and Applications of Fractional Differential Equations*; Elsevier: New York, NY, USA, 2006.

Article

Basic Properties for Certain Subclasses of Meromorphic p-Valent Functions with Connected q-Analogue of Linear Differential Operator

Sheza M. El-Deeb [1,2] and Luminiţa-Ioana Cotîrlă [3,*]

1 Department of Mathematics, College of Science and Arts, Al-Badaya, Qassim University, Buraidah 52571, Saudi Arabia
2 Department of Mathematics, Faculty of Science, Damietta University, New Damietta 34517, Egypt
3 Department of Mathematics, Technical University of Cluj-Napoca, 400114 Cluj-Napoca, Romania
* Correspondence: luminita.cotirla@math.utcluj.ro

Abstract: In this paper, we define three subclasses $\mathcal{M}_{p,\alpha}^{n,q}(\eta, A, B)$, $\mathcal{I}_{p,\alpha}^{n}(\lambda, \mu, \gamma)$, $R_{p}^{n,q}(\lambda, \mu, \gamma)$ connected with a q-analogue of linear differential operator $\mathcal{D}_{\alpha,p,\mathcal{G}}^{n,q}$ which consist of functions $\mathcal{F}$ of the form $\mathcal{F}(\zeta) = \zeta^{-p} + \sum_{j=1-p}^{\infty} a_j \zeta^j$ $(p \in \mathbb{N})$ satisfying the subordination condition $p - \frac{1}{\eta} \left\{ \frac{\zeta \left(\mathcal{D}_{\alpha,p,\mathcal{G}}^{n,q} \mathcal{F}(\zeta) \right)'}{\mathcal{D}_{\alpha,p,\mathcal{G}}^{n,q} \mathcal{F}(\zeta)} + p \right\} \prec p \frac{1+A\zeta}{1+B\zeta}$. Also, we study the various properties and characteristics of this subclass $\mathcal{M}_{p,\alpha}^{n,q,*}(\eta, A, B)$ such as coefficients estimate, distortion bounds and convex family. Also the concept of δ neighborhoods and partial sums of analytic functions to the class $\mathcal{M}_{p,\alpha}^{n,q}(\eta, A, B)$.

Keywords: fractional derivative; convolution; meromorphic function; q-analogue of linear differential operator; complex order; q-starlike; q-convex; neighborhoods; partial sums

MSC: 30C50; 30C45; 11B65; 47B38

1. Introduction

Let $\mathcal{M}_p$ is the class of p-valently meromorphic functions of the form:

$$\mathcal{F}(\zeta) = \zeta^{-p} + \sum_{j=1-p}^{\infty} a_j \zeta^j \quad (p \in \mathbb{N} = \{1, 2, \ldots\}), \tag{1}$$

which are analytic in the punctured open unit disk $\Delta^* := \{\zeta \in \mathbb{C} : 0 < |\zeta| < 1\} = \Delta \setminus \{0\}$. Let $\mathcal{F}$ and $\mathcal{E}$ are analytic functions in Δ, we say that $\mathcal{F}$ is subordinate to $\mathcal{E}$ if there exists an analytic function $\omega(\zeta)$ with $\omega(0) = 0$ and $|\omega(\zeta)| < 1$ $(\zeta \in \Delta)$ such that $\mathcal{F} = \mathcal{E}(\omega(\zeta))$. We denote by $\mathcal{F} \prec \mathcal{E}$ (see [1,2]).

Let the functions $\mathcal{F}(\zeta) \in \mathcal{M}_p$ defined by (1) and $\mathcal{G}(\zeta) \in \mathcal{M}_p$ defined by

$$\mathcal{G}(\zeta) = \zeta^{-p} + \sum_{j=1-p}^{\infty} b_j \zeta^j \quad (p \in \mathbb{N}). \tag{2}$$

The Hadamard product or convolution of $\mathcal{F}(\zeta)$ and $\mathcal{G}(\zeta)$ is defined by

$$(\mathcal{F} * \mathcal{G})(\zeta) = \zeta^{-p} + \sum_{j=1-p}^{\infty} a_j b_j \zeta^j = (\mathcal{G} * \mathcal{F})(\zeta). \tag{3}$$

In this paper, we define some concepts of fractional derivative, for any non-negative integer j, the q-factorial $[j]_q!$ is defined by (see [3]):

Assume that $0 < q < 1$, the q-number $[j]_q$ are defined by (see [3–9]). where

$$[j]_q := \frac{1-q^j}{1-q} = 1 + \sum_{r=1}^{j-1} q^r. \qquad (4)$$

El-Deeb et al. [10] defined the q-derivative operator for $\mathcal{F} * \mathcal{G}$ as follows (see [11])

$$\mathcal{D}_q(\mathcal{F} * \mathcal{G})(\zeta) := \begin{cases} \frac{(\mathcal{F}*\mathcal{G})(q\zeta) - (\mathcal{F}*\mathcal{G})(\zeta)}{\zeta(q-1)} & \zeta \neq 0 \\ \mathcal{F}'(0) & \zeta = 0. \end{cases} \qquad (5)$$

Also, we have

$$\lim_{q \to 1^-} \mathcal{D}_q(\mathcal{F} * \mathcal{G})(\zeta) := \lim_{q \to 1^-} \frac{(\mathcal{F} * \mathcal{G})(q\zeta) - (\mathcal{F} * \mathcal{G})(\zeta)}{\zeta(q-1)} = ((\mathcal{F} * \mathcal{G})(\zeta))'.$$

From (1) and (5), we get

$$\mathcal{D}_q(\mathcal{F} * \mathcal{G})(\zeta) := -\frac{[p]_q}{q^p}\zeta^{-p-1} + \sum_{j=1-p}^{\infty} [j]_q a_j b_j \zeta^{j-1}, \; \zeta \neq 0. \qquad (6)$$

Also, we define the linear differential operator $\mathcal{D}_{\alpha,p,\mathcal{G}}^{n,q} : \mathcal{M}_p \to \mathcal{M}_p$ as follows:

$$\mathcal{D}_{\alpha,p,\mathcal{G}}^{0,q}\mathcal{F}(\zeta) = (\mathcal{F} * \mathcal{G})(\zeta),$$

$$\begin{aligned}
\mathcal{D}_{\alpha,p,\mathcal{G}}^{1,q}\mathcal{F}(\zeta) &= \frac{\alpha q^p}{[p]_q}\zeta\, \mathcal{D}_q\left(\mathcal{D}_{\alpha,p,\mathcal{G}}^{0,q}\mathcal{F}(\zeta)\right) + (1-\alpha)(\mathcal{F} * \mathcal{G})(\zeta) + 2\alpha\zeta^{-p} \\
&= \zeta^{-p} + \sum_{j=1-p}^{\infty} \left(\frac{\alpha q^p [j]_q + (1-\alpha)[p]_q}{[p]_q}\right) a_j b_j \zeta^j \\
\mathcal{D}_{\alpha,p,\mathcal{G}}^{2,q}\mathcal{F}(\zeta) &= \frac{\alpha q^p}{[p]_q}\zeta\, \mathcal{D}_q\left(\mathcal{D}_{\alpha,p,\mathcal{G}}^{1,q}\mathcal{F}(\zeta)\right) + (1-\alpha)\mathcal{D}_{\alpha,p,\mathcal{G}}^{1,q}\mathcal{F}(\zeta) + 2\alpha\zeta^{-p} \\
&= \zeta^{-p} + \sum_{j=1-p}^{\infty} \left(\frac{\alpha q^p [j]_q + (1-\alpha)[p]_q}{[p]_q}\right)^2 a_j b_j \zeta^j
\end{aligned}$$

$$\begin{aligned}
\mathcal{D}_{\alpha,p,\mathcal{G}}^{n,q}\mathcal{F}(\zeta) &= \frac{\alpha q^p}{[p]_q}\zeta\, \mathcal{D}_q\left(\mathcal{D}_{\alpha,p,\mathcal{G}}^{n-1,q}\mathcal{F}(\zeta)\right) + (1-\alpha)\mathcal{D}_{\alpha,p,\mathcal{G}}^{n-1,q}\mathcal{F}(\zeta) + 2\alpha\zeta^{-p} \\
&= \zeta^{-p} + \sum_{j=1-p}^{\infty} \left(\frac{\alpha q^p [j]_q + (1-\alpha)[p]_q}{[p]_q}\right)^n a_j b_j \zeta^j \qquad (7)
\end{aligned}$$

$(p \in \mathbb{N}, \; n \in \mathbb{N}_0 = \mathbb{N} \cup \{0\}, \; 0 < q < 1, \; \alpha > 0).$

From (7), we obtain the following relations:

(i) $\mathcal{D}_{\alpha,p,\mathcal{G}}^{n+1,q}\mathcal{F}(\zeta) = \frac{\alpha q^p}{[p]_q}\zeta\, \mathcal{D}_q\left(\mathcal{D}_{\alpha,p,\mathcal{G}}^{n,q}\mathcal{F}(\zeta)\right) + (1-\alpha)\mathcal{D}_{\alpha,p,\mathcal{G}}^{n,q}\mathcal{F}(\zeta) + 2\alpha\zeta^{-p}, \; \zeta \in \Delta^*;$ (8)

(ii) $\mathcal{I}_{\alpha,p,\mathcal{G}}^{n}\mathcal{F}(\zeta) := \lim_{q \to 1^-}\mathcal{D}_{\alpha,p,\mathcal{G}}^{n,q}\mathcal{F}(\zeta) = \zeta^{-p} + \sum_{j=1-p}^{\infty}\left(\frac{j\alpha + p(1-\alpha)}{p}\right)^n a_j b_j \zeta^j, \; \zeta \in \Delta^*.$ (9)

Remark 1. *(i) By taking* $\mathcal{G}(\zeta) = \frac{\zeta^{-p}}{1-\zeta}$ *(or $b_j = 1$) in this operator $\mathcal{D}_{\alpha,p,\mathcal{G}}^{n,q}$, we have the linear differential operator $\mathcal{D}_{\alpha,p,q}^n$ defined by El-Deeb and El-Matary ([12], With $A = 1$);*

(ii) Put $\alpha = 1$ in the operator $\mathcal{D}_{\alpha,p,\mathcal{G}}^{n,q}$, we get the (p,q)-analogue of the operator $\mathcal{D}_{p,\mathcal{G}}^{n,q}$ defined as follows:

$$\mathcal{D}_{p,\mathcal{G}}^{n,q}\mathcal{F}(\zeta) = \zeta^{-p} + \sum_{j=1-p}^{\infty} \left(\frac{q^p [j]_q}{[p]_q}\right)^n a_j b_j \zeta^j \quad (p \in \mathbb{N}, \ n \in \mathbb{N}_0, \ 0 < q < 1, \ \zeta \in \Delta^*); \tag{10}$$

(iii) Let $\alpha = 1$ and $q \to 1$ in the operator $\mathcal{D}_{\alpha,p,\mathcal{G}}^{n,q}$, we have the operator $\mathcal{D}_{p,\mathcal{G}}^n$ defined as follows:

$$\mathcal{D}_{p,\mathcal{G}}^n \mathcal{F}(\zeta) := \lim_{q \to 1^-} \mathcal{D}_{1,p,q}^n \mathcal{F}(\zeta) = \zeta^{-p} + \sum_{j=1-p}^{\infty} \left(\frac{j}{p}\right)^n a_j b_j \zeta^j, \quad (p \in \mathbb{N}, \ n \in \mathbb{N}_0, \ \zeta \in \Delta^*); \tag{11}$$

(iv) Taking $\alpha = 1$ and $\mathcal{G}(\zeta) = \frac{\zeta^{-p}}{1-\zeta}$ (or $b_j = 1$) in the operator $\mathcal{D}_{\alpha,p,\mathcal{G}}^{n,q}$, we have the (p,q)-analogue of Salagean operator $\mathcal{D}_{p,q}^n$ defined as follows:

$$\mathcal{D}_{p,q}^n \mathcal{F}(\zeta) := \zeta^{-p} + \sum_{j=1-p}^{\infty} \left(\frac{q^p [j]_q}{[p]_q}\right)^n a_j \zeta^j \quad (p \in \mathbb{N}, \ n \in \mathbb{N}_0, \ 0 < q < 1, \ \zeta \in \Delta^*); \tag{12}$$

(v) Putting $q \to 1^-$ and $\alpha = 1$ in the operator $\mathcal{D}_{\alpha,p,\mathcal{G}}^{n,q}$, we get the operator in meromorphic $\mathcal{D}_{p,\mathcal{G}}^n$ defined as follows:

$$\mathcal{D}_{p,\mathcal{G}}^n \mathcal{F}(\zeta) := \lim_{q \to 1^-} \mathcal{D}_{1,p,\mathcal{G}}^{n,q} \mathcal{F}(\zeta) = \zeta^{-p} + \sum_{j=1-p}^{\infty} \left(\frac{j}{p}\right)^n a_j b_j \zeta^j, \quad (p \in \mathbb{N}, \ n \in \mathbb{N}_0, \ \zeta \in \Delta^*). \tag{13}$$

A function $\mathcal{F} \in \mathcal{M}_p$ is said to be in the subclass $\mathcal{MS}^*(\gamma)$ of meromorphic starlike functions of order γ in Δ^*, if it satisfies the following condition (see [13–16]):

$$\Re\left(\frac{\zeta \mathcal{F}'(\zeta)}{\mathcal{F}(\zeta)}\right) < -\gamma \quad (\zeta \in \Delta^*; \ 0 \leq \gamma < 1). \tag{14}$$

A function $\mathcal{F} \in \mathcal{M}_p$ is said to be in the subclass $MC(\gamma)$ of meromorphic convex functions of order γ in Δ^*, if it satisfies the following condition (see [17]):

$$\Re\left(1 + \frac{\zeta \mathcal{F}''(\zeta)}{\mathcal{F}'(\zeta)}\right) < -\gamma \quad (\zeta \in \Delta^*; \ 0 \leq \gamma < 1). \tag{15}$$

It is easy to observe from (14) and (15) that

$$\mathcal{F} \in MC(\gamma) \Leftrightarrow -\zeta \mathcal{F}' \in \mathcal{MS}^*(\gamma). \tag{16}$$

We will generalize these classes by using the new operator $\mathcal{D}_{\alpha,p,\mathcal{G}}^{n,q}$, we define the new class $\mathcal{M}_{p,\alpha}^{n,q}(\lambda, \mu, \gamma)$ and study some theorems for this class.

Definition 1. *Assume that $\mathcal{F} \in \mathcal{M}_p$ be in the class $\mathcal{M}_{p,\alpha}^{n,q}(\eta, A, B)$ if*

$$p - \frac{1}{\eta}\left\{\frac{\zeta\left(\mathcal{D}_{\alpha,p,\mathcal{G}}^{n,q}\mathcal{F}(\zeta)\right)'}{\mathcal{D}_{\alpha,p,\mathcal{G}}^{n,q}\mathcal{F}(\zeta)} + p\right\} \prec p\frac{1+A\zeta}{1+B\zeta} \tag{17}$$

or, equivalently, to

$$\left| \frac{\frac{\zeta \left(\mathcal{D}_{\alpha,p,\mathcal{G}}^{n,q} \mathcal{F}(\zeta) \right)'}{\mathcal{D}_{\alpha,p,\mathcal{G}}^{n,q} \mathcal{F}(\zeta)} + p}{B \frac{\zeta \left(\mathcal{D}_{\alpha,p,\mathcal{G}}^{n,q} \mathcal{F}(\zeta) \right)'}{\mathcal{D}_{\alpha,p,\mathcal{G}}^{n,q} \mathcal{F}(\zeta)} + p[(A-B)\eta + B]} \right| < 1 \qquad (18)$$

$(p \in \mathbb{N}, n \in \mathbb{N}_0, 0 < q < 1, \alpha > 0, \eta \in \mathbb{C}^*, -1 \leq B < A \leq 1, \zeta \in \Delta^*)$.

Let $\mathcal{M}_p^*$ is subclass of $\mathcal{M}_p$ which contains functions on the form:

$$\mathcal{F}(\zeta) := \zeta^{-p} + \sum_{j=p}^{\infty} a_j \zeta^j \quad (p \in \mathbb{N}). \qquad (19)$$

Also, we can write

$$\mathcal{M}_{p,\alpha}^{n,q,*}(\eta, A, B) = \mathcal{M}_{p,\alpha}^{n,q}(\eta, A, B) \cap \mathcal{M}_p^*.$$

Remark 2. *(i) Taking $q \to 1^-$, we get $\lim_{q \to 1^-} \mathcal{M}_{p,\alpha}^{n,q}(\lambda, \mu, \gamma) =: \mathcal{I}_{p,\alpha}^n(\lambda, \mu, \gamma)$, where $\mathcal{I}_{p,\alpha}^n(\lambda, \mu, \gamma)$ represents the function $\mathcal{F} \in \mathcal{M}_p$ that satisfies (18) for $\mathcal{D}_{\alpha,p,\mathcal{G}}^{n,q}$ replaced with $\mathcal{I}_{\alpha,p,\mathcal{G}}^n$ given by (9);*

(ii) Putting $\alpha = 1$, we get the subclass $R_p^{n,q}(\lambda, \mu, \gamma)$ represents the function $\mathcal{F} \in \mathcal{M}_p$ that satisfies (18) for $\mathcal{D}_{\alpha,p,\mathcal{G}}^{n,q}$ replaced with $\mathcal{D}_{p,\mathcal{G}}^{n,q}$ given by (10).

2. Basic Properties of the Subclass $\mathcal{M}_{p,\alpha}^{n,q,*}(\eta, A, B)$

Theorem 1. *The function $\mathcal{F}$ defined by (19) belongs to the subclass $\mathcal{M}_{p,\alpha}^{n,q,*}(\eta, A, B)$ if and only if*

$$\sum_{j=p}^{\infty} [(j+p)(1-B) - p|\eta|(A-B)] \left(\frac{\alpha q^p [j]_q + (1-\alpha)[p]_q}{[p]_q} \right)^n b_j |a_j| \leq p|\eta|(A-B). \qquad (20)$$

Proof. Let (20) holds true, we get

$$\left| \zeta \left(\mathcal{D}_{\alpha,p,\mathcal{G}}^{n,q} \mathcal{F}(\zeta) \right)' + p \mathcal{D}_{\alpha,p,\mathcal{G}}^{n,q} \mathcal{F}(\zeta) \right| - \left| B\zeta \left(\mathcal{D}_{\alpha,p,\mathcal{G}}^{n,q} \mathcal{F}(\zeta) \right)' + [Bp(1-\eta) + Ap\eta] \mathcal{D}_{\alpha,p,\mathcal{G}}^{n,q} \mathcal{F}(\zeta) \right|$$

$$= \left| \sum_{j=p}^{\infty} (j+p) \left(\frac{\alpha q^p [j]_q + (1-\alpha)[p]_q}{[p]_q} \right)^n a_j b_j \zeta^{j+p} \right| -$$

$$\left| p\eta(A-B) + \sum_{j=p}^{\infty} [B(j+p) + p\eta(A-B)] \left(\frac{\alpha q^p [j]_q + (1-\alpha)[p]_q}{[p]_q} \right)^n a_j b_j \zeta^{j+p} \right|$$

$$\leq \sum_{j=p}^{\infty} (j+p) \left(\frac{\alpha q^p [j]_q + (1-\alpha)[p]_q}{[p]_q} \right)^n b_j |a_j| r^{j+p} - p\eta(A-B)$$

$$- \sum_{j=p}^{\infty} [B(j+p) + p\eta(A-B)] \left(\frac{\alpha q^p [j]_q + (1-\alpha)[p]_q}{[p]_q} \right)^n b_j |a_j| r^{j+p}$$

$$= \sum_{j=p}^{\infty} [(1-B)(j+p) - p\eta(A-B)] \left(\frac{\alpha q^p [j]_q + (1-\alpha)[p]_q}{[p]_q} \right)^n b_j |a_j| r^{j+p} - p\eta(A-B). \qquad (21)$$

Since (21) holds for all $r \in (0,1)$. Letting $r \to 1^-$, we obtain

$$\left|\zeta\left(\mathcal{D}^{n,q}_{\alpha,p,\mathcal{G}}\mathcal{F}(\zeta)\right)' + p\mathcal{D}^{n,q}_{\alpha,p,\mathcal{G}}\mathcal{F}(\zeta)\right| - \left|B\zeta\left(\mathcal{D}^{n,q}_{\alpha,p,\mathcal{G}}\mathcal{F}(\zeta)\right)' + [Bp(1-\eta) + Ap\eta]\mathcal{D}^{n,q}_{\alpha,p,\mathcal{G}}\mathcal{F}(\zeta)\right|$$

$$\leq \sum_{j=p}^{\infty}[(1-B)(j+p) - p\eta(A-B)]\left(\frac{\alpha q^p[j]_q + (1-\alpha)[p]_q}{[p]_q}\right)^n b_j|a_j| - p\eta(A-B)$$

$$\leq 0 \quad \text{(by (20))}.$$

Hence, we get $\mathcal{F}(\zeta) \in \mathcal{M}^{n,q}_{p,\alpha}(\eta, A, B)$.

Conversely, Let $\mathcal{F}(\zeta)$ belongs to $\mathcal{M}^{n,q}_{p,\alpha}(\eta, A, B)$ with $\mathcal{F}(\zeta)$ of the form (19), we find from (18), that

$$\left|\frac{\zeta\left(\mathcal{D}^{n,q}_{\alpha,p,\mathcal{G}}\mathcal{F}(\zeta)\right)' + p\mathcal{D}^{n,q}_{\alpha,p,\mathcal{G}}\mathcal{F}(\zeta)}{B\zeta\left(\mathcal{D}^{n,q}_{\alpha,p,\mathcal{G}}\mathcal{F}(\zeta)\right)' + [Bp(1-b) + Apb]\mathcal{D}^{n,q}_{\alpha,p,\mathcal{G}}\mathcal{F}(\zeta)}\right|$$

$$= \left|\frac{\sum_{j=p}^{\infty}(j+p)\left(\frac{\alpha q^p[j]_q + (1-\alpha)[p]_q}{[p]_q}\right)^n a_j b_j \zeta^{j+p}}{p\eta(A-B) + \sum_{j=p}^{\infty}[B(j+p) + p\eta(A-B)]\left(\frac{\alpha q^p[j]_q + (1-\alpha)[p]_q}{[p]_q}\right)^n a_j b_j \zeta^{j+p}}\right| < 1. \quad (22)$$

Using the fact that $\Re\{\zeta\} \leq |\zeta|$ for all ζ, we get

$$\Re\left\{\frac{\frac{\zeta\left(\mathcal{D}^{n,q}_{\alpha,p,\mathcal{G}}\mathcal{F}(\zeta)\right)'}{\mathcal{D}^{n,q}_{\alpha,p,\mathcal{G}}\mathcal{F}(\zeta)} + p}{\frac{B\zeta\left(\mathcal{D}^{n,q}_{\alpha,p,\mathcal{G}}\mathcal{F}(\zeta)\right)'}{\mathcal{D}^{n,q}_{\alpha,p,\mathcal{G}}\mathcal{F}(\zeta)} + [Bp(1-\eta) + Ap\eta]}\right\} < 1, \; \zeta \in \Delta^*. \quad (23)$$

If we take ζ on real axis, so that $\frac{\zeta\left(\mathcal{D}^{n,q}_{\alpha,p,\mathcal{G}}\mathcal{F}(\zeta)\right)'}{\mathcal{D}^{n,q}_{\alpha,p,\mathcal{G}}\mathcal{F}(\zeta)}$ is real. Upon clearing the denominator in (23) and letting $\zeta \to 1^-$, we get

$$\sum_{j=p}^{\infty}[(j+p)(1-B) - p|\eta|(A-B)]\left(\frac{\alpha q^p[j]_q + (1-\alpha)[p]_q}{[p]_q}\right)^n b_j|a_j| \leq p|\eta|(A-B), \quad (24)$$

which we've got the assertion (20) of Theorem 1. □

Corollary 1. *The function $\mathcal{F}(\zeta)$ be defined by (19) belongs to $\mathcal{M}^{n,q,*}_{p,\alpha}(\eta, A, B)$, then*

$$|a_j| \leq \frac{p|\eta|(A-B)}{[(j+p)(1-B) - p|\eta|(A-B)]\left(\frac{\alpha q^p[j]_q + (1-\alpha)[p]_q}{[p]_q}\right)^n b_j} \quad (j \geq p). \quad (25)$$

This result is sharp for $\mathcal{F}$ given by

$$\mathcal{F}(\zeta) = \zeta^{-p} + \frac{p|\eta|(A-B)}{[(j+p)(1-B) - p|\eta|(A-B)]\left(\frac{\alpha q^p[j]_q + (1-\alpha)[p]_q}{[p]_q}\right)^n b_j}\zeta^j \quad (j \geq p). \quad (26)$$

Theorem 2. *The function $\mathcal{F}(\zeta)$ defined by (19) belongs $\mathcal{M}^{n,q,*}_{p,\alpha}(\eta, A, B)$, then for $|\zeta| = r < 1$, we have*

$$\left\{ \frac{(p+m-1)!}{(p-1)!} - \frac{p!|\eta|(A-B)}{[2(1-B)-|\eta|(A-B)](1+\alpha(q^p-1))^n(p-m)!b_p} r^{2p} \right\} r^{-(p+m)}$$
$$\leq \left|\mathcal{F}^{(m)}(\zeta)\right| \leq \left\{ \frac{(p+m-1)!}{(p-1)!} + \frac{p!|\eta|(A-B)}{[2(1-B)-|\eta|(A-B)](1+\alpha(q^p-1))^n(p-m)!b_p} r^{2p} \right\} r^{-(p+m)}. \quad (27)$$

This result is sharp for $\mathcal{F}$ given by

$$\mathcal{F}(\zeta) = \zeta^{-p} + \frac{|\eta|(A-B)}{[2(1-B)-|\eta|(A-B)](1+\alpha(q^p-1))^n b_p} \zeta^p. \quad (28)$$

Proof. Let $\mathcal{F}(\zeta) \in \mathcal{M}_{p,\alpha}^{n,q,*}(\eta, A, B)$, then

$$\frac{p[2(1-B)-|\eta|(A-B)](1+\alpha(q^p-1))^n(p-m)!b_p}{p!} \sum_{j=p}^{\infty} \frac{j!}{(j-m)!}|a_j|$$
$$\leq \sum_{j=p}^{\infty} [(j+p)(1-B) - p|\eta|(A-B)] \left(\frac{\alpha q^p [j]_q + (1-\alpha)[p]_q}{[p]_q} \right)^n b_j \cdot |a_j| \leq p|\eta|(A-B),$$

which yields

$$\sum_{j=p}^{\infty} \frac{j!}{(j-m)!}|a_j| \leq \frac{|\eta|(A-B)}{[2(1-B)-|\eta|(A-B)](1+\alpha(q^p-1))^n b_p} \frac{p!}{(p-m)!}. \quad (29)$$

Differentiating both sides of (19) m times with respect to ζ, we get

$$\mathcal{F}^{(m)}(\zeta) = (-1)^m \frac{(p+m-1)!}{(p-1)!} \zeta^{-(p+m)} + \sum_{j=p}^{\infty} \frac{j!}{(j-m)!}|a_j|\zeta^{j-m} \quad (p \in \mathbb{N},\ 0 \leq m < p) \quad (30)$$

and Theorem 2 follows easily from (29) and (30), and it is easy to have the bounds in (27) are attained for $\mathcal{F}$ given by (28). □

Theorem 3. *The function $\mathcal{F}$ defined by (19) belings to $\mathcal{M}_{p,\alpha}^{n,q,*}(\eta, A, B)$, then*

(i) $\mathcal{F}$ is meromorphically p-valent q-starlike of order ρ ($0 \leq \rho < [p]_q$) in the disc $|\zeta| < r_1$, that is,

$$\Re\left\{ -\frac{\zeta \mathcal{D}_q \mathcal{F}(\zeta)}{\mathcal{F}(\zeta)} \right\} > \rho \quad (|\zeta| < r_1,\ 0 \leq \rho < [p]_q,\ p \in \mathbb{N}), \quad (31)$$

where

$$r_1 = \inf_{j \geq p} \left\{ \frac{[(j+p)(1-B) - p|\eta|(A-B)] \left(\frac{\alpha q^p [j]_q + (1-\alpha)[p]_q}{[p]_q} \right)^n \left(\frac{[p]_q}{q^p} - \rho \right) b_j}{p|\eta|(A-B) \left([j]_q + \rho \right)} \right\}^{\frac{1}{j+p}}, \quad (32)$$

(ii) $\mathcal{F}$ is meromorphically p-valent q-convex of order ρ ($0 \leq \rho < [p]_q$) in the disc $|\zeta| < r_2$, that is,

$$\Re\left\{ -\left(\frac{\mathcal{D}_q(\zeta \mathcal{D}_q \mathcal{F}(\zeta))}{\mathcal{D}_q \mathcal{F}(\zeta)} \right) \right\} > \rho \quad (|\zeta| < r_2,\ 0 \leq \rho < [p]_q,\ p \in \mathbb{N}), \quad (33)$$

where

$$r_2 = \inf_{j \geq p} \left\{ \frac{[(j+p)(1-B) - p|\eta|(A-B)]\left(\frac{\alpha q^p[j]_q + (1-\alpha)[p]_q}{[p]_q}\right)^n \left(\frac{[p]_q}{q^p} - \rho\right)[p]_q b_j}{pq^p[j]_q \left([j]_q + \rho\right)|\eta|(A-B)} \right\}^{\frac{1}{j+p}}. \qquad (34)$$

Each of these results is sharp for the function $\mathcal{F}(\zeta)$ given by (26).

Proof. (i) From the definition (19), we easily get

$$\left| \frac{\frac{\zeta \mathcal{D}_q \mathcal{F}(\zeta)}{\mathcal{F}(\zeta)} + \frac{[p]_q}{q^p}}{\frac{\zeta \mathcal{D}_q \mathcal{F}(\zeta)}{\mathcal{F}(\zeta)} - \frac{[p]_q}{q^p} + 2\rho} \right| \leq \frac{\sum\limits_{j=p}^{\infty} ([j]_q + \frac{[p]_q}{q^p})|a_j||\zeta|^{j+p}}{2(\frac{[p]_q}{q^p} - \rho) - \sum\limits_{j=p}^{\infty} ([j]_q - \frac{[p]_q}{q^p} + 2\rho)|a_j||\zeta|^{j+p}}. \qquad (35)$$

We have the inequality

$$\left| \frac{\frac{\zeta \mathcal{D}_q \mathcal{F}(\zeta)}{\mathcal{F}(\zeta)} + \frac{[p]_q}{q^p}}{\frac{\zeta \mathcal{D}_q \mathcal{F}(\zeta)}{\mathcal{F}(\zeta)} - \frac{[p]_q}{q^p} + 2\rho} \right| \leq 1 \quad (0 \leq \rho < [p]_q;\ p \in \mathbb{N}), \qquad (36)$$

if

$$\sum_{j=p}^{\infty} \left(\frac{[j]_q + \rho}{\frac{[p]_q}{q^p} - \rho} \right) |a_j||\zeta|^{j+p} \leq 1. \qquad (37)$$

Hence, by Theorem 1, (37) will be true

$$\frac{\left([j]_q + \rho\right)}{\left(\frac{[p]_q}{q^p} - \rho\right)} |\zeta|^{j+p} \leq \frac{[(j+p)(1-B) - p|\eta|(A-B)]\left(\frac{\alpha q^p[j]_q + (1-\alpha)[p]_q}{[p]_q}\right)^n b_j}{p|\eta|(A-B)}$$

$$|\zeta| \leq \left\{ \frac{[(j+p)(1-B) - p|\eta|(A-B)]\left(\frac{\alpha q^p[j]_q + (1-\alpha)[p]_q}{[p]_q}\right)^n b_j \left(\frac{[p]_q}{q^p} - \rho\right)}{p|\eta|(A-B)\left([j]_q + \rho\right)} \right\}^{\frac{1}{j+p}}, \qquad (38)$$

the inequality leads us immediately to the disc $|\zeta| < r_1$, where r_1 is given by (32).

(ii) To prove the second assertion of Theorem 3, we get from the definition (19) that

$$\left| \frac{\frac{\mathcal{D}_q(\zeta \mathcal{D}_q \mathcal{F}(\zeta))}{\mathcal{D}_q \mathcal{F}(\zeta)} + \frac{[p]_q}{q^p}}{\frac{\mathcal{D}_q(\zeta \mathcal{D}_q \mathcal{F}(\zeta))}{\mathcal{D}_q \mathcal{F}(\zeta)} - \frac{[p]_q}{q^p} + 2\rho} \right| \leq \frac{\sum\limits_{j=p}^{\infty} [j]_q([j]_q + \frac{[p]_q}{q^p})|a_j||\zeta|^{j+p}}{2\frac{[p]_q}{q^p}(\frac{[p]_q}{q^p} - \rho) - \sum\limits_{j=p}^{\infty} [j]_q([j]_q - \frac{[p]_q}{q^p} + 2\rho)|a_j||\zeta|^{j+p}}. \qquad (39)$$

Thus, we have the desired inequality

$$\left| \frac{\frac{\mathcal{D}_q(\zeta \mathcal{D}_q \mathcal{F}(\zeta))}{\mathcal{D}_q \mathcal{F}(\zeta)} + \frac{[p]_q}{q^p}}{\frac{\mathcal{D}_q(\zeta \mathcal{D}_q \mathcal{F}(\zeta))}{\mathcal{D}_q \mathcal{F}(\zeta)} - \frac{[p]_q}{q^p} + 2\rho} \right| \leq 1 \quad (0 \leq \rho < [p]_q,\ p \in \mathbb{N}), \qquad (40)$$

if
$$\sum_{j=p}^{\infty} \frac{q^p [j]_q}{[p]_q} \left(\frac{[j]_q + \rho}{\frac{[p]_q}{q^p} - \rho} \right) |a_j| |\zeta|^{j+p} \leq 1. \tag{41}$$

From Theorem 1, (41) will be true if

$$\frac{q^p [j]_q}{[p]_q} \left(\frac{[j]_q + \rho}{\frac{[p]_q}{q^p} - \rho} \right) |\zeta|^{j+p} \leq \frac{[(j+p)(1-B) - p|\eta|(A-B)] \left(\frac{\alpha q^p [j]_q + (1-\alpha)[p]_q}{[p]_q} \right)^n b_j}{p|\eta|(A-B)}. \tag{42}$$

The inequality (42) readily yields the disc $|\zeta| < r_2$, where r_2 defined by (34), and the proof of Theorem 3 is completed. □

3. Neighborhoods and Partial Sums

By following the earlier works based upon the familiar concept of neighborhoods of analytic functions by Goodman [15] and Ruscheweyh [18] and (more recently) by Altintas et al. [19–21], Liu [22], Liu and Srivastava [23] and El-Ashwah et al. [24], we introduce here the δ-neighborhoods of a function $\mathcal{F} \in \mathcal{M}_p$ has the form (1) by means of the definition given by:

$$\mathcal{N}_\delta(\mathcal{F}) = \left\{ h : h \in \mathcal{M}_p, \, h(\zeta) = \zeta^{-p} + \sum_{j=1-p}^{\infty} c_j z^j \text{ and} \right.$$

$$\sum_{j=1-p}^{\infty} \frac{[(j+p)(1-B) - p|\eta|(A-B)] \left(\frac{\alpha q^p [j]_q + (1-\alpha)[p]_q}{[p]_q} \right)^n b_j}{p|\eta|(A-B)} |c_j - a_j| \leq \delta$$

$$\left. (n \in \mathbb{N}_0, \, 0 < q < 1, \, \alpha > 0, \, \eta \in \mathbb{C}^*, \, -1 \leq B < A \leq 1) \right\}. \tag{43}$$

Using the definition (43), we will obtain the following theorem:

Theorem 4. *The function $\mathcal{F}$ defined by (1) belongs to $M_{p,\alpha}^{n,q}(\eta, A, B)$. If $\mathcal{F}$ satisfies the condition*

$$\frac{\mathcal{F}(\zeta) + \epsilon \zeta^{-p}}{1 + \epsilon} \in M_{p,\alpha}^{n,q}(\eta, A, B) \quad (\epsilon \in \mathbb{C}, \, |\epsilon| < \delta, \, \delta > 0) \tag{44}$$

then

$$N_\delta(\mathcal{F}) \subset M_{p,\alpha}^{n,q}(\eta, A, B). \tag{45}$$

Proof. From (18), we obtain $h \in M_{p,\alpha}^{n,q}(\eta, A, B)$ if, for $\sigma \in \mathbb{C}$ with $|\sigma| = 1$, we have

$$\frac{\zeta \left(\mathcal{D}_{\alpha,p,\mathcal{G}}^{n,q} h(\zeta) \right)' + p \mathcal{D}_{\alpha,p,\mathcal{G}}^{n,q} h(\zeta)}{B\zeta \left(\mathcal{D}_{\alpha,p,\mathcal{G}}^{n,q} h(\zeta) \right)' + [Bp(1-b) + Apb] \mathcal{D}_{\alpha,p,\mathcal{G}}^{n,q} h(\zeta)} \neq \sigma \quad (\zeta \in \Delta), \tag{46}$$

which is equivalent to

$$\frac{(h * \psi)(\zeta)}{\zeta^{-p}} \neq 0 \quad (\zeta \in \Delta^*), \tag{47}$$

where, for convenience,

$$\psi(\zeta) = \zeta^{-p} + \sum_{j=1-p}^{\infty} y_j \zeta^j$$

$$= \zeta^{-p} + \sum_{j=1-p}^{\infty} \frac{[(j+p)(1-B\sigma) - p|\eta|\sigma(A-B)] \left(\frac{\alpha q^p [j]_q + (1-\alpha)[p]_q}{[p]_q}\right)^n b_j}{p\eta\sigma(A-B)} \zeta^j. \qquad (48)$$

From (48), we get

$$|y_j| = \left| \frac{[(j+p)(1-B\sigma) - p|\eta|\sigma(A-B)] \left(\frac{\alpha q^p [j]_q + (1-\alpha)[p]_q}{[p]_q}\right)^n b_j}{p\eta\sigma(A-B)} \right|$$

$$\leq \frac{[(j+p)(1+|B|) - p|\eta|(A-B)] \left(\frac{\alpha q^p [j]_q + (1-\alpha)[p]_q}{[p]_q}\right)^n b_j}{p|\eta|(A-B)} \quad (j \geq p,\ p \in \mathbb{N}). \qquad (49)$$

If $\mathcal{F}(\zeta) = \zeta^{-p} + \sum_{j=1-p}^{\infty} a_j \zeta^j \in \mathcal{M}_p$ holds the condition (44), then (47) yields

$$\left| \frac{(\mathcal{F} * \psi)(\zeta)}{\zeta^{-p}} \right| > \delta \quad (\zeta \in \Delta^*,\ \delta > 0). \qquad (50)$$

Let

$$\Phi(\zeta) = \zeta^{-p} + \sum_{j=1-p}^{\infty} d_j \zeta^j \in N_\delta(\mathcal{F}) \qquad (51)$$

we have

$$\left| \frac{[\Phi(\zeta) - \mathcal{F}(\zeta)] * \psi(\zeta)}{\zeta^{-p}} \right| = \left| \sum_{j=1-p}^{\infty} (d_j - a_j) y_j \zeta^{j+p} \right|$$

$$\leq |\zeta| \sum_{j=1-p}^{\infty} \frac{[(j+p)(1+|B|) - p|\eta|(A-B)]}{p|\eta|(A-B)} \left(\frac{\alpha q^p [j]_q + (1-\alpha)[p]_q}{[p]_q}\right)^n b_j |d_j - a_j| \qquad (52)$$

$$< \delta \quad (\zeta \in \Delta,\ \delta > 0).$$

We have (47), and hence also (46) for any σ, which implies that $\Phi \in M_{p,\alpha}^{n,q}(\eta, A, B)$. This evidently proves the assertion (45) of Theorem 4. □

Theorem 5. *Let $\mathcal{F} \in \mathcal{M}_p$ defined by (1) and $-1 \leq B \leq 0$, the partial sums $\mathcal{S}_1(\zeta)$ and $\mathcal{S}_m(\zeta)$ are given by*

$$\mathcal{S}_1(\zeta) = \zeta^{-p} \quad \text{and} \quad \mathcal{S}_m(\zeta) = \zeta^{-p} + \sum_{j=1-p}^{m-1} a_j \zeta^j \quad (m \in \mathbb{N} \setminus \{1\}). \qquad (53)$$

Also, suppose that

$$\sum_{j=1-p}^{\infty} y_{j+p}|a_j| \leq 1 \ \left(y_{j+p} = \frac{[(j+p)(1+|B|) - p|\eta|(A-B)]}{p|\eta|(A-B)} \left(\frac{\alpha q^p [j]_q + (1-\alpha)[p]_q}{[p]_q}\right)^n b_j \right), \qquad (54)$$

then

(i) $\mathcal{F}(\zeta) \in M_{p,\alpha}^{n,q}(\eta, A, B)$

(ii) $\operatorname{Re}\left\{\dfrac{\mathcal{F}(\zeta)}{\mathcal{S}_m(\zeta)}\right\} > 1 - \dfrac{1}{y_q}$ $(\zeta \in \Delta,\, m \in \mathbb{N})$ \hfill (55)

and

(iii) $\operatorname{Re}\left\{\dfrac{\mathcal{S}_m(\zeta)}{\mathcal{F}(\zeta)}\right\} > \dfrac{y_q}{1+y_q}$ $(\zeta \in \Delta,\, m \in \mathbb{N})$. \hfill (56)

The estimates in (55) and (56) are sharp.

Proof. Since $\dfrac{\zeta^{-p} + \varepsilon \zeta^{-p}}{1+\varepsilon} = \zeta^{-p} \in M_{p,\alpha}^{n,q}(\eta, A, B)$, $|\varepsilon| < 1$, then by Theorem 4, we have $N_\delta(\mathcal{F}) \subset M_{p,\alpha}^{n,q}(\eta, A, B)$, $p \in \mathbb{N}$. $N_1(\zeta^{-p})$ denoting the 1-neighbourhood). Now since

$$\sum_{j=1-p}^{\infty} y_j |a_j| \leq 1, \tag{57}$$

then $\mathcal{F} \in N_1(\zeta^{-p})$ and $\mathcal{F} \in M_{p,\alpha}^{n,q}(\eta, A, B)$. Since $\{y_j\}$ is an increasing sequence, we get

$$\sum_{j=1-p}^{m-p-1} |a_j| + y_m \sum_{j=m-p}^{\infty} |a_j| \leq \sum_{j=1-p}^{\infty} y_{j+p} |a_j| \leq 1, \tag{58}$$

we have used the hypothesis (54). Putting

$$h_1(\zeta) = y_m\left\{\dfrac{\mathcal{F}(\zeta)}{\mathcal{S}_m(\zeta)} - \left(1 - \dfrac{1}{y_m}\right)\right\} = 1 + \dfrac{y_m \sum_{j=m-p}^{\infty} |a_j| \zeta^{j+p}}{1 + \sum_{j=1-p}^{m-p-1} |a_j| \zeta^{j+p}}$$

and applying (58), we find that

$$\left|\dfrac{h_1(\zeta) - 1}{h_1(\zeta) + 1}\right| \leq \dfrac{y_m \sum_{j=m-p}^{\infty} |a_j|}{2 - 2\sum_{j=1-p}^{m-p-1} |a_j| - y_m \sum_{j=m-p}^{\infty} |a_j|} \leq 1 \quad (\zeta \in \Delta), \tag{59}$$

which readily yields the assertion (55) of Theorem 5. If we take

$$\mathcal{F}(\zeta) = \zeta^{-p} - \dfrac{\zeta^m}{y_m}, \tag{60}$$

then

$$\dfrac{\mathcal{F}(\zeta)}{\mathcal{S}_m(\zeta)} = 1 - \dfrac{\zeta^{p+m}}{y_m} \to 1 - \dfrac{1}{y_m},\ \text{as } \zeta \to 1^-,$$

which shows that the bound in (55) is the best possible for each $m \in \mathbb{N}$.

If we put

$$h_2(\zeta) = (1+y_m)\left\{\dfrac{\mathcal{S}_m(\zeta)}{\mathcal{F}(\zeta)} - \dfrac{y_m}{1+y_m}\right\} = 1 - \dfrac{(1+y_m)\sum_{j=m-p}^{\infty}|a_j|\zeta^{j+p}}{1 + \sum_{j=1-p}^{\infty}|a_j|\zeta^{j+p}}, \tag{61}$$

and make use of (58), we can deduce that

$$\left|\frac{h_2(\zeta)-1}{h_2(\zeta)+1}\right| \leq \frac{(1+y_m)\sum\limits_{j=m-p}^{\infty}|a_j|}{2-2\sum\limits_{j=1-p}^{m-p-1}|a_j|-(1-y_m)\sum\limits_{j=m-p}^{\infty}|a_j|} \leq 1,$$

leads us to the assertion (56) of Theorem 5. The bound in (56) is sharp. The proof of Theorem 5 is completed. □

4. Concluding Remarks and Observations

In our present investigation, we have introduced and studied the properties of some new subclasses of the class of meromorphic p-valent functions in the open unit disk Δ^* by using the combination of q-derivative and convolution and obtain the new operator $\mathcal{D}_{\alpha,p,g}^{n,q}$. Among other properties and results such as coefficients estimate, distortion bounds and convex family. Also the concept of δ neighborhoods and partial sums of analytic functions to the class $\mathcal{M}_{p,\alpha}^{n,q}(\eta, A, B)$.

Interesting results about meromorphic functions can be found in the works [25–31].

Author Contributions: Conceptualization, S.M.E.-D. and L.-I.C.; methodology, S.M.E.-D. and L.-I.C.; software, S.M.E.-D. and L.-I.C.; validation, S.M.E.-D. and L.-I.C.; formal analysis, S.M.E.-D. and L.-I.C.; investigation, S.M.E.-D. and L.-I.C.; resources, S.M.E.-D. and L.-I.C.; data curation, S.M.E.-D. and L.-I.C.; writing—original draft preparation, S.M.E.-D. and L.-I.C.; writing—review and editing, S.M.E.-D. and L.-I.C.; visualization, S.M.E.-D. and L.-I.C.; supervision, S.M.E.-D. and L.-I.C.; project administration, S.M.E.-D. and L.-I.C.; funding acquisition, L.-I.C. All authors have read and agreed to the published version of the manuscript.

Funding: Not applicable.

Data Availability Statement: Not applicable.

Conflicts of Interest: The authors declare no conflict of interest.

References

1. Bulboacă, T. *Differential Subordinations and Superordinations: Recent Results*; House of Scientific Book Publishing: Cluj-Napoca, Romania, 2005.
2. Miller, S.S.; Mocanu, P.T. *Differential Subordinations: Theory and Applications, Series on Monographs and Textbooks in Pure and Applied Mathematics*; Marcel Dekker Inc.: New York, NY, USA; Basel, Switzerland, 2000; Volume 225.
3. Jackson, F.H. On q-definite integrals. *Quart. J. Pure Appl. Math.* **1910**, *41*, 193–203.
4. Abu Risha, M.H.; Annaby, M.H.; Ismail, M.E.H.; Mansour, Z.S. Linear q-difference equations. *Z. Anal. Anwend.* **2007**, *26*, 481–494. [CrossRef]
5. Jackson, F.H. On q-functions and a certain difference operator. *Trans. Royal Soc. Edinburgh* **1909**, *46*, 253–281. [CrossRef]
6. Srivastava, H.M. Certain q−polynomial expansions for functions of several variables. I and II. *IMA J. Appl. Math.* **1983**, *30*, 205–209. [CrossRef]
7. Srivastava, H.M. Univalent functions, fractional calculus, and associated generalized hypergeometric functions. In *Univalent Functions, Fractional Calculus, and Their Applications*; Srivastava, H.M., Owa, S., Eds.; Halsted Press (Ellis Horwood Limited): Chichester, UK; John Wiley and Sons: New York, NY, USA; Chichester, UK; Brisbane, Australia; Toronto, ON, Canada, 1989; pp. 329–354.
8. Srivastava, H.M.; El-Deeb, S.M. A certain class of analytic functions of complex order with a q-analogue of integral operators. *Miskolc Math Notes* **2020**, *21*, 417–433. [CrossRef]
9. Srivastava, H.M.; Karlsson, P.W. *Multiple Gaussian Hypergeometric Series*; Wiley: New York, NY, USA, 1985.
10. El-Deeb, S.M.; Bulboacă, T.; El-Matary, B.M. Maclaurin Coefficient Estimates of Bi-Univalent Functions Connected with the q-Derivative. *Mathematics* **2020**, *8*, 418. [CrossRef]
11. Gasper, G.; Rahman, M. Basic hypergeometric series (with a Foreword by Richard Askey). In *Encyclopedia of Mathematics and Its Applications*; Cambridge University Press: Cambridge, UK, 1990; Volume 35.
12. El-Deeb, S.M.; El-Matary, B.M. Q-analogue of linear differential operator on meromorphic p-valent functions with connected sets. *Appl. Math. Sci.* **2020**, *14*, 621–634. [CrossRef]
13. Aouf, M.K. A certain subclass of meromorphically starlike functions with positive coefficients. *Rend. Mat.* **1989**, *9*, 225–235.
14. Clunie, J. On meromorphic Schlicht functions. *J. Lond. Math. Soc.* **1959**, *34*, 215–216. [CrossRef]

15. Goodman, A.W. Univalent functions and nonanalytic curves. *Proc. Am. Math. Soc.* **1957**, *8*, 898–901. [CrossRef]
16. Pommerenke, C. On meromorphic starlike functions. *Pacific J. Math.* **1963**, *13*, 221–235. [CrossRef]
17. Miller, J.E. Convex meromorphic mapping and related functions. *Proc. Am. Math. Soc.* **1970**, *25*, 220–228. [CrossRef]
18. Ruscheweyh, S. Neighborhoods of univalent functions. *Proc. Am. Math. Soc.* **1981**, *81*, 521–527. [CrossRef]
19. Altintas, O.; Owa, S. Neighborhoods of certain analytic functions with negative coefficients. *Int. J. Math. Math. Sci.* **1996**, *19*, 797–800. [CrossRef]
20. Altintas, O.; Özkan, Ö.; Srivastava, H.M. Neighborhoods of a class of analytic functions with negative coefficients. *Appl. Math. Lett.* **2000**, *13*, 63–67. [CrossRef]
21. Altintas, O.; Özkan, Ö.; Srivastava, H.M. Neighborhoods of a certain family of multivalent functions with negative coefficient. *Comput. Math. Appl.* **2004**, *47*, 1667–1672. [CrossRef]
22. Liu, J.-L. Properties of some families of meromorphic p-valent functions. *Math. Jpn.* **2000**, *52*, 425–434.
23. Liu, J.-L.; Srivastava, H.M. A linear operator and associated families of meromorphically multivalent functions. *J. Math. Anal. Appl.* **2000**, *259*, 566–581. [CrossRef]
24. El-Ashwah, R.M.; Aouf, M.K.; El-Deeb, S.M. Some properties of certain subclasses of meromorphic multivalent functions of complex order defined by certain linear operator. *Acta Univ. Apulensis* **2014**, *40*, 265–282.
25. Aouf, M.K. On a certain class of meromorphic univalent functions with positive coefficients. *Rend. Mat.* **1991**, *7*, 209–219.
26. Chen, M.P.; Irmak, H.; Srivastava, H.M.; Yu, C.S. Certain subclasses of meromorphically univalent functions with positive or negative coefficients. *Panam. Math. J.* **1996**, *6*, 65–77.
27. Breaz, D.; Cotîrlă, L.I.; Umadevi, E.; Karthikeyan, K.R. Properties of meromorphic spiral-like functions associated with symmetric functions. *J. Funct. Spaces* **2022**, *2022*, 344485. [CrossRef]
28. Irmak, H.; Cho, N.E.; Raina, R.K. Certain inequalities involving meromorphically multivalent functions. *Hacet. Bull. Nat. Sci. Eng. Ser. B* **2001**, *30*, 39–43.
29. Totoi, A.; Cotîrlă, L.I. Preserving classes of meromorphic functions through integral operators. *Symmetry* **2022**, *14*, 1545. [CrossRef]
30. Çağlar, M.; Orhan, H. Univalence criteria for meromorphic functions and quasiconformal extensions. *J. Inequalities Appl.* **2013**, *112*, 1732. [CrossRef]
31. Oros, G.I.; Cătaş, A.; Oros, G. On certain subclasses of meromorphic close-to-convex functions. *J. Funct. Spaces* **2008**. [CrossRef]

Disclaimer/Publisher's Note: The statements, opinions and data contained in all publications are solely those of the individual author(s) and contributor(s) and not of MDPI and/or the editor(s). MDPI and/or the editor(s) disclaim responsibility for any injury to people or property resulting from any ideas, methods, instructions or products referred to in the content.

Article

On a Coupled Differential System Involving (k, ψ)-Hilfer Derivative and (k, ψ)-Riemann–Liouville Integral Operators

Ayub Samadi [1], Sotiris K. Ntouyas [2], Bashir Ahmad [3] and Jessada Tariboon [4,*]

1. Department of Mathematics, Miyaneh Branch, Islamic Azad University, Miyaneh 5315836511, Iran; ayubtoraj1366@gmail.com
2. Department of Mathematics, University of Ioannina, 451 10 Ioannina, Greece; sntouyas@uoi.gr
3. Nonlinear Analysis and Applied Mathematics (NAAM)-Research Group, Department of Mathematices, Faculty of Science, King Abdulaziz University, P.O. Box 80203, Jeddah 21589, Saudi Arabia; bahmad@kau.edu.sa
4. Intelligent and Nonlinear Dynamic Innovations Research Center, Department of Mathematics, Faculty of Applied Science, King Mongkut's University of Technology North Bangkok, Bangkok 10800, Thailand
* Correspodence: jessada.t@sci.kmutnb.ac.th

Abstract: We investigate a nonlinear, nonlocal, and fully coupled boundary value problem containing mixed $(k, \hat{\psi})$-Hilfer fractional derivative and $(k, \hat{\psi})$-Riemann–Liouville fractional integral operators. Existence and uniqueness results for the given problem are proved with the aid of standard fixed point theorems. Examples illustrating the main results are presented. The paper concludes with some interesting findings.

Keywords: systems of (k, ψ) Hilfer fractional differential equations; fractional integrals; fractional derivatives; coupled nonlocal boundary conditions; existence of solutions; fixed point theorems

MSC: 26A33; 34A08; 34B15

Citation: Samadi, A.; Ntouyas, S.K.; Ahmad, B.; Tariboon, J. On a Coupled Differential System Involving (k, ψ)-Hilfer Derivative and (k, ψ)-Riemann–Liouville Integral Operators. *Axioms* **2023**, *12*, 229. https://doi.org/10.3390/axioms12030229

Academic Editors: Péter Kórus and Juan Eduardo Nápoles Valdés

Received: 11 January 2023
Revised: 13 February 2023
Accepted: 20 February 2023
Published: 22 February 2023

Copyright: © 2023 by the authors. Licensee MDPI, Basel, Switzerland. This article is an open access article distributed under the terms and conditions of the Creative Commons Attribution (CC BY) license (https://creativecommons.org/licenses/by/4.0/).

1. Introduction

We consider a nonlinear system of $(k, \hat{\psi})$-Hilfer fractional differential equations:

$$\begin{cases} {}^{k,H}\mathcal{D}^{\tilde{\alpha},\tilde{\beta};\hat{\psi}}\check{k}(s) = \check{L}(s, \check{k}(s), \check{I}(s)), & s \in [l_1, l_2], \\ {}^{k,H}\mathcal{D}^{\tilde{p},\tilde{q};\hat{\psi}}\check{I}(s) = \check{L}(s, \check{k}(s), \check{I}(s)), & s \in [l_1, l_2], \end{cases} \quad (1)$$

supplemented with coupled mixed boundary conditions containing $(k, \hat{\psi})$-derivative and integral operators

$$\begin{cases} \check{k}(l_1) = 0, \quad \check{k}(l_2) = \tilde{\lambda}\, {}^{k,H}\mathcal{D}^{\tilde{r},\tilde{s},\hat{\psi}}\check{I}(\tilde{\xi}) + \tilde{\mu}\, {}^k\mathcal{I}^{\tilde{v},\hat{\psi}}\check{I}(\tilde{\sigma}), \; \tilde{\lambda}, \tilde{\mu} \in \mathbb{R}, \\ \check{I}(l_1) = 0, \quad \check{I}(l_2) = \tilde{v}\, {}^{k,H}\mathcal{D}^{\tilde{z},\tilde{w},\hat{\psi}}\check{k}(\tilde{\eta}) + \tilde{\theta}\, {}^k\mathcal{I}^{\tilde{u},\hat{\psi}}\check{k}(\tilde{\tau}), \; \tilde{v}, \tilde{\theta} \in \mathbb{R}, \end{cases} \quad (2)$$

where ${}^{k,H}\mathcal{D}^{\varrho,\omega;\hat{\psi}}$ represents the $(k, \hat{\psi})$-Hilfer fractional derivative operator of order ϱ and parameter ω with $\varrho = \{\tilde{\alpha}, \tilde{p}, \tilde{r}, \tilde{z}\}$ and $\omega = \{\tilde{\beta}, \tilde{q}, \tilde{s}, \tilde{w}\}$, such that $1 < \tilde{\alpha}, \tilde{p} < 2, 0 < \tilde{r}, \tilde{z} < 1$, $0 < \omega < 1, 0 \le l_1 < l_2 < \infty$, $\check{L}, \check{L} \in C([l_1, l_2] \times \mathbb{R} \times \mathbb{R}, \mathbb{R})$, and ${}^k\mathcal{I}^{\tilde{v},\hat{\psi}}$, ${}^k\mathcal{I}^{\tilde{u},\hat{\psi}}$ are $(k, \hat{\psi})$-Riemann–Liouville fractional integrals of order $\tilde{v} > 0, \hat{u} > 0$, respectively, and $l_1 < \tilde{\tilde{\xi}}, \tilde{\sigma}, \tilde{\eta}, \tilde{\tau} < l_2$.

The objective of the present work is to develop the existence theory for the Problem (1) and (2) via the tools of the fixed point theory. A uniqueness result for the Problem (1) and (2) is proved by means of a fixed point theorem due to Banach, while the Leray–Schauder alternative and Krasnosel'skiĭ's fixed-point theorem are applied to derive the two existence results for the problem at hand. The results established in this paper will contribute significantly to the literature on coupled $(k, \hat{\psi})$-Hilfer fractional differential systems, which is indeed scarce and needs to be enriched and extended further in several directions.

Boundary value problems involving different kinds of fractional derivative operators such as Caputo–Liouville, Riemann–Liouville, $\hat{\psi}$-Riemann–Liouville [1], Hilfer [2], k-Riemann–Liouville, $(k, \hat{\psi})$-Riemann–Liouville [3], $\hat{\psi}$-Hilfer [4], etc., have been addressed by several authors. Some recent results on nonlocal multipoint single-valued and multi-valued boundary value problems containing Hilfer and Caputo–Hadamard type fractional derivative operators can be found in the papers [5–7]. For preliminary concepts of fractional calculus, for example, see the books [1,8]. Here we mention that the Hilfer fractional derivative unifies the definitions of both Riemann–Liouville and Caputo fractional derivatives. For some applications of Hilfer fractional derivative operator, see [2,9–11].

Let us now review some recent works on fractional differential equations and systems equipped with different boundary conditions. In [12], the authors proved the existence and uniqueness of solutions for a boundary value problem involving $(k, \hat{\psi})$-Hilfer type fractional derivative and integral operators of the form:

$$\begin{cases} {}^{k,H}D^{\alpha,\beta;\hat{\psi}}\check{k}(s) = \check{L}(s,\check{k}(s)), \quad s \in [l_1, l_2], \\ \check{k}(l_1) = 0, \quad \check{k}(l_2) = \tilde{\lambda}\,{}^{k,H}D^{p,q;\hat{\psi}}\check{k}(\tilde{\eta}) + \tilde{\mu}\,{}^{k}\mathfrak{J}^{v,\hat{\psi}}\check{k}(\tilde{\sigma}), \end{cases}$$

where ${}^{k,H}D^{\alpha,\beta;\hat{\psi}}$ and ${}^{k,H}D^{p,q;\hat{\psi}}$ represent the $(k, \hat{\psi})$-Hilfer type fractional derivative operators of orders $\alpha \in (1,2)$, and $p \in (0,1)$ with parameters $\beta, q \in [0,1]$, respectively, $\check{L} \in C([l_1, l_2] \times \mathbb{R}, \mathbb{R})$, ${}^{k}\mathfrak{J}^{v,\hat{\psi}}$ is the $(k, \hat{\psi})$-Riemann–Liouville fractional integral of order $v > 0$, $\tilde{\lambda}, \tilde{\mu} \in \mathbb{R}$, and $l_1 < \tilde{\xi}, \tilde{\sigma} < l_2$. For some recent results on $(k, \hat{\psi})$-Hilfer fractional differential equations, see [13].

In [14], the authors applied the standard tools of the fixed point theory to establish the existence and uniqueness results for the coupled (k, φ)-Hilfer type fractional differential system (1) equipped with nonlocal multipoint boundary conditions:

$$\check{k}(l_1) = 0, \quad \check{l}(l_1) = 0, \quad \check{k}(l_2) = \sum_{i=1}^{m} \tilde{\lambda}_i\,\check{l}(\tilde{\xi}_i), \check{l}(l_2) = \sum_{j=1}^{k} \tilde{\mu}_j\,\check{k}(\tilde{\eta}_j),$$

where $\tilde{\tilde{\lambda}}_i, \tilde{\mu}_j \in \mathbb{R}$, and $l_1 < \tilde{\xi}_i, \tilde{\eta}_j < l_2, i = 1, 2, \ldots, m, j = 1, 2, \ldots, k$.

As far as the authors know, the paper [14] is the only work in the literature dealing with coupled systems of $(k, \hat{\psi})$-Hilfer fractional derivative operator of the order in $(1,2]$. Our goal in the present paper is to enrich this new research area on coupled $(k, \hat{\psi})$-Hilfer fractional systems by introducing and investigating the new boundary value Problem (1) and (2).

Concerning the importance of coupled fractional differential systems, it is well-known that such systems appear in the mathematical models of many physical phenomena related to bio-engineering [15], fractional dynamics [16], financial economics [17], etc. In [18,19], some interesting results for $\hat{\psi}$-Hilfer fractional differential coupled systems were obtained.

The structure of the remaining paper is designed as follows. Section 2 contains basic definitions and an auxiliary lemma. Existence and uniqueness results for the given problem are presented in Section 3, while illustrative examples for these results are discussed in Section 4. In the last section, we indicate some new results arising as special cases of the present work.

2. A Preliminary Result

Let us begin this section with the definitions involved in the Problem (1) and (2).

Definition 1 ([3]). *The fractional integral of $(k, \hat{\psi})$-Riemann–Liouville type of order $\tilde{\alpha} > 0$ ($\tilde{\alpha} \in \mathbb{R}$) of a function $\check{L} \in L^1([l_1, l_2], \mathbb{R})$ is defined by*

$$^{k}\mathfrak{J}_{l_1^+}^{\tilde{\alpha};\hat{\psi}}\check{L}(s) = \frac{1}{k\Gamma_k(\tilde{\alpha})}\int_{l_1}^{s} \hat{\psi}'(v)(\hat{\psi}(s) - \hat{\psi}(v))^{\frac{\tilde{\alpha}}{k}-1}\check{L}(v)dv, \, k > 0, \quad (3)$$

where $\hat{\psi} : [l_1, l_2] \to \mathbb{R}$ is an increasing function with $\hat{\psi}'(s) \neq 0$ for all $s \in [l_1, l_2]$.

Definition 2 ([13]). *For $\tilde{\alpha}, k \in \mathbb{R}^+ = (0, +\infty)$, $\tilde{\beta} \in [0,1]$, $\hat{\psi} \in C^n([l_1, l_2], \mathbb{R})$, $\hat{\psi}'(s) \neq 0$, $s \in [l_1, l_2]$, the fractional derivative of $(k, \hat{\psi})$-Hilfer type for the function $\check{L} \in C^n([l_1, l_2], \mathbb{R})$ of order $\tilde{\alpha}$ and type $\tilde{\beta}$ is given by*

$$^{k,H}\mathcal{D}^{\tilde{\alpha},\tilde{\beta};\hat{\psi}}\check{L}(s) = {}^k\mathcal{J}_{l_1+}^{\tilde{\beta}(nk-\tilde{\alpha});\hat{\psi}}\left(\frac{k}{\hat{\psi}'(s)}\frac{d}{ds}\right)^n {}^k\mathcal{J}_{l_1+}^{(1-\tilde{\beta})(nk-\tilde{\alpha});\hat{\psi}}\check{L}(s), \quad n = \left\lceil \frac{\tilde{\alpha}}{k} \right\rceil. \quad (4)$$

We solve the linear variant of the nonlinear Problem (1) and (2) in the following lemma.

Lemma 1. *Let $\tilde{\vartheta}_k = \tilde{\alpha} + \tilde{\beta}(2k - \tilde{\alpha})$, $\tilde{\eta}_k = \tilde{p} + \tilde{q}(2k - \tilde{p})$, $\mathcal{B} \neq 0$, and $\check{L}, \check{L} \in C([l_1, l_2], \mathbb{R})$. Then the pair $(\check{k}, \check{l})$ is a solution of the linear version of the Problem (1) and (2) given by*

$$\begin{cases} {}^{k,H}\mathcal{D}^{\tilde{\alpha},\tilde{\beta};\hat{\psi}}\check{k}(s) = \check{L}(s), & s \in (l_1, l_2], \\ {}^{k,H}\mathcal{D}^{\tilde{p},\tilde{q};\hat{\psi}}\check{l}(s) = \check{L}(s), & s \in (l_1, l_2], \\ \check{k}(l_1) = 0, \quad \check{k}(l_2) = \tilde{\lambda}\,{}^{k,H}\mathcal{D}^{\tilde{r},\tilde{s};\hat{\psi}}\check{l}(\tilde{\xi}) + \tilde{\mu}\,{}^k\mathcal{I}^{\tilde{v},\hat{\psi}}\check{l}(\tilde{\sigma}), \\ \check{l}(l_1) = 0, \quad \check{l}(l_2) = \tilde{v}\,{}^{k,H}\mathcal{D}^{\tilde{z},\tilde{w};\hat{\psi}}\check{k}(\tilde{\eta}) + \tilde{\theta}\,{}^k\mathcal{I}^{\tilde{u},\hat{\psi}}\check{k}(\tilde{\tau}), \end{cases} \quad (5)$$

if and only if

$$\begin{aligned}
\check{k}(s) &= {}^k\mathcal{I}^{\tilde{\alpha},\hat{\psi}}\check{L}(s) \\
&+ \frac{(\hat{\psi}(s) - \hat{\psi}(l_1))^{\frac{\tilde{\vartheta}_k}{k}-1}}{\mathcal{B}\Gamma_k(\tilde{\vartheta}_k)}\left[\mathcal{B}_4\left(\tilde{\mu}\,{}^k\mathcal{I}^{\tilde{p}+\tilde{v},\hat{\psi}}\check{L}(\tilde{\sigma}) + \tilde{\lambda}\,{}^k\mathcal{I}^{\tilde{p}-\tilde{r},\hat{\psi}}\check{L}(\tilde{\xi}) - {}^k\mathcal{I}^{\tilde{p},\hat{\psi}}\check{L}(l_2)\right) \right. \quad (6) \\
&\left. + \mathcal{B}_2\left(\tilde{\theta}\,{}^k\mathcal{I}^{\tilde{\alpha}+\tilde{u},\hat{\psi}}\check{L}(\tilde{\tau}) + \tilde{v}\,{}^k\mathcal{I}^{\tilde{\alpha}-\tilde{z},\hat{\psi}}\check{L}(\tilde{\eta}) - {}^k\mathcal{I}^{\tilde{p},\hat{\psi}}\check{L}(l_2)\right)\right],
\end{aligned}$$

and

$$\begin{aligned}
\check{l}(s) &= {}^k\mathcal{I}^{\tilde{p},\hat{\psi}}\check{L}(s) \\
&+ \frac{(\hat{\psi}(s) - \hat{\psi}(l_1))^{\frac{\tilde{\eta}_k}{k}-1}}{\mathcal{B}\Gamma_k(\tilde{\eta}_k)}\left[\mathcal{B}_1\left(\tilde{\theta}\,{}^k\mathcal{I}^{\tilde{\alpha}+\tilde{u},\hat{\psi}}\check{L}(\tilde{\tau}) + \tilde{v}\,{}^k\mathcal{I}^{\tilde{\alpha}-\tilde{z},\hat{\psi}}\check{L}(\tilde{\eta}) - {}^k\mathcal{I}^{\tilde{p},\hat{\psi}}\check{L}(l_2)\right) \right. \quad (7) \\
&\left. + \mathcal{B}_3\left(\tilde{\mu}\,{}^k\mathcal{I}^{\tilde{p}+\tilde{v},\hat{\psi}}\check{L}(\tilde{\sigma}) + \tilde{\lambda}\,{}^k\mathcal{I}^{\tilde{p}-\tilde{r},\hat{\psi}}\check{L}(\tilde{\xi}) - {}^k\mathcal{I}^{\tilde{\alpha},\hat{\psi}}\check{L}(l_2)\right)\right],
\end{aligned}$$

where

$$\mathcal{B} := \mathcal{B}_1\mathcal{B}_4 - \mathcal{B}_2\mathcal{B}_3 \neq 0, \quad (8)$$

$$\begin{aligned}
\mathcal{B}_1 &= \frac{(\hat{\psi}(l_2) - \hat{\psi}(l_1))^{\frac{\tilde{\vartheta}_k}{k}-1}}{\Gamma_k(\tilde{\vartheta}_k)}, \\
\mathcal{B}_2 &= \frac{\tilde{\lambda}(\hat{\psi}(\tilde{\xi}) - \hat{\psi}(l_1))^{\frac{\tilde{\eta}_k-\tilde{r}}{k}-1}}{\Gamma_k(\tilde{\eta}_k - \tilde{r})} + \frac{\tilde{\mu}(\hat{\psi}(\tilde{\sigma}) - \hat{\psi}(l_1))^{\frac{\tilde{\eta}_k+\tilde{v}}{k}-1}}{\Gamma_k(\tilde{\eta}_k + \tilde{v})}, \\
\mathcal{B}_3 &= \frac{\tilde{v}(\hat{\psi}(\tilde{\eta}) - \hat{\psi}(l_1))^{\frac{\tilde{\vartheta}_k-\tilde{z}}{k}-1}}{\Gamma_k(\tilde{\vartheta}_k - \tilde{z})} + \frac{\tilde{\theta}(\hat{\psi}(\tilde{\tau}) - \hat{\psi}(l_1))^{\frac{\tilde{\vartheta}_k+\tilde{u}}{k}-1}}{\Gamma_k(\tilde{\vartheta}_k + \tilde{u})}, \quad (9) \\
\mathcal{B}_4 &= \frac{(\hat{\psi}(l_2) - \hat{\psi}(l_1))^{\frac{\tilde{\eta}_k}{k}-1}}{\Gamma_k(\tilde{\eta}_k)}.
\end{aligned}$$

Proof. Assume that the pair $(\check{k}, \check{l})$ is the solution of the System (5). As argued in [12], operating fractional integrals ${}^k\mathcal{I}^{\tilde{\alpha},\hat{\psi}}$ and ${}^k\mathcal{I}^{\tilde{p},\hat{\psi}}$ on the first and second $(k, \hat{\psi})$-Hilfer fractional differential equations in system (5), respectively, we obtain

$$\check{k}(s) = {}^k\mathcal{I}^{\tilde{\alpha},\hat{\psi}}\check{L}(s) + c_0\frac{(\hat{\psi}(s) - \hat{\psi}(a))^{\frac{\tilde{\vartheta}_k}{k} - 1}}{\Gamma_k(\tilde{\vartheta}_k)} + c_1\frac{(\hat{\psi}(s) - \hat{\psi}(l_1))^{\frac{\tilde{\vartheta}_k}{k} - 2}}{\Gamma_k(\tilde{\vartheta}_k - k)},$$

$$\check{l}(s) = {}^k\mathcal{I}^{\tilde{p},\hat{\psi}}\check{L}(s) + d_0\frac{(\hat{\psi}(s) - \hat{\psi}(l_1))^{\frac{\tilde{\eta}_k}{k} - 1}}{\Gamma_k(\tilde{\eta}_k)} + d_1\frac{(\hat{\psi}(s) - \hat{\psi}(l_1))^{\frac{\tilde{\eta}_k}{k} - 2}}{\Gamma_k(\tilde{\eta}_k - k)}, \tag{10}$$

where c_0, c_1, d_0 and d_1 are constants. Making use of the boundary conditions $\check{k}(l_1) = 0$ and $\check{l}(l_2) = 0$ in Equations (10), we find that $c_1 = 0$ and $d_1 = 0$ since $\frac{\tilde{\vartheta}_k}{k} - 2 < 0$, $\frac{\tilde{\eta}_k}{k} - 2 < 0$.

On the other hand, due to the conditions $\check{k}(l_2) = \tilde{\lambda}\, {}^{k,H}\mathcal{D}^{\tilde{r},\tilde{s},\hat{\psi}}\check{l}(\tilde{\xi}) + \tilde{\mu}\, {}^k\mathcal{I}^{\tilde{v},\hat{\psi}}\check{l}(\tilde{\sigma})$ and $\check{l}(l_2) = \tilde{v}\, {}^{k,H}\mathcal{D}^{\tilde{z},\tilde{w},\hat{\psi}}\check{k}(\tilde{\eta}) + \tilde{\theta}\, {}^k\mathcal{I}^{\tilde{u},\hat{\psi}}\check{k}(\tilde{\tau})$, we obtain from Equations (10) after inserting $c_1 = 0$ and $d_1 = 0$ that

$${}^k\mathcal{I}^{\tilde{\alpha},\hat{\psi}}\check{L}(l_2) + c_0\frac{(\hat{\psi}(l_2) - \hat{\psi}(l_1))^{\frac{\tilde{\vartheta}_k}{k} - 1}}{\Gamma_k(\tilde{\vartheta}_k)} = \tilde{\lambda}\, {}^k\mathcal{I}^{\tilde{p}-\tilde{r},\hat{\psi}}\check{L}(\tilde{\xi}) + \tilde{\lambda}\, d_0\frac{(\hat{\psi}(\tilde{\xi}) - \hat{\psi}(l_1))^{\frac{\tilde{\eta}_k - \tilde{r}}{k} - 1}}{\Gamma_k(\tilde{\eta}_k - \tilde{r})}$$

$$+\tilde{\mu}\, {}^k\mathcal{I}^{\tilde{p}+\tilde{v},\hat{\psi}}\check{L}(\tilde{\sigma}) + \tilde{\mu}\, d_0\frac{(\hat{\psi}(\tilde{\sigma}) - \hat{\psi}(l_1))^{\frac{\tilde{\eta}_k + \tilde{v}}{k} - 1}}{\Gamma_k(\tilde{\eta}_k + \tilde{v})}, \tag{11}$$

and

$${}^k\mathcal{I}^{\tilde{p},\hat{\psi}}\check{L}(l_2) + d_0\frac{(\hat{\psi}(l_2) - \hat{\psi}(l_1))^{\frac{\tilde{\eta}_k}{k} - 1}}{\Gamma_k(\tilde{\eta}_k)} = \tilde{v}\, {}^k\mathcal{I}^{\tilde{\alpha}-\tilde{z},\hat{\psi}}\check{L}(\tilde{\eta}) + \tilde{v}\, c_0\frac{(\hat{\psi}(\tilde{\eta}) - \hat{\psi}(l_1))^{\frac{\tilde{\vartheta}_k - \tilde{z}}{k} - 1}}{\Gamma_k(\tilde{\vartheta}_k - \tilde{z})}$$

$$+\tilde{\theta}\, {}^k\mathcal{I}^{\tilde{\alpha}+\tilde{u},\hat{\psi}}\check{L}(\tilde{\tau}) + \tilde{\theta}\, c_0\frac{(\hat{\psi}(\tilde{\tau}) - \hat{\psi}(l_1))^{\frac{\tilde{\vartheta}_k + \tilde{u}}{k} - 1}}{\Gamma_k(\tilde{\vartheta}_k + \tilde{u})}. \tag{12}$$

In view of the Notation (9), we can rewrite Equations (11) and (12) as

$$\begin{aligned}\mathcal{B}_1 c_0 - \mathcal{B}_2 d_0 &= \tilde{\mu}\, {}^k\mathcal{I}^{\tilde{p}+\tilde{v},\hat{\psi}}\check{L}(\tilde{\sigma}) + \tilde{\lambda}\, {}^k\mathcal{I}^{\tilde{p}-\tilde{r},\hat{\psi}}\check{L}(\tilde{\xi}) - {}^k\mathcal{I}^{\tilde{\alpha},\hat{\psi}}\check{L}(l_2),\\ -\mathcal{B}_3 c_0 + \mathcal{B}_4 d_0 &= \tilde{\theta}\, {}^k\mathcal{I}^{\tilde{\alpha}+\tilde{u},\hat{\psi}}\check{L}(\tilde{\tau}) + \tilde{v}\, {}^k\mathcal{I}^{\tilde{\alpha}-\tilde{z},\hat{\psi}}\check{L}(\tilde{\eta}) - {}^k\mathcal{I}^{\tilde{p},\hat{\psi}}\check{L}(l_2).\end{aligned} \tag{13}$$

Solving the System (13) for c_0 and d_0, we obtain

$$c_0 = \frac{1}{\mathcal{B}}\left[\mathcal{B}_4\left(\tilde{\mu}\, {}^k\mathcal{I}^{\tilde{p}+\tilde{v},\hat{\psi}}\check{L}(\tilde{\sigma}) + \tilde{\lambda}\, {}^k\mathcal{I}^{\tilde{p}-\tilde{r},\hat{\psi}}\check{L}(\tilde{\xi}) - {}^k\mathcal{I}^{\tilde{\alpha},\hat{\psi}}\check{L}(l_2)\right)\right.$$

$$\left.+ \mathcal{B}_2\left(\tilde{\theta}\, {}^k\mathcal{I}^{\tilde{\alpha}+\tilde{u},\hat{\psi}}\check{L}(\tilde{\tau}) + \tilde{v}\, {}^k\mathcal{I}^{\tilde{\alpha}-\tilde{z},\hat{\psi}}\check{L}(\tilde{\eta}) - {}^k\mathcal{I}^{\tilde{p},\hat{\psi}}\check{L}(l_2)\right)\right],$$

$$d_0 = \frac{1}{\mathcal{B}}\left[\mathcal{B}_1\left(\tilde{\theta}\, {}^k\mathcal{I}^{\tilde{\alpha}+\tilde{u},\hat{\psi}}\check{L}(\tilde{\tau}) + \tilde{v}\, {}^k\mathcal{I}^{\tilde{\alpha}-\tilde{z},\hat{\psi}}\check{L}(\tilde{\eta}) - {}^k\mathcal{I}^{\tilde{p},\hat{\psi}}\check{L}(l_2)\right)\right.$$

$$\left.+ \mathcal{B}_3\left(\tilde{\mu}\, {}^k\mathcal{I}^{\tilde{p}+\tilde{v},\hat{\psi}}\tilde{h}(\tilde{\sigma}) + \tilde{\lambda}\, {}^k\mathcal{I}^{\tilde{p}-\tilde{r},\hat{\psi}}\check{L}(\tilde{\xi}) - {}^k\mathcal{I}^{\tilde{\alpha},\hat{\psi}}\check{L}(l_2)\right)\right].$$

Replacing c_0 and d_0 in Equation (10) by the above values, we obtain Equations (6) and (7). The converse is obtained by direct calculation. This ends the proof. $\square$

3. Existence and Uniqueness Results

Suppose that $\mathbb{X} = C([l_1, l_2], \mathbb{R})$ is the Banach space consisting of all continuous real-valued functions on $[l_1, l_2]$ to $\mathbb{R}$, equipped with the norm $\|\check{k}\| = \max\{|\check{k}(s)|; s \in [l_1, l_2]\}$. Then $(\mathbb{X} \times \mathbb{X}, \|(\check{k}, \check{l})\|)$ is also a Banach space endowed with the norm $\|(\check{k}, \check{l})\| = \|\check{k}\| + \|\check{l}\|$.

Using Lemma 1, an operator $\mathcal{F} : \mathbb{X} \times \mathbb{X} \longrightarrow \mathbb{X} \times \mathbb{X}$ can be defined as

$$\mathcal{F}(\check{k},\check{l})(s) = \begin{pmatrix} \mathcal{F}_1(\check{k},\check{l})(s) \\ \mathcal{F}_2(\check{k},\check{l})(s) \end{pmatrix}, \tag{14}$$

where

$$\begin{aligned}
\mathcal{F}_1(\check{k},\check{l})(s) &= {}^k\mathcal{I}^{\tilde{\alpha},\hat{\psi}}\check{L}(s,\check{k}(s),\check{l}(s)) + \frac{(\hat{\psi}(s)-\hat{\psi}(l_1))^{\frac{\tilde{\vartheta}_k}{k}-1}}{\mathcal{B}\Gamma_k(\tilde{\vartheta}_k)} \times \\
&\quad \left[\mathcal{B}_4\left(\tilde{\mu}\,{}^k\mathcal{I}^{\tilde{p}+\tilde{v},\hat{\psi}}\check{L}(\tilde{\sigma},\check{k}(\tilde{\sigma}),\check{l}(\tilde{\sigma})) + \tilde{\lambda}\,{}^k\mathcal{I}^{\tilde{p}-\tilde{r},\hat{\psi}}\check{L}(\tilde{\xi},\check{k}(\tilde{\xi}),\check{l}(\tilde{\xi})) - {}^k\mathcal{I}^{\tilde{\alpha},\hat{\psi}}\check{L}(l_2,\check{k}(l_2),\check{l}(l_2))\right) \right. \\
&\quad \left. + \mathcal{B}_2\left(\tilde{\theta}\,{}^k\mathcal{I}^{\tilde{\alpha}+\tilde{u},\hat{\psi}}\check{L}(\tilde{\tau},\check{k}(\tilde{\tau}),\check{l}(\tilde{\tau})) + \tilde{v}\,{}^k\mathcal{I}^{\tilde{\alpha}-\tilde{z},\hat{\psi}}\check{L}(\tilde{\eta},\check{r}(\tilde{\eta}),\check{l}(\tilde{\eta})) - {}^k\mathcal{I}^{\tilde{p},\hat{\psi}}\check{L}(l_2,\check{k}(l_2),\check{l}(l_2))\right)\right],
\end{aligned}$$

and

$$\begin{aligned}
\mathcal{F}_2(\check{k},\check{l})(s) &= {}^k\mathcal{I}^{\tilde{p},\hat{\psi}}L_{\check{k},\check{l}}(s) + \frac{(\hat{\psi}(s)-\hat{\psi}(l_1))^{\frac{\tilde{\eta}_k}{k}-1}}{\mathcal{B}\Gamma_k(\tilde{\eta}_k)} \times \\
&\quad \left[\mathcal{B}_1\left(\tilde{\theta}\,{}^k\mathcal{I}^{\tilde{\alpha}+\tilde{u},\hat{\psi}}\check{L}(\tilde{\tau},\check{k}(\tilde{\tau}),\check{l}(\tilde{\tau})) + \tilde{v}\,{}^k\mathcal{I}^{\tilde{\alpha}-\tilde{z},\hat{\psi}}\check{L}(\tilde{\eta},\check{k}(\tilde{\eta}),\check{l}(\tilde{\eta})) - {}^k\mathcal{I}^{\tilde{p},\hat{\psi}}\check{L}(l_2,\check{k}(l_2),\check{l}(l_2))\right) \right. \\
&\quad \left. + \mathcal{B}_3\left(\tilde{\mu}\,{}^k\mathcal{I}^{\tilde{p}+\tilde{v},\hat{\psi}}\check{L}(\tilde{\sigma},\check{k}(\tilde{\sigma}),\check{l}(\tilde{\sigma})) + \tilde{\lambda}\,{}^k\mathcal{I}^{\tilde{p}-\tilde{r},\hat{\psi}}\check{L}(\tilde{\xi},\check{k}(\tilde{\xi}),\check{l}(\tilde{\xi})) - {}^k\mathcal{I}^{\tilde{\alpha},\hat{\psi}}\check{L}(l_2,\check{k}(l_2),\check{l}(l_2))\right)\right].
\end{aligned}$$

Here one can notice that the fixed point problem $\mathcal{F}(\check{k},\check{l}) = (\check{k},\check{l})$ is equivalent to the nonlinear Problem (1) and (2).

For the sake of computational convenience, we introduce the notation:

$$\begin{aligned}
\mathfrak{R}_1 &= \frac{(\hat{\psi}(l_2)-\hat{\psi}(l_1))^{\frac{\tilde{\alpha}}{k}}}{\Gamma_k(\tilde{\alpha}+k)} + \frac{(\hat{\psi}(l_2)-\hat{\psi}(l_1))^{\frac{\tilde{\vartheta}_k}{k}-1}}{|\mathcal{B}|\Gamma_k(\tilde{\vartheta}_k)}\left[\mathcal{B}_4\frac{(\hat{\psi}(l_2)-\hat{\psi}(l_1))^{\frac{\tilde{\alpha}}{k}}}{\Gamma_k(\tilde{\alpha}+k)}\right. \\
&\quad \left. + \mathcal{B}_2\left(|\tilde{\theta}|\frac{(\hat{\psi}(\tilde{\tau})-\hat{\psi}(l_1))^{\frac{\tilde{\alpha}+\tilde{u}}{k}}}{\Gamma_k(\tilde{\alpha}+\tilde{u}+k)} + |\tilde{v}|\frac{(\hat{\psi}(\tilde{\eta})-\hat{\psi}(l_1))^{\frac{\tilde{\alpha}-\tilde{z}}{k}}}{\Gamma_k(\tilde{\alpha}-\tilde{z}+k)}\right)\right], \\
\mathfrak{R}_2 &= \frac{(\hat{\psi}(l_2)-\hat{\psi}(l_1))^{\frac{\tilde{\vartheta}_k}{k}-1}}{|\mathcal{B}|\Gamma_k(\tilde{\vartheta}_k)}\left[\mathcal{B}_4\left(|\tilde{\mu}|\frac{(\hat{\psi}(\tilde{\sigma})-\hat{\psi}(l_1))^{\frac{\tilde{p}+\tilde{v}}{k}}}{\Gamma_k(\tilde{p}+\tilde{v}+k)} + |\tilde{\lambda}|\frac{(\hat{\psi}(\tilde{\xi})-\hat{\psi}(l_1))^{\frac{\tilde{p}-\tilde{r}}{k}}}{\Gamma_k(\tilde{p}-\tilde{r}+k)}\right) \right. \\
&\quad \left. + \mathcal{B}_2\frac{(\hat{\psi}(l_2)-\hat{\psi}(l_1))^{\frac{\tilde{p}}{k}}}{\Gamma_k(\tilde{p}+k)}\right], \quad (15) \\
\mathfrak{R}_3 &= \frac{(\hat{\psi}(l_2)-\hat{\psi}(l_1))^{\frac{\tilde{\eta}_k}{k}-1}}{|\mathcal{B}|\Gamma_k(\tilde{\eta}_k)}\left[\mathcal{B}_1\left(|\tilde{\theta}|\frac{(\hat{\psi}(\tilde{\tau})-\hat{\psi}(l_1))^{\frac{\tilde{\alpha}+\tilde{u}}{k}}}{\Gamma_k(\tilde{\alpha}+\tilde{u}+k)} + |\tilde{v}|\frac{(\hat{\psi}(\tilde{\eta})-\hat{\psi}(l_1))^{\frac{\tilde{\alpha}-\tilde{z}}{k}}}{\Gamma_k(\tilde{\alpha}-\tilde{z}+k)}\right) \right. \\
&\quad \left. + \mathcal{B}_3\frac{(\hat{\psi}(l_2)-\hat{\psi}(l_1))^{\frac{\tilde{\alpha}}{k}}}{\Gamma_k(\tilde{\alpha}+k)}\right], \\
\mathfrak{R}_4 &= \frac{(\hat{\psi}(l_2)-\hat{\psi}(l_1))^{\frac{\tilde{p}}{k}}}{\Gamma_k(\tilde{p}+k)} + \frac{(\hat{\psi}(l_2)-\hat{\psi}(l_1))^{\frac{\tilde{\vartheta}_k}{k}-1}}{|\mathcal{B}|\Gamma_k(\tilde{\vartheta}_k)}\left[\mathcal{B}_1\frac{(\hat{\psi}(l_2)-\hat{\psi}(l_1))^{\frac{\tilde{p}}{k}}}{\Gamma_k(\tilde{p}+k)}\right. \\
&\quad \left. + \mathcal{B}_3\left(|\tilde{\mu}|\frac{(\hat{\psi}(\tilde{\sigma})-\hat{\psi}(l_1))^{\frac{\tilde{p}+\tilde{v}}{k}}}{\Gamma_k(\tilde{p}+\tilde{v}+k)} + |\tilde{\lambda}|\frac{(\hat{\psi}(\tilde{\xi})-\hat{\psi}(l_1))^{\frac{\tilde{p}-\tilde{r}}{k}}}{\Gamma_k(\tilde{p}-\tilde{r}+k)}\right)\right]
\end{aligned}$$

and

$$\mathfrak{R}_1^* = \mathfrak{R}_1 - \frac{(\hat{\psi}(l_2) - \hat{\psi}(l_1))^{\frac{\tilde{\alpha}}{k}}}{\Gamma_k(\tilde{\alpha} + k)}, \quad \mathfrak{R}_4^* = \mathfrak{R}_4 - \frac{(\hat{\psi}(l_2) - \hat{\psi}(l_1))^{\frac{\tilde{p}}{k}}}{\Gamma_k(\tilde{p} + k)}. \tag{16}$$

3.1. Existence of a Unique Solution

In the following result, the Banach's fixed point theorem is applied to establish the uniqueness of solutions for the System (1) and (2).

Theorem 1. *Let* $\check{L}, \check{L} : [l_1, l_2] \times \mathbb{R} \times \mathbb{R} \longrightarrow \mathbb{R}$ *satisfy the Lipschitz condition, that is, for all* $s \in [l_1, l_2]$ *and* $\check{k}_i, \check{l}_i \in \mathbb{R}, i = 1, 2,$

$$\begin{aligned}|\check{L}(s, \check{k}_1, \check{k}_2) - \check{L}(s, \check{l}_1, \check{l}_2)| &\leq \hat{m}_1 |\check{k}_1 - \check{l}_1| + \hat{m}_2 |\check{k}_2 - \check{l}_2|, \\ |\check{f}(s, \check{k}_1, \check{k}_2) - \check{f}(s, \check{l}_1, \check{l}_2)| &\leq \hat{n}_1 |\check{k}_1 - \check{l}_1| + \hat{n}_2 \check{k}_2 - \check{l}_2|,\end{aligned} \tag{17}$$

where $\hat{m}_i, \hat{n}_i, i = 1, 2$ *are real constants. Moreover, we suppose that*

$$(\mathfrak{R}_1 + \mathfrak{R}_3)(\hat{m}_1 + \hat{m}_2) + (\mathfrak{R}_2 + \mathfrak{R}_4)(\hat{n}_1 + \hat{n}_2) < 1, \tag{18}$$

where $\mathfrak{R}_i, i = 1, 2, 3, 4$, *are defined in Equation (15). Then, the System (1) and (2) has a unique solution on* $[l_1, l_2]$.

Proof. Let us consider a closed ball $\mathbb{B}_r = \{(\check{k}, \check{l}) \in \mathbb{X} \times \mathbb{X} : \|(\check{k}, \check{l})\| \leq r\}$, where

$$r \geq \frac{(\mathfrak{R}_1 + \mathfrak{R}_3)\mathfrak{D} + (\mathfrak{R}_2 + \mathfrak{R}_4)\mathfrak{D}_1}{1 - [(\mathfrak{R}_1 + \mathfrak{R}_3)(\hat{m}_1 + \hat{m}_2) + (\mathfrak{R}_2 + \mathfrak{R}_4)(\hat{n}_1 + \hat{n}_2)]},$$

$\sup_{s \in [l_1, l_2]} |\check{L}(s, 0, 0)| = \mathfrak{D} < \infty$ and $\sup_{s \in [l_1, l_2]} |\check{L}(s, 0, 0)| = \mathfrak{D}_1 < \infty$. Then we show that $\mathcal{F}\mathbb{B}_r \subseteq \mathbb{B}_r$. For $(\check{k}, \check{l}) \in \mathbb{B}_r$, we obtain

$$\begin{aligned}&|\mathcal{F}_1(\check{k}, \check{l})(s)| \\ \leq\ & {}^k\mathcal{I}^{\tilde{\alpha}, \hat{\psi}} [|\check{L}(s, \check{k}(s), \check{l}(s)) - \check{L}(s, 0, 0)| + |\check{L}(s, 0, 0)|] \\ &+ \frac{(\hat{\psi}(s) - \hat{\psi}(l_1))^{\frac{\tilde{\vartheta}_k}{k} - 1}}{|\mathcal{B}|\Gamma_k(\tilde{\vartheta}_k)} \Bigg[\mathcal{B}_4 \bigg(|\tilde{\mu}|\ {}^k\mathcal{I}^{\tilde{p}+\tilde{\vartheta}, \hat{\psi}} [|\check{L}(\tilde{\sigma}, \check{k}(\tilde{\sigma}), \check{l}(\tilde{\sigma})) - \check{L}(\tilde{\sigma}, 0, 0)| + |\check{L}(\tilde{\sigma}, 0, 0)|] \\ &+ |\tilde{\lambda}|\ {}^k\mathcal{I}^{\tilde{p}-\tilde{r}, \hat{\psi}} [|\check{L}(\tilde{\xi}, \check{k}(\tilde{\xi}), \check{l}(\tilde{\xi})) - \check{L}(\tilde{\xi}, 0, 0)| + |\check{L}(\tilde{\xi}, 0, 0)|] \\ &+ {}^k\mathcal{I}^{\tilde{\alpha}, \hat{\psi}} [|\check{L}(l_2, \check{k}(l_2), \check{l}(l_2)) - \check{L}(l_2, 0, 0)| + |\check{L}(l_2, 0, 0)|] \bigg) \\ &+ \mathcal{B}_2 \bigg(|\tilde{\vartheta}|\ {}^k\mathcal{I}^{\tilde{\alpha}+\tilde{u}, \hat{\psi}} [|\check{L}(\tilde{\tau}, \check{k}(\tilde{\tau}), \check{l}(\tilde{\tau})) - \check{L}(\tilde{\tau}, 0, 0)| + |\check{L}(\tilde{\tau}, 0, 0)|] \\ &+ |\tilde{v}|\ {}^k\mathcal{I}^{\tilde{\alpha}-\tilde{z}, \hat{\psi}} [|\check{L}(\tilde{\eta}, \check{k}(\tilde{\eta}), \check{l}(\tilde{\eta})) - \check{L}(\tilde{\eta}, 0, 0)| + |\check{L}(\tilde{\eta}, 0, 0)|] \\ &+ {}^k\mathcal{I}^{\tilde{p}, \hat{\psi}} [|\check{L}(l_2, \check{k}(l_2), \check{l}(l_2)) - \check{L}(l_2, 0, 0)| + |\check{L}(l_2, 0, 0)|] \bigg) \Bigg] \\ \leq\ & \frac{(\hat{\psi}(l_2) - \hat{\psi}(l_1))^{\frac{\tilde{\alpha}}{k}}}{\Gamma_k(\tilde{\alpha} + k)} [\hat{m}_1 \|\check{k}\| + \hat{m}_2 \|\check{l}\| + \mathfrak{D}] \\ &+ \frac{(\hat{\psi}(l_2) - \hat{\psi}(l_1))^{\frac{\tilde{\vartheta}_k}{k} - 1}}{|\mathcal{B}|\Gamma_k(\tilde{\vartheta}_k)} \Bigg[\mathcal{B}_4 \bigg(|\tilde{\mu}| \frac{(\hat{\psi}(\tilde{\sigma}) - \hat{\psi}(l_1))^{\frac{\tilde{p}+\tilde{\vartheta}}{k}}}{\Gamma_k(\tilde{p} + \tilde{\vartheta} + k)} [\hat{n}_1 \|\check{k}\| + \hat{n}_2 \|\check{l}\| + \mathfrak{D}_1] \\ &+ |\tilde{\lambda}| \frac{(\hat{\psi}(\tilde{\xi}) - \hat{\psi}(l_1))^{\frac{\tilde{p}-\tilde{r}}{k}}}{\Gamma_k(\tilde{p} - \tilde{r} + k)} [\hat{n}_1 \|\check{k}\| + \hat{n}_2 \|\check{l}\| + \mathfrak{D}_1] \\ &+ \frac{(\hat{\psi}(l_2) - \hat{\psi}(l_1))^{\frac{\tilde{\alpha}}{k}}}{\Gamma_k(\tilde{\alpha} + k)} [\hat{m}_1 \|\check{k}\| + \hat{m}_2 \|\check{l}\| + \mathfrak{D}] \bigg)\end{aligned}$$

$$
\begin{aligned}
&+ \mathcal{B}_2\bigg(|\tilde{\theta}|\,\frac{(\hat{\psi}(\tilde{\tau}) - \hat{\psi}(l_1))^{\frac{\tilde{\alpha}+\tilde{u}}{k}}}{\Gamma_k(\tilde{\alpha}+\tilde{u}+k)}[\hat{m}_1\|\check{k}\| + \hat{m}_2\|\check{l}\| + \mathfrak{D}]\\
&+ |\tilde{v}|\,\frac{(\hat{\psi}(\tilde{\eta}) - \hat{\psi}(l_1))^{\frac{\tilde{\alpha}-\tilde{z}}{k}}}{\Gamma_k(\tilde{\alpha}-\tilde{z}+k)}[\hat{m}_1\|\check{k}\| + \hat{m}_2\|\check{l}\| + \mathfrak{D}]\\
&+ \frac{(\hat{\psi}(l_2)-\hat{\psi}(l_1))^{\frac{\tilde{p}}{k}}}{\Gamma_k(\tilde{p}+k)}[\hat{n}_1\|\check{k}\| + \hat{n}_2\|\check{l}\| + \mathfrak{D}_1]\bigg)\bigg]\\
=\;&\bigg\{\frac{(\hat{\psi}(l_2) - \hat{\psi}(l_1))^{\frac{\tilde{\alpha}}{k}}}{\Gamma_k(\tilde{\alpha}+k)} + \frac{(\hat{\psi}(l_2)-\hat{\psi}(l_1))^{\frac{\tilde{\vartheta}_k}{k}-1}}{|\mathcal{B}|\Gamma_k(\tilde{\vartheta}_k)}\bigg[\mathcal{B}_4\,\frac{(\hat{\psi}(l_2)-\hat{\psi}(l_1))^{\frac{\tilde{\alpha}}{k}}}{\Gamma_k(\tilde{\alpha}+k)}\\
&+ \mathcal{B}_2\Big(|\tilde{\theta}|\,\frac{(\hat{\psi}(\tilde{\tau})-\hat{\psi}(l_1))^{\frac{\tilde{\alpha}+\tilde{u}}{k}}}{\Gamma_k(\tilde{\alpha}+\tilde{u}+k)} + |\tilde{v}|\,\frac{(\hat{\psi}(\tilde{\eta})-\hat{\psi}(l_1))^{\frac{\tilde{\alpha}-\tilde{z}}{k}}}{\Gamma_k(\tilde{\alpha}-\tilde{z}+k)}\Big)\bigg]\bigg\}[\hat{m}_1\|\check{r}\| + \hat{m}_2\|\check{l}\| + \mathfrak{D}]\\
&+ \bigg\{\frac{(\hat{\psi}(l_2)-\hat{\psi}(l_1))^{\frac{\tilde{\vartheta}_k}{k}-1}}{|\mathcal{B}|\Gamma_k(\tilde{\vartheta}_k)}\bigg[\mathcal{B}_4\Big(|\tilde{\mu}|\,\frac{(\hat{\psi}(\tilde{\sigma})-\hat{\psi}(l_1))^{\frac{\tilde{p}+\tilde{v}}{k}}}{\Gamma_k(\tilde{p}+\tilde{v}+k)} + |\tilde{\lambda}|\,\frac{(\hat{\psi}(\tilde{\xi})-\hat{\psi}(l_1))^{\frac{\tilde{p}-\tilde{r}}{k}}}{\Gamma_k(\tilde{p}-\tilde{r}+k)}\Big)\bigg]\\
&+ \mathcal{B}_2\,\frac{(\hat{\psi}(l_2)-\hat{\psi}(l_1))^{\frac{\tilde{p}}{k}}}{\Gamma_k(\tilde{p}+k)}\bigg\}[\hat{n}_1\|\check{r}\| + \hat{n}_2\|\check{l}\| + \mathfrak{D}_1]\\
=\;&\mathfrak{R}_1[\hat{m}_1\|\check{k}\| + \hat{m}_2\|\check{l}\| + \mathfrak{D}] + \mathfrak{R}_2[\hat{n}_1\|\check{k}\| + \hat{n}_2\|\check{l}\| + \mathfrak{D}_1]\\
=\;&(\mathfrak{R}_1\hat{m}_1 + \mathfrak{R}_2\hat{n}_1)\|\check{k}\| + (\mathfrak{R}_1\hat{m}_2 + \mathfrak{R}_2\hat{n}_2)\|\check{l}\| + \mathfrak{R}_1\mathfrak{D} + \mathfrak{R}_2\mathfrak{D}_1\\
\leq\;&\mathfrak{R}_1\hat{m}_1 + \mathfrak{R}_2\hat{n}_1 + \mathfrak{R}_1\hat{m}_2 + \mathfrak{R}_2\hat{n}_2)r + \mathfrak{R}_1\mathfrak{D} + \mathfrak{R}_2\mathfrak{D}_1.
\end{aligned}
$$

Analogously, we have

$$
\begin{aligned}
&|\mathcal{F}_2(\check{k},\check{l})(s)|\\
\leq\;&\bigg\{\frac{(\hat{\psi}(l_2)-\hat{\psi}(l_1))^{\frac{\tilde{\eta}_k}{k}-1}}{|\mathcal{B}|\Gamma_k(\tilde{\eta}_k)}\bigg[\mathcal{B}_1\Big(|\tilde{\theta}|\,\frac{(\hat{\psi}(\tilde{\tau})-\hat{\psi}(l_1))^{\frac{\tilde{\alpha}+\tilde{u}}{k}}}{\Gamma_k(\tilde{\alpha}+\tilde{u}+k)} + |\tilde{v}|\,\frac{(\hat{\psi}(\tilde{\eta})-\hat{\psi}(l_1))^{\frac{\tilde{\alpha}-\tilde{z}}{k}}}{\Gamma_k(\tilde{\alpha}-\tilde{z}+k)}\Big)\\
&+ \mathcal{B}_3\,\frac{(\hat{\psi}(l_2)-\hat{\psi}(l_1))^{\frac{\tilde{\alpha}}{k}}}{\Gamma_k(\tilde{\alpha}+k)}\bigg]\bigg\}[\hat{m}_1\|\check{k}\| + \hat{m}_2\|\check{l}\| + \mathfrak{D}]\\
&+ \bigg\{\frac{(\hat{\psi}(l_2)-\hat{\psi}(l_1))^{\frac{\tilde{p}}{k}}}{\Gamma_k(\tilde{p}+k)} + \frac{(\hat{\psi}(l_2)-\hat{\psi}(l_1))^{\frac{\tilde{\vartheta}_k}{k}-1}}{|\mathcal{B}|\Gamma_k(\tilde{\vartheta}_k)}\bigg[\mathcal{B}_1\,\frac{(\hat{\psi}(l_2)-\hat{\psi}(l_1))^{\frac{\tilde{p}}{k}}}{\Gamma_k(\tilde{p}+k)}\\
&+ \mathcal{B}_3\Big(|\tilde{\mu}|\,\frac{(\hat{\psi}(\tilde{\sigma})-\hat{\psi}(l_1))^{\frac{\tilde{p}+\tilde{v}}{k}}}{\Gamma_k(\tilde{p}+\tilde{v}+k)} + |\tilde{\lambda}|\,\frac{(\hat{\psi}(\tilde{\xi})-\hat{\psi}(l_1))^{\frac{\tilde{p}-\tilde{r}}{k}}}{\Gamma_k(\tilde{p}-\tilde{r}+k)}\Big)\bigg]\bigg\}[\hat{n}_1\|\check{k}\| + \hat{n}_2\|\check{l}\| + \mathfrak{D}_1]\\
=\;&(\mathfrak{R}_3\hat{m}_1 + \mathfrak{R}_4\hat{n}_1)\|\check{k}\| + (\mathfrak{R}_3\hat{m}_2 + \mathfrak{R}_4\hat{n}_2)\|\check{l}\| + \mathfrak{R}_3\mathfrak{D} + \mathfrak{R}_4\mathfrak{D}_1\\
\leq\;&\mathfrak{R}_3\hat{m}_1 + \mathfrak{R}_4\hat{n}_1 + \mathfrak{R}_3\hat{m}_2 + \mathfrak{R}_4\hat{n}_2)r + \mathfrak{R}_3\mathfrak{D} + \mathfrak{R}_4\mathfrak{D}_1.
\end{aligned}
$$

Accordingly, we obtain

$$
\begin{aligned}
\|\mathcal{F}(\check{k},\check{l})\| &= \|\mathcal{F}_1(\check{k},\check{l})\| + \|\mathcal{F}_2(\check{k},\check{l})\|\\
&\leq [(\mathfrak{R}_1+\mathfrak{R}_3))(\hat{m}_1+\hat{m}_2) + (\mathfrak{R}_2+\mathfrak{R}_4)(\hat{n}_1+\hat{n}_2)]r\\
&\quad + (\mathfrak{R}_1+\mathfrak{R}_3))\mathfrak{D} + (\mathfrak{R}_2+\mathfrak{R}_4))\mathfrak{D}_1 \leq r,
\end{aligned}
$$

which implies that $\mathcal{F}(\mathbb{B}_r) \subseteq \mathbb{B}_r$ since $(\check{k},\check{l}) \in \mathbb{B}_r$ is an arbitrary element. On the other hand, for $(\check{k}_2,\check{l}_2),(\check{k}_1,\check{l}_1) \in \mathbb{X} \times \mathbb{X}$ and $s \in [l_1, l_2]$, we obtain

$$
\begin{aligned}
&|\mathcal{F}_1(\check{k}_2,\check{l}_2)(s) - \mathcal{F}_1(\check{k}_1,\check{l}_1)(s)|\\
\leq\;&{}^k\mathcal{I}^{\tilde{\alpha},\hat{\psi}}|\check{L}(s,\check{k}_2(s),\check{l}_2(s)) - \check{L}(s,\check{k}_1(s),\check{l}_1(s))|\\
&+ \frac{(\hat{\psi}(s)-\hat{\psi}(l_1))^{\frac{\tilde{\vartheta}_k}{k}-1}}{|\mathcal{B}|\Gamma_k(\tilde{\vartheta}_k)}\bigg[\mathcal{B}_4\Big(|\tilde{\mu}|\,{}^k\mathcal{I}^{\tilde{p}+\tilde{v},\hat{\psi}}|\check{L}(\tilde{\sigma},\check{k}_2(\tilde{\sigma}),\check{l}_2(\tilde{\sigma})) - \check{L}(\tilde{\sigma},\check{k}_1(\tilde{\sigma}),\check{l}_1(\tilde{\sigma}))|\\
&+ |\tilde{\lambda}|\,{}^k\mathcal{I}^{\tilde{p}-\tilde{r},\hat{\psi}}|\check{L}(\tilde{\xi},\check{k}_2(\xi),\check{l}_2(\xi)) - \check{L}(\tilde{\xi},\check{k}_1(\xi),\check{l}_1(\xi))|
\end{aligned}
$$

$$+ {}^k\mathcal{I}^{\tilde{\alpha},\hat{\psi}}|\check{L}(l_2,\check{k}_2(l_2),\check{l}_2(l_2)) - \check{L}(l_2,\check{k}_1(l_2),\check{l}_1(l_2))|\Big)$$

$$+ \mathcal{B}_2\Big(|\tilde{\vartheta}|\,{}^k\mathcal{I}^{\tilde{\alpha}+\tilde{u},\hat{\psi}}|\check{L}(\tilde{\tau},\check{k}_2(\tilde{\tau}),\check{l}_2(\tilde{\tau})) - \check{L}(\tilde{\tau},\check{k}_1(\tilde{\tau}),\check{l}_1(\tilde{\tau}))|$$

$$+|\tilde{v}|\,{}^k\mathcal{I}^{\tilde{\alpha}-\tilde{z},\hat{\psi}}|\check{L}(\tilde{\eta},\check{k}_2(\tilde{\eta}),\check{l}_2(\tilde{\eta})) - \check{L}(\tilde{\eta},\check{k}_1(\tilde{\eta}),\check{l}_1(\tilde{\eta}))|$$

$$+{}^k\mathcal{I}^{\tilde{p},\hat{\psi}}|\check{f}(l_2,\check{k}_2(l_2),\check{l}_2(l_2)) - \check{L}(l_2,\check{k}_1(l_2),\check{l}_1(l_2))|\Big)\Big]$$

$$\leq \quad {}^k\mathcal{I}^{\tilde{\alpha},\hat{\psi}}[\hat{m}_1\|\check{k}_2-\check{k}_1\| + \hat{m}_2\|\check{l}_2-\check{l}_1\|]$$

$$+ \frac{(\hat{\psi}(l_2)-\hat{\psi}(l_1))^{\frac{\tilde{\vartheta}_k}{k}-1}}{|\mathcal{B}|\Gamma_k(\tilde{\vartheta}_k)}\Big[\mathcal{B}_4\Big(|\tilde{\mu}|\,{}^k\mathcal{I}^{\tilde{p}+\tilde{v},\hat{\psi}}[\hat{n}_1\|\check{k}_2-\check{k}_1\| + \hat{n}_2\|\check{l}_2-\check{l}_1\|]$$

$$+|\tilde{\lambda}|\,{}^k\mathcal{I}^{\tilde{p}-\tilde{r},\hat{\psi}}[\hat{n}_1\|\check{k}_2-\check{k}_1\| + n_2\|\check{l}_2-\check{l}_1\|]$$

$$+{}^k\mathcal{I}^{\tilde{\alpha},\hat{\psi}}[\hat{m}_1\|\check{k}_2-\check{k}_1\| + \hat{m}_2\|\check{l}_2-\check{l}_1\|]\Big)$$

$$+ \mathcal{B}_2\Big(|\tilde{\vartheta}|\,{}^k\mathcal{I}^{\tilde{\alpha}+\tilde{u},\hat{\psi}}[\hat{m}_1\|\check{k}_2-\check{k}_1\| + \hat{m}_2\|\check{l}_2-\check{l}_1\|]$$

$$+|\tilde{v}|\,{}^k\mathcal{I}^{\tilde{\alpha}-\tilde{z},\hat{\psi}}[\hat{m}_1\|\check{k}_2-\check{k}_1\| + \hat{m}_2\|\check{l}_2-\check{l}_1\|]$$

$$+{}^k\mathcal{I}^{\tilde{p},\hat{\psi}}[\hat{n}_1\|\check{k}_2-\check{k}_1\| + \hat{n}_2\|\check{l}_2-\check{l}_1\|]\Big)\Big]$$

$$= \quad \left\{\frac{(\hat{\psi}(l_2)-\hat{\psi}(l_1))^{\frac{\tilde{\alpha}}{k}}}{\Gamma_k(\tilde{\alpha}+k)} + \frac{(\hat{\psi}(l_2)-\hat{\psi}(l_1))^{\frac{\tilde{\vartheta}_k}{k}-1}}{|\mathcal{B}|\Gamma_k(\tilde{\vartheta}_k)}\Big[\mathcal{B}_4\frac{(\hat{\psi}(l_2)-\hat{\psi}(l_1))^{\frac{\tilde{\alpha}}{k}}}{\Gamma_k(\tilde{\alpha}+k)}\right.$$

$$+ \mathcal{B}_2\Big(|\tilde{\vartheta}|\frac{(\hat{\psi}(\tilde{\tau})-\hat{\psi}(l_1))^{\frac{\tilde{\alpha}+\tilde{u}}{k}}}{\Gamma_k(\tilde{\alpha}+\tilde{u}+k)} + |\tilde{v}|\frac{(\hat{\psi}(\tilde{\eta})-\hat{\psi}(l_1))^{\frac{\tilde{\alpha}-\tilde{z}}{k}}}{\Gamma_k(\tilde{\alpha}-\tilde{z}+k)}\Big)\Big]\Big\}$$

$$\times [\hat{m}_1\|\check{k}_2-\check{k}_1\| + \hat{m}_2\|\check{l}_2-\check{l}_1\|]$$

$$+ \left\{\frac{(\hat{\psi}(l_2)-\hat{\psi}(l_1))^{\frac{\tilde{\vartheta}_k}{k}-1}}{|\mathcal{B}|\Gamma_k(\tilde{\vartheta}_k)}\Big[\mathcal{B}_4\Big(|\mu|\frac{(\hat{\psi}(\tilde{\sigma})-\hat{\psi}(l_1))^{\frac{\tilde{p}+\tilde{v}}{k}}}{\Gamma_k(\tilde{p}+\tilde{v}+k)} + |\tilde{\lambda}|\frac{(\hat{\psi}(\tilde{\xi})-\hat{\psi}(l_1))^{\frac{\tilde{p}-\tilde{r}}{k}}}{\Gamma_k(\tilde{p}-\tilde{r}+k)}\Big)\Big]\right.$$

$$+ \mathcal{B}_2\frac{(\hat{\psi}(l_2)-\hat{\psi}(l_1))^{\frac{\tilde{p}}{k}}}{\Gamma_k(\tilde{p}+k)}\Big\}[\hat{n}_1\|\check{k}_2-\check{k}_1\| + \hat{n}_2\|\check{l}_2-\check{l}_1\|]$$

$$= \quad (\mathfrak{R}_1\hat{m}_1 + \mathfrak{R}_2\hat{n}_1)(\|\check{k}_2-\check{k}_1\|) + (\mathfrak{R}_1\hat{m}_2 + \mathfrak{R}_2\hat{n}_2)(\|\check{l}_2-\check{l}_1\|).$$

Thus, we obtain

$$\|\mathcal{F}_1(\check{k}_2,\check{l}_2) - \mathcal{F}_1(\check{k}_1,\check{l}_1)\|$$
$$\leq (\mathfrak{R}_1\hat{m}_1 + \mathfrak{R}_2\hat{n}_1 + \mathfrak{R}_1\hat{m}_2 + \mathfrak{R}_2\hat{n}_2)[\|\check{k}_2-\check{k}_1\| + \|\check{l}_2-\check{l}_1\|]. \quad (19)$$

Similarly, one can find that

$$\|\mathcal{F}_2(\check{k}_2,\check{l}_2) - \mathcal{F}_2(\check{k}_1,\check{l}_1)\|$$
$$\leq (\mathfrak{R}_3\hat{m}_1 + \mathfrak{R}_4\hat{n}_1 + \mathfrak{R}_3\hat{m}_2 + \mathfrak{R}_4\hat{n}_2)[\|\check{k}_2-\check{k}_1\| + \|\check{l}_2-\check{l}_1\|]. \quad (20)$$

Then, it follows from from Equations (19) and (20) that

$$\|\mathcal{F}(\check{k}_2,\check{l}_2) - \mathcal{F}(\check{k}_1,\check{k}_1)\|$$
$$\leq [(\mathfrak{R}_1+\mathfrak{R}_3)(\hat{m}_1+\hat{m}_2) + (\mathfrak{R}_2+\mathfrak{R}_4)(\hat{n}_1+n_2)](\|\check{k}_2-\check{k}_1\| + \|\check{l}_2-\check{l}_1\|),$$

which, in view of the Condition (18), verifies that the operator $\mathcal{F}$ is a contraction. Hence, by Banach's contraction mapping principle, the operator $\mathcal{F}$ has a unique fixed point. Therefore, the System (1) and (2) has a unique solution on $[l_1,l_2]$. □

3.2. Existence Results

We rely on the Leray–Schauder alternative [20] to establish our first existence result.

Theorem 2. *Let $\check{L}, \check{L} : [l_1, l_2] \times \mathbb{R} \longrightarrow \mathbb{R}$ be two continuous functions such that, for all $s \in [l_1, l_2]$ and $\check{k}_i, \check{l}_i \in \mathbb{R}, i = 1, 2$,*

$$|\check{L}(s, \check{k}_1, \check{l}_1)| \leq \hat{l}_0 + \hat{l}_1 |\check{k}_1| + \hat{l}_2 |\check{l}_1|,$$
$$|\check{L}(s, \check{k}_2, \check{l}_2)| \leq \hat{q}_0 + \hat{q}_1 |\check{k}_2| + \hat{q}_2 |\check{l}_2|,$$

where $\hat{l}_i, \hat{q}_i, i = 0, 1, 2$, are real constants with $\hat{l}_0, \hat{q}_0 > 0$. Then, the System (1) and (2) has at least one solution on $[l_1, l_2]$ provided that

$$(\mathfrak{R}_1 + \mathfrak{R}_3)\hat{l}_1 + (\mathfrak{R}_2 + \mathfrak{R}_4)\hat{q}_1 < 1 \text{ and } (\mathfrak{R}_1 + \mathfrak{R}_3)\hat{l}_2 + (\mathfrak{R}_2 + \mathfrak{R}_4)\hat{q}_2 < 1, \quad (21)$$

where $\mathfrak{R}_i, i = 1, 2, 3, 4$, are defined in Equations (15).

Proof. Notice that continuity of the functions $\check{L}$ and $\check{L}$ implies that of the operator $\mathcal{F}$. Next, it will be shown that the operator $\mathcal{F}$ is completely continuous. Consider a bounded set $\mathcal{S}$ of $\mathbb{X} \times \mathbb{X}$. Then, there exist positive constants $\mathcal{L}_1$ and $\mathcal{L}_2$ such that $|\check{L}(s, \check{k}(s), \check{l}(s)| \leq \mathcal{L}_1, |\check{L}(s, \check{k}(s), \check{l}(s)| \leq \mathcal{L}_2, \forall (\check{k}, \check{l}) \in \mathcal{S}$. In consequence, for all $(\check{k}, \check{l}) \in \mathcal{S}$, we obtain

$$\begin{aligned}|\mathcal{F}_1(\check{k}, \check{l})(s)| &\leq \left\{\frac{(\hat{\psi}(l_2) - \hat{\psi}(l_1))^{\frac{\check{\alpha}}{k}}}{\Gamma_k(\tilde{\alpha} + k)} + \frac{(\hat{\psi}(l_2) - \hat{\psi}(l_1))^{\frac{\check{\theta}_k}{k} - 1}}{|\mathcal{B}|\Gamma_k(\tilde{\theta}_k)}\left[\mathcal{B}_4 \frac{(\hat{\psi}(l_2) - \hat{\psi}(l_1))^{\frac{\check{\alpha}}{k}}}{\Gamma_k(\tilde{\alpha} + k)}\right.\right.\\ &\quad \left.\left. + \mathcal{B}_2\left(|\tilde{\theta}|\frac{(\hat{\psi}(\tilde{\tau}) - \hat{\psi}(l_1))^{\frac{\check{\alpha}+\tilde{u}}{k}}}{\Gamma_k(\tilde{\alpha}+\tilde{u}+k)} + |\tilde{\nu}|\frac{(\hat{\psi}(\tilde{\eta}) - \hat{\psi}(l_1))^{\frac{\check{\alpha}-\tilde{z}}{k}}}{\Gamma_k(\tilde{\alpha}-\tilde{z}+k)}\right)\right]\right\}\mathcal{L}_1\\ &\quad + \left\{\frac{(\hat{\psi}(l_2) - \hat{\psi}(l_1))^{\frac{\check{\theta}_k}{k} - 1}}{|\mathcal{B}|\Gamma_k(\tilde{\theta}_k)}\left[\mathcal{B}_4\left(|\tilde{\mu}|\frac{(\hat{\psi}(\tilde{\sigma}) - \hat{\psi}(l_1))^{\frac{\tilde{p}+\tilde{\sigma}}{k}}}{\Gamma_k(\tilde{p}+\tilde{\sigma}+k)}\right.\right.\right.\\ &\quad \left.\left.\left.+ |\tilde{\lambda}|\frac{(\hat{\psi}(\tilde{\xi}) - \hat{\psi}(l_1))^{\frac{\tilde{p}-\tilde{r}}{k}}}{\Gamma_k(\tilde{p}-\tilde{r}+k)}\right)\right] + \mathcal{B}_2\frac{(\hat{\psi}(l_2) - \hat{\psi}(l_1))^{\frac{\tilde{p}}{k}}}{\Gamma_k(\tilde{p}+k)}\right\}\mathcal{L}_2\\ &\leq \mathfrak{R}_1 \mathcal{L}_1 + \mathfrak{R}_2 \mathcal{L}_2,\end{aligned}$$

which yields

$$\|\mathcal{F}_1(\check{k}, \check{l})\| \leq \mathfrak{R}_1 \mathcal{L}_1 + \mathfrak{R}_2 \mathcal{L}_2.$$

Analogously, one can obtain

$$\|\mathcal{F}_2(\check{k}, \check{l})\| \leq \mathfrak{R}_3 \mathcal{L}_1 + \mathfrak{R}_4 \mathcal{L}_2.$$

Hence, we have

$$\|\mathcal{F}(\check{k}, \check{l})\| = \|\mathcal{F}_1(\check{k}, \check{l})\| + \|\mathcal{F}_2(\check{k}, \check{l})\| \leq (\mathfrak{R}_1 + \mathfrak{R}_3)\mathcal{L}_1 + (\mathfrak{R}_2 + \mathfrak{R}_4)\mathcal{L}_2.$$

Consequently, the operator $\mathcal{F}$ is uniformly bounded. To establish equicontinuity property of the operator $\mathcal{F}$, let $s_1, s_2 \in [l_1, l_2]$ with $s_1 < s_2$. Then, we have

$$\begin{aligned}&|\mathcal{F}_1(\check{k}(s_2), \check{l}(s_2)) - \mathcal{F}_1(\check{k}(s_1), \check{l}(s_1))|\\ &\leq \frac{1}{\Gamma_k(\tilde{\alpha})}\left|\int_{s_1}^{s_2} \hat{\psi}'(s)[(\hat{\psi}(s_2) - \hat{\psi}(s))^{\frac{\check{\alpha}}{k}-1} - (\hat{\psi}(s_1) - \hat{\psi}(s))^{\frac{\check{\alpha}}{k}-1}]\check{L}(s, \check{k}(s), \check{l}(s))ds\right.\\ &\quad \left. + \int_{s_1}^{s_2} \hat{\psi}'(s)(\hat{\psi}(s_2) - \hat{\psi}(s))^{\frac{\check{\alpha}}{k}-1}\check{L}(s, \check{k}(s), \check{l}(s))ds\right|\end{aligned}$$

$$+\frac{(\hat{\psi}(s_2)-\hat{\psi}(l_1))^{\frac{\tilde{\vartheta}_k}{k}-1}-(\hat{\psi}(s_1)-\hat{\psi}(l_1))^{\frac{\tilde{\vartheta}_k}{k}-1}}{|\mathcal{B}|\Gamma_k(\tilde{\vartheta}_k)}\bigg[\mathcal{B}_4\bigg(|\tilde{\mu}|\,{}^k\mathcal{I}^{\tilde{p}+\tilde{v},\hat{\psi}}|\check{L}(\tilde{\sigma},\check{k}(\tilde{\sigma}),\check{I}(\tilde{\sigma}))|$$

$$+|\tilde{\lambda}|\,{}^k\mathcal{I}^{\tilde{p}-\tilde{r},\hat{\psi}}|\check{L}(\tilde{\sigma},\check{k}(\tilde{\sigma}),\check{I}(\tilde{\sigma}))|+{}^k\mathcal{I}^{\tilde{\alpha},\hat{\psi}}|\check{L}(l_2,\check{k}(l_2),\check{I}(l_2))|\bigg)$$

$$+\mathcal{B}_2\bigg(|\tilde{\theta}|\,{}^k\mathcal{I}^{\tilde{\alpha}+\tilde{u},\hat{\psi}}|\check{L}(\tilde{\tau},\check{k}(\tilde{\tau}),\check{I}(\tilde{\tau}))+|\tilde{\nu}|\,{}^k\mathcal{I}^{\tilde{\alpha}-\tilde{z},\hat{\psi}}|\check{L}(\tilde{\eta},\check{k}(\tilde{\eta}),\check{I}(\tilde{\eta}))|$$

$$+{}^k\mathcal{I}^{\tilde{p},\hat{\psi}}|\check{L}(l_2,\check{k}(l_2),\check{I}(l_2))|\bigg)\bigg]$$

$$\leq\frac{\mathcal{L}_1}{\Gamma_k(\tilde{\alpha}+k)}[2(\hat{\psi}(s_2)-\hat{\psi}(s_1))^{\frac{\tilde{\alpha}}{k}}+|(\hat{\psi}(s_2)-\hat{\psi}(l_2))^{\frac{\tilde{\alpha}}{k}}-(\hat{\psi}(s_1)-\hat{\psi}(l_2))^{\frac{\tilde{\alpha}}{k}}|]$$

$$+\frac{(\hat{\psi}(s_2)-\hat{\psi}(l_1))^{\frac{\tilde{\vartheta}_k}{k}-1}-(\hat{\psi}(s_1)-\hat{\psi}(l_1))^{\frac{\tilde{\vartheta}_k}{k}-1}}{|\mathcal{B}|\Gamma_k(\tilde{\vartheta}_k)}\bigg[\mathcal{B}_4\bigg(|\tilde{\mu}|\,\frac{(\hat{\psi}(\tilde{\sigma})-\hat{\psi}(l_1))^{\frac{\tilde{p}+\tilde{v}}{k}}}{\Gamma_k(\tilde{p}+\tilde{v}+k)}\mathcal{L}_2$$

$$+|\tilde{\lambda}|\,\frac{(\hat{\psi}(\tilde{\xi})-\hat{\psi}(l_1))^{\frac{\tilde{p}-\tilde{r}}{k}}}{\Gamma_k(\tilde{p}-\tilde{r}+k)}\mathcal{L}_2+\frac{(\hat{\psi}(l_2)-\hat{\psi}(l_1))^{\frac{\tilde{\alpha}}{k}}}{\Gamma_k(\tilde{\alpha}+k)}\mathcal{L}_1\bigg)$$

$$+\mathcal{B}_2\bigg(|\tilde{\theta}|\,\frac{(\hat{\psi}(\tilde{\tau})-\hat{\psi}(l_1))^{\frac{\tilde{\alpha}+\tilde{u}}{k}}}{\Gamma_k(\tilde{\alpha}+\tilde{\tau}+k)}\mathcal{L}_1+|\nu|\,\frac{(\hat{\psi}(\tilde{\eta})-\hat{\psi}(l_1))^{\frac{\tilde{\alpha}-\tilde{z}}{k}}}{\Gamma_k(\tilde{\alpha}-\tilde{z}+k)}\mathcal{L}_1$$

$$+\frac{(\hat{\psi}(l_2)-\hat{\psi}(l_1))^{\frac{\tilde{p}}{k}}}{\Gamma_k(\tilde{p}+k)}\mathcal{L}_2\bigg)\bigg]\to 0 \text{ as } s_2-s_1\to 0,$$

independently of $(\check{k},\check{I})\in\mathcal{S}$. Hence, $\mathcal{F}_1(\check{k},\check{I})$ is equicontinuous. Similarly, it can be shown that $\mathcal{F}_2(\check{k},\check{I})$ is equicontinuous. Thus, it follows by the foregoing arguments that the operator $\mathcal{F}(\check{k},\check{I})$ is completely continuous.

Lastly, it will be shown that the set $\mathcal{D}=\{(\check{k},\check{I})\in\mathbb{X}\times\mathbb{X}:(\check{k},\check{I})=\omega\mathcal{F}(\check{k},\check{I}),0\leq\omega\leq 1\}$ is bounded. Let $(\check{k},\check{I})\in\mathcal{D}$, then $(\check{k},\check{I})=\omega\mathcal{F}(\check{k},\check{I})$ for all $s\in[l_1,l_2]$ and that

$$\check{k}(s)=\omega\mathcal{F}_1(\check{k},\check{I})(s),\quad \check{I}(s)=\omega\mathcal{F}_2(\check{k},\check{I})(s).$$

Thus, we have

$$|\check{k}(s)|\leq\bigg\{\frac{(\hat{\psi}(l_2)-\hat{\psi}(l_1))^{\frac{\tilde{\alpha}}{k}}}{\Gamma_k(\tilde{\alpha}+k)}+\frac{(\hat{\psi}(l_2)-\hat{\psi}(l_1))^{\frac{\tilde{\vartheta}_k}{k}-1}}{|\mathcal{B}|\Gamma_k(\tilde{\vartheta}_k)}\bigg[\mathcal{B}_4\frac{(\hat{\psi}(l_2)-\hat{\psi}(l_1))^{\frac{\tilde{\alpha}}{k}}}{\Gamma_k(\tilde{\alpha}+k)}$$

$$+\mathcal{B}_2\bigg(|\tilde{\theta}|\,\frac{(\hat{\psi}(\tilde{\tau})-\hat{\psi}(l_1))^{\frac{\tilde{\alpha}+\tilde{u}}{k}}}{\Gamma_k(\tilde{\alpha}+\tilde{u}+k)}+|\tilde{\nu}|\,\frac{(\hat{\psi}(\tilde{\eta})-\hat{\psi}(l_1))^{\frac{\tilde{\alpha}-\tilde{z}}{k}}}{\Gamma_k(\tilde{\alpha}-\tilde{z}+k)}\bigg)\bigg]\bigg\}[\hat{l}_0+\hat{l}_1|\check{k}|+\hat{l}_2|\check{I}|]$$

$$+\bigg\{\frac{(\hat{\psi}(l_2)-\hat{\psi}(l_1))^{\frac{\tilde{\vartheta}_k}{k}-1}}{|\mathcal{B}|\Gamma_k(\tilde{\vartheta}_k)}\bigg[\mathcal{B}_4\bigg(|\tilde{\mu}|\,\frac{(\hat{\psi}(\tilde{\sigma})-\hat{\psi}(l_1))^{\frac{\tilde{p}+\tilde{v}}{k}}}{\Gamma_k(\tilde{p}+\tilde{v}+k)}$$

$$+|\tilde{\lambda}|\,\frac{(\hat{\psi}(\tilde{\xi})-\hat{\psi}(l_1))^{\frac{\tilde{p}-\tilde{r}}{k}}}{\Gamma_k(\tilde{p}-\tilde{r}+k)}\bigg)\bigg]+\mathcal{B}_2\frac{(\hat{\psi}(l_2)-\hat{\psi}(l_1))^{\frac{\tilde{p}}{k}}}{\Gamma_k(\tilde{p}+k)}\bigg\}[\hat{q}_0+\hat{q}_1|\check{k}|+\hat{q}_2|\check{I}|],$$

$$|\check{I}(s)|\leq\bigg\{\frac{(\hat{\psi}(l_2)-\hat{\psi}(l_1))^{\frac{\tilde{\eta}_k}{k}-1}}{|\mathcal{B}|\Gamma_k(\tilde{\eta}_k)}\bigg[\mathcal{B}_1\bigg(|\tilde{\theta}|\,\frac{(\hat{\psi}(\tilde{\tau})-\hat{\psi}(l_1))^{\frac{\tilde{\alpha}+\tilde{u}}{k}}}{\Gamma_k(\tilde{\alpha}+\tilde{u}+k)}$$

$$+|\tilde{\nu}|\,\frac{(\hat{\psi}(\tilde{\eta})-\hat{\psi}(l_1))^{\frac{\tilde{\alpha}-\tilde{z}}{k}}}{\Gamma_k(\tilde{\alpha}-\tilde{z}+k)}\bigg)+\mathcal{B}_3\frac{(\hat{\psi}(l_2)-\hat{\psi}(l_1))^{\frac{\tilde{\alpha}}{k}}}{\Gamma_k(\tilde{\alpha}+k)}\bigg]\bigg\}[\hat{l}_0+\hat{l}_1|\check{k}|+\hat{l}_2|\check{I}|]$$

$$+\bigg\{\frac{(\hat{\psi}(l_2)-\hat{\psi}(l_1))^{\frac{\tilde{p}}{k}}}{\Gamma_k(\tilde{p}+k)}+\frac{(\hat{\psi}(l_2)-\hat{\psi}(l_1))^{\frac{\tilde{\vartheta}_k}{k}-1}}{|\mathcal{B}|\Gamma_k(\tilde{\vartheta}_k)}\bigg[\mathcal{B}_1\frac{(\hat{\psi}(l_2)-\hat{\psi}(l_1))^{\frac{\tilde{p}}{k}}}{\Gamma_k(\tilde{p}+k)}$$

$$+\mathcal{B}_3\bigg(|\tilde{\mu}|\,\frac{(\hat{\psi}(\tilde{\sigma})-\hat{\psi}(l_1))^{\frac{\tilde{p}+\tilde{v}}{k}}}{\Gamma_k(\tilde{p}+\tilde{v}+k)}$$

$$+|\tilde{\lambda}|\frac{(\hat{\psi}(\tilde{\xi})-\hat{\psi}(l_1))^{\frac{\tilde{p}-\tilde{r}}{k}}}{\Gamma_k(\tilde{p}-\tilde{r}+k)}\Big)\Big]\Big\}[\hat{q}_0+\hat{q}_1|\check{k}|+\hat{q}_2|\check{l}|].$$

Consequently, we obtain

$$\|\check{k}\|+\|\check{l}\| \leq (\mathfrak{R}_1+\mathfrak{R}_3)\hat{l}_0+(\mathfrak{R}_2+\mathfrak{R}_4)\hat{q}_0+[((\mathfrak{R}_1+\mathfrak{R}_3)\hat{l}_1+(\mathfrak{R}_2+\mathfrak{R}_4)\hat{q}_1]\|\check{k}\|$$
$$+[((\mathfrak{R}_1+\mathfrak{R}_3)\hat{l}_2+(\mathfrak{R}_2+\mathfrak{R}_4)\hat{q}_2]\|\check{l}\|,$$

which can be expressed as

$$\|(\check{k},\check{l})\| \leq \frac{(\mathfrak{R}_1+\mathfrak{R}_3)\hat{l}_0+(\mathfrak{R}_2+\mathfrak{R}_4)\hat{q}_0}{\mathcal{M}_0},$$

where

$$\mathcal{M}_0 = \min\{1-[(\mathfrak{R}_1+\mathfrak{R}_3)\hat{l}_1+(\mathfrak{R}_2+\mathfrak{R}_4)\hat{q}_1], 1-[(\mathfrak{R}_1+\mathfrak{R}_3)\hat{l}_2+(\mathfrak{R}_2+\mathfrak{R}_4)\hat{q}_2]\}.$$

Thus, the Leray–Schauder alternative applies and hence its conclusion implies that the operator $\mathcal{F}$ has at least one fixed point. Hence the System (1) and (2) has at least one solution on $[l_1, l_2]$. □

The proof of the next existence result relies on Krasnosel'skiĭ's fixed point theorem [21].

Theorem 3. *Assume that $\check{L}, \check{L} : [l_1, l_2] \times \mathbb{R} \times \mathbb{R} \to \mathbb{R}$ are two continuous functions which satisfy Condition (17) of Theorem 1. Moreover, it is assumed that*

($\mathcal{H}$) There exist P and $Q \in C([l_1, l_2], \mathbb{R}_+)$ such that

$$|\check{L}(s,\check{k},\check{l})| \leq P(s), \ |\check{L}(s,\check{k},\check{l})| \leq Q(s), \ \text{for each } (s,\check{k},\check{l}) \in [l_1, l_2] \times \mathbb{R} \times \mathbb{R}.$$

Then, the Problem (1) and (2) has at least one solution on $[l_1, l_2]$, provided that

$$[\mathfrak{R}_1^* + \mathfrak{R}_3](\hat{m}_1 + \hat{m}_2) + [\mathfrak{R}_2 + \mathfrak{R}_4^*](\hat{n}_1 + \hat{n}_2) < 1. \tag{22}$$

Proof. Let us first decompose the operator $\mathcal{F}$ into four operators $\mathcal{F}_{1,1}, \mathcal{F}_{1,2}, \mathcal{F}_{2,1}$ and $\mathcal{F}_{2,2}$ as

$$\mathcal{F}_{1,1}(\check{k},\check{l})(s) = {}^k\mathcal{I}^{\tilde{\alpha},\hat{\psi}}\check{L}(s,\check{k}(s),\check{l}(s)), \ s \in [l_1, l_2],$$

$$\mathcal{F}_{1,2}(\check{k},\check{l})(s) = \frac{(\hat{\psi}(s)-\hat{\psi}(l_1))^{\frac{\tilde{\theta}_k}{k}-1}}{\mathcal{B}\Gamma_k(\tilde{\theta}_k)}\bigg[\mathcal{B}_4\bigg(\tilde{\mu}\ {}^k\mathcal{I}^{\tilde{p}+\tilde{\sigma},\hat{\psi}}\check{L}(\tilde{\sigma},\check{k}(\tilde{\sigma}),\check{l}(\tilde{\sigma}))$$
$$+\tilde{\lambda}\ {}^k\mathcal{I}^{\tilde{p}-\tilde{r},\hat{\psi}}\check{L}(\tilde{\xi},\check{k}(\tilde{\xi}),\check{l}(\tilde{\xi})) - {}^k\mathcal{I}^{\tilde{\alpha},\hat{\psi}}\check{L}(l_2,\check{k}(l_2),\check{l}(l_2))\bigg)$$
$$+\mathcal{B}_2\bigg(\tilde{\theta}\ {}^k\mathcal{I}^{\tilde{\alpha}+\tilde{u},\hat{\psi}}\check{L}(\tilde{\tau},\check{k}(\tilde{\tau}),\check{l}(\tilde{\tau}))) + \tilde{v}\ {}^k\mathcal{I}^{\tilde{\alpha}-\tilde{z},\hat{\psi}}\check{L}(\tilde{\eta},\check{k}(\tilde{\eta}),\check{l}(\tilde{\eta}))$$
$$-{}^k\mathcal{I}^{\tilde{p},\hat{\psi}}\check{L}(l_2,\check{k}(l_2),\check{l}(l_2))\bigg)\bigg], \ s \in [l_1, l_2],$$

$$\mathcal{F}_{2,1}(\check{k},\check{l})(s) = {}^k\mathcal{I}^{\tilde{p},\hat{\psi}}\check{L}(s,\check{k}(s),\check{l}(s)), \ s \in [l_1, l_2],$$

$$\mathcal{F}_{2,2}(\check{k},\check{l})(s) = \frac{(\hat{\psi}(s)-\hat{\psi}(l_1))^{\frac{\tilde{\eta}_k}{k}-1}}{\mathcal{B}\Gamma_k(\tilde{\eta}_k)}\bigg[\mathcal{B}_1\bigg(\tilde{\theta}\ {}^k\mathcal{I}^{\tilde{\alpha}+\tilde{u},\hat{\psi}}\check{L}(\tilde{\tau},\check{k}(\tilde{\tau}),\check{l}(\tilde{\tau}))$$
$$+\tilde{v}\ {}^k\mathcal{I}^{\tilde{\alpha}-\tilde{z},\hat{\psi}}\check{L}(\tilde{\eta},\check{k}(\tilde{\eta}),\check{l}(\tilde{\eta})) - {}^k\mathcal{I}^{\tilde{p},\hat{\psi}}\check{L}(l_2,\check{k}(l_2),\check{l}(l_2))\bigg)$$
$$+\mathcal{B}_3\bigg(\tilde{\mu}\ {}^k\mathcal{I}^{\tilde{p}+\tilde{\sigma},\hat{\psi}}\check{L}(\tilde{\sigma},\check{k}(\tilde{\sigma}),\check{l}(\tilde{\sigma})) + \tilde{\lambda}\ {}^k\mathcal{I}^{\tilde{p}-\tilde{r},\hat{\psi}}\check{L}(\tilde{\xi},\check{k}(\tilde{\xi}),\check{l}(\tilde{\xi}))$$

$$-{}^k\mathcal{I}^{\tilde{\alpha},\hat{\psi}}\check{L}(l_2,\check{k}(l_2),\check{l}(l_2))\Big)\Big], \quad s\in[l_1,l_2].$$

Observe that $\mathcal{F}_1 = \mathcal{F}_{1,1} + \mathcal{F}_{1,2}$ and $\mathcal{F}_2 = \mathcal{F}_{2,1} + \mathcal{F}_{2,2}$. Consider a closed ball $\mathcal{B}_{\hat{\rho}} = \{(\check{k},\check{l}) \in \mathbb{X} \times \mathbb{X} : \|(\check{k},\check{l})\| \leq \hat{\rho}\}$ with $\hat{\rho} \geq (\mathfrak{R}_1 + \mathfrak{R}_3)\|P\| + (\mathfrak{R}_2 + \mathfrak{R}_4)\|Q\|$. As in the proof of Theorem 2, one can obtain

$$|\mathcal{F}_{1,1}(\check{k}_1,\check{k}_2)(s) + \mathcal{F}_{1,2}(\check{l}_1,\check{l}_2)(s)| \leq \mathfrak{R}_1\|P\| + \mathfrak{R}_2\|Q\|,$$

and

$$|\mathcal{F}_{1,1}(\check{k}_1,\check{k}_2)(t) + \mathcal{F}_{2,2}(\check{k}_1,\check{k}_2)(t)| \leq \mathfrak{R}_3\|P\| + \mathfrak{R}_4\|Q\|.$$

Therefore, we obtain

$$\|\mathcal{F}_1(\check{k}_1,\check{k}_2) + \mathcal{F}_2(\check{l}_1,\check{l}_2)\| \leq (\mathfrak{R}_1 + \mathfrak{R}_3)\|P\| + (\mathfrak{R}_2 + \mathfrak{R}_4)\|Q\| < \hat{\rho}.$$

Consequently, $\mathcal{F}_1(\check{k}_1,\check{k}_2) + \mathcal{F}_2(\check{l}_1,\check{l}_2) \in \mathcal{B}_{\hat{\rho}}$. Next, it will be accomplished that the $(F_{1,2}, F_{2,2})$ is a contraction. As argued in proving Theorem 1, for $(\check{k}_1,\check{l}_1), (\check{k}_2,\check{l}_2) \in \mathcal{B}_{\hat{\rho}}$, one can find that

$$
\begin{aligned}
&|\mathcal{F}_{1,2}(\check{k}_1,\check{k}_2)(s) - \mathcal{F}_{1,2}(\check{l}_1,\check{l}_2)(s)| \\
&\leq \left\{ \frac{(\hat{\psi}(l_2) - \hat{\psi}(l_1))^{\frac{\tilde{\vartheta}_k}{k}-1}}{|\mathcal{B}|\Gamma_k(\tilde{\vartheta}_k)}\left[\mathcal{B}_4 \frac{(\hat{\psi}(l_2) - \hat{\psi}(l_1))^{\frac{\tilde{\alpha}}{k}}}{\Gamma_k(\tilde{\alpha}+k)} + \mathcal{B}_2\Big(|\tilde{\theta}|\frac{(\hat{\psi}(\tilde{\tau}) - \hat{\psi}(l_1))^{\frac{\tilde{\alpha}+\tilde{u}}{k}}}{\Gamma_k(\tilde{\alpha}+\tilde{u}+k)}\right.\right. \\
&\quad\left.\left. +|\tilde{v}|\frac{(\hat{\psi}(\tilde{\eta}) - \hat{\psi}(l_1))^{\frac{\tilde{\alpha}-\tilde{z}}{k}}}{\Gamma_k(\tilde{\alpha}-\tilde{z}+k)}\Big)\right]\right\}[\hat{m}_1\|\check{k}_1-\check{l}_1\| + \hat{m}_2\|\check{k}_2-\check{l}_2\|] \\
&\quad + \left\{\frac{(\hat{\psi}(l_2)-\hat{\psi}(l_1))^{\frac{\tilde{\vartheta}_k}{k}-1}}{|\mathcal{B}|\Gamma_k(\tilde{\vartheta}_k)}\left[\mathcal{B}_4\Big(|\tilde{\mu}|\frac{(\hat{\psi}(\tilde{\sigma})-\hat{\psi}(l_1))^{\frac{\tilde{p}+\tilde{v}}{k}}}{\Gamma_k(\tilde{p}+\tilde{v}+k)} + |\tilde{\lambda}|\frac{(\hat{\psi}(\tilde{\xi})-\hat{\psi}(l_1))^{\frac{\tilde{p}-\tilde{r}}{k}}}{\Gamma_k(\tilde{p}-\tilde{r}+k)}\Big)\right]\right. \\
&\quad\left. +\mathcal{B}_2\frac{(\hat{\psi}(l_2)-\hat{\psi}(l_1))^{\frac{\tilde{p}}{k}}}{\Gamma_k(\tilde{p}+k)}\right\}[\hat{n}_1\|\check{k}_1-\check{l}_1\|+\hat{n}_2\|\check{k}_2-\check{l}_2\|] \\
&= \mathfrak{R}_1^*(\hat{m}_1\|\check{k}_1-\check{l}_1\| + \hat{m}_2\|\check{k}_2-\check{l}_2\|) \\
&\quad + \mathfrak{R}_2(\hat{n}_1\|\check{k}_1-\check{l}_1\| + \hat{n}_2\|\check{k}_2-\check{l}_2\|) \\
&= [\mathfrak{R}_1^*\hat{m}_1 + \mathfrak{R}_2\hat{n}_1]\|\check{k}_1-\check{l}_1\| + [\mathfrak{R}_1^*\hat{m}_2 + \mathfrak{R}_2\hat{n}_2]\|\check{k}_2-\check{l}_2\|,
\end{aligned}
\tag{23}
$$

and

$$
\begin{aligned}
&|\mathcal{F}_{2,2}(\check{k}_1,\check{k}_2)(s) - \mathcal{F}_{2,2}(\check{l}_1,\check{l}_2)(s)| \\
&\leq [\mathfrak{R}_3\hat{m}_1 + \mathfrak{R}_4^*\hat{n}_1]\|\check{k}_1-\check{l}_1\| + [\mathfrak{R}_3\hat{m}_2 + \mathfrak{R}_4^*\hat{n}_2]\|\check{k}_2-\check{l}_2\|.
\end{aligned}
\tag{24}
$$

From Equations (23) and (24), we obtain

$$
\begin{aligned}
&\|(\mathcal{F}_{1,2},\mathcal{F}_{2,2})(\check{k}_1,\check{k}_2) - (\mathcal{F}_{1,2},\mathcal{F}_{2,2})(\check{l}_1,\check{l}_2)\| \\
&\leq \left\{[\mathfrak{R}_1^* + \mathfrak{R}_3](\hat{m}_1+\hat{m}_2) + [\mathfrak{R}_2 + \mathfrak{R}_4^*](\hat{n}_1+\hat{n}_2)\right\}(\|\check{k}_1-\check{l}_1\| + \|\check{k}_2-\check{l}_2\|),
\end{aligned}
$$

which, owing to the Condition (22), shows that the operator $(\mathcal{F}_{1,2}, \mathcal{F}_{2,1})$ is a contraction. In view of the continuity property of $\check{L}$ and $\check{L}$, the operator $(\mathcal{F}_{1,1}, \mathcal{F}_{2,1})$ is continuous. Moreover,

$$\|(\mathcal{F}_{1,1},\mathcal{F}_{2,1})(\check{k},\check{l})\| \leq \frac{(\hat{\psi}(l_2)-\hat{\psi}(l_1))^{\frac{\tilde{\alpha}}{k}}}{\Gamma_k(\tilde{\alpha}+k)}\|P\| + \frac{(\hat{\psi}(l_2)-\hat{\psi}(l_1))^{\frac{\tilde{p}}{k}}}{\Gamma_k(\tilde{p}+k)}\|Q\|,$$

as $\|\mathcal{F}_{1,1}(\check{k},\check{l})\| \leq \dfrac{\hat{\psi}(l_2)-\hat{\psi}(l_1))^{\frac{\tilde{\alpha}}{k}}}{\Gamma_k(\tilde{\alpha}+k)}\|P\|$ and $\|\mathcal{F}_{2,1}(\check{k},\check{l})\| \leq \dfrac{\hat{\psi}(l_2)-\hat{\psi}(l_1))^{\frac{\tilde{p}}{k}}}{\Gamma_k(\tilde{p}+k)}\|Q\|$.

Thus, $(\mathcal{F}_{1,1},\mathcal{F}_{2,1})\mathcal{B}_\rho$ is uniformly bounded.

In the next step, we establish that the set $(\mathcal{F}_{1,1},\mathcal{F}_{2,1})\mathcal{B}_\rho$ is equicontinuous. For $s_1, s_2 \in [l_1, l_2]$, $s_1 < s_2$ and for all $(\check{k},\check{l}) \in \mathcal{B}_\rho$, we have

$$
\begin{aligned}
&|\mathcal{F}_{1,1}(\check{k},\check{l})(s_2) - \mathcal{F}_{1,1}(\check{k},\check{l})(s_1)| \\
&\leq \dfrac{1}{\Gamma_k(\hat{\tilde{\alpha}})}\bigg|\int_{s_1}^{s_2}\hat{\psi}'(s)[(\hat{\psi}(s_2)-\hat{\psi}(s))^{\frac{\tilde{\alpha}-k}{k}} - (\hat{\psi}(s_1)-\hat{\psi}(s))^{\frac{\tilde{\alpha}-k}{k}}]\check{L}(s,\check{k}(s),\check{l}(s))ds \\
&\quad + \int_{s_1}^{s_2}\hat{\psi}'(s)(\hat{\psi}(s_2)-\hat{\psi}(s))^{\frac{\tilde{\alpha}-k}{k}}\check{f}(s,\check{k}(s),\check{l}(s))ds\bigg| \\
&\leq \dfrac{\|P\|}{\Gamma_k(\tilde{\alpha}+k)}[2(\hat{\psi}(s_2)-\hat{\psi}(s_1))^{\frac{\tilde{\alpha}}{k}} + |(\hat{\psi}(s_2)-\hat{\psi}(l_1))^{\frac{\tilde{\alpha}}{k}} - (\hat{\psi}(s_1)-\hat{\psi}(l_1))^{\frac{\tilde{\alpha}}{k}}|] \\
&\longrightarrow 0 \text{ as } s_1 \longrightarrow s_2,
\end{aligned}
$$

independently of $(\check{k},\check{l}) \in \mathcal{B}_\rho$. Analogously, one can obtain that

$$|(\mathcal{F}_{2,1}(\check{k},\check{l})(s_2) - \mathcal{F}_{2,1}(\check{k},\check{l})(s_1)| \to 0 \text{ as } s_1 \longrightarrow s_2.$$

Thus, $|(\mathcal{F}_{1,1},\mathcal{F}_{2,1})(\check{k},\check{l})(s_2) - (\mathcal{F}_{1,1},\mathcal{F}_{2,1})(\check{k},\check{l})(s_1)| \to 0$ as $s_1 \longrightarrow s_2$. So, $(\mathcal{F}_{1,1},\mathcal{F}_{2,1})$ is equicontinuous. Hence, we deduce by the Arzelá–Ascoli theorem that the operator $(\mathcal{F}_{1,1},\mathcal{F}_{2,1})$ is compact on $\mathcal{B}_\rho$. Thus, the hypotheses of Krasnosel'skiĭ fixed point theorem is verified. Therefore, the System (1) and (2) has at least one solution on $[l_1,l_2]$. □

4. Examples

Consider the following boundary value problem after fixing the parameters in the System (1) and (2):

$$
\begin{cases}
{}^{\frac{6}{7},H}\mathcal{D}^{\frac{9}{7},\frac{4}{5};s^2+1}\check{k}(s) = \check{L}(s,\check{k}(s),\check{l}(s)), & \frac{2}{5} < s < \frac{8}{5}, \\
{}^{\frac{6}{7},H}\mathcal{D}^{\frac{11}{7},\frac{2}{5};s^2+1}\check{l}(s) = \check{L}(s,\check{k}(s),\check{l}(s)), & \frac{2}{5} < s < \frac{8}{5}, \\
\check{k}\left(\dfrac{2}{5}\right) = 0, \quad \check{k}\left(\dfrac{8}{5}\right) = \dfrac{1}{\sqrt{\pi}}{}^{\frac{6}{7},H}\mathcal{D}^{\frac{6}{7},\frac{3}{5};s^2+1}\check{l}\left(\dfrac{4}{5}\right) + \dfrac{2}{59}{}^{\frac{6}{7}}\mathcal{I}^{\frac{1}{4};s^2+1}\check{l}\left(\dfrac{7}{5}\right), \\
\check{l}\left(\dfrac{2}{5}\right) = 0, \quad \check{l}\left(\dfrac{8}{5}\right) = \dfrac{4}{79}{}^{\frac{6}{7},H}\mathcal{D}^{\frac{5}{7},\frac{1}{5};s^2+1}\check{k}\left(\dfrac{3}{5}\right) + \dfrac{1}{\sqrt{e}}{}^{\frac{6}{7}}\mathcal{I}^{\frac{3}{4};s^2+1}\check{k}\left(\dfrac{6}{5}\right).
\end{cases} \quad (25)
$$

Here, $k = 6/7$, $\tilde{\alpha} = 9/7$, $\tilde{p} = 11/7$, $\tilde{r} = 6/7$, $\tilde{z} = 5/7$, $\tilde{\beta} = 4/5$, $\tilde{q} = 2/5$, $\tilde{s} = 3/5$, $\tilde{w} = 1/5$, $\tilde{v} = 1/4$, $\tilde{u} = 3/4$, $\hat{\psi}(s) = s^2+1$, $\tilde{\lambda} = 1/\sqrt{\pi}$, $\tilde{\mu} = 2/59$, $\tilde{\nu} = 4/79$, $\tilde{\theta} = 1/\sqrt{e}$ and $l_1 = 2/5$, $l_2 = 8/5$, $\tilde{\xi} = 4/5$, $\tilde{\sigma} = 7/5$, $\tilde{\eta} = 3/5$, $\tilde{\tau} = 6/5$. Using the given values, we find that $\tilde{\vartheta}_k = \tilde{\eta}_k = 57/35$, $\Gamma_k(\tilde{\vartheta}_k) = \Gamma_k(\tilde{\eta}_k) \approx 0.8371768940$, $\Gamma_k(\tilde{\vartheta}_k+\tilde{u}) \approx 1.248828596$, $\Gamma_k(\tilde{\vartheta}_k-\tilde{z}) \approx 0.9557910248$, $\Gamma_k(\tilde{\eta}_k+\tilde{v}) \approx 0.9127761461$, $\Gamma_k(\tilde{\eta}_k-\tilde{r}) \approx 1.085229307$, $\Gamma_k(\tilde{\alpha}+k) \approx 1.054911472$, $\Gamma_k(\tilde{p}+k) \approx 1.299979244$, $\Gamma_k(\tilde{\alpha}+\tilde{u}+k) \approx 2.012923279$, $\Gamma_k(\tilde{\alpha}-\tilde{z}+k) \approx 2.968888877$, $\Gamma_k(\tilde{p}+\tilde{v}+k) \approx 1.622489113$, $\Gamma_k(\tilde{p}-\tilde{r}+k) \approx 6.329317026$, $\mathcal{B}_1 \approx 2.626472658$, $\mathcal{B}_2 \approx 0.6342926434$, $\mathcal{B}_3 \approx 0.8003297566$, $\mathcal{B}_4 \approx 2.626472658$, $\mathcal{B} \approx 6.390715346$ ($\mathcal{B}_i, i = 1,2,3,4$, and $\mathcal{B}$ are, respectively, given in Equations (9) and (8)), $\mathfrak{R}_1 \approx 7.483199257$, $\mathfrak{R}_2 \approx 1.254247333$, $\mathfrak{R}_3 \approx 1.797703986$, $\mathfrak{R}_4 \approx 8.040757033$ ($\mathfrak{R}_i, i = 1,2,3,4$, are defined in (15)), $\mathfrak{R}_1^* \approx 3.958672213$, $\mathfrak{R}_4^* \approx 4.211473493$ ($\mathfrak{R}_1^*$ and $\mathfrak{R}_2^*$ are defined in (16)).

Example 1. Let $\check{L}, \hat{L} : [(2/5), (8/5)] \times \mathbb{R} \times \mathbb{R} \longrightarrow \mathbb{R}$ be the nonlinear Lipschitzian unbounded functions given by

$$\check{L}(s, \check{k}, \check{l}) = \frac{e^{-(5s-2)}}{(40s+21)} \left(\frac{|\check{k}|}{1+|\check{k}|} \right) + \frac{\cos^2 \pi s (\check{l}^2 + 2|\check{l}|)}{(2(5s+4)^2 + 6)(1+|\check{l}|)} + \frac{1}{3}s + 1, \qquad (26)$$

$$\hat{L}(s, \check{k}, \check{l}) = \frac{\sin^2 \pi t (\check{k}^2 + 2|\check{k}|)}{2(5s+4)^2(1+|\check{k}|)} + \frac{\tan^{-1}(\check{l})}{2(35t+5)} + \frac{1}{4}s + 2, \qquad (27)$$

which satisfy the Lipschitz condition:

$$|\check{L}(s, \check{k}_1, \check{l}_1) - \check{L}(s, \check{k}_2, \check{l}_2)| \leq \frac{1}{37}|\check{k}_1 - \check{k}_2| + \frac{1}{39}|\check{l}_1 - \check{l}_2|,$$

$$|\hat{L}(s, \check{k}_1, \check{l}_1) - \hat{L}(s, \check{k}_2, \check{l}_2)| \leq \frac{1}{36}|\tilde{r}_1 - \tilde{r}_2| + \frac{1}{38}|\hat{z}_1 - \hat{z}_2|,$$

with Lipschitz constants $\hat{m}_1 = 1/37$, $\hat{m}_2 = 1/39$, $\hat{n}_1 = 1/36$ and $\hat{n}_2 = 1/38$. Furthermore, $(\mathfrak{R}_1 + \mathfrak{R}_3)(\hat{m}_1 + \hat{m}_2) + (\mathfrak{R}_2 + \mathfrak{R}_4)(\hat{n}_1 + \hat{n}_2) \approx 0.9916070446 < 1$. Thus, the hypotheses of Theorem 1 are satisfied and hence its conclusion implies that the Problem (25) with functions $\check{L}$ and $\hat{L}$ given by Equations (26) and (27), respectively, has a unique solution on the interval $[(2/5), (8/5)]$.

Example 2. Consider the functions $\check{L}, \hat{L} : [(2/5), (8/5)] \times \mathbb{R} \times \mathbb{R} \longrightarrow \mathbb{R}$ as

$$\check{L}(s, \check{k}, \check{l}) = \frac{1 + \cos^2(s\check{k}\check{l})}{2\pi s} + \frac{e^{-|s\check{l}|}|\check{k}|^{33}}{20(1+\check{k}^{32})} + \frac{\sin|\check{l}|}{(5s+19)}, \qquad (28)$$

$$\hat{L}(s, \check{k}, \check{l}) = \frac{1 + \sin^2(s\check{k}\check{l})}{4\pi s} + \frac{\check{k}(1+\cos^4 \check{l})}{(5s+36)} + \frac{e^{-|s\check{k}|}\check{l}^{38}}{22(1+|\check{l}|^{37})}. \qquad (29)$$

Clearly $|\tilde{f}(s, \check{k}, \check{l})| \leq (5/2\pi) + (1/20)|\check{k}| + (1/21)|\check{l}|$ and $|\hat{L}(s, \check{k}, \check{l})| \leq (5/4\pi) + (1/19)|\check{k}| + (1/22)|\check{l}|$, with $\hat{l}_0 = 5/2\pi$, $\hat{l}_1 = 1/20$, $\hat{l}_2 = 1/21$, $\hat{q}_0 = 5/4\pi$, $\hat{q}_1 = 1/19$, $\hat{q}_2 = 1/22$. Moreover, $(\mathfrak{R}_1 + \mathfrak{R}_3)\hat{l}_1 + (\mathfrak{R}_2 + \mathfrak{R}_4)\hat{q}_1 \approx 0.9532559183 < 1$ and $(\mathfrak{R}_1 + \mathfrak{R}_3)\hat{l}_2 + (\mathfrak{R}_2 + \mathfrak{R}_4)\hat{q}_2 \approx 0.8644479720 < 1$. Therefore, by the conclusion of Theorem 2, the Problem (25) with functions $\check{L}$, $\hat{L}$ given by Equations (28) and (29), respectively, has at least one solution on $[(2/5), (8/5)]$.

Example 3. Let the nonlinear Lipschitzian functions $\check{L}, \hat{L} : [(2/5), (8/5)] \times \mathbb{R} \times \mathbb{R} \longrightarrow \mathbb{R}$ be defined by

$$\check{L}(s, \check{k}, \check{l}) = \frac{1}{2\pi} \sin^4 \pi s + \frac{|\check{k}|}{24(1+|\check{k}|)} + \frac{1}{22} e^{-(5s-2)} \tan^{-1} \check{l}, \qquad (30)$$

$$\hat{L}(s, \check{k}, \check{l}) = \frac{1}{4\pi} \cos^4 \pi s + \frac{\sin \check{k}}{(10s+19)} + \frac{2|\check{l}|}{105s(1+|\check{l}|)}. \qquad (31)$$

Then, we have

$$|\check{L}(s, \check{k}, \check{l})| \leq \frac{1}{2\pi} \sin^4 \pi s + \frac{\pi}{44} e^{-(5s-2)} + \frac{1}{24},$$

$$|\hat{L}(s, \check{k}, \check{l})| \leq \frac{1}{4\pi} \cos^4 \pi s + \frac{1}{10s+19} + \frac{2}{105s},$$

and

$$|\check{L}(s, \check{k}_1, \check{l}_1) - \check{L}(s, \check{k}_2, \check{l}_2)| \leq \frac{1}{24}|\check{k}_1 - \check{k}_2| + \frac{1}{22}|\check{l}_1 - \check{l}_2|,$$

$$|\hat{L}(s, \check{k}_1, \check{l}_1) - \hat{L}(s, \check{k}_2, \check{l}_2)| \leq \frac{1}{23}|\check{k}_1 - \check{k}_2| + \frac{1}{21}|\check{l}_1 - \check{l}_2|.$$

Setting $\hat{m}_1 = 1/24$, $\hat{m}_2 = 1/22$, $\hat{n}_1 = 1/23$, $\hat{n}_2 = 1/21$, we find that $[\mathfrak{R}_1^* + \mathfrak{R}_3](\hat{m}_1 + \hat{m}_2) + [\mathfrak{R}_2 + \mathfrak{R}_4^*](\hat{n}_1 + \hat{n}_2) \approx 0.9994149281 < 1$. Therefore, by Theorem 3, the Problem (25) with the functions $\check{L}$, $\check{L}$ given by Equations (30) and (31), respectively, has at least one solution.

It is interesting to note that the functions given in Equations (30) and (31) satisfy the Lipschitz condition. However, the uniqueness of the solution to the problem at hand does not follow since $(\mathfrak{R}_1 + \mathfrak{R}_3)(\hat{m}_1 + \hat{m}_2) + (\mathfrak{R}_2 + \mathfrak{R}_4)(\hat{n}_1 + \hat{n}_2) \approx 1.655313420 > 1$.

5. Conclusions

In this work, we have established the existence and uniqueness results for a nonlinear nonlocal boundary value problem involving $(k, \hat{\psi})$-Hilfer fractional derivative and $(k, \hat{\psi})$-Riemann–Liouville fractional integral operators. In order to apply the fixed-point technique to the given problem, we first transform it into a fixed-point problem, which facilitates the application of the fixed point theorems chosen for the present analysis. Our problem is novel in the given configuration and the results obtained for it are of more general form. Some new results arising as special cases from our work are listed below.

1. By letting $\tilde{\mu} = 0 = \tilde{\theta}$ in the present results, we obtain the ones for coupled boundary conditions involving only $(k, \hat{\psi})$-Hilfer derivative operators:

$$\check{k}(l_1) = 0, \ \check{l}(l_1) = 0, \ \check{k}(l_2) = \tilde{\lambda}\,^{k,H}\mathcal{D}^{\tilde{r},\tilde{s},\hat{\psi}}\check{l}(\tilde{\xi}), \ \check{l}(l_2) = \tilde{v}\,^{k,H}\mathcal{D}^{\tilde{z},\tilde{w},\hat{\psi}}\check{k}(\tilde{\eta}).$$

2. For $\tilde{\lambda} = 0 = \tilde{v}$, our results correspond to the $(k, \hat{\psi})$-Riemann–Liouville fractional type integral boundary conditions:

$$\check{k}(l_1) = 0, \ \check{l}(l_1) = 0, \ \check{k}(l_2) = \tilde{\mu}\,^{k}\mathcal{I}^{\tilde{v},\hat{\psi}}\check{l}(\tilde{\sigma}), \ \check{l}(l_2) = \tilde{\theta}\,^{k}\mathcal{I}^{\tilde{u},\hat{\psi}}\check{k}(\tilde{\tau}).$$

3. Fixing $\tilde{\mu} = 0$ and $\tilde{v} = 0$ in the present results, we obtain the ones for the mixed boundary conditions of the form:

$$\check{k}(l_1) = 0, \ \check{l}(l_1) = 0, \ \check{k}(l_2) = \tilde{\lambda}\,^{k,H}\mathcal{D}^{\tilde{r},\tilde{s},\hat{\psi}}\check{l}(\tilde{\xi}), \ \check{l}(l_2) = \tilde{\theta}\,^{k}\mathcal{I}^{\tilde{u},\hat{\psi}}\check{k}(\tilde{\tau}).$$

4. Letting $\tilde{\lambda} = 0$ and $\tilde{\theta} = 0$ in the present results, we obtain the ones for the mixed boundary condition:

$$\check{k}(l_1) = 0, \ \check{l}(l_1) = 0, \ \check{k}(l_2) = \tilde{\mu}\,^{k}\mathcal{I}^{\tilde{v},\hat{\psi}}\check{l}(\tilde{\sigma}), \ \check{l}(l_2) = \tilde{v}\,^{k,H}\mathcal{D}^{\tilde{z},\tilde{w},\hat{\psi}}\check{k}(\tilde{\eta}).$$

Author Contributions: Conceptualization, S.K.N.; methodology, A.S., S.K.N., B.A. and J.T.; validation, A.S., S.K.N., B.A. and J.T.; formal analysis, A.S., S.K.N., B.A. and J.T. writing—original draft preparation, A.S., S.K.N., B.A. and J.T. All authors have read and agreed to the published version of the manuscript.

Funding: This research was funded by National Science, Research and Innovation Fund (NSRF) and King Mongkut's University of Technology North Bangkok with Contract no. KMUTNB-FF-66-11.

Institutional Review Board Statement: Not applicable.

Informed Consent Statement: Not applicable.

Data Availability Statement: Not applicable.

Acknowledgments: The authors thank the reviewers for their constructive remarks on their work.

Conflicts of Interest: The authors declare no conflict of interest.

References

1. Kilbas, A.A.; Srivastava, H.M.; Trujillo, J.J. *Theory and Applications of the Fractional Differential Equations*; North-Holland Mathematics Studies: Amsterdam, The Netherlands, 2006.
2. Hilfer, R. *Applications of Fractional Calculus in Physics*; World Scientific: Singapore, 2000.
3. Dorrego, G.A. An alternative definition for the k-Riemann-Liouville fractional derivative. *Appl. Math. Sci.* **2015**, *9*, 481–491. [CrossRef]

4. da Sousa, J.V.C.; de Oliveira, E.C. On the $\hat{\psi}$-Hilfer fractional derivative. *Commun. Nonlinear Sci. Numer. Simul.* **2018**, *60*, 72–91. [CrossRef]
5. Nuchpong, C.; Ntouyas, S.K.; Tariboon, J. Boundary value problems of Hilfer-type fractional integro-differential equations and inclusions with nonlocal integro-multipoint boundary conditions. *Open Math.* **2020**, *18*, 1879–1894. [CrossRef]
6. Subramanian, M.; Gopal, T.N. Analysis of boundary value problem with multi-point conditions involving Caputo-Hadamard fractional derivative. *Proyecciones* **2020**, *39*, 155–1575. [CrossRef]
7. Belbali, H.; Benbachir, M.; Etemad, S.; Park, C.S. Rezapour, Existence theory and generalized Mittag-Leffler stability for a nonlinear Caputo-Hadamard FIVP via the Lyapunov method. *AIMS Math.* **2022**, *7*, 14419–14433. [CrossRef]
8. Zhou, Y. *Basic Theory of Fractional Differential Equations*; World Scientific: Singapore, 2014.
9. Ali, I.; Malik, N. Hilfer fractional advection-diffusion equations with power-law initial condition; a numerical study using variational iteration method. *Comput. Math. Appl.* **2014**, *68*, 1161–1179. [CrossRef]
10. Hilfer, R. Experimental evidence for fractional time evolution in glass forming materials. *Chem. Phys.* **2002**, *284*, 399–408. [CrossRef]
11. Garra, R.; Gorenflo, R.; Polito, F.Z. Tomovski, Hilfer-Prabhakar derivatives and some applications. *Appl. Math. Comput.* **2014**, *242*, 576–589.
12. Ntouyas, S.K.; Ahmad, B.; Tariboon, J. On $(k, \hat{\psi})$-Hilfer fractional differential equations and inclusions with mixed $(k, \hat{\psi})$-derivative and integral boundary conditions. *Axioms* **2022**, *11*, 403. [CrossRef]
13. Kucche, K.D.; Mali, A.D. On the nonlinear $(k, \hat{\psi})$-Hilfer fractional differential equations. *Chaos Solitons Fractals* **2021**, *152*, 111335. [CrossRef]
14. Samadi, A.; Ntouyas, S.K.; Tariboon, J. Nonlocal coupled system for (k, φ)-Hilfer fractional differential equations. *Fractal Fract.* **2022**, *6*, 234. [CrossRef]
15. Magin, R.L. *Fractional Calculus in Bioengineering*; Begell House Publishers: Danbury, CT, USA, 2006.
16. Zaslavsky, G.M. *Hamiltonian Chaos and Fractional Dynamics*; Oxford University Press: Oxford, UK, 2005.
17. Fallahgoul, H.A.; Focardi, S.M.; Fabozzi, F.J. *Fractional Calculus and Fractional Processes with Applications to Financial Economics: Theory and Application*; Elsevier/Academic Press: London, UK, 2017.
18. Almalahi, M.A.; Abdo, M.S.; Panchal, S.K. Existence and Ulam-Hyers stability results of a coupled system of $\hat{\psi}$-Hilfer sequential fractional differential equations. *Results Appl. Math.* **2021**, *10*, 100142. [CrossRef]
19. Wongcharoen, A.; Ntouyas, S.K.; Wongsantisuk, P.; Tariboon, J. Existence results for a nonlocal coupled system of sequential fractional differential equations involving $\hat{\psi}$-Hilfer fractional derivatives. *Adv. Math. Phys.* **2021**, *2021*, 5554619. [CrossRef]
20. Granas, A.; Dugundji, J. *Fixed Point Theory*; Springer: New York, NY, USA, 2003.
21. Krasnosel'skiĭ, M.A. Two remarks on the method of successive approximations. *Uspekhi Mat. Nauk.* **1955**, *10*, 123–127.

Disclaimer/Publisher's Note: The statements, opinions and data contained in all publications are solely those of the individual author(s) and contributor(s) and not of MDPI and/or the editor(s). MDPI and/or the editor(s) disclaim responsibility for any injury to people or property resulting from any ideas, methods, instructions or products referred to in the content.

Article

Controllability for Fractional Evolution Equations with Infinite Time-Delay and Non-Local Conditions in Compact and Noncompact Cases

Ahmed Salem [1,*] and Kholoud N. Alharbi [2]

[1] Department of Mathematics, Faculty of Science, King Abdulaziz University, P.O. Box 80203, Jeddah 21589, Saudi Arabia

[2] Department of Mathematics, College of Science and Arts in Uglat Asugour, Qassim University, Buraydah 51411, Saudi Arabia

* Correspondence: asaalshreef@kau.edu.sa

Abstract: The goal of this dissertation is to explore a system of fractional evolution equations with infinitesimal generator operators and an infinite time delay with non-local conditions. It turns out that there are two ways to regulate the solution. To demonstrate the presence of the controllability of mild solutions, it is usual practice to apply Krasnoselskii's theorem in the compactness case and the Sadvskii and Kuratowski measure of noncompactness. A fractional Caputo approach of order between 1 and 2 was used to construct our model. The families of linear operators cosine and sine, which are strongly continuous and uniformly bounded, are used to achieve the mild solution. To make our results seem to be applicable, a numerical example is provided.

Keywords: Caputo fractional derivative; evolution equation; infinite time-delay; mild solution; countability; Kuratowski measure of noncompactness

MSC: 34A08; 34A12; 34G99; 34K99; 34A60

Citation: Salem, A.; Alharbi, K.N. Controllability for Fractional Evolution Equations with Infinite Time-Delay and Non-Local Conditions in Compact and Noncompact Cases. *Axioms* **2023**, *12*, 264. https://doi.org/10.3390/axioms12030264

Academic Editors: Péter Kórus and Juan Eduardo Nápoles Valdes

Received: 20 January 2023
Revised: 28 February 2023
Accepted: 1 March 2023
Published: 3 March 2023

Copyright: © 2023 by the authors. Licensee MDPI, Basel, Switzerland. This article is an open access article distributed under the terms and conditions of the Creative Commons Attribution (CC BY) license (https://creativecommons.org/licenses/by/4.0/).

1. Introduction

Fractional calculus is a branch of mathematics that studies derivatives and integrals of arbitrary order, which are known as fractional derivatives and fractional integrals [1–3]. It is a generalization of classical calculus, which studies derivatives and integrals of integer order. Fractional calculus can be used to model various physical phenomena, such as diffusion and wave propagation, and can also be used to solve certain types of differential equations. It has applications in many fields, such as engineering, physics, chemistry, economics, and finance. Fractional studies based on the economic and financial systems have been investigated by [4,5].

Calculating the targets to which one can influence the state of a dynamical system using a control parameter that appears in the equation is the mathematical problem of controllability. It is the ability to control the evolution of a system by manipulating its parameters. This concept is used in many areas, such as control theory, dynamic systems, and engineering. Controllability is a key factor in the analysis and design of systems and can help to ensure that the system behaves as desired. Understanding the controllability of evolution equations can help us to better understand and control the behavior of complex systems [6,7]. Controllability results for impulsive neutral differential evolution inclusions with infinite delay have been discussed in [8].

Non-local conditions are also used to incorporate the effect of external influences, such as boundary conditions, on the system. By combining fractional derivatives and non-local conditions, we can gain a better understanding of the behavior of the system (see [9–13]).

Therefore, fractional evolution equations with infinite delay are a type of differential equation that can be used to model a variety of physical phenomena. These equations involve a fractional derivative of a certain order, which is a generalization of the standard derivative. The infinite delay term in the equation allows for the consideration of memory effects, which can be important in many real-world systems. Solving these equations can be challenging, but they can provide valuable insights into the behavior of complex systems [14–17]. In more detail, the existence and uniqueness of mild solutions for impulsive fractional equations with non-local conditions and infinite delay have been concerned in [14]. The existence of solutions for neutral fractional differential equations with indefinite delay is examined using the Banach fixed point theorem and the nonlinear alternative of the Leray-Schauder type [15]. In [16], Santra et al. have discovered a few necessary and sufficient criteria for the oscillation of the solutions to a second-order neutral differential equation. Local estimates, fixed point arguments, and a novel Halanay-type inequality are used to address the dissipativity, stability, and weak stability of solutions for non-local differential equations involving infinite delays [17].

In 2021, Bedi et al. [18] introduced a study about controllability and stability results for fractional evolution equations involving generalized Hilfer fractional derivatives such as

$$\begin{cases} \mathbb{D}_{0+}^{\mathfrak{r},\mathfrak{y};\mathfrak{x}} \mathscr{E}\mathfrak{U}(t) = \mathbb{A}\mathfrak{U}(t) + \mathscr{E}\mathfrak{H}(t,\mathfrak{U}(t)) + \mathscr{E}(\mathfrak{K}\mathfrak{V}(t)), & t \in \mathfrak{J} = [0,a], \\ \mathscr{E}I_{0+}^{(1-\mathfrak{r})(1-\mathfrak{y});\mathfrak{x}} \mathfrak{U}(0) = \mathscr{E}\mathfrak{U}_0, & \mathfrak{U}_0 \in D(\mathscr{E}). \end{cases} \quad (1)$$

Such that $\mathbb{D}_{0+}^{\mathfrak{r},\mathfrak{y};\mathfrak{x}}$ portray the Hilfer fractional derivative of order $0 < \mathfrak{r} < 1$ and type $0 \leq \mathfrak{y} \leq 1$. The control function $\mathfrak{V}(\cdot)$ is defined in the Banach space of admissible control functions $\mathbb{L}^\infty(\mathfrak{J},\mathbb{U})$ and the state $\mathfrak{U}(\cdot)$ takes value in Banach space Ω. Furthermore, $\mathfrak{K}\colon \mathbb{U} \to D(\mathscr{E})$ is bounded linear operator and $\mathfrak{H}\colon \mathfrak{J} \times \Omega \to D(\mathscr{E}) \subset \Omega$. Therefore, $(\mathbb{A},\mathscr{E})$ is closed linear operator generates an exponentially bounded propagation family $\{T(t), t \leq 0\}$ from $D(\mathscr{E})$ to Ω. $I_{0+}^{(1-\mathfrak{r})(1-\mathfrak{y});\mathfrak{x}}$ is the Riemann–Liouville fractional integral of order $(1-\mathfrak{r})(1-\mathfrak{y})$.

In [19], the researchers examined the existence of solutions and the approximate controllability of the Atangana–Baleanu fractional neutral stochastic inclusion with an infinite delay of the form

$$\begin{cases} {}^{ABC}D_{0+}^{\mathfrak{v}}[p(\xi) - N(\xi, p_t)] \in \mathfrak{A}[p(\xi) - N(\xi, p_t)] + Bu(\xi) \\ +\mathcal{F}(\xi, p_\xi) + G(\xi, p_\xi)\frac{dW(\xi)}{d\xi}, & \xi \in J = [0,c], \\ p(\xi) = \phi(\xi) \in \mathbb{L}^\infty(\Omega, \mathfrak{P}_j U), & \xi \in (-\infty, 0]. \end{cases}$$

As above, ${}^{ABC}D^{\mathfrak{v}}$ is the ABC fractional derivative of order $\mathfrak{v} \in (0,1)$, $\mathfrak{A}\colon D(\mathfrak{A}) \subset H \to H$ is infinitesimal generator of an q-resolvent operator $\{S_q(\xi)\}_{\xi \geq 0}$, $\{T_\rho(\xi)\}_{\xi \geq 0}$ is a solution on separable Hilbert space $(H, \|\cdot\|)$.

We are inspired by these masterpieces and hope to establish controllability of mild solution with infinite delay and non-local conditions of the evolution equation

$$\begin{cases} {}_c\mathfrak{D}_0^{\mathfrak{v}}\mathscr{U}(\xi) = \mathbb{A}\mathscr{U}(\xi) + \mathscr{F}(\xi, \mathscr{U}(\xi), \mathscr{U}_\xi) + \mathfrak{B}y(\xi), & \xi \in J = [0,a], \\ \mathscr{U}(\xi) = \phi(\xi), & \xi \in (-\infty, 0], \\ \mathscr{U}'(0) + \eta(\mathscr{U}) = \xi_0, & \xi \in \mathfrak{X} \end{cases} \quad (2)$$

where ${}_c\mathfrak{D}_0^{\mathfrak{v}}(\cdot)$ is the Caputo fractional derivative of order $1 < \mathfrak{v} \leq 2$, $\mathscr{F}\colon [0,a] \times \mathfrak{X} \times \mathcal{P}_\mathfrak{h} \to \mathfrak{X}$ is a continuous function, $\phi(\xi) \in \mathcal{P}_\mathscr{H}$ ($\mathcal{P}_\mathscr{H}$ later judgment will be made over the phase space that is acceptable), a is a finite positive number, the state $\mathscr{U}(\cdot)$ takes values in a Banach space $\mathfrak{X}$, the control function $y(\cdot)$ is given in a Banach space $\mathbb{L}^2(J, \mathbb{U})$ and $\eta(\cdot)$ is a continuous function on $\mathfrak{X}$. Furthermore, $\mathscr{U}_\xi$ represents the state function's history up to the present time ξ, i.e., $\mathscr{U}_\xi(\mathfrak{K}) = \mathscr{U}(\xi + \mathfrak{K})$ for all $\mathfrak{K} \in (-\infty, 0]$.

Let $\mathbb{A}$ be an infinitesimal generator of a strongly continuous cosine family $\{\mathscr{K}(\xi)\}_{\xi \geq 0}$ of uniformly bounded linear operators defined on a Banach space $\mathfrak{X}$. The Banach space of continuous and bounded functions from $(-\infty, a]$ into $\mathfrak{X}$ provided with the topology of uniform convergence is denoted by $\mathcal{C} = \mathcal{C}_a((-\infty, a], \mathfrak{X})$ with the norm

$$\|\mathscr{U}\|_{\mathcal{C}} = \sup_{\xi \in (-\infty, a]} |\mathscr{U}(\xi)|$$

and let $(\mathcal{B}(\mathfrak{X}), \|\cdot\|_{(\mathcal{B}(\mathfrak{X}))})$ be the Banach space of all linear and bounded operators from $\mathfrak{X}$ to $\mathfrak{X}$. As $\{\mathscr{K}(\xi)\}_{\xi \geq 0}$ is cosine family on $\mathfrak{X}$, then there exists $\mathfrak{M} \geq 1$ where

$$\|\mathscr{K}(\xi)\| \leq \mathfrak{M}. \tag{3}$$

The fractional derivatives have many different types of definitions, among them Riemann–Liouville, Caputo, Hadamard, Conformable, Katugampola, Hilfer, etc. Riemann–Liouville and Caputo fractional derivatives are the most important ones in the applications of fractional calculus. A close relationship exists between the Riemann–Liouville fractional derivative and the Caputo fractional derivative. The Riemann–Liouville fractional derivative can be converted to the Caputo fractional derivative under some regularity assumptions of the function. However, the Caputo derivative is the most appropriate fractional operator to be used in modeling real-world problems. The Caputo derivative is of use in modeling phenomena that take account of interactions within the past and also problems with non-local properties. Furthermore, the initial conditions take the same form as that for integer-order differential equations, namely, the initial values of integer-order derivatives of functions at starting point [20]. However, the Riemann–Liouville approach needs initial conditions containing the limit values of the Riemann–Liouville fractional derivative at the starting point, whose physical meanings are not very clear.

Partial differential equations with time t as one of the independent variables, or nonlinear evolution equations, can be found in many areas of mathematics as well as in other scientific disciplines including physics, mechanics, and material science. Nonlinear evolution equations include, among others, the Navier–Stokes and Euler equations from fluid mechanics, the nonlinear reaction-diffusion equations from heat transfers and biological sciences, the nonlinear Klein-Gordon equations and nonlinear Schrodinger equations from quantum mechanics, and the Cahn-Hilliard equations from material science (see [21–23] and references cited therein).

Functional evolution equations with infinite-time delay arise often in mathematical modeling of a wide range of real-world issues, and as a result, research into these equations has gotten a lot of interest in recent years (see [24–28]. The time delay in the robot teleoperation system occurs when the system operator and the remote robot are far apart [29]. Zhang et al. [30] used the principle of compressed mapping to discuss the existence and uniqueness of the fractional diffusion equation with time delay. Anilkumar and Jose [31] analyzed a discrete-time queueing inventory model with service time and back-order in inventory. Some results of the existence and uniqueness of fixed points for a C-class of mappings satisfying an inequality of rational type in b-metric spaces have been studied by Asadi and Afsha [32].

The remainder of the text is organized as follows. We introduce some basic ideas and lemmas in Section 2. In Section 3, we formulate the mild solution of (2) by assuming that $\mathbb{A}$ is an infinitesimal generator of a strongly continuous cosine family $\{\mathscr{K}(\xi)\}_{\xi \geq 0}$. In Section 4, we handle the infinite delay by phase space. Section 5 provides the results of our analysis using two cases first in a compact case and second by the measure of the non-compactness technique. Section 6 offers an example that can be used as an application.

2. Preliminaries

In this section, a few concepts and terms related to the components of the research report are offered.

Definition 1 ([33]). *The expression of the Caputo derivative of fractional order q for at least nth continuously differentiable function $g : [0, \infty) \to \mathbb{R}$ is*

$$_c\mathfrak{D}^{\mathfrak{q}} g(t) = \frac{1}{\Gamma(n-\mathfrak{q})} \int_0^t (t-s)^{n-\mathfrak{q}-1} g^{(n)}(s) ds, \ n-1 < \mathfrak{q} < n, n = [\mathfrak{q}] + 1,$$

where $[\mathfrak{q}]$ denote the integer part of the real number $\mathfrak{q}$.

Definition 2 ([33]). *Given below is the Laplace transform for the Caputo derivative of order $\mathfrak{q} \in (1, 2]$*

$$\mathcal{L}\{_c\mathfrak{D}_t^{\mathfrak{q}} g(t)\} = \lambda^{\mathfrak{q}} G(\lambda) - \lambda^{\mathfrak{q}-1} G(0) + \lambda^{\mathfrak{q}-2} G'(0),$$

where $G(\lambda) = \int_0^{\infty} e^{-\lambda t} g(t) dt$.

Definition 3 ([33]). *The left fractional integrals of the function f is*

$$\mathcal{I}_a^{\mathfrak{q}} f(t) = \frac{1}{\Gamma(\mathfrak{q})} \int_a^t (t^{\rho} - s^{\rho})^{\mathfrak{q}-1} f(s) ds, \ t > a, \ \mathfrak{q} > 0.$$

Lemma 1 ([34]). *Let $n \in \mathbb{N}$, $n-1 < \mathfrak{q} \le n$ and $x(t) \in C^n[0, 1]$. Then,*

$$I_c^{\mathfrak{q}} \mathfrak{D}^{\mathfrak{q}} x(t) = x(t) + a_0 + a_1 t + \cdots + a_{n-1} t^{n-1}.$$

Definition 4 ([35]). *The Kuratowski measure of noncompactness $\mu(\cdot)$ is defined on bounded set S of Banach space $\mathfrak{X}$ as*

$$\mu(S) := \inf \left\{ \delta > 0 : S \subset \bigcup_{i=1}^m S_i, S_i \subset \mathfrak{X}, diam(S_i) < \delta \ \text{for} \ i = 1, 2, \ldots, m; m \in \mathbb{N} \right\}$$

where

$$diam(S_i) = \sup\{\|x_1 - x_2\| : x_1, x_2 \in S_i\}.$$

The following properties of the Kuratowski measure of noncompactness are well-known.

Lemma 2 ([35]). *Let $\mathscr{T}, \mathscr{R}$ be bounded in Banach space $\mathfrak{X}$. The following properties are satisfied:*

(i) $\mu(\mathscr{T}) = 0$, if and only if $\overline{\mathscr{T}}$ is compact, where $\overline{\mathscr{T}}$ means the closure hull of $\mathscr{T}$;
(ii) $\mu(\mathscr{T}) = \mu(\overline{\mathscr{T}}) = \mu(conv\mathscr{T})$, where $conv\mathscr{T}$ means the convex hull of $\mathscr{T}$;
(iii) $\mu(k\mathscr{T}) = |k|\mu(\mathscr{T})$ for any $k \in \mathbb{R}$;
(iv) $\mathscr{T} \subset \mathscr{R}$ implies $\mu(\mathscr{T}) \le \mu(\mathscr{R})$;
(v) $\mu(\mathscr{T} + \mathscr{R}) \le \mu(\mathscr{T}) + \mu(\mathscr{R})$, where $\mathscr{T} + \mathscr{R} = \{x | x = y + z, y \in \mathscr{T}, z \in \mathscr{R}\}$;
(vi) $\mu(\mathscr{T} \cup \mathscr{R}) = \max\{\mu\mathscr{T}, \mu\mathscr{R}\}$;
(vii) *If the map $H : D(H) \subset \mathfrak{X} \to \mathfrak{Y}$ is Lipschitz continuous with constant c, then $\mu(H(U)) \le c\mu(U)$ for any bounded subset $U \in D(H)$, where $\mathfrak{Y}$ is another Banach space.*

Lemma 3 (Sadovskii fixed point theorem [35]). *Let Ψ be bounded closed and convex subset in Banach space $\mathfrak{X}$. If the operator $\mathscr{Q} : \Psi \to \Psi$ is continuous μ-condensing, which means that $\mu(\mathscr{Q}(\Psi)) < \mu(\Psi)$. Then, $\mathscr{Q}$ has at least one fixed point in Ψ.*

Definition 5 ([36]). *Claim that the family of bounded linear operators $\{\mathscr{K}(t)\}_{t \in \mathbb{R}_+}$, namely maps the Banach space $\mathfrak{X} \to \mathfrak{X}$, has just one parameter, is referred to as a strongly continuous cosine family if and only if*

(i) $\mathcal{K}(0) = I$;
(ii) $\mathcal{K}(s+t) + \mathcal{K}(s-t) = 2\mathcal{L}(s)\mathcal{K}(t)$ for all $s, t \in \mathbb{R}_+$;
(iii) $\mathcal{K}(t)x$ is a continuous on $\mathbb{R}_+$ for any $x \in \mathfrak{X}$.

The substantially continuous cosine family $\{\mathcal{K}(t)\}_{t \in \mathbb{R}_+}$, which is connected to the sine family $\{\mathcal{L}(t)\}_{t \in \mathbb{R}_+}$, is defined by

$$\mathcal{L}(t)x = \int_0^t \mathcal{K}(s)x\,ds, \quad x \in \mathfrak{X}, t \in \mathbb{R}_+.$$

Lemma 4 ([36]). *Unless $\mathbb{A}$ is an infinitesimal generator of a strongly continuous cosine family $\{\mathcal{K}(t)\}_{t \in \mathbb{R}_+}$ on a Banach space $\mathfrak{X}$, then $\|\mathcal{K}(t)\|_{\mathcal{B}(\mathfrak{X})} \leq Me^{\xi t}, t \in \mathbb{R}_+$ will be obtained. Then, given the value of $\lambda > \xi$ and $(\xi^2, \infty) \subset \varrho(\mathbb{A})$ (the resolvent set of the operator $\mathbb{A}$), we obtain*

$$\lambda R(\lambda^2; \mathbb{A})x = \int_0^\infty e^{-\lambda t} \mathcal{K}(t)x\,dt, \qquad R(\lambda^2; \mathbb{A})x = \int_0^\infty e^{-\lambda t} \mathcal{L}(t)x\,dt, \quad x \in \mathfrak{X}$$

where the operator $R(\lambda; \mathbb{A}) = (\lambda I - \mathbb{A})^{-1}$ is the resolvent of the operator $\mathbb{A}$ and $\lambda \in \varrho(\mathbb{A})$.

The operator $\mathbb{A}$ is characterized by

$$\mathbb{A}x = \frac{d^2}{dt^2}\mathcal{K}(0)x, \quad \forall\, x \in \mathcal{D}(\mathbb{A})$$

where $\mathcal{D}(\mathbb{A}) = \{x \in \mathfrak{X} : \mathcal{K}(t)x \in \mathcal{C}^2(\mathbb{R}, \mathfrak{X})\}$. Clearly, the infinitesimal generator $\mathbb{A}$ is a densely defined operator in $\mathfrak{X}$ and closed.

Definition 6. *The Mainardi–Wright-type function when $t > 0$ is*

$$M_\rho(t) = \sum_{n=0}^\infty \frac{(-t)^n}{n!\Gamma(1 - \rho(n+1))}, \quad \rho \in (0,1), \; t \in \mathbb{C}$$

and achieves

$$M_\rho(t) \geq 0, \qquad \int_0^\infty \theta^\xi M_\rho(\theta)\,d\theta = \frac{\Gamma(1+\xi)}{\Gamma(1+\rho\xi)}, \qquad \xi > -1.$$

3. Setting of Mild Solution

We first illustrate the following lemma before giving a formulation of the moderate solution of (2).

Lemma 5. *Allow (2) to hold. Then, there is*

$$\mathscr{U}(\xi) = \begin{cases} \mathcal{K}_q(\xi)\phi(0) + \int_0^\xi \mathcal{K}_q(t)(\xi_0 - \eta(\mathscr{U}))\,dt + \int_0^\xi (\xi-t)^{q-1}\mathcal{L}_q(\xi,t)\mathscr{F}(t)\,dt \\ \quad + \int_0^\xi (\xi-t)^{q-1}\mathcal{L}_q(\xi,t)\mathfrak{B}y(t)\,dt, & \xi \in [0,a], \\ \phi(\xi), & \xi \in (-\infty, 0], \end{cases}$$

where $1/2 < q = \frac{v}{2} < 1$,

$$\mathcal{K}_q(\xi) = \int_0^\infty M_q(\theta)\mathcal{K}(\xi^q \theta)\,d\theta,$$

$$\mathcal{L}_q(\xi, s) = q\int_0^\infty \theta M_q(\theta)\mathcal{L}((\xi-s)^q \theta)\,d\theta,$$

and M_q is a probability density function defined by Definition 6.

Proof. Presume that $\lambda > 0$

$$U(\lambda) = \int_0^\infty e^{-\lambda \xi} \mathscr{U}(\xi) d\xi, \qquad F(\lambda) + \mathfrak{B}Y(\lambda) = \int_0^\infty e^{-\lambda \xi}(\mathscr{F}(\xi) + \mathfrak{B}y(\xi)) d\xi.$$

Let $\lambda^\mathfrak{v} \in \varrho(\mathbb{A})$. Now, that (2) has been transformed using Laplace and Lemma 4, we attain

$$U(\lambda) = (\lambda^\mathfrak{v} - \mathbb{A})^{-1} \Big[F(\lambda) + \mathfrak{B}Y(\lambda) + \lambda^{-1} \phi(0) + \lambda^{-2} (\xi_0 - \eta(\mathscr{U})) \Big]$$
$$= \lambda^{q-1} \int_0^\infty e^{-\lambda^q s} \mathscr{K}(s) \phi(0) ds + \lambda^{q-2} \int_0^\infty e^{-\lambda^q s} \mathscr{K}(t)(\xi_0 - \eta(\mathscr{U})) ds$$
$$+ \int_0^\infty e^{-\lambda^q s} \mathscr{L}(s)[F(\lambda) + \mathfrak{B}Y(\lambda)] ds.$$

Let $\theta \in (0,\infty)$, $q \in (\frac{1}{2}, 1)$ and $\Psi_q(\theta) = \frac{q}{\theta^{q+1}} M_q(\theta^{-q})$. Then,

$$\int_0^\infty e^{-\lambda \theta} \Psi_q(\theta) d\theta = e^{-\lambda^q}, \text{ for } q \in (\frac{1}{2}, 1).$$

If we take $\rho \to 0$, we will still have the same answer for the first term in Lemma 5 in [37]. Afterward, we can write:

$$\lambda^{q-1} \int_0^\infty e^{-\lambda^q s} \mathscr{K}(s) \phi(0) ds = \int_0^\infty e^{-\lambda \xi} \mathscr{K}_q(\xi) \phi(0) d\xi.$$

In addition, since $\mathcal{L}[1](\lambda) = \lambda^{-1}$, we obtain

$$\lambda^{-1} \lambda^{q-1} \int_0^\infty e^{-\lambda^q s} \mathscr{K}(s)(\xi_0 - \eta(\mathscr{U})) ds = \int_0^\infty e^{-\lambda \xi} \left\{ \int_0^\xi \mathscr{K}_q(t)(\xi_0 - \eta(\mathscr{U})) dt \right\} d\xi.$$

The last term, $\int_0^\infty e^{-\lambda^q s} \mathscr{L}(s)[F(\lambda) + \mathfrak{B}Y(\lambda)] ds$, is identical to the final term in [37] if we set $\rho \to 0$ and set $f(p) = F(\lambda) + \mathfrak{B}Y(\lambda)$, we get

$$\int_0^\infty e^{-\lambda^q s} \mathscr{L}(s)[F(\lambda) + \mathfrak{B}Y(\lambda)] ds = \int_0^\infty e^{-\lambda \xi} \left\{ \int_0^\xi (\xi - t)^{q-1} \mathscr{L}_q(\xi, t)[\mathscr{F}(t) + \mathfrak{B}y(t)] dt \right\} d\xi.$$

To sum up, we can obtain

$$\int_0^\infty e^{-\lambda \xi} \mathscr{U}(\xi) d\xi = \int_0^\infty e^{-\lambda \xi} \bigg\{ \mathscr{K}_q(\xi) \phi(0) + \int_0^\xi \mathscr{K}_q(t)(\xi_0 - \eta(\mathscr{U})) dt$$
$$+ \int_0^\xi (\xi - t)^{q-1} \mathscr{L}_q(\xi, t)[\mathscr{F}(t) + \mathfrak{B}y(t)] dt \bigg\} d\xi.$$

The intended outcome is attained by using the inverse Laplace transform. □

Definition 7. *A function $\mathscr{U}(\xi) \in (\mathcal{C}(-\infty, a]; \mathfrak{X})$ is considered to be the mild solution of (2) if it fulfills*

$$\mathscr{U}(\xi) = \begin{cases} \mathscr{K}_q(\xi) \phi(0) + \int_0^\xi \mathscr{K}_q(t)(\xi_0 - \eta(\mathscr{U})) dt \\ + \int_0^\xi (\xi - t)^{q-1} \mathscr{L}_q(\xi, t)[\mathscr{F}(t, \mathscr{U}, \mathscr{U}_t) + \mathfrak{B}y(t)] dt, & \xi \in [0, a], \\ \phi(\xi), & \xi \in (-\infty, 0]. \end{cases}$$

Remark 1 ([37]). *It is obvious to infer from the linearity of $\mathscr{K}(\xi)$ and $\mathscr{L}(\xi)$ for any $\xi \geq 0$ that $\mathscr{K}_q(\xi)$ and $\mathscr{L}_q(\xi, s)$ are also linear operators where $0 < s < \xi$.*

As a corollary, when ρ approaches 1, the proofs of all subsequent Lemmas are identical.

Lemma 6 ([37]). *The following estimates for $\mathscr{K}_q(\xi)$ and $\mathscr{L}_q(\xi,s)$ are verified for any fixed $\xi \geq 0$ and $0 < s < \xi$*

$$|\mathscr{K}_q(\xi)x| \leq \mathfrak{M}|x| \quad \text{and} \quad |\mathscr{L}_q(\xi,s)x| \leq \frac{\mathfrak{M}a^q}{\Gamma(2q)}|x|.$$

Lemma 7 ([37]). *For any $0 < s < \xi$ and $\xi > 0$, the operators $\mathscr{K}_q(\xi)$ and $\mathscr{L}_q(s,\xi)$ are strongly continuous.*

Lemma 8 ([37]). *Pretend that $\mathscr{K}(\xi)$ and $\mathscr{L}(\xi,s)$ are compact for every $0 < s < t$. In that case, for any $0 < s < \xi$, the operators $\mathscr{K}_q(\xi)$ and $\mathscr{L}_q(s,\xi)$ are compact.*

4. Abstract Phases Space $\mathscr{P}_\mathscr{H}$ and Infinite Delay

By using the handy method of [14,15], we demonstrate the abstract phase $\mathscr{P}_\mathscr{H}$. Let us say that $\mathscr{H} = \mathcal{C}((-\infty,0],[0,\infty))$ with $\int_{-\infty}^{0} \mathscr{H}(t)dt < \infty$ are used. Finally, we have stated that for every $c > 0$

$$\mathscr{P} = \{\mathfrak{A} : [-c,0] \to \mathfrak{X}, \quad \mathfrak{A} \text{ is bounded and measurable}\}$$

identically, create the space $\mathscr{P}$ with

$$\|\mathfrak{A}\|_\mathscr{P} = \sup_{s \in [-c,0]} |\mathfrak{A}(s)|, \quad \text{for all} \quad \mathfrak{A} \in \mathscr{P}.$$

Let us specify the space

$$\mathscr{P}_\mathscr{H} = \left\{\mathfrak{A} : (-\infty,0] \to \mathfrak{X} \text{ such that for any } c > 0, \mathfrak{A}|_{[-c,0]} \in \mathscr{P} \text{ and } \int_{-\infty}^{0} \mathscr{H}(t)\sup_{t \leq s \leq 0}\mathfrak{A}(s)dt < \infty\right\}.$$

If $\mathscr{P}_\mathscr{H}$ are configured as

$$\|\mathfrak{A}\|_{\mathscr{P}_\mathscr{H}} = \int_{-\infty}^{0} \mathscr{H}(t)\sup_{t \leq s \leq 0}\|\mathfrak{A}(s)\|dt, \quad \forall \mathfrak{A} \in \mathscr{P}_\mathscr{H},$$

then $(\mathscr{P}_\mathscr{H}, \|\cdot\|_{\mathscr{P}_\mathscr{H}})$ is a Banach space.

The space is the first thing we consider

$$\overline{\mathscr{P}}_\mathscr{H} = \left\{v : (-\infty,a] \to \mathfrak{X} \text{ such that } v|_{[0,a]} \text{ is continuous}, v|_{(-\infty,0]} = \phi \in \mathscr{P}_\mathscr{H}\right\}$$

which has the norm

$$\|x\|_{\overline{\mathscr{P}}_\mathscr{H}} = \sup_{s \in [0,a]} \|v(s)\| + \|\phi\|_{\mathscr{P}_\mathscr{H}}.$$

Definition 8 ([38]). *The prerequisites are true $\forall t \in [0,a]$. If $v : (-\infty,a] \to \mathfrak{X}$, $a > 0$, such that $\phi \in \mathscr{P}_\mathscr{H}$:*

1. $v_\tau \in \mathscr{P}_\mathscr{H}$;
2. *There are two function $\beta_1(t), \beta_2(t)$ such that $\beta_1(t): [0,\infty) \to [0,\infty)$ is a continuous function and $\beta_2(t): [0,\infty) \to [0,\infty)$ is a locally bounded function which are independent to $v(\cdot)$ whereas*

$$\|v_t\|_{\mathscr{P}_\mathscr{H}} \leq \beta_1(t)\sup_{0 < s < t}\|v(s)\| + \beta_2(t)\|\phi\|_{\mathscr{P}_\mathscr{H}};$$

3. $\|v(t)\| \leq H\|v_t\|_{\mathscr{P}_\mathscr{H}}$, *where $H > 0$ is constant.*

Currently, the operator is defined $\mathscr{H}: \overline{\mathscr{P}}_{\mathscr{H}} \to \overline{\mathscr{P}}_{\mathscr{H}}$ as follows

$$\mathscr{H}(\mathscr{U})(\xi) = \begin{cases} \mathscr{K}_q(\xi)\phi(0) + \int_0^\xi \mathscr{K}_q(t)(\xi_0 - \eta(\mathscr{U}))dt \\ \quad + \int_0^\xi (\xi-t)^{q-1}\mathscr{L}_q(\xi,t)[\mathscr{F}(t) + \mathfrak{B}y(t)]dt, & \xi \in [0,a], \\ \phi(\xi), & \xi \in (-\infty, 0]. \end{cases}$$

The function represented by $\varkappa(\cdot) : (-\infty, a] \to \mathfrak{X}$ should be considered as

$$\varkappa(\xi) = \begin{cases} 0, & \xi \in (0,a], \\ \phi(\xi), & \xi \in (-\infty, 0]. \end{cases}$$

After that, $\varkappa(0) = \phi(0)$. We indicate the function defined by κ for each $\mathscr{Z} \in \mathcal{C}([0,a], \mathfrak{X})$ with $\mathscr{Z}(0) = 0$ and

$$\kappa(\xi) = \begin{cases} \mathscr{Z}(\xi), & \xi \in [0,a], \\ 0, & \xi \in (-\infty, 0]. \end{cases}$$

If $\mathscr{U}(\cdot)$ satisfies that $\mathscr{U}(\xi) = \mathscr{H}(\mathscr{U})(\xi)$ for all $\xi \in (-\infty, a]$, we can decompose that $\mathscr{U}(\xi) = \kappa(\xi) + \varkappa(\xi)$, $\xi \in (-\infty, a]$, it denotes $\mathscr{U}_\xi = \kappa_\xi + \varkappa_\xi$ for every $\xi \in (-\infty, a]$ and the function $\mathscr{Z}(\cdot)$ satisfies

$$\mathscr{Z}(\xi) = \mathscr{K}_q(\xi)\phi(0) + \int_0^\xi \mathscr{K}_q(t)(\xi_0 - \eta(\kappa + \varkappa))dt$$
$$+ \int_0^\xi (\xi-t)^{q-1}\mathscr{L}_q(\xi,t)[\mathscr{F}(t, \kappa + \varkappa, \kappa_t + \varkappa_t) + \mathfrak{B}y(t)]dt.$$

Set the space $\Theta = \{\mathscr{Z} \in \mathcal{C}([0,a], \mathfrak{X}), \mathscr{Z}(0) = 0\}$ equipped the norm

$$\|\mathscr{Z}\|_\Theta = \sup_{\xi \in [0,a]} \|\mathscr{Z}(\xi)\|.$$

Therefore, $(\Theta, \|\cdot\|_\Theta)$ is a Banach space. Assume that the operator $\mathfrak{G}$ is defined as follows: Let the operator $\mathfrak{G} : \Theta \to \Theta$ be formulated as follows:

$$\mathfrak{G}(\mathscr{Z})(\xi) = \mathscr{K}_q(\xi)\phi(0) + \int_0^\xi \mathscr{K}_q(t)(\xi_0 - \eta(\kappa + \varkappa))dt$$
$$+ \int_0^\xi (\xi-t)^{q-1}\mathscr{L}_q(\xi,t)[\mathscr{F}(t, \kappa + \varkappa, \kappa_t + \varkappa_t) + \mathfrak{B}y(t)]dt.$$

The argument that the operator $\mathscr{H}$ appears to have a fixed point is similar to the claim that $\mathfrak{G}$ has a fixed point. Therefore, we continue to demonstrate this.

The subsequent assumptions, we make:

$(\mathcal{I}_1)$ The function $\mathscr{F} : J \times \mathfrak{X} \times \mathscr{P}_{\mathscr{H}} \to \mathfrak{X}$ is a continuous and there exist $d_{1f}, d_{2f} \geq 0$ such that for all $(\xi, \mathscr{U}, \mathscr{U}_\xi), (\xi, \mathscr{V}, \mathscr{V}_\xi) \in J \times \mathfrak{X} \times \mathscr{P}_{\mathscr{H}}$,

$$\|\mathscr{F}(\xi, \mathscr{U}, \mathscr{U}_\xi) - \mathscr{F}(\xi, \mathscr{V}, \mathscr{V}_\xi)\| \leq d_{1f}\|\mathscr{U} - \mathscr{V}\|_{\mathfrak{X}} + d_{2f}\|\mathscr{U}_\xi - \mathscr{V}_\xi\|_{\mathscr{P}_{\mathscr{H}}}.$$

$(\mathcal{I}_2)$ The linear operator $\mathscr{B} : \mathbb{U} \to \mathfrak{X}$ is bounded, and let $\mathbb{W} : \mathbb{L}^2(J, \mathbb{U}) \to \mathfrak{X}$ be the linear operator defined by

$$\mathbb{W}y = \int_0^a (a-t)^{q-1}\mathscr{L}_q(a,t)\mathfrak{B}y(t)dt,$$

has an invertible operator $\mathbb{W}^{-1}$ which takes value in $\mathbb{L}^2(J, \mathbb{U})/ker\mathbb{W}$, and there exist two positive constant $\mathfrak{D}_1$ and $\mathfrak{D}_1$ such that

$$\|\mathfrak{B}\| \leq \mathfrak{D}_1, \qquad \|\mathbb{W}^{-1}\| \leq \mathfrak{D}_2.$$

($\mathcal{I}_3$) The function $\eta\colon \mathfrak{X} \to \mathfrak{X}$ is continuous and there exist there exist a positive constant L_η such that
$$\|\eta(\mathscr{U}) - \eta(\mathscr{V})\| \leq L_\eta \|\mathscr{U} - \mathscr{V}\|.$$

Lemma 9. Let $\beta_1^* = \sup_{\xi \in [0,a]} \beta_1(\xi)$ and $\beta_2^* = \sup_{\xi \in [0,a]} \beta_2(\xi)$ where $\beta_1(\cdot)$ and $\beta_2(\cdot)$ be defined in Definition (8). Assume that the assumptions ($\mathcal{I}_1$) and ($\mathcal{I}_3$) are satisfied with $\mathfrak{c} = \max_{\xi \in [0,a]} |\mathscr{F}(\xi, 0, 0)|$ and $\gamma_\eta = |\eta(0)|$. Then,

$$\|\mathscr{F}(\xi, \kappa + \varkappa, \kappa_\xi + \varkappa_\xi)\| \leq \left(d_{1f} H + d_{2f}\right)\left(\beta_1(\xi)\|\mathscr{Z}\|_\Theta + \beta_2(\xi)\|\phi\|_{\mathscr{P}_{\mathscr{H}}}\right) + \mathfrak{c}$$
$$\leq \left(d_{1f} H + d_{2f}\right)\left(\beta_1^* \|\mathscr{Z}\|_\Theta + \beta_2^* \|\phi\|_{\mathscr{P}_{\mathscr{H}}}\right) + \mathfrak{c} \triangleq \ell$$

and

$$\eta(\mathscr{U})\| \leq L_\eta \|\mathscr{U}\| + \gamma_\eta.$$

Proof. By the same way in Lemma 9 in [37], we can easily reach the desired result. □

5. Controllability Results

Definition 9 ([39]). *The system (2) is said to be controllable on the interval J if for any $\phi(0) \in \mathscr{P}_{\mathscr{H}}$ and $\xi_0, y_a \in \mathfrak{X}$, there exists a control $y \in \mathbb{L}^2(J, \mathbb{U})$ such that a mild solution $\mathscr{Z}(\cdot)$ of system (2) satisfies $\mathscr{Z}(a) = y_a$.*

Lemma 10. *If the assumptions ($\mathcal{I}_1$) and ($\mathcal{I}_3$) hold, and $y_a \in \mathfrak{X}$ is target point. Then the control function*

$$y(\xi) = \mathbb{W}^{-1}\left[y_a - \mathscr{K}_q(a)\phi(0) + \int_0^a \mathscr{K}_q(t)(\xi_0 - \eta(\kappa + \varkappa))dt \right.$$
$$\left. + \int_0^a (a-t)^{q-1} \mathscr{L}_q(a,t) \mathscr{F}(t, \kappa + \varkappa, \kappa_t + \varkappa_t)dt\right].$$

steers the state $\mathscr{Z}(\xi)$ of the system (2) from initial points $\phi(0)$ and ξ_0 to target point y_a at time a. Furthermore, the control function $y(\xi)$ has an estimate $\|y(\xi)\| \leq \Pi$ where

$$\Pi = \mathfrak{D}_2[\|y_a\| + \mathscr{T}_0 + \mathscr{M}_0 \ell], \quad \mathscr{T}_0 = \mathfrak{M}(\|\phi(0)\| + a(\|\xi_0\| + \gamma_\eta)), \quad \text{and} \quad \mathscr{M}_0 = \frac{a^{2q}\mathfrak{M}}{q\Gamma(2q)}.$$

Proof. Consider the solution $\mathscr{Z}(\xi)$ of (2) defined by (7). For $\xi = a$, we get

$$\mathscr{Z}(a) = \mathscr{K}_q(a)\phi(0) + \int_0^a \mathscr{K}_q(t)(\xi_0 - \eta(\kappa + \varkappa))dt + \int_0^a (a-t)^{q-1} \mathscr{L}_q(a,t) \mathscr{F}(\tau, \kappa + \varkappa, \kappa_\tau + \varkappa_\tau)d\tau dt$$
$$+ \int_0^a (a-t)^{q-1} \mathscr{L}_q(a,t) \mathfrak{B} \mathbb{W}^{-1}\left[y_a - \mathscr{K}_q(a)\phi(0) + \int_0^a \mathscr{K}_q(\tau)(\xi_0 - \eta(\kappa + \varkappa))d\tau\right.$$
$$\left. + \int_0^a (a-\tau)^{q-1} \mathscr{L}_q(a,t) \mathscr{F}(\tau, \kappa + \varkappa, \kappa_\tau + \varkappa_\tau)d\tau\right]dt$$
$$= \mathscr{K}_q(a)\phi(0) + \int_0^a \mathscr{K}_q(t)(\xi_0 - \eta(\kappa + \varkappa))dt + \int_0^a (a-t)^{q-1} \mathscr{L}_q(a,t) \mathscr{F}(\tau, \kappa + \varkappa, \kappa_\tau + \varkappa_\tau)d\tau dt$$
$$+ \mathbb{W}\mathbb{W}^{-1}\left[y_a - \mathscr{K}_q(a)\phi(0) + \int_0^a \mathscr{K}_q(\tau)(\xi_0 - \eta(\kappa + \varkappa))d\tau\right.$$
$$\left. + \int_0^a (a-\tau)^{q-1} \mathscr{L}_q(a,\tau) \mathscr{F}(\tau, \kappa + \varkappa, \kappa_\tau + \varkappa_\tau)d\tau\right] = y_a.$$

Furthermore, by using Lemma 9 the control function estimate

$$\|y(\xi)\| \leq \|\mathbb{W}^{-1}\|\bigg[\|y_a\| + \|\mathcal{K}_q(a)\phi(0)\| + \int_0^a \|\mathcal{K}_q(t)\|(\|\xi_0\| + \|\eta(\kappa+\varkappa)\|)dt$$
$$+ \int_0^a (a-t)^{q-1}\|\mathcal{L}_q(a,t)\|\|\mathcal{F}(t,\kappa+\varkappa,\kappa_t+\varkappa_t)\|dt\bigg]$$
$$\leq \mathfrak{D}_2\bigg[\|y_a\| + \mathfrak{M}(\|\phi(0)\| + a(\|\xi_0\| + \gamma_\eta)) + \frac{a^{2q}\mathfrak{M}\ell}{q\Gamma(2q)}\bigg] = \Pi$$

which ends the proof. □

5.1. Compactness Case

In this subsection, we assume the compactness of controllability of mild solution and investigate its existence of it by employing Krasnoselskii's fixed point theorem to deduce the first result about the existence of the solution of the problem (2).

Theorem 1. *Assume that* $(\mathcal{I}_1)$, $(\mathcal{I}_2)$ *and* $(\mathcal{I}_3)$ *are satisfied. Then the problem (2) is controllable on J if*

$$\mathcal{L}_\mathfrak{v} = \mathcal{M}_1\Big[a\mathfrak{M}L_\eta + \mathcal{M}_0\beta_1^*(d_{1f}H + d_{2f})\Big] < 1$$

where $\mathcal{M}_1 = \mathfrak{D}_1\mathfrak{D}_2\mathcal{M}_0$.

Proof. Designate

$$Y_\rho = \{\mathscr{X} \in \theta : \|\mathscr{X}\|_\theta \leq \rho\}$$

where

$$\rho \geq \frac{(1+\mathcal{M}_1)\Big\{\mathscr{T}_0 + \mathcal{M}_0[(d_{1f}H + d_{2f})\beta_2^*\|\phi\|_{\mathscr{P}_{\mathscr{H}}} + \mathfrak{c}]\Big\} + \mathcal{M}_1\|y_a\|}{1 - \mathcal{L}_\mathfrak{v}}.$$

The operator $\mathfrak{G}$ can be divided as a sum of two operators $\mathfrak{G}_1$ and $\mathfrak{G}_2$ which can be defined as

$$(\mathfrak{G}_1\mathscr{X})(\xi) = \mathcal{K}_q(\xi)\phi(0) + \int_0^\xi \mathcal{K}_q(t)(\xi_0 - \eta(\kappa+\varkappa))dt$$
$$+ \int_0^\xi (\xi-t)^{q-1}\mathcal{L}_q(\xi,t)\Big[\mathcal{F}(t,\kappa+\varkappa,\kappa_t+\varkappa_t) + \mathfrak{B}\mathbb{W}^{-1}(y_a - \mathcal{K}_q(a)\phi(0))\Big]dt,$$
$$(\mathfrak{G}_2\mathscr{X})(\xi) = \mathfrak{B}\mathbb{W}^{-1}\int_0^\xi (\xi-t)^{q-1}\mathcal{L}_q(\xi,t)\bigg[\int_0^a \mathcal{K}_q(\tau)(\xi_0 - \eta(\kappa+\varkappa))d\tau$$
$$+ \int_0^a (a-\tau)^{q-1}\mathcal{L}_q(a,\tau)\mathcal{F}(\tau,\kappa+\varkappa,\kappa_\tau+\varkappa_\tau)d\tau\bigg]dt.$$

Then, for $u, v \in Y_\rho$, it follows that $\|\mathfrak{G}_1(\mathscr{X})u + \mathfrak{G}_2(\mathscr{X})v\| \leq \rho$, which concludes that $\mathfrak{G}_1(u) + \mathfrak{G}_2(v) \in Y_\rho$. Now, we want to show that $\mathfrak{G}$ maps bounded sets into the bounded set. For any $\rho \geq 0$ and for any $\mathscr{X} \in Y_\rho$ and in light of Lemma 9, we have

$$\|(\mathfrak{G}\mathscr{Z})(\xi)\| \leq \mathfrak{M}(\|\phi(0)\| + a(\|\xi_0\| + \gamma_\eta)))$$
$$+ \mathscr{M}_0\left[\left(d_{1f}H + d_{2f}\right)\left(\beta_1^*\|\mathscr{Z}\|_\Theta + \beta_2^*\|\phi\|_{\mathscr{P}_\mathscr{H}}\right) + \mathfrak{c}\right]$$
$$+ \mathscr{M}_1\left[\|y_a\| + \mathfrak{M}(\|\phi(0)\| + a(\|\xi_0\| + \gamma_\eta))\right.$$
$$+ \mathscr{M}_0\left[\left(d_{1f}H + d_{2f}\right)\left(\beta_1^*\|\mathscr{Z}\|_\Theta + \beta_2^*\|\phi\|_{\mathscr{P}_\mathscr{H}}\right) + \mathfrak{c}\right]\bigg]$$
$$= (1 + \mathscr{M}_1)\left\{\mathscr{T}_0 + \mathscr{M}_0[\left(d_{1f}H + d_{2f}\right)\beta_2^*\|\phi\|_{\mathscr{P}_\mathscr{H}} + \mathfrak{c}]\right\} + \mathscr{M}_1\|y_a\|$$
$$+ \rho\mathscr{M}_0\beta_1^*(1 + \mathscr{M}_1)(d_{1f}H + d_{2f})\rho \leq \rho.$$

The following step is to confirm that the operator $\mathfrak{G}_1$ is equicontinuous. In the light of the situations $(\mathcal{I}_1)$ and $(\mathcal{I}_3)$, $\mathfrak{G}_1$ is continuous. Let $v_1, v_2 \in J$ such that $0 \leq v_1 < v_2 \leq a$, then the following scenarios are therefore possible.

$$\|(\mathfrak{G}_1\mathscr{Z})(v_2) - (\mathfrak{G}_1\mathscr{Z})(v_1)\| \leq \|\mathscr{K}_q(v_2) - \mathscr{K}_q(v_1)\|\|\phi(0)\| + \mathfrak{M}(\|\xi_0\| + \gamma_\eta)(v_2 - v_1)$$
$$\left[\frac{\mathfrak{M}\ell}{q\Gamma(2q)} + \frac{\mathfrak{M}\mathfrak{D}_1\mathfrak{D}_2}{q\Gamma(2q)}(\|y_a\| + \mathfrak{M}\|\phi(0)\|)\right](v_2 - v_1)^q$$
$$+ (\ell + \mathfrak{D}_1\mathfrak{D}_2(\|y_a\| + \mathfrak{M}\|\phi(0)\|))\int_0^{v_1}\left\|(v_2 - t)^{q-1}\mathscr{L}_q(v_2,t) - (v_1 - t)^{q-1}\mathscr{L}_q(v_1,t)\right\|dt.$$

To evaluate the last term, we can follow the steps

$$I = \int_0^{v_1}\left\|(v_2 - t)^{q-1}\mathscr{L}_q(v_2,t) - (v_1 - t)^{q-1}\mathscr{L}_q(v_2,t) + (v_1 - t)^{q-1}\mathscr{L}_q(v_2,t) - (v_1 - t)^{q-1}\mathscr{L}_q(v_1,t)\right\|dt$$
$$\leq \int_0^{v_1}[(v_1 - t)^{q-1} - (v_2 - t)^{q-1}]\|\mathscr{L}_q(v_2,t)\|dt + \int_0^{v_1}(v_1 - t)^{q-1}\|\mathscr{L}_q(v_2,t) - \mathscr{L}_q(v_1,t)\|dt$$
$$= \frac{\mathfrak{M}}{q\Gamma(2q)}\left[(v_2 - v_1)^q + (v_1^q - v_2^q)\right] + \int_0^{v_1}(v_1 - t)^{q-1}\|\mathscr{L}_q(v_2,t) - \mathscr{L}_q(v_1,t)\|dt$$

which implies that

$$\|(\mathfrak{G}_1\mathscr{Z})(v_2) - (\mathfrak{G}_1\mathscr{Z})(v_1)\| \leq \|\mathscr{K}_q(v_2) - \mathscr{K}_q(v_1)\|\|\phi(0)\| + \mathfrak{M}(\|\xi_0\| + \gamma_\eta)(v_2 - v_1)$$
$$+ \left[\frac{\mathfrak{M}\ell}{q\Gamma(2q)} + \frac{\mathfrak{M}\mathfrak{D}_1\mathfrak{D}_2}{q\Gamma(2q)}(\|y_a\| + \mathfrak{M}\|\phi(0)\|)\right](v_2 - v_1)^q$$
$$+ (\ell + \mathfrak{D}_1\mathfrak{D}_2(\|y_a\| + \mathfrak{M}\|\phi(0)\|))\frac{\mathfrak{M}}{q\Gamma(2q)}\left[(v_2 - v_1)^q + (v_1^q - v_2^q)\right]$$
$$+ (\ell + \mathfrak{D}_1\mathfrak{D}_2(\|y_a\| + \mathfrak{M}\|\phi(0)\|))\int_0^{v_1}\left\|(v_2 - t)^{q-1}\mathscr{L}_q(v_2,t) - (v_1 - t)^{q-1}\mathscr{L}_q(v_1,t)\right\|dt.$$

Due to compactness of operator $\mathscr{K}_q(y)$ and $\mathscr{L}_q(t,y)$ (see Lemma 8), we infer that $\|\mathfrak{G}_1(z)(v_1) - \mathfrak{G}_1(z)(v_2)\| \to 0$ as $v_2 \to v_1$. Thus, $\mathfrak{G}_1$ is a relatively compact on Y_ρ. By Arezela Ascoli Theorem the operator $\mathfrak{G}_1$ is completely continuous on Y_ρ. The only thing left to do is provide evidence that $\mathfrak{G}_2$ is a contraction mapping. Consider $\mathscr{Z}, \mathscr{Z}^* \in Y$. Then, for any $\xi \in [0,a]$,

$$\|(\mathfrak{G}_2\mathscr{Z})(\xi) - (\mathfrak{G}_2\mathscr{Z}^*)(\xi)\|_Y$$
$$\leq \frac{\mathfrak{D}_1\mathfrak{D}_2\mathfrak{M}}{\Gamma(2q)} \int_0^\xi (\xi-t)^{q-1}\left[\mathfrak{M}\int_0^a \|\eta(\kappa+\varkappa) - \eta(\kappa^*+\varkappa)\|d\tau\right.$$
$$+ \frac{\mathfrak{M}}{\Gamma(2q)} \int_0^a (a-\tau)^{q-1} \|\mathscr{F}(\tau,\kappa+\varkappa,\kappa_\tau+\varkappa_\tau) - \mathscr{F}(\tau,\kappa^*+\varkappa,\kappa_\tau^*+\varkappa_\tau)\|d\tau\right]$$
$$\leq \mathscr{M}_1\left[a\mathfrak{M}L_\eta\|\kappa-\kappa^*\|_Y + \frac{\mathfrak{M}}{\Gamma(2q)}\int_0^a(a-\tau)^{q-1}(d_{1f}\|\kappa-\kappa^*\|_Y + d_{2f}\|\kappa_\tau-\kappa_\tau^*\|_{\mathscr{P}_{\mathscr{H}}})d\tau\right]$$
$$\leq \mathscr{M}_1\left[a\mathfrak{M}L_\eta\|\kappa-\kappa^*\|_Y + \frac{\mathfrak{M}}{\Gamma(2q)}\int_0^a(a-\tau)^{q-1}(d_{1f}H+d_{2f})\|\kappa_\tau-\kappa_\tau^*\|_{\mathscr{P}_{\mathscr{H}}}d\tau\right]$$
$$\leq \mathscr{M}_1\left[a\mathfrak{M}L_\eta + \mathscr{M}_0\beta_1^*(d_{1f}H+d_{2f})\right]\|\kappa-\kappa^*\|_Y$$
$$= \mathcal{L}_\mathfrak{v}\|\kappa-\kappa^*\|_Y.$$

In a sense, the fractional evolution equation with non-instantaneous impulsive (2) has at least one mild solution on Y, according to the Krasnoselskii Theorem. In view of the results in Lemma 10 and our results here, the evolution system (2) is controllable on J. The evidence is now complete. □

5.2. Noncompactness Case

The existence of a solution in the case of noncompactness of controllability of mild solution can be further explored by utilizing Kuratowski's measure of noncompactness through applying Sadovskii's fixed point Theorem 3. This matter can be addressed by considering the next existence result.

Theorem 2. *Assume that* $(\mathcal{I}_1)$, $(\mathcal{I}_2)$ *and* $(\mathcal{I}_3)$ *are satisfied. Furthermore, suppose that the following inequality holds*

$$\mathfrak{P}_\mathfrak{v} = (1+\mathscr{M}_1)\left[a\mathfrak{M}L_\eta + \mathscr{M}_0\beta_1^*(d_{1f}H+d_{2f})\right] < 1.$$

Then, the evolution system (2) is controllable on J.

Proof. Firstly, we show that $\mathfrak{G}: Y_\rho \to Y_\rho$ is continuous where $Y_\rho \subset \theta$ is defined in the proof of Theorem 1. Plainly, the subset Y_ρ is a closed, bounded, and convex nonempty subset of the Banach space θ. Let the sequence $\{\mathscr{Z}^n\}_{n\in\mathbb{N}}$ of a Banach space θ such that $\mathscr{Z}^n \to \mathscr{Z}$ as $n \to \infty$. For $0 \leq \xi \leq a$, by the strongly continuity of $\mathscr{K}_q(\xi)$ and $\mathscr{L}_q(\xi,t)$ and Lemma 9, we get

$$\|(\mathfrak{G}\mathscr{Z}^n)(\xi) - (\mathfrak{G}\mathscr{Z})(\xi)\| \leq \mathfrak{M}\int_0^\xi \|\eta(\kappa^n+\varkappa) - \eta(\kappa+\varkappa)\|dt$$
$$+ \frac{\mathfrak{M}}{\Gamma(2q)}\int_0^\xi (\xi-t)^{q-1}\|\mathscr{F}(t,\kappa^n+\varkappa,\kappa_t^n+\varkappa_t) - \mathscr{F}(t,\kappa+\varkappa,\kappa_t+\varkappa_t)\|dt$$
$$\leq \mathfrak{M}L_\eta\int_0^\xi \|\kappa^n-\kappa\|_Y dt + \frac{\mathfrak{M}}{\Gamma(2q)}\int_0^\xi (\xi-t)^{q-1}\left(d_{1f}\|\kappa^n-\kappa\|_Y + d_{2f}\|\kappa_t^n-\kappa_t\|_{\mathscr{P}_{\mathscr{H}}}\right)dt$$
$$\leq \mathfrak{M}L_\eta\int_0^\xi \|\kappa^n-\kappa\|_Y dt + \frac{\mathfrak{M}}{\Gamma(2q)}\int_0^\xi (\xi-t)^{q-1}\left(d_{1f}H+d_{2f}\right)\|\kappa_t^n-\kappa_t\|_{\mathscr{P}_{\mathscr{H}}}dt$$
$$\leq \left[a\mathfrak{M}L_\eta + \mathscr{M}_0\beta_1^*\left(d_{1f}H+d_{2f}\right)\right]\|\mathscr{Z}^n-\mathscr{Z}\|_Y \to 0$$

as $n \to \infty$ which implies that $\mathfrak{G}: Y_\rho \to Y_\rho$ is continuous.

Next, we show $\mathfrak{G}$ maps Y_ρ into itself. It is verified as in Theorem 1. The operator $\mathfrak{G}$ must be shown to satisfy the inequality of the Kuratowski measure of noncompactness in

Lemma 3 as the last phase of this argument. Indeed, consider $\mathscr{L}, \mathscr{L}^* \in Y_r$. Then, for any $\xi \in [0, a]$, with using the assumptions $(\mathcal{I}_1)$-$(\mathcal{I}_3)$, we get

$$\|(\mathfrak{G}_1 \mathscr{L})(\xi) - (\mathfrak{G}_1 \mathscr{L}^*)(\xi)\|_Y \leq \mathfrak{M} \int_0^\xi \|\eta(\kappa + \varkappa) - \eta(\kappa^* + \varkappa)\| dt$$
$$+ \frac{\mathfrak{M} a^q}{\Gamma(2q)} \int_0^\xi (\xi - t)^{q-1} \|\mathscr{F}(t, \kappa + \varkappa, \kappa_t + \varkappa_t) - \mathscr{F}(t, \kappa^* + \varkappa, \kappa_t^* + \varkappa_t)\| dt$$
$$\leq \left[a \mathfrak{M} L_\eta + \mathscr{M}_0 \beta_1^* \left(d_{1f} H + d_{2f} \right) \right] \|\mathscr{L} - \mathscr{L}^*\|_Y.$$

By exploiting the results obtained in the previous theorem, we find that

$$\|(\mathfrak{G} \mathscr{L})(\xi) - (\mathfrak{G} \mathscr{L}^*)(\xi)\|_Y \leq \|(\mathfrak{G}_1 \mathscr{L})(\xi) - (\mathfrak{G}_1 \mathscr{L}^*)(\xi)\|_Y + \|(\mathfrak{G}_2 \mathscr{L})(\xi) - (\mathfrak{G}_2 \mathscr{L}^*)(\xi)\|_Y$$
$$\leq (1 + \mathscr{M}_1) \left[a \mathfrak{M} L_\eta + \mathscr{M}_0 \beta_1^* (d_{1f} H + d_{2f}) \right] \|\mathscr{L} - \mathscr{L}^*\|_Y$$

which implies that

$$\|(\mathfrak{G} \mathscr{L})(\xi) - (\mathfrak{G} \mathscr{L}^*)(\xi)\|_Y \leq \mathfrak{P}_\rho \|\mathscr{L} - \mathscr{L}^*\|_Y.$$

Let $U \subset Y_\rho$ be closed such that there are U_i, $i = 1, 2, \ldots, n$; $n \in \mathbb{N}$ and $U \subseteq \bigcup_{i=1}^n U_i$. Then, according to the definitions of diameter and Kuratowski measure of noncompactness, we conclude that

$$\mu(\mathfrak{G} U) = \inf \left\{ r : diam(\mathfrak{G} U_i) \leq r, U \subseteq \bigcup_{i=1}^n U_i \right\}$$
$$= \inf \left\{ r : \sup\{\|(\mathfrak{G} \mathscr{L})(\xi) - (\mathfrak{G} \mathscr{L}^*)(\xi)\|_Y\} \leq r, \mathscr{L}, \mathscr{L}^* \in U_i, U \subseteq \bigcup_{i=1}^n U_i \right\}$$
$$\leq \mathfrak{P}_\rho \inf \left\{ r : \sup\{\|\mathscr{L}(\xi) - \mathscr{L}^*(\xi)\|_Y\} \leq r, \mathscr{L}, \mathscr{L}^* \in U_i, U \subseteq \bigcup_{i=1}^n U_i \right\}$$
$$= \mathfrak{P}_\rho \inf \left\{ r : diam(U_i) \leq r, U \subseteq \bigcup_{i=1}^n U_i \right\}$$
$$= \mathfrak{P}_\rho \mu(U).$$

By Lemma 2 (vii), we know that for any bounded $U \in Y_\rho$

$$\mu(\mathfrak{G}(U)) \leq \mathfrak{P}_\mathfrak{v} \mu(U).$$

This means that the operator $\mathfrak{G} \colon Y_\rho \to Y_\rho$ is μ-condensing. It follows from Sadovskii fixed point theorem the operator $\mathfrak{G}$ has at least one fixed point $\mathscr{L} \in Y_\rho$, which is just a mild solution to problem (2). This with Lemma 10 completes the proof. □

6. An Application

Consider the following fractional evolution with infinite delay

$$\begin{cases} {}_c\mathcal{D}_0^{\frac{5}{3}} \mathscr{U}(\xi, x) = \mathbb{A} \mathscr{U}(\xi, x) + \mathscr{F}(\xi, \mathscr{U}(\xi, x), \mathscr{U}_\xi(\xi, x)) + \mathfrak{B} y(\xi, x), & \xi \in [0, 1], x \in [0, \pi] \\ \mathscr{U}(\xi, x) = \frac{1}{5} e^{-0.5 \xi}, & \xi \in (-\infty, 0], x \in [0, \pi] \\ \mathscr{U}'(0, x) + \frac{1}{13} \sin \mathscr{U}(\xi, x) = \frac{1}{2}, & \xi \in [0, 1], x \in [0, \pi] \\ \mathscr{U}(\xi, 0) = \mathscr{U}(\xi, 1) = 0, & \xi \in [0, 1]. \end{cases}$$

Let the space $\mathfrak{X} = C([0, 1] \times [0, \pi], \mathbb{R})$ and $\mathbb{U} = L^2[0, 1]$ the space of a square-integrable function equipped with the norm

$$\|\mathscr{U}\|_{L^2[0,1]} = \left(\int_0^1 |\mathscr{U}(\xi)|^2 d\xi \right)^{\frac{1}{2}}.$$

Furthermore, the operator $\mathbb{A}\colon D(\mathbb{A}) \subset \mathfrak{X} \to \mathfrak{X}$ is defined as $\mathbb{A} = \frac{\partial^2}{\partial x^2}$ with a domain

$$D(\mathbb{A}) = \left\{ \mathscr{U} \in \mathfrak{X} \Big| \frac{\partial}{\partial x}\mathscr{U}, \frac{\partial^2}{\partial x^2}\mathscr{U} \in \mathfrak{X} \right\}$$

Apparently, the operator $\mathbb{A}$ is densely defined in $\mathfrak{X}$ and is the infinitesimal generator of a resolvent cosine family $\mathscr{K}(\xi), \xi > 0$ on $\mathfrak{X}$. Here, we take $\mathfrak{v} = \frac{5}{3}$ which implies $q = \frac{5}{6}$ and $\mathbb{A} = \frac{\partial^2}{\partial x^2}, x \in [0, \pi]$, we take $H = \frac{1}{16}, \beta_1(\xi) = \frac{\xi^2+1}{5} \to \beta_1^* = \frac{2}{5}, \beta_2(\xi) = \frac{1}{\sqrt{\xi+1}}, \beta_2^* = \frac{1}{\sqrt{2}}$, $\|\mathscr{K}_q(\xi)\| \le 1, \|\mathscr{L}_q(\xi,t)\| \le 0.36 \ \forall\, 0 < s < \xi \le 1$.

The non-local function given by $\eta(\mathscr{U}(\xi,\cdot)) = \frac{1}{13}\sin\mathscr{U}(\xi,\cdot)$, so we have

$$\left\| \frac{1}{13}\sin\mathscr{U} - \frac{1}{13}\sin\mathscr{V} \right\| \le \frac{1}{13}\|\mathscr{U} - \mathscr{V}\|$$

then, $L_\eta = \frac{1}{13}$.

Let $h(s) = e^{7s}, s < 0$, then $\int_{-\infty}^0 h(s)ds = \frac{1}{7}$, we define

$$\|\phi\|_{\mathscr{P}_\mathscr{H}} = \int_{-\infty}^0 e^{7s} \sup_{s \le \xi \le 0} \|\phi(\xi)\| ds.$$

Then, we can say

$$\|\phi\|_{\mathscr{P}_\mathscr{H}} = \left\| \frac{1}{5} e^{-0.5\xi} \right\|_{\mathscr{P}_\mathscr{H}} = \frac{1}{35}.$$

Assume that the operator $\mathfrak{B} = \mathfrak{D}_1 I$ where I is the identity operator. For $x \in [0, \pi]$, we also assume the operator $\mathbb{W}\colon (\mathbb{U}, \mathbb{R}) \to \mathfrak{X}$ is defined as

$$\mathbb{W}y = \mathfrak{D}_1 \int_0^1 (1-\xi)^{\frac{-1}{6}} \mathscr{L}_q(1,\xi) I y(\xi, x) d\xi$$

and its norm can be given easily by

$$\|\mathbb{W}y\| = \left\| \int_0^1 (1-\xi)^{\frac{-1}{6}} \mathscr{L}_q(1,\xi) \mathfrak{B} y(\xi, x) d\xi \right\| \le \frac{6\mathfrak{D}_1}{5\Gamma(\frac{5}{3})} \|y\|.$$

Plainly, $\mathbb{W}$ is linear and bounded operator with $\mathbb{W} \le \frac{6\mathfrak{D}_1}{5\Gamma(\frac{5}{3})}$. Therefore Assumption 2 holds for a suitable constant $\mathfrak{D}_2 > 0$.

Finally, suppose that

$$\mathscr{F}(\xi, \mathscr{U}(\xi), \mathscr{U}_\xi) = \frac{1}{15} \xi^{\frac{1}{3}} \sin\mathscr{U} + \frac{\mathscr{U}_\xi}{5 + \xi^{\frac{3}{2}}}$$

Clearly $\mathscr{F}\colon [0,1] \times \mathfrak{X} \times \mathscr{P}_\mathscr{H} \to \mathfrak{X}$ is continuous and satisfies

$$\|\mathscr{F}(\xi, \mathscr{U}(\xi), \mathscr{U}_\xi) - \mathscr{F}(\xi, \mathscr{V}(\xi), \mathscr{V}_\xi)\| \le \frac{1}{15}\xi^{\frac{1}{3}} \|\sin\mathscr{U} - \sin\mathscr{V}\|_{\mathfrak{X}} + \frac{1}{5+\xi^{\frac{3}{2}}} \|\mathscr{U}_\xi - \mathscr{V}_\xi\|_{\mathscr{P}_\mathscr{H}}.$$

Then, we have $d_{1f} = \frac{1}{15}$ and $d_{2f} = \frac{1}{6}$ and

$$a\mathfrak{M}L_\eta + \mathscr{M}_0 \beta_1^*(d_{1f}H + d_{2f}) \sim 0.167757.$$

- Case I: Krasnoselskii fixed point theorem:
  To check the presumption of Theorem 1, we have $\mathscr{L}_\mathfrak{v} \sim 0.167757.\mathscr{M}_1 < 1$ which is true for all $0 < \mathfrak{D}_1 < 4.48439/\mathfrak{D}_2$. Thus, all assumptions of this theorem are satisfied. Therefore, the problem (2) has a unique mild solution and is controllable on $(-\infty, 1]$.

- Case II: Sadovskii fixed point theorem:
  To check the presumption of Theorem 2, we have $\mathfrak{P}_\rho \sim 0.167757(1 + \mathcal{M}_1) < 1$ which is true for all $0 < \mathfrak{D}_1 < 3.7321/\mathfrak{D}_2$. Thus, all assumptions of this theorem are satisfied. Therefore, the problem (2) has a unique mild solution and is controllable on $(-\infty, 1]$.

7. Conclusions

In the current study, we analyzed an infinitely delaying system of fractional evolution equations. The foundation for our observations is furnished by current functional analysis approaches. In order to provide a reasonable remedy, we employ the unbounded operator $\mathbb{A}$ as the generator of the strongly continuous Cosine family. In the case of the problem (2), we had to examine a moderate controllability solution by two different arguments, the first of which used compactness technology and the second, noncompactness. By using the Sadovskii fixed point theorem and the measure of non-compactness, we present a new approach to analyzing the controllability of mild solutions. The first argument is based on Krasnoselskii's theorem, which allows $\mathscr{F}(\xi, \mathscr{U}, \mathscr{U}_\xi)$ to behave as

$$\|\mathscr{F}(\xi, \mathscr{U}, \mathscr{U}_\xi) - \mathscr{F}(\xi, \mathscr{V}, \mathscr{V}_\xi)\| \leq d_{1f}\|\mathscr{U} - \mathscr{V}\|_{\mathfrak{X}} + d_{2f}\|\mathscr{U}_\xi - \mathscr{V}_\xi\|_{\mathscr{P}_{\mathscr{H}}}.$$

The tools of fixed point theory in the case of simple assumptions are simple to install and enhance the range of results offered to meet our demands. The second result, which is rooted in the Kuratowski measure of noncompactness and the Sadovskii fixed point theorem, establishes a stipulation to utilize the operator of the solution is a condensing map in order to comply with the Lipschitz continuance, ensuring that the problem at hand has no prior solutions. Our conclusion is then illustrated with a numerical example that looks at a function that meets all the requirements.

Author Contributions: Conceptualization, A.S. and K.N.A.; methodology, K.N.A.; software, K.N.A.; validation, A.S.; formal analysis, A.S. and K.N.A.; investigation, A.S.; resources, K.N.A.; data curation, K.N.A.; writing—original draft preparation, K.N.A.; writing—review and editing, A.S.; visualization, A.S.; supervision, A.S.; project administration, A.S.; funding acquisition, A.S. All authors have read and agreed to the published version of the manuscript.

Funding: The Deanship of Scientific Research (DSR) at King Abdulaziz University (KAU), Jeddah, Saudi Arabia has funded this Project, under grant no. (G:046-130-1443).

Conflicts of Interest: The authors declare no conflict of interest.

References

1. Baghani, H. An analytical improvement of a study of nonlinear Langevin equation involving two fractional orders in different intervals. *J. Fixed Point Theory Appl.* **2019**, *21*, 1–11. [CrossRef]
2. Salem, A.; Babusail, R. Finite-Time Stability in Nonhomogeneous Delay Differential Equations of Fractional Hilfer Type. *Mathematics* **2022**, *10*, 1520. [CrossRef]
3. Salem, A.; Abdullah, S. Non-Instantaneous Impulsive BVPs Involving Generalized Liouville–Caputo Derivative. *Mathematics* **2022**, *10*, 291. [CrossRef]
4. Chen, Q.; Sabir, Z.; Raja, M.A.Z.; Gao, W.; Baskonus, H.M. A fractional study based on the economic and environmental mathematical model. *Alex. Eng. J.* **2023**, *65*, 761–770. [CrossRef]
5. Gao, W.; Veeresha, P.; Baskonus, H.M. Dynamical analysis fractional-order financial system using efficient numerical methods. *Appl. Math. Sci. Eng.* **2023**, *31*, 2155152. [CrossRef]
6. Hannabou, M.; Bouaouid, M.; Hilal, K. Controllability of mild solution of non-local conformable fractional differential equations. *Adv. Math. Phys.* **2022**, *2022*, 3671909. [CrossRef]
7. Dineshkumar, C.; Udhayakumar, R.; Vijayakumar, V.; Nisar, K.S. A discussion on the approximate controllability of Hilfer fractional neutral stochastic integro-differential systems. *Chaos Solitons Fractals* **2021**, *142*, 110472. [CrossRef]
8. Vijayakumar, V.; Panda, S.K.; Nisar, K.S.; Baskonus, H.M. Results on approximate controllability results for second-order Sobolev-type impulsive neutral differential evolution inclusions with infinite delay. *Numer. Methods Partial. Differ. Equ.* **2021**, *37*, 1200–1221. [CrossRef]
9. Salem, A.; Alghamdi, B. Multi-Strip and Multi-Point Boundary Conditions for Fractional Langevin Equation. *Fractal Fract.* **2020**, *4*, 18. [CrossRef]

10. Salem, A. Existence results of solutions for anti-periodic fractional Langevin equation. *J. Appl. Anal. Comput.* **2020**, *10*, 2557–2574. [CrossRef]
11. Li, T.; Viglialoro, G. Boundedness for a non-local reaction chemotaxis model even in the attraction-dominated regime. *Differ. Integral Equ.* **2021**, *34*, 315–336
12. Iqbal, N.; Niazi, A.U.; Khan, I.U.; Shah, R.; Botmart, T. Cauchy problem for non-autonomous fractional evolution equations with non-local conditions of order (1,2). *AIMS Math.* **2022**, *7*, 8891–8913. [CrossRef]
13. Salem, A.; Alzahrani, F.; Alnegga, M. Coupled system of non-linear fractional Langevin equations with multi-point and non-local integral boundary conditions. *Math. Problen. Eng.* **2020**, *2020*, 7345658.
14. Zhang, X.; Huanga, X.; Liu, Z. The existence and uniqueness of mild solutions for impulsive fractional equations with non-local conditions and infinite delay. *Nonlinear Anal. Hybrid Syst.* **2010**, *4*, 775–781. [CrossRef]
15. Benchohra, M.; Henderson, J.; Ntouyas, S.K.; Ouahaba, A. Existence results for fractional order functional differential equations with infinite delay. *J. Math. Anal. Appl.* **2008**, *338*, 1340–1350. [CrossRef]
16. Santra, S.S.; Alotaibi, H.; Bazighifan, O. On the qualitative behavior of the solutions to second-order neutral delay differential equations. *J. Inequal. Appl.* **2020**, *2020*, 256. [CrossRef]
17. Nguyen, N.T.; Tran, D.K.; Nguyen, V.D. Stability analysis for non-local evolution equations involving infinite delays. *J. Fixed Point Theory Appl.* **2023**, *25*, 22. [CrossRef]
18. Bedi, P.; Kumar, A.; Abdeljawad, T.; Khan, A. Study of Hilfer fractional evolution equations by the properties of controllability and stability. *Alex. Eng. J.* **2021**, *60*, 3741–3749. [CrossRef]
19. Dineshkumar, C.; Udhayakumar, R.; Vijayakumar, V.; Nisar, K.S.; Shukla, A. A note concerning to approximate controllability of Atangana–Baleanu fractional neutral stochastic systems with infinite delay. *Chaos Solitons Fractals* **2022**, *157*, 111916. [CrossRef]
20. Salem, A.; Almaghamsi, L. Existence Solution for Coupled System of Langevin Fractional Differential Equations of Caputo Type with Riemann-Stieltjes Integral Boundary Conditions. *Symmetry* **2021**, *13*, 2123. [CrossRef]
21. Abbas, S.; Benchohra, M. *Advanced Functional Evolution Equations and Inclusions, Developments in Mathematics, 39*; Springer: Cham, Switzerland, 2015; Volume 20.
22. Diop, M.A.; Ezzinbi, K.; Ly, M.P. Non-local problems for integro-differential equations via resolvent operators and optimal controls. *Discuss. Math. Differ. Inclusions Control. Optim.* **2022**, *42*, 5–25. [CrossRef]
23. Salem, A.; Al-Dosari, A. Hybrid Differential Inclusion Involving Two Multi-Valued operators with Non-local Multi-Valued Integral Condition. *Fractal Fract.* **2022**, *6*, 109. [CrossRef]
24. Bensalem, A.; Salim, A.; Benchohra, M.; Guerekata, G.M.N. Functional Integro-Differential Equations with State-Dependent Delay and Non-Instantaneous Impulsions: Existence and Qualitative Results. *Fractal Fract.* **2022**, *6*, 615. [CrossRef]
25. Santos, J.P.C.D. On state-dependent delay partial neutral functional integro-differential equations. *Appl. Math. Comput.* **2010**, *100*, 1637–1644. [CrossRef]
26. Hernandez, E.; McKibben, M.A. On state-dependent delay partial neutral functional-differential equations. *Appl. Math. Comput.* **2017**, *186*, 294–301. [CrossRef]
27. Hernandez, E.; Prokopczyk, A.; Ladeira, L. A note on partial functional differential equations with state-dependent delay. *Nonlin. Anal.* **2006**, *7*, 510–519. [CrossRef]
28. Hino, Y.; Murakami, S.; Naito, T. Functional-differential equations with infinite delay. In *Lecture Notes in Mathematics, 1473*; Stahy, S., Ed.; Springer: Berlin, Germany, 1991; Volume 19.
29. Wang, C.; Shi, F.; Li, L.; Alhamami, M. Research on Stability of Time-delay Force Feedback Teleoperation System Based on Scattering Matrix. *Appl. Math. Nonlinear Sci.* **2022**. Available online: https://doi.org/10.2478/amns.2022.2.00017 (accessed on 1 December 2022).
30. Zhang, D.; Yang, L.; Arbab, A. The Uniqueness of Solutions of Fractional Differential Equations in University Mathematics Teaching Based on the Principle of Compression Mapping. *Appl. Math. Nonlinear Sci.* **2022**, 1–7. [CrossRef]
31. Anilkumar, M.P.; Jose, K.P. Analysis of a discrete time queueing-inventory model with back-order of items. *3c Empresa Investig. y Pensam. Crtico* **2022**, *11*, 50–62. Available online: https://dialnet.unirioja.es/servlet/articulocodigo=8749994 (accessed on 1 December 2022). [CrossRef]
32. Asadi, M.; Afshar, M. Fixed point theorems in the generalized rational type of C-class functions in b-metric spaces with Application to Integral Equation. *3C Empresa Investigacin y Pensamiento Crtico* **2022**, *11*, 64–74. [CrossRef]
33. Podlubny, I. *Fractional Differential Equations*; Acadmic Press: New York, NY, USA, 1999.
34. Kilbas, A.A.; Srivastava, H.M.; Trujillo, J.J. *Theory and Applications of Fractional Differential Equations*; Elsevier: Amsterdam, The Netherlands, 2006.
35. Chen, P.; Li, X.Z.Y. Non-autonomous parabolic evolution equations with non-instantaneous impulses governed by noncompact evolution families. *J. Fixed Point Theory App.* **2019**, *21*, 21–84. [CrossRef]
36. Travis, C.C.; Webb, G.F. Cosine families and abstract nonlinear second order differential equations. *Acta Math. Hungar.* **1978**, *32*, 75–96. [CrossRef]
37. Salem, A.; Alharbi, K.N.; Alshehri, H.M. Fractional Evolution Equations with Infinite Time Delay in Abstract Phase Space. *Mathematics* **2022**, *10*, 1332. [CrossRef]

38. Hale, J.; Kato, J. Phase space for retarded equations with infinite delay. *Funkcial. Ekvac.* **1978**, *21*, 11–41.
39. Zhou, Y.; He, J.W. New results on controllability of fractional systems with order $\alpha \in (1,2)$. *Evol. Equ. Control Theory* **2021**, *10*, 491–509. [CrossRef]

Disclaimer/Publisher's Note: The statements, opinions and data contained in all publications are solely those of the individual author(s) and contributor(s) and not of MDPI and/or the editor(s). MDPI and/or the editor(s) disclaim responsibility for any injury to people or property resulting from any ideas, methods, instructions or products referred to in the content.

Article

Fractional–Order Modeling and Control of COVID-19 with Shedding Effect

Isa A. Baba [1,2], Usa W. Humphries [2,*], Fathalla A. Rihan [3,4] and J. E. N. Valdés [5]

Citation: Baba, I.A.; Humphries, U.W.; Rihan, F.A.; Valdés, J.E.N. Fractional–Order Modeling and Control of COVID-19 with Shedding Effect. *Axioms* 2023, 12, 321. https://doi.org/10.3390/axioms12040291

Academic Editors: Darjan Karabašević and Martin Bohner

Received: 19 December 2022
Revised: 30 January 2023
Accepted: 1 February 2023
Published: 24 March 2023

Copyright: © 2023 by the authors. Licensee MDPI, Basel, Switzerland. This article is an open access article distributed under the terms and conditions of the Creative Commons Attribution (CC BY) license (https://creativecommons.org/licenses/by/4.0/).

[1] Department of Mathematics, Bayero University, Kano 700241, Nigeria
[2] Department of Mathematics, Faculty of Science, King Mongkuts University of Science and Technology Thonburi (KMUTT), Bangkok 10140, Thailand
[3] Department of Mathematical Sciences, College of Science, UAE University, Al Ain 15551, United Arab Emirates
[4] Department of Mathematics, Faculty of Science, Helwan University, Cairo 11795, Egypt
[5] Facultad de Ciencias Exactas y Naturales y Agrimensura, Universidad Nacional del Nordeste, Corrientes Capital 3400, Argentina
* Correspondence: usa.wan@kmutt.ac.th

Abstract: A fractional order COVID-19 model consisting of six compartments in Caputo sense is constructed. The indirect transmission of the virus through susceptible populations by the shedding effect is studied. Equilibrium solutions are calculated, and basic reproduction ratio (that depends both on direct and indirect mode of transmission), existence and uniqueness, as well as stability analysis of the solution of the model, are studied. The paper studies the effect of optimal control policy applied to shedding effect. The control is the observation of standard hygiene practices and chemical disinfectants in public spaces. Numerical simulations are carried out to support the analytic result and to show the significance of the fractional order from the biological viewpoint.

Keywords: mathematical model; fractional order; Caputo; optimal control; shedding effect; COVID-19

MSC: 92B05

1. Introduction

COVID-19 surfaced in the world at the end of the year 2019. It undermined many sectors such as transport, the economy, education systems, sports, entertainment, etc. The pandemic killed and infected many. The nature and mode of the spread of COVID-19 outbreak are still not completely understood. Researchers are geared towards finding vaccines to curtail the spread of the virus. The idea is to limit the number of new infections and subsequent deaths due to the pandemic. Due to the scarcity of vaccines, many countries in the world adopt non-pharmaceutical measures such as lockdown, airport closures, use of sanitizers and social distancing. There is a great deal of research in the literature with regard to the pandemic, both from a theoretical and practical point of view [1–7].

It is estimated that 75% of infected individuals recover without showing serious symptoms and many achieve e natural recovery [8]. Throat infection, chest pain, runny nose or nasal congestion, losing smell and taste, vomiting, diarrhea and nausea are some of the symptoms of COVID-19. In most cases, these symptoms appear slowly. It is also believed that elderly people can observe serious complications compared to their younger counterparts. On average, infected individuals spend 7–14 days before showing symptoms [9]. In many cases, it takes 14 days before mild cases recover [10]. The transmission of COVID-19 occurs mostly via either a direct (through contaminated air by tiny droplets and airborne particles containing the virus) or an indirect (through contaminated surfaces) method. The virus is released from the mouth of infected individuals through either sneezing or coughing and is shed into the environment in the form of micro-particles in the air. This shedding effect is of paramount significance in studying COVID-19 transmission. Although diagnostic tests and vaccine treatments are now available to curb the spread of the disease, the use of standard hygiene practices and chemical disinfectants in public places must still be maintained.

Many fields of study such as epidemiology, economics and finance, aeronautical engineering, robotics, etc., use optimal control as an effective mathematical tool to optimize control problems [11]. However, there is little in the literature about the use of an optimal control approach to study COVID-19, since control in a real sense varies with time [12–18].

Fractional order derivatives and fractional integrals are very important tools that are used in the study of mathematical modeling due to their hereditary properties and ability in memory description. In the last few decades, the fractional differential has been used in mathematical modeling of biological phenomena [19,20]. This is because fractional calculus can explain and process the retention and heritage properties of various materials more accurately than integer-order models [21,22]. Due to the effectiveness of mathematical models in studying infectious diseases, recently many scientists have been investigating mathematical models of the COVID-19 pandemic with fractional order derivatives; they have produced excellent results [23,24]. The Caputo fractional order derivative is based on the exponential kernel and details on its operation and its applications can be found in [25–28]. Caputo fractional derivative gives less noise when compared with other operators [29]. In this paper, we use Caputo fractional order to model the spread and control of COVID-19 with emphasis on shedding effect.

The main contribution of this paper is to mathematically demonstrate the fact that an uninfected population can become infected by both direct and indirect methods by the exposed or infected class. Infected and exposed individuals can contaminate the environment by shedding pathogens. It is also our aim to show the effect of healthy hygiene practices, i.e., using alcohol-based hand sanitizers and effective chemical disinfectants in public areas in curbing the spread of COVID-19.

This paper is organized as follows: the introduction is given in Section 1, formulation of the model is given in Section 2, analysis of the model is given in Section 3, construction and analysis of the optimal control problem is given in Section 4, numerical simulation is given in Section 5 and finally conclusions are given in Section 6.

2. Definition of Terms

In this section we give definitions of the Caputo derivative as in [30].

Definition 1. *The Caputo fractional left-sided derivative is defined as*

$$ {}^C_*D^\alpha_{a+}(f(t)) = \frac{1}{\Gamma(n-\alpha)} \int_a^t (t-\tau)^{n-\alpha-1} \frac{d^n}{d\tau^n}[f(\tau)]d\tau, \ t \geq a $$

Caputo fractional right-sided derivative is defined as

$$ {}^C_*D^\alpha_{b-}(f(t)) = \frac{(-1)^n}{\Gamma(n-\alpha)} \int_t^b (\tau-t)^{n-\alpha-1} \frac{d^n}{d\tau^n}[f(\tau)]d\tau, \ t \leq b. $$

3. Formulation of the Model

We adopted and modified the model in [28]. The transmission of COVID-19 occurs through primary and secondary routes. The primary route is through person–person contact and the secondary route is through contaminated surfaces (shedding effect). While much research on the control of pathogen transmission through the primary route are available in the literature, little considers the secondary route. The control of the transmission through the secondary route involves healthy hygiene practices which include using hand sanitizers, face masks and effective chemical disinfectants in public areas.

The model consists of a system of fractional order differential equation in the Caputo sense with six compartments. The compartments are: $S(t)$, $E(t)$, $I(t)$, $H(t), R(t)$ and $V(t)$ which stands for Susceptible, Exposed, Infected, Hospitalized, and Recovered compartments, respectively. To study the shedding effect, another compartment for contaminated surfaces is added as Virus class $V(t)$.

First, we will consider and analyze the fractional order model in Caputo sense without the optimal control and then in Section 5 we will introduce and analyze the optimal control function.

The model is given below

$$\begin{aligned}
{}_0^C D_t^\alpha S(t) &= Y^\alpha - \beta^\alpha SI - \theta^\alpha SV - \mu^\alpha S, \\
{}_0^C D_t^\alpha E(t) &= \beta^\alpha SI + \theta^\alpha SV - (\mu^\alpha + \gamma^\alpha + \eta_1^\alpha) E, \\
{}_0^C D_t^\alpha I &= \gamma^\alpha E - (\mu^\alpha + \pi^\alpha + \xi_1^\alpha + \eta_2^\alpha) I, \\
{}_0^C D_t^\alpha H &= \pi^\alpha I - (\mu^\alpha + \xi_2^\alpha + \eta_3^\alpha) H, \\
{}_0^C D_t^\alpha R(t) &= \eta_1^\alpha E + \eta_2^\alpha I + \eta_3^\alpha H - \mu^\alpha R, \\
{}_0^C D_t^\alpha V(t) &= q_1^\alpha E + q_2^\alpha I - r^\alpha V,
\end{aligned} \quad (1)$$

with the following initial conditions

$$S(0) = a_1, E(0) = a_2, I(0) = a_3, H(0) = a_4, \; R(0) = a_5 \text{ and } V(0) = a_6$$

The meaning of the parameters involved in the model is given in Table 1 below.

Table 1. Meaning of Parameters.

Parameter	Meaning
Y	Recruitment rate into susceptible class
β	Transmission rate of COVID-19 from human to human
θ	Transmission rate of COVID-19 from environment to human
μ	Natural death rate
γ	Rate at which exposed individuals move to Infected class
η_1, η_2, η_3	Natural recovery rate in Exposed, Infected and Hospitalized classes respectively
π	Rate of hospitalization
ξ_1, ξ_2	Rate of COVID-19 caused death in Infected and Hospitalized classes respectively
q_1, q_2	Rate of virus shedding from Exposed and Infected classes respectively
r	Rate of sanitization
$0 < \alpha \leq 1$	Fractional order

4. Analysis of the Model

In this section, some mathematical properties of the model are explored. This consists of positivity and boundedness, computation of Equilibria, basic reproduction number, existence and uniqueness analysis of the solution of the model, and local stability analysis.

4.1. Positivity and Boundedness

To show positivity, considering Equation (1), we have

$$\begin{aligned}
{}_0^C D_t^\alpha S(t)|_{S=0} &= Y^\alpha > 0, \\
{}_0^C D_t^\alpha E(t)|_{E=0} &= \beta^\alpha SI + \theta^\alpha SV \geq 0, \\
{}_0^C D_t^\alpha I(t)|_{I=0} &= \gamma^\alpha E \geq 0, \\
{}_0^C D_t^\alpha H(t)|_{H=0} &= \pi^\alpha I \geq 0, \text{ and} \\
{}_0^C D_t^\alpha R(t)|_{R=0} &= \eta_1^\alpha E + \eta_2^\alpha I + \eta_3^\alpha H \geq 0.
\end{aligned}$$

Therefore, we can observe that the solution of (1) is non-negative.

For the boundedness, we can observe that the overall dynamics of the human population is obtained by adding the first five Equations of (1). Let

$$N(t) = S(t) + E(t) + I(t) + H(t) + R(t)$$

Then,
$$^C_0D^\alpha_t N(t) = {^C_0D^\alpha_t} S(t) + {^C_0D^\alpha_t} E(t) + {^C_0D^\alpha_t} I(t) + {^C_0D^\alpha_t} H(t) + {^C_0D^\alpha_t} R(t),$$

which simplifies to,
$$^C_0D^\alpha_t N(t) = Y^\alpha - \mu^\alpha N - (\xi^\alpha_1 I + \xi^\alpha_2 H),$$

hence,
$$^C_0D^\alpha_t N(t) \leq Y^\alpha - \mu^\alpha N.$$

We apply the lap-lace transform method to solve the Gronwall's like inequality with initial condition $N(t_0) \geq 0$. We have,
$$\mathcal{L}\left\{^C_0D^\alpha_t N(t) + \mu^\alpha N\right\} \leq \mathcal{L}\{Y^\alpha\}.$$

By linearity of the Laplace transform, we get
$$\mathcal{L}\left\{^C_0D^\alpha_t N(t)\right\} + \mu^\alpha \mathcal{L}\{N(t)\} \leq \mathcal{L}\{Y^\alpha\},$$

Then we get,
$$S^\alpha \mathcal{L}\{N(t)\} - \sum_{k=0}^{n-1} S^{\alpha-k-1} N^k(t_0) + \mu^\alpha \mathcal{L}\{N(t)\} \leq \frac{Y^\alpha}{S}.$$

Simplifying, we get
$$\mathcal{L}\{N(t)\} \leq Y^\alpha \left(\frac{1}{S} - \frac{1}{S}\frac{1}{\left(1 + \frac{\mu^\alpha}{S^\alpha}\right)}\right) + \sum_{k=0}^{n-1} \frac{1}{S^{k+1}} \frac{1}{\left(1 + \frac{\mu^\alpha}{S^\alpha}\right)} N^k(t_0).$$

Using Taylor series expansion, we have
$$\frac{1}{\left(1 + \frac{\mu^\alpha}{S^\alpha}\right)} = \sum_{n=0}^{\infty} \left(\frac{-\mu^\alpha}{S^\alpha}\right)^n$$

Therefore,
$$\mathcal{L}\{N(t)\} \leq Y^\alpha \left(\frac{1}{S} - \frac{1}{S}\sum_{n=0}^{\infty}\left(\frac{-\mu^\alpha}{S^\alpha}\right)^n\right) + \sum_{k=0}^{n-1} \frac{1}{S^{k+1}} N^k(t_0) \sum_{n=0}^{\infty}\left(\frac{-\mu^\alpha}{S^\alpha}\right)^n.$$

Taking, Laplace inverse, we get
$$N(t) \leq Y^\alpha - Y^\alpha \sum_{n=0}^{\infty} \frac{-(\mu^\alpha t^\alpha)^n}{\Gamma(\alpha n + 1)} + \sum_{k=0}^{n-1}\sum_{n=0}^{\infty} \frac{-(\mu^\alpha t^\alpha)^n}{\Gamma(\alpha n + k + 1)} t^k N^k(t_0).$$

Substituting the Mittag-Leffler function, we get
$$N(t) \leq Y^\alpha[1 - E_1(-\mu^\alpha t^\alpha)] + \sum_{k=0}^{n-1} E_{k+1}(-\mu^\alpha t^\alpha) t^k N^k(t_0).$$

where $E_1(-\mu^\alpha t^\alpha)$, $E_{k+1}(-\mu^\alpha t^\alpha)$ are the series of Mittag-Leffler functions which converge for any argument; hence we say that the solution to the model is bounded.

Thus we define,

$$\omega = \{(S(t), E(t), I(t), H(t), R(t)) \in R_+^5 : S(t), E(t), I(t), H(t), R(t)$$
$$\leq Y^\alpha[1 - E_1(-\mu^\alpha t^\alpha)] + \sum_{k=0}^{n-1} E_{k+1}(-\mu^\alpha t^\alpha) t^k N^k(t_0)\}$$

Hence, all solutions of (1) commencing in ω stay in ω for all $t \geq 0$. Positivity of solutions means that the population thrives, while boundedness means that the population growth is restricted naturally due to limited resources.

4.2. Equilibria and Basic Reproduction Number

The equilibrium solutions are obtained by equating the equations in the model to zero and solving the system simultaneously. We obtain two equilibrium solutions; disease free and endemic equilibrium solutions.

i. Disease free equilibrium (E^0)

$$E^0 = \{S_0, E_0, I_0, H_0, R_0, V_0\} = \left\{\frac{Y^\alpha}{\mu^\alpha}, 0, 0, 0, 0, 0\right\}$$

ii. Endemic equilibrium (E^1)

$$E^1 = \{S_1, E_1, I_1, H_1, R_1, V_1\},$$

where,

$$S_1 = \frac{r^\alpha (\pi^\alpha + \eta_2^\alpha + \mu^\alpha + \xi_1^\alpha)(\mu^\alpha + \eta_1^\alpha + \gamma^\alpha) E_1}{\beta^\alpha \gamma^\alpha r^\alpha + \theta^\alpha (q_1^\alpha (\pi^\alpha + \eta_2^\alpha + \mu^\alpha + \xi_1^\alpha) + q_2^\alpha \gamma^\alpha)},$$

$$I_1 = \frac{\gamma^\alpha E_1}{\pi^\alpha + \eta_2^\alpha + \mu^\alpha + \xi_1^\alpha},$$

$$H_1 = \frac{\gamma^\alpha \pi^\alpha E_1}{(\eta_3^\alpha + \mu^\alpha + \xi_2^\alpha)(\pi^\alpha + \eta_2^\alpha + \mu^\alpha + \xi_1^\alpha)},$$

$$R_1 = \frac{1}{\mu^\alpha}\left[\eta_1^\alpha + \frac{\eta_3^\alpha \pi^\alpha \gamma^\alpha}{(\eta_3^\alpha + \mu^\alpha + \xi_2^\alpha)(\pi^\alpha + \eta_2^\alpha + \mu^\alpha + \xi_1^\alpha)} + \frac{\eta_2^\alpha \gamma^\alpha}{\pi^\alpha + \eta_2^\alpha + \mu^\alpha + \xi_1^\alpha}\right] E_1,$$

$$V_1 = \frac{1}{r^\alpha}\left[q_1^\alpha + \frac{q_2^\alpha \gamma^\alpha}{\pi^\alpha + \eta_2^\alpha + \mu^\alpha + \xi_1^\alpha}\right] E_1,$$

and E_1 is defined as

$$E_1 = \frac{1}{(\mu^\alpha + \eta_1^\alpha + \gamma^\alpha)}\left[Y^\alpha - \frac{\mu^\alpha r^\alpha (\pi^\alpha + \eta_2^\alpha + \mu^\alpha + \xi_1^\alpha)(\mu^\alpha + \eta_1^\alpha + \gamma^\alpha)}{\beta^\alpha \gamma^\alpha r^\alpha + \theta^\alpha (q_1^\alpha (\pi^\alpha + \eta_2^\alpha + \mu^\alpha + \xi_1^\alpha) + q_2^\alpha \gamma^\alpha)}\right]$$

4.3. Computation of Basic Reproduction Ratio

In this section, a threshold quantity called basic reproduction ratio is computed using the method of next generation matrix. Consider the following Equations from (1):

$$\begin{aligned}
{}_0^C D_t^\alpha E(t) &= \beta^\alpha SI + \theta^\alpha SV - (\mu^\alpha + \gamma^\alpha + \eta_1^\alpha) E, \\
{}_0^C D_t^\alpha I &= \gamma^\alpha E - (\mu^\alpha + \pi^\alpha + \xi_1^\alpha + \eta_2^\alpha) I, \\
{}_0^C D_t^\alpha V(t) &= q_1 E + q_2 I - rV.
\end{aligned} \quad (2)$$

Let $A_i(X)$ and $B_i(X)$ be the rate of appearance of new infection and rate of other transitions in the ith compartment respectively. Then

$$A_i(X) = \begin{pmatrix} \beta^\alpha SI + \theta^\alpha SV \\ 0 \\ 0 \end{pmatrix}, \text{ and } B_i(X)$$

$$= \begin{pmatrix} (\mu^\alpha + \gamma^\alpha + \eta_1^\alpha)E \\ -\gamma^\alpha E + (\mu^\alpha + \pi^\alpha + \xi_1^\alpha + \eta_2^\alpha)I \\ -q_1^\alpha E - q_2^\alpha I + r^\alpha V \end{pmatrix}.$$

Then Equation (2) can be written as

$$\dot{X} = A_i(X) - B_i(X), \ i = 1, 2, 3.$$

Now, define

$$A = \left(\frac{\partial A_i}{\partial x_j}\right)(E_0) = \begin{pmatrix} 0 & \frac{\gamma^\alpha \beta^\alpha}{\mu^\alpha} & \frac{\theta^\alpha \beta^\alpha}{\mu^\alpha} \\ 0 & 0 & 0 \\ 0 & 0 & 0 \end{pmatrix}, \text{ and}$$

$$B = \left(\frac{\partial B_i}{\partial x_j}\right)(E_0) = \begin{pmatrix} \mu^\alpha + \gamma^\alpha + \eta_1^\alpha & 0 & 0 \\ -\gamma^\alpha E & \mu^\alpha + \pi^\alpha + \xi_1^\alpha + \eta_2^\alpha & 0 \\ -q_1^\alpha & -q_2^\alpha & r^\alpha \end{pmatrix}.$$

The basic reproduction ratio, which is the spectral radius of the matrix AB^{-1}, defined as $\rho(AB^{-1})$, is calculated as

$$R_0 = R_1 + R_2 + R_3,$$

where

$$R_1 = \frac{\gamma^\alpha \beta^\alpha \gamma^\alpha}{\mu^\alpha (\mu^\alpha + \pi^\alpha + \xi_1^\alpha + \eta_2^\alpha)(\mu^\alpha + \gamma^\alpha + \eta_1^\alpha)},$$

$$R_2 = \frac{\gamma^\alpha \theta^\alpha q_1^\alpha}{\mu^\alpha r^\alpha (\mu^\alpha + \gamma^\alpha + \eta_1^\alpha)}, \text{ and}$$

$$R_3 = \frac{\theta^\alpha \gamma^\alpha q_2^\alpha \gamma^\alpha}{\mu^\alpha r^\alpha (\mu^\alpha + \pi^\alpha + \xi_1^\alpha + \eta_2^\alpha)(\mu^\alpha + \gamma^\alpha + \eta_1^\alpha)}$$

where R_1, R_2 and R_3 are related with the endowment of direct human-to-human contact routes, exposed-to-environment and infected-to-environment, respectively.

4.4. Existence and Uniqueness of Solution of the Model

Consider the system

$$S(t) - S(0) = {}^C_0D^\alpha_t S(t)\{\gamma^\alpha - \beta^\alpha SI - \theta^\alpha SV - \mu^\alpha S\},$$

$$E(t) - E(0) = {}^C_0D^\alpha_t E(t)\{\beta^\alpha SI + \theta^\alpha SV - (\mu^\alpha + \gamma^\alpha + \eta_1^\alpha)E\},$$

$$I(t) - I(0) = {}^C_0D^\alpha_t I\{\gamma^\alpha E - (\mu^\alpha + \pi^\alpha + \xi_1^\alpha + \eta_2^\alpha)I\},$$

$$H(t) - H(0) = {}^C_0D^\alpha_t H\{\pi^\alpha I - (\mu^\alpha + \xi_2^\alpha + \eta_3^\alpha)H\},$$

$$R(t) - R(0) = {}^C_0D^\alpha_t R(t)\{\eta_1^\alpha E + \eta_2^\alpha I + \eta_3^\alpha H - \mu^\alpha R\},$$

$$V(t) - V(0) = {}^C_0D^\alpha_t V(t)\{q_1^\alpha E + q_2^\alpha I - r^\alpha V\},$$

and
$$S(t) - S(0) = M(\alpha) \int_0^1 (t-\tau)^{-\alpha} F_1(t,S) d\tau,$$
$$E(t) - E(0) = M(\alpha) \int_0^1 (t-\tau)^{-\alpha} F_2(t,E) d\tau,$$
$$I(t) - I(0) = M(\alpha) \int_0^1 (t-\tau)^{-\alpha} F_3(t,I) d\tau,$$
$$H(t) - H(0) = M(\alpha) \int_0^1 (t-\tau)^{-\alpha} F_4(t,H) d\tau,$$
$$R(t) - R(0) = M(\alpha) \int_0^1 (t-\tau)^{-\alpha} F_5(t,R) d\tau,$$
$$V(t) - V(0) = M(\alpha) \int_0^1 (t-\tau)^{-\alpha} F_6(t,V) d\tau,$$

where
$$^C_0 D^\alpha_t S(t) = F_1(t,S),$$
$$^C_0 D^\alpha_t E(t) = F_2(t,E),$$
$$^C_0 D^\alpha_t I(t) = F_3(t,I),$$
$$^C_0 D^\alpha_t H(t) = F_4(t,H),$$
$$^C_0 D^\alpha_t R(t) = F_5(t,R),$$
$$^C_0 D^\alpha_t V(t) = F_6(t,V).$$

Now, we can easily show that $F_1, \ldots, F_6$ satisfy Lipschitz continuity using the following theorem
$$0 \leq \beta^\alpha k_1 + \theta^\alpha k_2 + \mu^\alpha < 1,$$

This is a contraction.

Proof.

$$\|F_1(t,S) - F_1(t,S_1)\|$$
$$= \|Y^\alpha - \beta^\alpha S(t)I(t) - \theta^\alpha S(t)V(t) - \mu^\alpha S(t) - Y^\alpha$$
$$+ \beta^\alpha S_1(t)I(t) + \theta^\alpha S_1(t)V(t) + \mu^\alpha S_1(t)\|$$
$$= \| - \beta^\alpha I(t)(S(t) - S_1(t)) - \theta^\alpha V(t)(S(t) - S_1(t)) - \mu^\alpha(S(t) - S_1(t))\|$$
$$\leq \beta^\alpha \|I(t)\| \|S(t) - S_1(t)\| + \theta^\alpha V(t)\|S(t) - S_1(t)\| + \mu^\alpha \|S(t) - S_1(t)\|$$
$$\leq (\beta^\alpha k_1 + \theta^\alpha k_2 + \mu^\alpha) \|S(t) - S_1(t)\|$$
$$\leq L_1 \|S(t) - S_1(t)\|,$$

where $L_1 = \beta^\alpha k_1 + \theta^\alpha k_2 + \mu^\alpha$, $k_1 \geq \|I(t)\|$ and $k_2 \geq \|V(t)\|$. □

Similarly, we find the remaining Lipschitz constants $L_2, \ldots, L_6$ show the Lischitz continuity and contraction of $F_2, \ldots, F_6$.

Recursively, let
$$\begin{aligned} p_{1n}(t) &= S_n(t) - S_{n-1}(t) \\ &= \frac{2(1-\alpha)}{(2-\alpha)M(\alpha)}(F_1(t,S_{n-1}) - F_1(t,S_{n-2})) \\ &+ \frac{2\alpha}{(2-\alpha)M(\alpha)} \int_0^t (F_1(\vartheta, S_{n-1}) - F_1(\vartheta, S_{n-2})) d\vartheta, \end{aligned}$$

$$\begin{aligned} p_{2n}(t) &= E_n(t) - E_{n-1}(t) \\ &= \frac{2(1-\alpha)}{(2-\alpha)M(\alpha)}(F_2(t,E_{n-1}) - F_2(t,E_{n-2})) \\ &+ \frac{2\alpha}{(2-\alpha)M(\alpha)} \int_0^t (F_2(\vartheta, E_{n-1}) - F_2(\vartheta, E_{n-2})) d\vartheta, \end{aligned}$$

$$\begin{aligned}
p_{3n}(t) &= I_n(t) - I_{n-1}(t) \\
&= \frac{2(1-\alpha)}{(2-\alpha)M(\alpha)}(F_3(t, I_{n-1}) - F_3(t, I_{n-2})) \\
&\quad + \frac{2\alpha}{(2-\alpha)M(\alpha)} \int_0^t (F_3(\vartheta, I_{n-1}) - F_3(\vartheta, I_{n-2})) d\vartheta, \\
p_{4n}(t) &= H_n(t) - H_{n-1}(t) \\
&= \frac{2(1-\alpha)}{(2-\alpha)M(\alpha)}(F_4(t, H_{n-1}) - F_4(t, H_{n-2})) \\
&\quad + \frac{2\alpha}{(2-\alpha)M(\alpha)} \int_0^t (F_4(\vartheta, H_{n-1}) - F_4(\vartheta, H_{n-2})) d\vartheta, \\
p_{5n}(t) &= R_n(t) - R_{n-1}(t) \\
&= \frac{2(1-\alpha)}{(2-\alpha)M(\alpha)}(F_5(t, R_{n-1}) - F_5(t, R_{n-2})) \\
&\quad + \frac{2\alpha}{(2-\alpha)M(\alpha)} \int_0^t (F_5(\vartheta, R_{n-1}) - F_5(\vartheta, R_{n-2})) d\vartheta, \\
p_{6n}(t) &= V_n(t) - V_{n-1}(t) \\
&= \frac{2(1-\alpha)}{(2-\alpha)M(\alpha)}(F_6(t, V_{n-1}) - F_6(t, V_{n-2})) \\
&\quad + \frac{2\alpha}{(2-\alpha)M(\alpha)} \int_0^t (F_6(\vartheta, V_{n-1}) - F_5(\vartheta, V_{n-2})) d\vartheta,
\end{aligned}$$

with initial conditions

$$S_0(t) = S(0), E_0(t) = E(0), I_0(t) = I(0), H_0(0) = H(0), R_0(0) = R(0) \text{ and } V_0(0) = V(0)$$

Consider q_{1n} and take the norm, we have

$$\begin{aligned}
\|q_{1n}(t)\| &= \|S_n(t) - S_{n-1}(t)\| \\
&= \left\| \frac{2(1-\alpha)}{(2-\alpha)M(\alpha)}(F_1(t, S_{n-1}) - F_1(t, S_{n-2})) \right. \\
&\quad \left. + \frac{2\alpha}{(2-\alpha)M(\alpha)} \int_0^t (F_1(\vartheta, S_{n-1}) - F_1(\vartheta, S_{n-2})) d\vartheta \right\|
\end{aligned}$$

Applying triangular inequality, we have

$$\begin{aligned}
\|p_{1n}(t)\| &= \|S_n(t) - S_{n-1}(t)\| \\
&= \frac{2(1-\alpha)}{(2-\alpha)M(\alpha)} \|F_1(t, S_{n-1}) - F_1(t, S_{n-2})\| \\
&\quad + \frac{2\alpha}{(2-\alpha)M(\alpha)} \left\| \int_0^t (F_1(\vartheta, S_{n-1}) - F_1(\vartheta, S_{n-2})) d\vartheta \right\| \\
&\leq \frac{2(1-\alpha)}{(2-\alpha)M(\alpha)} L_1 \|S_n - S_{n-1}\| \\
&\quad + \frac{2\alpha}{(2-\alpha)M(\alpha)} L_1 \int_0^t \|S_n - S_{n-1}\| d\vartheta.
\end{aligned}$$

This implies

$$\begin{aligned}
\|p_{1n}(t)\| &\leq \frac{2(1-\alpha)}{(2-\alpha)M(\alpha)} L_1 \|p_{1n-1}(t)\| \\
&\quad + \frac{2\alpha}{(2-\alpha)M(\alpha)} L_1 \int_0^t \|p_{1n-1}(t)\| d\vartheta.
\end{aligned}$$

In the same way,

$$\|p_{2n}(t)\| \le \frac{2(1-\alpha)}{(2-\alpha)M(\alpha)}L_2\|p_{2n-1}(t)\| + \frac{2\alpha}{(2-\alpha)M(\alpha)}L_2\int_0^t \|p_{2n-1}(t)\|d\vartheta,$$

$$\|p_{3n}(t)\| \le \frac{2(1-\alpha)}{(2-\alpha)M(\alpha)}L_3\|p_{3n-1}(t)\| + \frac{2\alpha}{(2-\alpha)M(\alpha)}L_3\int_0^t \|p_{3n-1}(t)\|d\vartheta,$$

$$\|p_{4n}(t)\| \le \frac{2(1-\alpha)}{(2-\alpha)M(\alpha)}L_4\|p_{4n-1}(t)\| + \frac{2\alpha}{(2-\alpha)M(\alpha)}L_4\int_0^t \|p_{4n-1}(t)\|d\vartheta,$$

$$\|p_{5n}(t)\| \le \frac{2(1-\alpha)}{(2-\alpha)M(\alpha)}L_5\|p_{5n-1}(t)\| + \frac{2\alpha}{(2-\alpha)M(\alpha)}L_5\int_0^t \|p_{5n-1}(t)\|d\vartheta,$$

$$\|p_{6n}(t)\| \le \frac{2(1-\alpha)}{(2-\alpha)M(\alpha)}L_6\|p_{6n-1}(t)\| + \frac{2\alpha}{(2-\alpha)M(\alpha)}L_6\int_0^t \|p_{6n-1}(t)\|d\vartheta.$$

Hence, we have

$$S_n(t) = \sum_{i=1}^n p_{1i}(t),$$
$$E_n(t) = \sum_{i=1}^n p_{2i}(t),$$
$$I_n(t) = \sum_{i=1}^n p_{3i}(t),$$
$$H_n(t) = \sum_{i=1}^n p_{4i}(t),$$
$$R_n(t) = \sum_{i=1}^n p_{5i}(t),$$
$$V_n(t) = \sum_{i=1}^n p_{6i}(t).$$

The following theorem gives the condition for the existence of the solution:

Theorem 1. *The solution exists if t_1 exists, such that the following inequality is true,*

$$\frac{2(1-\alpha)}{(2-\alpha)M(\alpha)}L_i + \frac{2\alpha t_1}{(2-\alpha)M(\alpha)}L_i < 1, \; i = 1, \ldots, 6$$

Proof. Recursively, we have

$$\|p_{1n}(t)\| \le \|S_n(0)\|\left[\frac{2(1-\alpha)}{(2-\alpha)M(\alpha)}L_1 + \frac{2\alpha}{(2-\alpha)M(\alpha)}L_1\right]^n,$$

$$\|p_{2n}(t)\| \le \|E_n(0)\|\left[\frac{2(1-\alpha)}{(2-\alpha)M(\alpha)}L_2 + \frac{2\alpha}{(2-\alpha)M(\alpha)}L_2\right]^n,$$

$$\|p_{3n}(t)\| \le \|I_n(0)\|\left[\frac{2(1-\alpha)}{(2-\alpha)M(\alpha)}L_3 + \frac{2\alpha}{(2-\alpha)M(\alpha)}L_3\right]^n,$$

$$\|p_{4n}(t)\| \le \|H_n(0)\|\left[\frac{2(1-\alpha)}{(2-\alpha)M(\alpha)}L_4 + \frac{2\alpha}{(2-\alpha)M(\alpha)}L_4\right]^n,$$

$$\|p_{5n}(t)\| \le \|R_n(0)\|\left[\frac{2(1-\alpha)}{(2-\alpha)M(\alpha)}L_5 + \frac{2\alpha}{(2-\alpha)M(\alpha)}L_5\right]^n,$$

$$\|p_{6n}(t)\| \le \|V_n(0)\|\left[\frac{2(1-\alpha)}{(2-\alpha)M(\alpha)}L_6 + \frac{2\alpha}{(2-\alpha)M(\alpha)}L_6\right]^n,$$

□

Hence solutions exist and are continuous. To show that the functions above construct the solutions, consider

$$S(t) - S(0) = S_n(t) - M_{1_n}(t),$$
$$E(t) - E(0) = E_n(t) - M_{2_n}(t),$$
$$I(t) - I(0) = I_n(t) - M_{3_n}(t),$$
$$H(t) - H(0) = H_n(t) - M_{4_n}(t),$$
$$R(t) - R(0) = R_n(t) - M_{5_n}(t).$$
$$V(t) - V(0) = V_n(t) - M_{6_n}(t).$$

Hence,

$$\|M_{1_n}(t)\| = \left\| \frac{2(1-\alpha)}{(2-\alpha)M(\alpha)}(F_1(t, S_{n-1}) - F_1(t, S_{n-2})) + \frac{2\alpha}{(2-\alpha)M(\alpha)} \int_0^t (F_1(\vartheta, S_{n-1}) - F_1(\vartheta, S_{n-2}))d\vartheta \right\|$$
$$\leq \frac{2(1-\alpha)}{(2-\alpha)M(\alpha)} \|F_1(t, S_{n-1}) - F_1(t, S_{n-2})\| + \frac{2\alpha}{(2-\alpha)M(\alpha)} \left\| \int_0^t (F_1(\vartheta, S_{n-1}) - F_1(\vartheta, S_{n-2}))d\vartheta \right\|$$
$$\leq \frac{2(1-\alpha)}{(2-\alpha)M(\alpha)} L_1 \|S - S_{n-1}\| + \frac{2\alpha}{(2-\alpha)M(\alpha)} L_1 \|S - S_{n-1}\| t.$$

Carrying out the procedure, we get

$$\|M_{1_n}(t)\| \leq \left[\frac{2(1-\alpha)}{(2-\alpha)M(\alpha)} + \frac{2\alpha t}{(2-\alpha)M(\alpha)} \right]^{n+1} L_1^{n+1} h.$$

At $t = t_1$, we get

$$\|M_{1_n}(t)\| \leq \left[\frac{2(1-\alpha)}{(2-\alpha)M(\alpha)} + \frac{2\alpha t_1}{(2-\alpha)M(\alpha)} \right]^{n+1} L_1^{n+1} h$$

Taking limit as $n \to \infty$, we get

$$\|M_{1_n}(t)\| \to 0.$$

Similarly, we have

$$\|M_{2_n}(t)\|, \|M_{3_n}(t)\|, \|M_{4_n}(t)\|, \|M_{5_n}(t)\|, \|M_{6_n}(t)\| \to 0.$$

To show uniqueness, assume we have some other solutions, $S^1(t), E^1(t), I^1(t), H^1(t), R^1(t),$ and $V^1(t)$, then

$$\|S(t) - S^1(t)\| \left(1 - \frac{2(1-\alpha)}{(2-\alpha)M(\alpha)} L_1 - \frac{2\alpha t}{(2-\alpha)M(\alpha)} L_1 \right) \leq 0.$$

The completion of the proof is given by the following theorem.

Theorem 2. *If*

$$\left(1 - \frac{2(1-\alpha)}{(2-\alpha)M(\alpha)} L_1 - \frac{2\alpha t}{(2-\alpha)M(\alpha)} L_1 \right) > 0,$$

then the solution is unique.

Proof. Consider

$$\|S(t) - S^1(t)\| \left(1 - \frac{2(1-\alpha)}{(2-\alpha)M(\alpha)} L_1 - \frac{2\alpha t}{(2-\alpha)M(\alpha)} L_1 \right) \leq 0$$

Since,

$$\left(1 - \frac{2(1-\alpha)}{(2-\alpha)M(\alpha)} L_1 - \frac{2\alpha t}{(2-\alpha)M(\alpha)} L_1 \right) > 0,$$

Then
$$\|S(t) - S^1(t)\| = 0$$
Hence,
$$S(t) = S^1(t)$$
□

This is true for the remaining solutions.

4.5. Stability Analysis of the Equilibria

Here, we show the local stability of Disease-free equilibrium (E^0) and Endemic equilibrium (E^1) respectively. For details see [31,32].

Consider the Jacobian matrix obtained from (1), we have

$$J = \begin{bmatrix} -\beta^\alpha I - \theta^\alpha V - \mu^\alpha & 0 & -\beta^\alpha S & 0 & -\theta^\alpha S \\ \beta^\alpha I + \theta^\alpha V & -(\mu^\alpha + \gamma^\alpha + \eta_1^\alpha) & \beta^\alpha S & 0 & \theta^\alpha S \\ 0 & \gamma^\alpha & -(\mu^\alpha + \pi^\alpha + \xi_1^\alpha + \eta_2^\alpha) & 0 & 0 \\ 0 & 0 & \pi^\alpha & -(\mu^\alpha + \xi_2^\alpha + \eta_3^\alpha) & 0 \\ 0 & q_1^\alpha & q_2^\alpha & 0 & -r^\alpha \end{bmatrix}. \quad (3)$$

Theorem 3. *Disease-free equilibrium (E^0) is locally asymptotically stable when $R_0 < 1$.*

Proof. Consider (3) at (E^0), we have

$$J(E^0) = \begin{bmatrix} -\mu^\alpha & 0 & -\beta^\alpha S_0 & 0 & -\theta^\alpha S_0 \\ 0 & -(\mu^\alpha + \gamma^\alpha + \eta_1^\alpha) & \beta^\alpha S_0 & 0 & \theta^\alpha S_0 \\ 0 & \gamma^\alpha & -(\mu^\alpha + \pi^\alpha + \xi_1^\alpha + \eta_2^\alpha) & 0 & 0 \\ 0 & 0 & \pi^\alpha & -(\mu^\alpha + \xi_2^\alpha + \eta_3^\alpha) & 0 \\ 0 & q_1^\alpha & q_2^\alpha & 0 & -r^\alpha \end{bmatrix}.$$

□

The Eigen–values are

$$\lambda_1 = -\mu^\alpha, \ \lambda_2 = -(\mu^\alpha + \eta_3^\alpha + \xi_2^\alpha),$$

λ_3, λ_4 and λ_5 can be found by solving the polynomial equation,

$$\lambda^3 + \lambda^2[(\mu^\alpha + \pi^\alpha + \xi_1^\alpha + \eta_2^\alpha) + (\mu^\alpha + \gamma^\alpha + \eta_1^\alpha) + r^\alpha]$$
$$+ \lambda[(\mu^\alpha + \pi^\alpha + \xi_1^\alpha + \eta_2^\alpha)(\mu^\alpha + \gamma^\alpha + \eta_1^\alpha) + (\mu^\alpha + \pi^\alpha + \xi_1^\alpha + \eta_2^\alpha)r^\alpha$$
$$+ (\mu^\alpha + \gamma^\alpha + \eta_1^\alpha)r^\alpha - q_1^\alpha \theta^\alpha S_0 - \gamma^\alpha \beta^\alpha S_0]$$
$$+ [(\mu^\alpha + \pi^\alpha + \xi_1^\alpha + \eta_2^\alpha)(\mu^\alpha + \gamma^\alpha + \eta_1^\alpha)r^\alpha$$
$$- [(\mu^\alpha + \pi^\alpha + \xi_1^\alpha + \eta_2^\alpha)q_1^\alpha \theta^\alpha S_0 + \gamma^\alpha \beta^\alpha S_0 r^\alpha + \gamma^\alpha \beta^\alpha S_0 q_1^\alpha \theta^\alpha S_0]] = 0.$$

By Routh-Hurwitz criterion, Eigen-values of $f(s) = a_0 s^3 + a_1 s^2 + a_2 s + a_3$, are all negative if $a_1 > 0$, $a_3 > 0$, and $a_1 a_2 > a_3$.

In this case,

$$a_1 = (\mu^\alpha + \pi^\alpha + \xi_1^\alpha + \eta_2^\alpha) + (\mu^\alpha + \gamma^\alpha + \eta_1^\alpha) + r^\alpha > 0,$$
$$a_3 = (\mu^\alpha + \pi^\alpha + \xi_1^\alpha + \eta_2^\alpha)(\mu^\alpha + \gamma^\alpha + \eta_1^\alpha)r^\alpha$$
$$- [(\mu^\alpha + \pi^\alpha + \xi_1^\alpha + \eta_2^\alpha)q_1^\alpha \theta^\alpha S_0 + \gamma^\alpha \beta^\alpha S_0 r^\alpha$$
$$+ \gamma^\alpha \beta^\alpha S_0 q_1^\alpha \theta^\alpha S_0] > 0,$$

if
$$\frac{[(\mu^\alpha + \pi^\alpha + \xi_1^\alpha + \eta_2^\alpha)q_1^\alpha \theta^\alpha S_0 + \gamma^\alpha \beta^\alpha S_0 r^\alpha + \gamma^\alpha \beta^\alpha S_0 q_1^\alpha \theta^\alpha S_0]}{(\mu^\alpha + \pi^\alpha + \xi_1^\alpha + \eta_2^\alpha)(\mu^\alpha + \gamma^\alpha + \eta_1^\alpha)r^\alpha} < 1. a_1 a_2 - a_3 > 0,$$

if
$$\frac{a_3}{a_1 a_2} < 1.$$

In conclusion, all the Eigen-values are negative if $R_0 < 1$.

Theorem 4. *Endemic equilibrium* (E^1) *is locally asymptotically stable when* $R_0 > 1$.

Proof. Consider (3) at (E^1), we have

$$J(E^1) = \begin{bmatrix} -\beta^\alpha I_1 - \theta^\alpha V_1 - \mu^\alpha & 0 & -\beta^\alpha S_1 & 0 & -\theta^\alpha S_1 \\ \beta^\alpha I_1 + \theta^\alpha V_1 & -(\mu^\alpha + \gamma^\alpha + \eta_1^\alpha) & \beta^\alpha S_1 & 0 & \theta^\alpha S_1 \\ 0 & \gamma^\alpha & -(\mu^\alpha + \pi^\alpha + \xi_1^\alpha + \eta_2^\alpha) & 0 & 0 \\ 0 & 0 & \pi^\alpha & -(\mu^\alpha + \xi_2^\alpha + \eta_3^\alpha) & 0 \\ 0 & q_1^\alpha & q_2^\alpha & 0 & -r^\alpha \end{bmatrix}.$$

□

The Eigen values are $\lambda_1 = -(\mu^\alpha + \eta_3^\alpha + \xi_2^\alpha)$, and $\lambda_2, \lambda_3, \lambda_4$ and λ_5 can be found by solving the polynomial equation,

$$\lambda^4 + \lambda^3[(\mu^\alpha + \pi^\alpha + \xi_1^\alpha + \eta_2^\alpha) + (\beta^\alpha I_1 + \theta^\alpha V_1 + \mu^\alpha) + r^\alpha + (\mu^\alpha + \gamma^\alpha \eta_1^\alpha)]$$
$$+ \lambda^2[\beta^\alpha S_1 + (\mu^\alpha + \pi^\alpha + \xi_1^\alpha + \eta_2^\alpha)(\beta^\alpha I_1 + \theta^\alpha V_1 + \mu^\alpha) + (\mu^\alpha + \pi^\alpha + \xi_1^\alpha + \eta_2^\alpha)r^\alpha$$
$$+ (\mu^\alpha + \pi^\alpha + \xi_1^\alpha + \eta_2^\alpha)(\mu^\alpha + \gamma^\alpha \eta_1^\alpha) + (\beta^\alpha I_1 + \theta^\alpha V_1 + \mu^\alpha)\mu^\alpha$$
$$+ (\beta^\alpha I_1 + \theta^\alpha V_1 + \mu^\alpha)(\mu^\alpha + \gamma^\alpha \eta_1^\alpha) + (\mu^\alpha + \gamma^\alpha \eta_1^\alpha)r^\alpha - ((\mu^\alpha + \xi_2^\alpha + \eta_3^\alpha)\theta^\alpha S_1)]$$
$$+ \lambda[\beta^\alpha S_1 r^\alpha + \beta^\alpha S_1(\beta^\alpha I_1 + \theta^\alpha V_1 + \mu^\alpha)$$
$$+ (\mu^\alpha + \pi^\alpha + \xi_1^\alpha + \eta_2^\alpha)(\beta^\alpha I_1 + \theta^\alpha V_1 + \mu^\alpha)(r^\alpha + (\mu^\alpha + \gamma^\alpha \eta_1^\alpha))$$
$$+ r^\alpha(\mu^\alpha + \gamma^\alpha \eta_1^\alpha)((\mu^\alpha + \pi^\alpha + \xi_1^\alpha + \eta_2^\alpha) + (\beta^\alpha I_1 + \theta^\alpha V_1 + \mu^\alpha))$$
$$+ (\mu^\alpha + \xi_2^\alpha + \eta_3^\alpha)\theta^\alpha S_1 \beta^\alpha I_1 + \theta^\alpha V_1)$$
$$- (\gamma^\alpha q_2^\alpha \theta^\alpha S_1 + \beta^\alpha S_1(\beta^\alpha I_1 + \theta^\alpha V_1) + (\mu^\alpha + \pi^\alpha + \xi_1^\alpha + \eta_2^\alpha)\theta^\alpha S_1(\mu^\alpha + \xi_2^\alpha + \eta_3^\alpha)$$
$$+ \theta^\alpha S_1(\mu^\alpha + \xi_2^\alpha + \eta_3^\alpha)(\beta^\alpha I_1 + \theta^\alpha V_1 + \mu^\alpha))]$$
$$+ [\gamma^\alpha q_2^\alpha \theta^\alpha S_1(\beta^\alpha I_1 + \theta^\alpha V_1) + r^\alpha \beta^\alpha S_1(\beta^\alpha I_1 + \theta^\alpha V_1 + \mu^\alpha)$$
$$+ (\beta^\alpha I_1 + \theta^\alpha V_1 + \mu^\alpha)(\mu^\alpha + \pi^\alpha + \xi_1^\alpha + \eta_2^\alpha)r^\alpha(\mu^\alpha + \gamma^\alpha + \eta_1^\alpha)$$
$$+ (\mu^\alpha + \pi^\alpha + \xi_1^\alpha + \eta_2^\alpha)\theta^\alpha S_1(\mu^\alpha + \xi_2^\alpha + \eta_3^\alpha)(\beta^\alpha I_1 + \theta^\alpha V_1)$$
$$- [(\mu^\alpha + \pi^\alpha + \xi_1^\alpha + \eta_2^\alpha)\theta^\alpha S_1(\mu^\alpha + \xi_2^\alpha + \eta_3^\alpha)(\beta^\alpha I_1 + \theta^\alpha V_1 + \mu^\alpha)$$
$$+ r^\alpha \beta^\alpha S_1(\beta^\alpha I_1 + \theta^\alpha V_1) + \gamma^\alpha q_2^\alpha \theta^\alpha S_1(\beta^\alpha I_1 + \theta^\alpha V_1 + \mu^\alpha)]] = 0$$

By the Routh-Hurwitz stability criterion, the remaining Eigen values of $f(s) = a_0 s^4 + a_1 s^3 + a_2 s^2 + a_3 s + a_4$, are all negative if

$$a_1 > 0, \ a_3 > 0, \ a_4 > 0, \ \text{and} \ a_1 a_2 a_3 - a_3^2 + a_1^2 a_4 > 0$$

Clearly, all the Eigen-values are negative if $R_0 > 1$.

5. Optimal Control Analysis

The formation and analysis of optimal control function is given in this chapter.

5.1. Formation of Optimal Control Problem

The dynamics of the control system can be described by the following system of Fractional order differential equation in the Caputo sense

$$\begin{aligned}
{}^C_0D^\alpha_t S(t) &= \Upsilon^\alpha - \beta^\alpha SI - \theta^\alpha SV - \mu^\alpha S + \varnothing uV, \\
{}^C_0D^\alpha_t E(t) &= \beta^\alpha SI + \theta^\alpha SV - (\mu^\alpha + \gamma^\alpha + \eta_1^\alpha)E, \\
{}^C_0D^\alpha_t I &= \gamma^\alpha E - (\mu^\alpha + \pi^\alpha + \zeta_1^\alpha + \eta_2^\alpha)I, \\
{}^C_0D^\alpha_t H &= \pi^\alpha I - (\mu^\alpha + \zeta_2^\alpha + \eta_3^\alpha)H, \\
{}^C_0D^\alpha_t R(t) &= \eta_1^\alpha E + \eta_2^\alpha I + \eta_3^\alpha H - \mu^\alpha R, \\
{}^C_0D^\alpha_t V(t) &= q_1^\alpha E + q_2^\alpha I - r^\alpha V - \varnothing uV,
\end{aligned} \quad (4)$$

where $u =$ is the observation of standard hygiene practices and chemical disinfectants in public spaces.

The objective function to be minimized is given as:

$$J(u) = \int_0^{t_f} (aV + bu^2) dt, \quad (5)$$

The objective here is minimizing V at the same time to minimize the cost of the control u. Hence, we need to get the optimal control u^* such that:

$$J(u^*) = \min_u \{J(u) | u \in \Omega\}. \quad (6)$$

The set containing control is:

$$\Omega = \left\{ u : [0, t_f] \to [0, \infty) \text{ Lebesgue measurable} \right\}.$$

The expense of minimizing V is represented by the term aV. Likewise, all the expenses associated with the control u is represented by bu^2. The sufficient conditions required for the optimal control to be fulfilled can be found by using the most popular PMP. The said principle can be used to turn Equations (3) and (5) into a point-wise minimizing problem of the Hamiltonian H with respect to u as stated below:

$$H = aV + bu^2 + \lambda \{q_1^\alpha E + q_2^\alpha I - r^\alpha V - \varnothing uV\} \quad (7)$$

where λ is the adjoint variable or co-state variable.

$$-\frac{d\lambda}{dt} = \frac{\partial H}{\partial V} = a + \lambda\{-r^\alpha - \varnothing u\} \quad (8)$$

The transversality condition is $\lambda(t_f) = 0$, for $0 < u < 1$.
From the interior of the control, we have:

$$\frac{\partial H}{\partial u} = 2bu - \lambda \varnothing V = 0 \quad (9)$$

from where

$$u^* = \frac{1}{2b} \lambda \varnothing V \quad (10)$$

5.2. Existence of Optimal Solutions

For the existence of the optimal control, we give the following theorem

Theorem 5. *The control values u^* which can minimize $J(u)$ over U are given by,*

$$u^* = \max\left\{0, \min\left[1, \frac{1}{2b}\lambda\varnothing V\right]\right\}, \quad (11)$$

where

$$u^* = \begin{cases} 0, & if\ u \leq 0, \\ u, & if\ 0 < u < 1 \\ 1, & if\ u \geq 0. \end{cases} \quad (12)$$

Proof. To prove the existence of the optimal control solution, we use the convexity of the integrand of J with respect to control u for the boundedness of the solutions and the Lipschitz property of the system of the state with respect to the variables of the state. Hence, we apply PMP and get the following:

$$^C_0 D^\alpha_t \lambda_S(t) = \frac{\partial H}{\partial S} \quad (13)$$

with $\lambda_S(t_f) = 0$. □

We can obtain the conditions for the optimality by differentiating the Hamiltonian H with respect to u:

$$\frac{\partial H}{\partial u} = 0 \quad (14)$$

The adjoint System (7) and (8) comes from the solution of Equation (4) and the optimal controls Equation (10) can be gotten from Equation (11). The optimal system comprises the controlled System (4) and its initial conditions, System of adjoint (7) and conditions for transversality.

6. Numerical Scheme and Numerical Simulation and Discussions

Here, the method proposed in [33] is reviewed. Consider the proposed algorithm using the following initial value problem (IVP):

$$^C_0 D^\alpha_t(y(t)) = f(t, u(t)),\ 0 < \alpha < 1,\ t \in [0, T]\ y^k(a) = y^k_0. \quad (15)$$

The above IVP is equivalent to the following Volterra integral equation:

$$y(t) = u(t) + \frac{\rho^{1-\alpha}}{\Gamma(\alpha)} \int_0^t (s)^{\rho-1}(t^\rho - s^\rho)^{\alpha-1} ds$$

where

$$u(t) = \sum_{n=0}^{m-1} \frac{1}{\rho^n n!}(t^\rho - a^\rho)^n \left[\left(x^{1-\rho}\frac{d}{dx}\right)^n y(x)\right]_{x=a}.$$

First, we assume that the solution exists on the interval $[a, T]$. Using the mesh points we divide $[a, T]$ into n subintervals equally $[t_k, t_{k+1}]$, where $k = 0, 1, \ldots, N-1$,

$$t_0 = a,\ t_{k+1} = \left(t^p_k + h\right)^{\frac{1}{p}},\ k = 0, 1, 2, \ldots, N-1,$$

and $h = \dfrac{(T^p - a^p)}{N}$. To solve (15) numerically, we generate the approximations y_k, $k = 0, 1, \ldots, N$. By means of the following integral equation and by assuming we already get the approximation $y_i \approx y(t_j)$, $j = 1, 2, \ldots, k$, we want to approximate $y_k \approx y(t_{k+1})$. The integral equation is given as

$$y(t_{k+1}) = u(t_{k+1}) + \frac{\rho^{-\alpha}}{\Gamma(\alpha)} \int_a^{t_{k+1}} (s)^{\rho-1} \left(t_{k+1}^\rho - s^\rho\right)^{\alpha-1} f(s, y(s)) ds$$

Substituting $z = (s)^\rho$, we have

$$y(t_{k+1}) = u(t_{k+1}) + \frac{\rho^{-\alpha}}{\Gamma(\alpha)} \int_a^{t_{k+1}^\rho} \left(t_{k+1}^\rho - z\right)^{\alpha-1} f\left(z^{\frac{1}{\rho}}, y\left(z^{\frac{1}{\rho}}\right)\right) dz,$$

equivalently,

$$y(t_{k+1}) = u(t_{k+1}) + \frac{\rho^{-\alpha}}{\Gamma(\alpha)} \sum_{j=0}^{k} \int_{t_j^\rho}^{t_{j+1}^\rho} \left(t_{k+1}^\rho - z\right)^{\alpha-1} f\left(z^{\frac{1}{\rho}}, y\left(z^{\frac{1}{\rho}}\right)\right) dz. \quad (16)$$

We then use the Trapezoidal quadrature rule by considering the weight function $\left(t_{k+1}^\rho - z\right)^{\alpha-1}$ to approximate the above integral. Using t_j^ρ ($j = 0, 1, \ldots, k+1$) to replace $f\left(z^{\frac{1}{\rho}}, y\left(z^{\frac{1}{\rho}}\right)\right)$, we get

$$\int_{t_j^\rho}^{t_{j+1}^\rho} \left(t_{k+1}^\rho - z\right)^{\alpha-1} f\left(z^{\frac{1}{\rho}}, y\left(z^{\frac{1}{\rho}}\right)\right) dz$$
$$\approx \frac{h^\alpha}{\alpha(\alpha+1)} [((k-j)^{\alpha+1}$$
$$- (k-j-\alpha)(k-j+1)^\alpha) f(t_j, y(t_j))$$
$$+ ((k-j+1)^{\alpha+1}$$
$$- (k-j-\alpha+1)(k-j)^\alpha) f(t_{j+1}, y(t_{j+1}))]$$

Substituting the integral into Equation (16), we obtain the following as the corrector formula:

$$y(t_{k+1}) \approx u(t_{k+1}) + \frac{\rho^{-\alpha}}{\Gamma(\alpha+2)} \sum_{j=0}^{k} a_{j,k+1} f(t_j, y(t_j)) + \frac{\rho^{-\alpha} h^\alpha}{\Gamma(\alpha+2)} f(t_{j+1}, y(t_{j+1})) \quad (17)$$

where

$$a_{j,k+1} = \begin{cases} k^{\alpha+1} - (k-\alpha)(k+1)^\alpha & \text{for } j = 0 \\ (k-j+2)^{\alpha+1} + (k-j)^{\alpha+1} - 2(k-j+1)^{\alpha+1} & \text{for } 1 \leq j < k. \end{cases}$$

Now, substituting $y(t_{k+1})$ with $y^p(t_{k+1})$ obtained by applying the one step Adams-Bashforth method and also substituting $f\left(z^{\frac{1}{\rho}}, y\left(z^{\frac{1}{\rho}}\right)\right)$ with $f(t_j, y(t_j))$, we obtain

$$y^p(t_{k+1}) \approx u(t_{k+1}) + \frac{\rho^{-\alpha} h^\alpha}{\Gamma(\alpha+1)} \sum_{j=0}^{k} \left[(k+1-j)^\alpha - (k-j)^\alpha\right] f(t_j, y(t_j)) \quad (18)$$

Hence, the predictor-corrector method is given as

$$y_{k+1} \approx u(t_{k+1}) + \frac{\rho^{-\alpha} h^\alpha}{\Gamma(\alpha+2)} \sum_{j=0}^{k} a_{j,k+1} f(t_j, y(t_j)) + \frac{\rho^{-\alpha} h^\alpha}{\Gamma(\alpha+2)} f\left(t_{k+1}, y_{k+1}^p\right).$$

To implement the above scheme, we solve Equation (1) numerically. The approximations $S_{k+1}, E_{k+1}, I_{k+1}, H_{k+1}, R_{k+1}, V_{k+1}$ can simply be obtained using the iterative formulas above for $N \in \mathbb{N}$ and $T > 0$,

$$S_{k+1} = S_0 + \frac{\rho^{-\alpha} h^\alpha}{\Gamma(\alpha+2)} \sum_{j=0}^{k} a_{j,k+1} [Y^\alpha - \beta^\alpha S_j I_j - \theta^\alpha S_j V_j - \mu^\alpha S_j]$$
$$+ \frac{\rho^{-\alpha} h^\alpha}{\Gamma(\alpha+2)} [Y^\alpha - \beta^\alpha S_{k+1} I_{k+1} - \theta^\alpha S_{k+1} V_{k+1} - \mu^\alpha S_{k+1}]$$

$$E_{k+1} = E_0 + \frac{\rho^{-\alpha} h^\alpha}{\Gamma(\alpha+2)} \sum_{j=0}^{k} a_{j,k+1} [\beta^\alpha S_j I_j + \theta^\alpha S_j V_j - (\mu^\alpha + \gamma^\alpha + \eta_1^\alpha) E_j]$$
$$+ \frac{\rho^{-\alpha} h^\alpha}{\Gamma(\alpha+2)} [\beta^\alpha S_{k+1} I_{k+1} + \theta^\alpha S_{k+1} V_{k+1} - (\mu^\alpha + \gamma^\alpha + \eta_1^\alpha) E_{k+1}],$$

$$I_{k+1} = I_0 + \frac{\rho^{-\alpha} h^\alpha}{\Gamma(\alpha+2)} \sum_{j=0}^{k} a_{j,k+1} [\gamma^\alpha E_j - (\mu^\alpha + \pi^\alpha + \xi_1^\alpha + \eta_2^\alpha) I_j]$$
$$+ \frac{\rho^{-\alpha} h^\alpha}{\Gamma(\alpha+2)} [\gamma^\alpha E_{k+1} - (\mu^\alpha + \pi^\alpha + \xi_1^\alpha + \eta_2^\alpha) I_{k+1}],$$

$$H_{k+1} = H_0 + \frac{\rho^{-\alpha} h^\alpha}{\Gamma(\alpha+2)} \sum_{j=0}^{k} a_{j,k+1} [\pi^\alpha I_j - (\mu^\alpha + \xi_2^\alpha + \eta_3^\alpha) H_j]$$
$$+ \frac{\rho^{-\alpha} h^\alpha}{\Gamma(\alpha+2)} [\pi^\alpha I_{k+1} - (\mu^\alpha + \xi_2^\alpha + \eta_3^\alpha) H_{k+1}],$$

$$R_{k+1} = R_0 + \frac{\rho^{-\alpha} h^\alpha}{\Gamma(\alpha+2)} \sum_{j=0}^{k} a_{j,k+1} [\eta_1^\alpha E_j + \eta_2^\alpha I_j + \eta_3^\alpha H_j - \mu^\alpha R_j]$$
$$+ \frac{\rho^{-\alpha} h^\alpha}{\Gamma(\alpha+2)} [\eta_1^\alpha E_{k+1} + \eta_2^\alpha I_{k+1} + \eta_3^\alpha H_{k+1} - \mu^\alpha R_{k+1}],$$

$$V_{k+1} = V_0 + \frac{\rho^{-\alpha} h^\alpha}{\Gamma(\alpha+2)} \sum_{j=0}^{k} a_{j,k+1} [q_1{}^\alpha E_j + q_2{}^\alpha I_j - r^\alpha V_j]$$
$$+ \frac{\rho^{-\alpha} h^\alpha}{\Gamma(\alpha+2)} [q_1{}^\alpha E_{k+1} + q_2{}^\alpha I_{k+1} - r^\alpha V_{k+1}].$$

where $h = \frac{T^p}{N}$ and

$$S_{k+1}^p \approx S_0 + \frac{\rho^{-\alpha} h^\alpha}{\Gamma(\alpha+1)} \sum_{j=0}^{k} [(k+1-j)^\alpha - (k-j)^\alpha] [Y^\alpha - \beta^\alpha S_j I_j - \theta^\alpha S_j V_j - \mu^\alpha S_j]$$

$$E_{k+1}^p \approx E_0 + \frac{\rho^{-\alpha} h^\alpha}{\Gamma(\alpha+1)} \sum_{j=0}^{k} [(k+1-j)^\alpha - (k-j)^\alpha] [\beta^\alpha S_j I_j + \theta^\alpha S_j V_j - (\mu^\alpha + \gamma^\alpha + \eta_1^\alpha) E_j],$$

$$I_{k+1}^p \approx I_0 + \frac{\rho^{-\alpha} h^\alpha}{\Gamma(\alpha+1)} \sum_{j=0}^{k} [(k+1-j)^\alpha - (k-j)^\alpha] [\gamma^\alpha E_j - (\mu^\alpha + \pi^\alpha + \xi_1^\alpha + \eta_2^\alpha) I_j],$$

$$H^p_{k+1} \approx H_0 + \frac{\rho^{-\alpha} h^\alpha}{\Gamma(\alpha+1)} \sum_{j=0}^{k} \left[(k+1-j)^\alpha - (k-j)^\alpha\right] \left[\pi^\alpha I_j - (\mu^\alpha + \xi_2^\alpha + \eta_3^\alpha) H_j\right],$$

$$R^p_{k+1} \approx R_0 + \frac{\rho^{-\alpha} h^\alpha}{\Gamma(\alpha+1)} \sum_{j=0}^{k} \left[(k+1-j)^\alpha - (k-j)^\alpha\right] \left[\eta_1^\alpha E_j + \eta_2^\alpha I_j + \eta_3^\alpha H_j - \mu^\alpha R_j\right],$$

$$V^p_{k+1} \approx V_0 + \frac{\rho^{-\alpha} h^\alpha}{\Gamma(\alpha+1)} \sum_{j=0}^{k} \left[(k+1-j)^\alpha - (k-j)^\alpha\right] \left[q_1^\alpha E_j + q_2^\alpha I_j - r^\alpha V_j\right].$$

For the numerical simulation, we use the following parameter values from [28]; $Y = 130$, $\beta = 0.11$, $\theta = 0.025$, $\mu = 0.0395$, $\gamma = 0.0689$, $\eta_1 = 0.157$, $\eta_2 = 0.098$, $\eta_3 = 0.0714$, $\pi = 0.009$, $\xi_1 = 0.015$, $\xi_2 = 0.015$, $q_1 = 0.001$, $q_2 = 0.000398$, $r = 0.06$, $\alpha \in (0,1]$.

Figure 1 depicts the dynamics of the model. It can clearly be seen that, without shedding effect control, the susceptible populations all go to extinction, whereas infected exposed populations and viral populations proliferate. This clearly shows the need for the application of shedding effect control measures to control the pandemic.

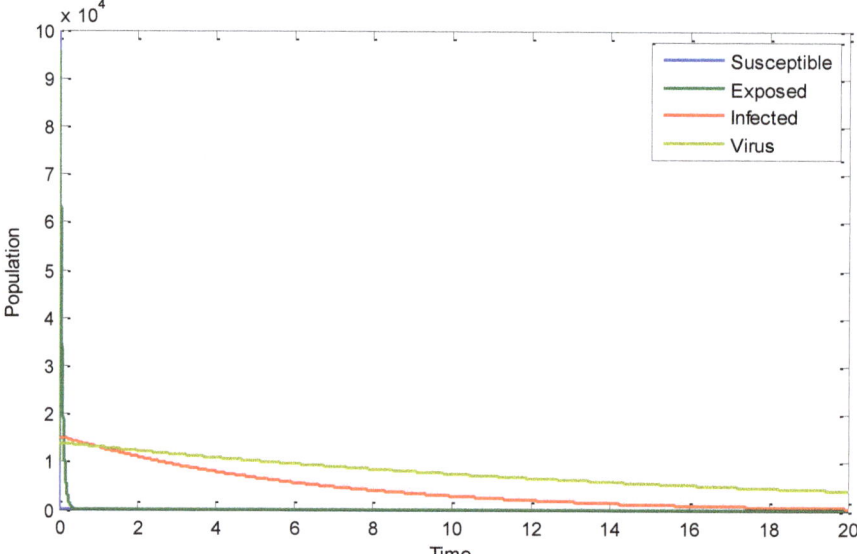

Figure 1. Dynamics of the model.

Figure 2 shows the extinction of the variation susceptible population. This means if no control of the shedding effect is observed, subsequently all people in the population will become infected.

From Figure 3, it can be observed that application of shedding effect control increases the susceptible population. It is clear that there may be a decrease in the population which can be attributed to direct infection of the disease, but the control prevents the population from extinction.

Figure 4 compares the exposed population with and without shedding effect control. It can clearly be seen that application of the control measure has a positive effect on the exposed class as it minimizes it. The proliferation of the disease can be attributed to the direct infection.

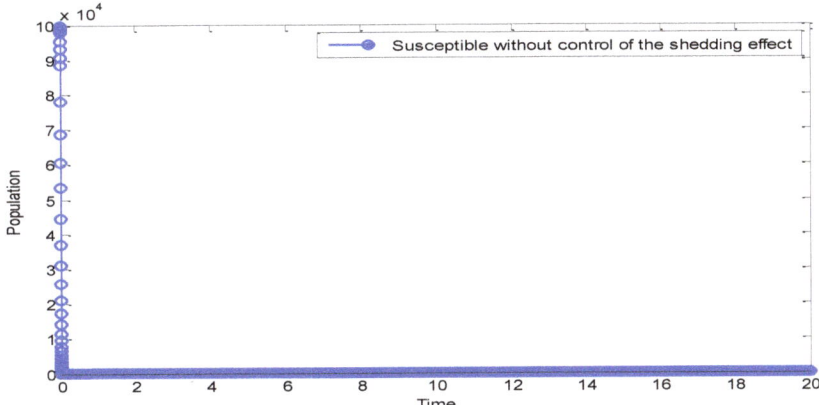

Figure 2. Dynamics of susceptible population without control.

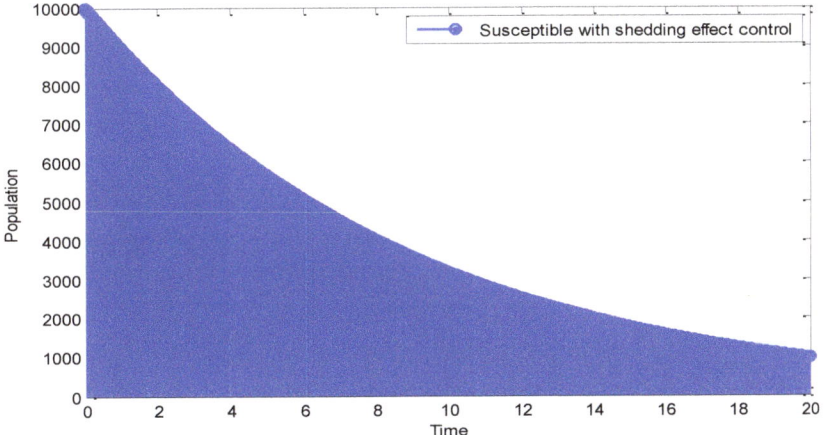

Figure 3. Dynamics of susceptible population with control.

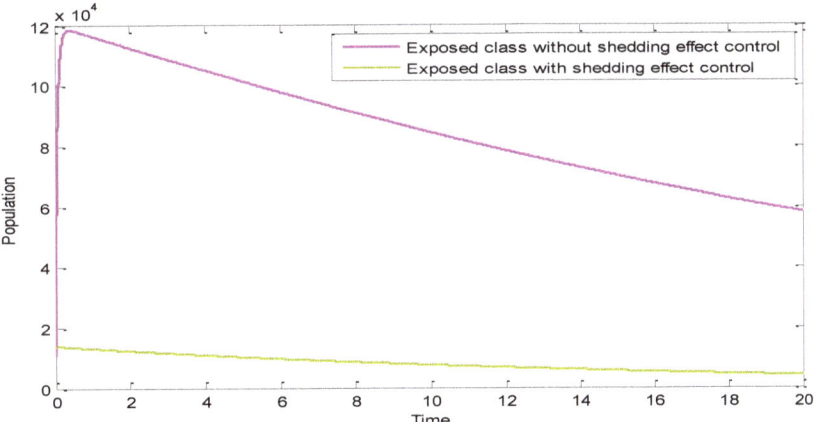

Figure 4. Comparing the dynamics of exposed population with and without control.

Figure 5 compares the infected population with and without shedding effect control. It can clearly be seen that application of the control measure has a positive effect on the infected class as it minimizes it. The proliferation of the disease can be attributed to the direct infection.

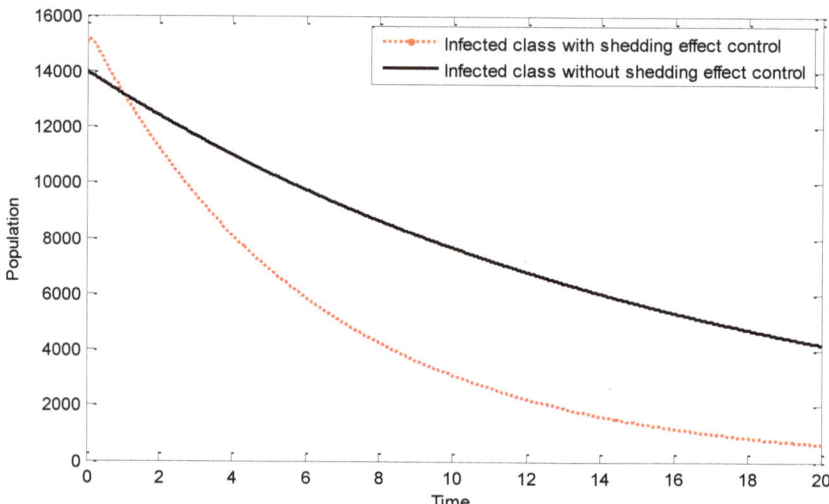

Figure 5. Comparing the dynamics of infected population with and without control.

Figure 6 shows the influence of the variation in the fractional-order α on the biological behavior of the infected population. It is clear from this Figure that the population has a decreasing effect when α is increased from 0.2 to 1. Hence, the memory effect can be seen clearly.

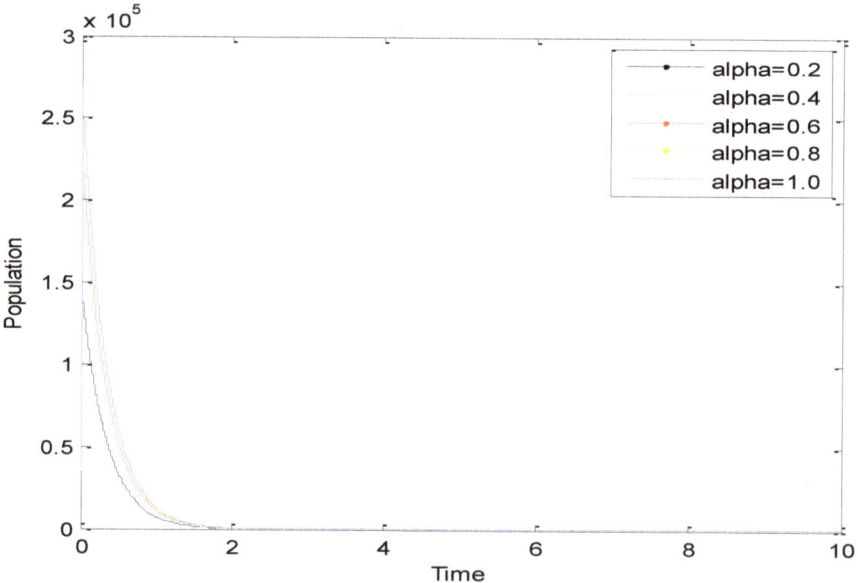

Figure 6. Dynamics of infected population for various values of α.

Daily infected cases for Nigeria are used to fit the model. The data are collected from daily new infected cases for Nigeria from 30 January 2020 to 10 April 2020, which is available at the WHO website [34]. Some parameter values were estimated to give the best fit for the model. We fit the curve for daily confirmed cases in Figure 7.

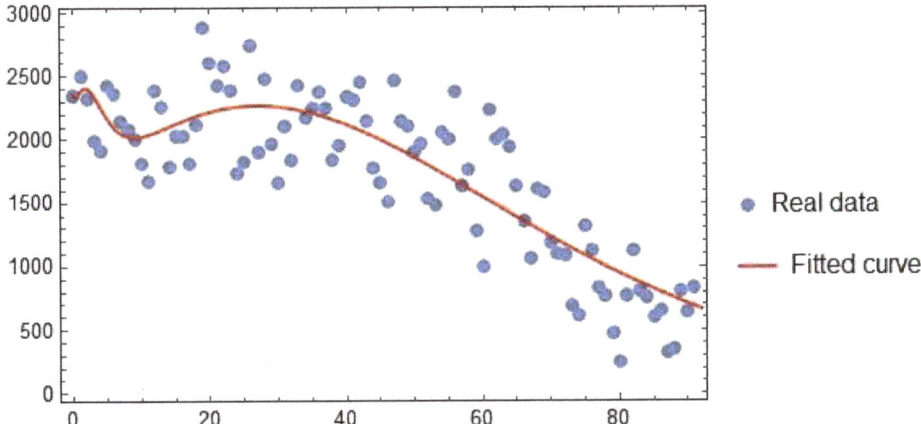

Figure 7. Model fitting using the real data.

To disclose the plenary scenario of the error analysis, a tabular exposure of the statistical ingredients of error analysis, including minimum value, maximum value, average, and standard deviation (SD) of the relative errors (RE), is provided in Table 2.

Table 2. Error Analysis of the data prediction for the Infected population.

Minimum Value of RE (%)	Maximum Value of RE (%)	Average RE (%)	SD of RE (%)
0.064410718	5.380764019	1.623503267	1.386483902

From the table the error indicated that the result demonstrated better validation of the model in comparison with real data.

7. Summary and Conclusions

This work consists of the transmission dynamics of COVID-19 represented using a fractional order SIR model in the Caputo sense. The model integrates the indirect mode of transmission of COVID-19 which is caused as a result of shedding effect. The indirect mode of transmission of the virus through shedding is an essential factor that needs to be studied. Equilibrium solutions, basic reproduction ratio (that depends both on direct and indirect mode of transmission), existence and uniqueness of the solution of the model and their stabilities were studied. The paper studied the effect of optimal control policy applied to shedding effect. The control is the observation of standard hygiene practices and chemical disinfectants in public spaces. Numerical simulations were carried out and the significance of the fractional order from the biological point of view was established. By applying shedding effect control, it was clear that while the population of susceptible individuals is increased, the populations of exposed and infected individuals are drastically decreased.

The public must follow the government rules or public health care policies to mitigate the spread of the virus. The limitation of this work lies in the absence of more reliable data. This is because more accurate data is needed to obtain better prediction.

We recommend that the fractal approach be used in future to consider the analysis of the model.

Author Contributions: Conceptualization, I.A.B., U.W.H., F.A.R. and J.E.N.V.; methodology, I.A.B.; software, F.A.R.; validation, I.A.B., U.W.H., F.A.R. and J.E.N.V.; formal analysis, I.A.B., U.W.H., F.A.R. and J.E.N.V.; investigation, F.A.R. and J.E.N.V.; resources, U.W.H.; data curation, I.A.B. and F.A.R.; writing—original draft preparation, I.A.B.; writing—review and editing, I.A.B., U.W.H., F.A.R. and J.E.N.V.; visualization, U.W.H., F.A.R. and J.E.N.V.; supervision, U.W.H.; project administration, F.A.R.; funding acquisition, U.W.H. All authors have read and agreed to the published version of the manuscript.

Funding: This research received no external funding.

Informed Consent Statement: Not applicable.

Data Availability Statement: Data is available on request.

Acknowledgments: This research was supported by King Mongkut's University of Science and Technology Thonburi's Postdoctoral Fellowship.

Conflicts of Interest: The authors declare no conflict of interest.

References

1. Al-Sheikh, S.; Musali, F.; Alsolami, M. Stability Analysis of an HIV/AIDS Epidemic model with screening. *Int. Math. Forum* **2011**, *6*, 3251–3273.
2. Owolabi, K.M.; Atangana, A. Mathematical analysis and computational experiments for an epidemic system with nonlocal and nonsingular derivative. *Chaos Solitons Fractals* **2019**, *126*, 41–49. [CrossRef]
3. Do, T.S.; Lee, Y.S. Modeling the Spread of Ebola. *Osong Public Health Res. Perspect.* **2016**, *7*, 43–48. [CrossRef]
4. Chowell, D.; Chavez, C.C.; Krishna, S.X.; Qiu, K.; Anderson, S. Modelling the effect of early detection of Ebola. *Lancet. Infect. Dis.* **2015**, *15*, 148–149. [CrossRef]
5. Liu, Z.; Magal, P.; Seydi, O.; Webb, G. Predicting the cumulative number of cases for the COVID-19 epidemic in China from early data. *Math. Biosci. Eng.* **2020**, *17*, 3040–3051. [CrossRef] [PubMed]
6. Chen, T.M.; Rui, J.; Wang, Q.P.; Zhao, Z.Y.; Cui, J.A.; Yin, L. A mathematical model for simulating the phase—Based transmissibility of a novel coronavirus. *Infect. Dis. Poverty* **2020**, *9*, 24. [CrossRef]
7. Khan, M.A.; Atangana, A. Modeling the dynamics of novel coronavirus (2019-nCov) with fractional derivative. *Alex. Eng. J.* **2020**, *59*, 2379–2389. [CrossRef]
8. Ivorra, B.; Ferrandez, M.R.; Vela-Perez, M.; Ramos, A.M. Mathematical modeling of the spread of the coronavirus disease 2019, (COVID-19) considering its particular characteristics: The case of China. *MOMAT* **2020**, *88*, 105303.
9. Zamir, M.; Nadeem, F.; Abdeljawad, T.; Hammouch, Z. Threshold condition and non pharmaceutical interventions's control strategies for elimination of COVID-19. *Res. Phys.* **2020**, *20*, 103698. [CrossRef]
10. Report of the WHO-China Joint Mission on Coronavirus Disease 2019 (COVID-19). Available online: https://www.who.int/china/news/detail/09-01-2020 (accessed on 10 November 2022).
11. Becerra, V.M. Optimal control. *Scholarpedia* **2008**, *3*, 5354. [CrossRef]
12. Jajarmi, A.; Ghanbari, B.; Baleanu, D. A new efficient numerical method for the fractional modeling and optimal control of diabetes and tuberculosis co-existence. *CHAOS* **2019**, *29*, 093111. [CrossRef] [PubMed]
13. Baleanu, D.; Jajarmi, A.; Sajjadi, S.S. A new fractional model and optimal control of a tumor-immune surveillance with non-singular derivative operator. *CHAOS* **2019**, *29*, 083127. [CrossRef] [PubMed]
14. Sweilam, N.H.; Al-Mekhlafi, S.M.; Baleanu, D. Optimal control for a fractional tuberculosis infection model including the impact of diabetes and resistant strains. *J. Adv. Res.* **2019**, *17*, 125–137. [CrossRef] [PubMed]
15. Akman, Y.T.; Arshad, S.; Baleanu, D. New observations on optimal cancer treatments for a fractional tumor growth model with and without singular kernel. *Chaos Solitons Fractals* **2018**, *117*, 226–239. [CrossRef]
16. Akman, Y.T.; Arshad, S.; Baleanu, D. Optimal chemotherapy and immunotherapy schedules for a cancer obesity model with caputo time fractional derivative. *Math. Methods Appl. Sci.* **2018**, *18*, 9390–9407. [CrossRef]
17. Baleanu, D.; Joseph, C.; Mophou, G. Low-regret control for a fractional wave equation with incomplete data. *Adv. Differ. Equ.* **2016**, *2016*, 240. [CrossRef]
18. Baba, I.A.; Abdulkadir, R.A.; Esmaili, P. Analysis of tuberculosis model with saturated incidence rate and optimal control. *Phys. A Stat. Mech. Its Appl.* **2019**, *540*, 123237. [CrossRef]
19. Martnez, J.E.E.; Aguilar, J.F.G.; Ramn, C.C.; Melndez, A.A.; Longoria, P.P. Synchronized bioluminescence behavior of a set of fireflies involving fractional operators of LiouvilleCaputo type. *Int. J. Biomath.* **2018**, *11*, 1850041. [CrossRef]

20. Martnez, J.E.E.; Aguilar, J.F.G.; Ramn, C.C.; Melndez, A.A.; Longoria, P.P. A mathematical model of circadian rhythms synchronization using fractional differential equations system of coupled van der Pol oscillators. *Int. J. Biomath.* **2018**, *11*, 1850014. [CrossRef]
21. Ullah, S.; Khan, M.A.; Farooq, M. A fractional model for the dynamics of TB virus. *Chaos Solitons Fractals* **2018**, *116*, 63–71. [CrossRef]
22. Aguilar, J.F.G. Fundamental solutions to electrical circuits of non-integer order via fractional derivatives with and without singular kernels. *Eur. Phys. J. Plus* **2018**, *133*, 197. [CrossRef]
23. Ahmad, S.; Ullah, A.; Al-Mdallal, Q.M.; Khan, H.; Shah, K.; Khan, A. Fractional order mathematical modeling of COVID-19 transmission. *Chaos Solitons Fractals* **2020**, *139*, 110256. [CrossRef] [PubMed]
24. Higazy, M. Novel fractional order SIDARTHE mathematical model of COVID-19 pandemic. *Chaos Solitons Fractals* **2020**, *138*, 110007. [CrossRef] [PubMed]
25. Gao, G.H.; Sun, Z.Z.; Zhang, H.W. A new fractional numerical differentiation formula to approximate the Caputo fractional derivative and its applications. *J. Comput. Phys.* **2014**, *259*, 33–50. [CrossRef]
26. Rabei, E.M.; Almayteh, I.; Muslih, S.I.; Baleanu, D. Hamilton–Jacobi formulation of systems within Caputo's fractional derivative. *Phys. Scr.* **2007**, *77*, 015101. [CrossRef]
27. Bonyah, E.; Atangana, A.; Khan, M.A. Modeling the spread of computer virus via Caputo fractional derivative and the beta-derivative. *Asia Pac. J. Comput. Eng.* **2017**, *4*, 1. [CrossRef]
28. Abdeljawad, T.; Baleanu, D. On fractional derivatives with exponential kernel and their discrete versions. *J. Rep. Math. Phy.* **2017**, *80*, 11–27. [CrossRef]
29. Atangana, A.; Gómez-Aguilar, J.F. Decolonisation of fractional calculus rules: Breaking commutativity and associativity to capture more natural phenomena. *Eur. Phys. J. Plus* **2018**, *133*, 166. [CrossRef]
30. Singh, A.; Deolia, P. COVID-19 outbreak: A predictive mathematical study incorporating shedding effect. *J. Appl. Math. Comput.* **2022**, *69*, 1239–1268. [CrossRef]
31. Caputo, M.; Fabrizio, M. A new definition of fractional derivative without singular kernel. *Prog. Fract. Differ. Appl.* **2015**, *1*, 73–85.
32. De Oliveira, E.C.; Tenreiro Machado, J.A. A review of definitions for fractional derivatives and integral. *Math. Probl. Eng.* **2014**, *2014*, 238459. [CrossRef]
33. Odibat, Z.; Baleanu, D. Numerical simulation of initial value problems with generalized Caputo-type fractional derivatives. *Appl. Numer. Math.* **2020**, *156*, 94–110. [CrossRef]
34. World Health Organization (WHO) Situation Report. (30 January 2020–30 April 2020). Available online: http://www.who.int (accessed on 1 December 2022).

Disclaimer/Publisher's Note: The statements, opinions and data contained in all publications are solely those of the individual author(s) and contributor(s) and not of MDPI and/or the editor(s). MDPI and/or the editor(s) disclaim responsibility for any injury to people or property resulting from any ideas, methods, instructions or products referred to in the content.

Article

Fractional Step Scheme to Approximate a Non-Linear Second-Order Reaction–Diffusion Problem with Inhomogeneous Dynamic Boundary Conditions

Constantin Fetecău [1] and Costică Moroşanu [2,*]

[1] Academy of Romanian Scientists, 54 Splaiul Independentei, 050094 Bucharest, Romania
[2] Department of Mathematics, "Alexandru Ioan Cuza" University, Bd. Carol I, 11, 700506 Iaşi, Romania
* Correspondence: costica.morosanu@uaic.ro

Abstract: Two main topics are addressed in the present paper, first, a rigorous qualitative study of a second-order reaction–diffusion problem with non-linear diffusion and cubic-type reactions, as well as inhomogeneous dynamic boundary conditions. Under certain assumptions about the input data: $g_d(t,x)$, $g_{fr}(t,x)$, $U_0(x)$ and $\zeta_0(x)$, we prove the well-posedness (the existence, a priori estimates, regularity and uniqueness) of a solution in the space $W_p^{1,2}(Q) \times W_p^{1,2}(\Sigma)$. Here, we extend previous results, enabling new mathematical models to be more suitable to describe the complexity of a wide class of different physical phenomena of life sciences, including moving interface problems, material sciences, digital image processing, automatic vehicle detection and tracking, the spread of an epidemic infection, semantic image segmentation including U-Net neural networks, etc. The second goal is to develop an iterative splitting scheme, corresponding to the non-linear second-order reaction–diffusion problem. Results relating to the convergence of the approximation scheme and error estimation are also established. On the basis of the proposed numerical scheme, we formulate the algorithm **alg-frac_sec-ord_dbc**, which represents a delicate challenge for our future works. The benefit of such a method could simplify the process of numerical computation.

Citation: Fetecău, C.; Moroşanu, C. Fractional Step Scheme to Approximate a Non-Linear Second-Order Reaction–Diffusion Problem with Inhomogeneous Dynamic Boundary Conditions. *Axioms* **2023**, *12*, 406. https://doi.org/10.3390/axioms12040406

Academic Editors: Péter Kórus and Juan Eduardo Nápoles Valdes

Received: 26 February 2023
Revised: 7 April 2023
Accepted: 19 April 2023
Published: 21 April 2023

Copyright: © 2023 by the authors. Licensee MDPI, Basel, Switzerland. This article is an open access article distributed under the terms and conditions of the Creative Commons Attribution (CC BY) license (https://creativecommons.org/licenses/by/4.0/).

Keywords: boundary value problems for non-linear parabolic PDE; fractional step method; convergence of numerical methods; numerical algorithm; error analysis; dynamic boundary conditions

MSC: 35K55; 65N06; 65N12; 65YXX; 80AXX

1. Introduction

Considering the following non-linear second-order reaction–diffusion problem:

$$\begin{cases} p_1 \dfrac{\partial}{\partial t} U(t,x) - p_2 \mathrm{div}\Big(K(t,x,U(t,x)) \, \nabla U(t,x) \Big) \\ \qquad = p_r \big[U(t,x) - U^3(t,x) \big] + p_s g_d(t,x) & \text{in } Q \\ p_2 \dfrac{\partial}{\partial \mathbf{n}} U + p_1 \dfrac{\partial}{\partial t} U - \Delta_\Gamma U + p_t U = g_{fr}(t,x) & \text{on } \Sigma \\ U(0,x) = U_0(x) & \text{on } \Omega, \end{cases} \quad (1)$$

where $\Omega \subset \mathbf{R}^n$, $n \leq 3$ is a compact domain with a C^2 boundary $\partial\Omega = \Gamma$, $[0,T]$ a generic time interval, $Q = (0,T) \times \Omega$, $\Sigma = (0,T) \times \partial\Omega$ and:

- $t \in (0,T]$, $x = (x_1, \ldots, x_n) \in \Omega$;
- p_1, p_2, p_r, p_s and p_t are positive parameters;

- $\frac{\partial}{\partial s}U(s,\cdot)$ (U_s in short) is the partial derivative of $U(s,\cdot)$ (U in short) relative to $s \in (0,T]$;
- $U(s,y)$, $(s,y) \in Q$, is the unknown function (the order parameter in Q, for example). $\nabla U(s,y) = U_y(s,y)$ ($\nabla U = U_y$) denotes the gradient of $U(s,y)$ in y, $y \in \Omega$ (see [1–3] for more details);
- $K(s,y,U(s,y))$ is the mobility (attached to the solution $U(s,y)$, $(s,y) \in Q$, to Equation (1)) (see [2–4] for more details);
- $g_d(s,y) \in L^p(Q)$ is the distributed control (see Remark 1 below), where

$$p \geq 2; \tag{2}$$

- $g_{fr}(s,y) \in W_p^{1-\frac{1}{2p},2-\frac{1}{p}}(\Sigma)$ is the boundary control (see Remark 1 below);
- $U_0 \in W_\infty^{2-\frac{2}{p}}(\Omega)$ verifying

$$p_2 \frac{\partial}{\partial n}U_0 - \Delta_\Gamma U_0 + p_t U_0 = g_{fr}(0,x);$$

- $\mathbf{n} = n(x)$ has the same meaning as in [5];
- Δ_Γ has the same meaning as in [6];

Remark 1. *The given functions g_d and g_{fr} in (1), can be interpreted as distributed and boundary control, respectively, opening a large field of applications for the non-linear second-order problem (1), such as optimal control.*

For convenience, let us write (1) in the following form

$$\begin{cases} p_1 \frac{\partial}{\partial t}U(t,x) - p_2 \frac{\partial}{\partial U_{x_j}}\left[K(t,x,U(t,x))U_{x_i}\right]U_{x_j x_i} \\ \quad = A\left(t,x,U(t,x),U_{x_i}(t,x)\right) + p_r\left[U(t,x) - U^3(t,x)\right] + p_s g_d(t,x) & \text{in } Q \\ p_2 \frac{\partial}{\partial \mathbf{n}}U + p_1 \frac{\partial}{\partial t}U - \Delta_\Gamma U + p_t U = g_{fr}(t,x) & \text{on } \Sigma \\ U(0,x) = U_0(x) & \text{on } \Omega, \end{cases} \tag{3}$$

where $U_{x_j x_i} = \frac{\partial^2}{\partial x_j \partial x_i}U(t,x)$, $i,j = 1,\ldots,n$, and

$$A(t,x,U(t,x),U_{x_i}(t,x)) = \frac{\partial}{\partial U}(K(t,x,U)U_{x_i})U_{x_i} + \frac{\partial}{\partial x_i}(K(t,x,U)U_{x_i}), \quad i=1,\ldots,n. \tag{4}$$

As in [1–3,5–9], we recall that Equation $(1)_1$ is a quasi-linear one, i.e.,

$$a_i(t,x,U(t,x),U_x(t,x)) = K(t,x,U(t,x))U_{x_i}(t,x), \quad i=1,\ldots,n$$

and

$$a(t,x,U(t,x),U_x(t,x)) = -p_r\left[U(t,x) - U^3(t,x)\right] - p_s g_d(t,x).$$

On the other hand, the problem in $(3)_1$ is similar to in [10] (p. 3, relation (2.4)), where, for $i = 1,\ldots,n$,

$$a_{ij}(t,x,U(t,x),U_x(t,x)) = \frac{\partial}{\partial U_{x_j}}a_i(t,x,U(t,x),U_x(t,x)) = \frac{\partial}{\partial U_{x_j}}\left[K(t,x,U(t,x))U_{x_i}(t,x)\right],$$

and

$$a(t,x,U(t,x),U_x(t,x)) = -A(t,x,U(t,x),U_x(t,x)) - p_r\left[U(t,x) - U^3(t,x)\right] - p_s g_d(t,x),$$

while $(3)_2$ are of the second type, namely

$$\frac{\partial}{\partial \mathbf{n}} U(t,x) = a_{ij}(t,x,U(t,x),U_x(t,x))U_{x_j}(t,x)\cos\alpha_i,$$

and

$$\psi(t,x,U)|_\Sigma = p_1 \frac{\partial}{\partial t} U - \Delta_\Gamma U + p_t U - g_{fr}(t,x) \tag{5}$$

(see [10] (p. 475, relation (7.2))).

Moreover, we consider that Equations $(1)_1$ and $(3)_1$ are uniformly parabolic, i.e.,

$$\nu_1(|U|)\zeta^2 \leq \frac{\partial}{\partial z_j} a_i(s,y,U(s,y),z(s,y))\zeta_i\zeta_j \leq \nu_2(|U|)\zeta^2 \tag{6}$$

for arbitrary $U(s,y)$ and $z(s,y)$, $(s,y) \in Q$, and $\zeta = (\zeta_1,\ldots,\zeta_n)$ for an arbitrary real vector (see [5] for more details).

Equation $(1)_1$ was initially introduced by Allen and Cahn (see [5,11] and references therein) to describe the motion of anti-phase boundaries in crystalline solids. In fact, the Allen–Cahn model is widely applied to moving interface problems, such as the mixture of two incompressible fluids, the nucleation of solids, vesicle membranes, etc. Furthermore, the non-linear parabolic Equation $(1)_1$ appears in the Caginalp's phase-field transition system (see [2–9,11–22]), describing the transition between phases (solid and liquid) (see [17], for example).

In the present paper we investigate the solvability of boundary value problems of the form (1) or (3) in the class $W_p^{1,2}(Q)$. The new model expressed in (1) stands out by the presence of parameters $p_1, p_2, p_r, p_s, p_t, K(s,y,U(s,y))$, and $(s,y) \in Q$, the principal part being in the divergence form and by considering a non-linear reaction term (see [5,11] and references therein). The most important aspect in our paper concerns inhomogeneous dynamic boundary conditions. Thus, we more precisely define the significant aspects of the physical features. In this regard, we advise applying (1) or (3), to the moving interface problems (see [5,7,8,11–15]), anisotropy effects (see [3–6,9,11,16–22]), image de-noising and segmentation (see [2,4] and references therein), etc. Let us point out that the following assumption is satisfied (see [20]):

$$H_0: \ (U - U^3)|U|^{3p-4}U \leq 1 + |U|^{3p-1} - |U|^{3p}.$$

2. Results—Theorem 1

In order to approach the problem in (3) (or (1)), we use the same ideas as in [1,6,7,9]. In this respect we introduce a new variable $\zeta(t,x) = U(t,x)$, $\zeta(0,x) = U_0(x)$ on Γ (see [10] (6.2)). Correspondingly, $(3)_2$ is approached in the following

$$\begin{cases} U(t,x) = \zeta(t,x) & \text{on } \Sigma \\ p_2 \frac{\partial}{\partial \mathbf{n}} U + p_1 \frac{\partial}{\partial t}\zeta(t,x) - \Delta_\Gamma \zeta(t,x) + p_t \zeta(t,x) = g_{fr}(t,x) & \text{on } \Sigma \\ \zeta(0,x) = \zeta_0(x) & x \in \Gamma. \end{cases} \tag{7}$$

Accordingly, the non-linear second-order boundary value problem (3) can be written suitably as follows

$$\begin{cases} p_1 \dfrac{\partial}{\partial t} U(t,x) - p_2 \dfrac{\partial}{\partial U_{x_j}} \left[K(t,x,U(t,x)) U_{x_i}(t,x) \right] U_{x_j x_i} \\ \quad = A\left(t,x,U(t,x),U_{x_i}(t,x)\right) + p_r \left[U(t,x) - U^3(t,x) \right] + p_s g_d(t,x) & \text{in } Q \\ U(t,x) = \zeta(t,x) & \text{on } \Sigma \\ p_2 \dfrac{\partial}{\partial \mathbf{n}} U + p_1 \dfrac{\partial}{\partial t} \zeta - \Delta_\Gamma \zeta + p_t \zeta = g_{fr}(t,x) & \text{on } \Sigma \\ U(0,x) = U_0(x) & \text{on } \Omega \\ \zeta(0,x) = \zeta_0(x) & x \in \Gamma, \end{cases} \quad (8)$$

where $A\left(t,x,U(t,x),U_{x_i}(t,x)\right)$ is defined by (4), $U_0(x) = \zeta_0(x)$ on Γ and $\zeta_0(x) \in W_\infty^{2-\frac{2}{p}}(\Gamma)$.

Definition 1. *Any solution $(U(t,x), \zeta(t,x))$ to problem (8) is called the* classical solution *if it is continuous in $\bar{Q}$, with continuous derivatives U_t, U_x and U_{xx} in Q and ζ_t, ζ_x, and ζ_{xx} in Σ, satisfying Equation $(8)_1$ at all points $(t,x) \in Q$ and satisfying conditions $(8)_{2-3}$ and $(8)_{4-5}$ on the lateral surface Σ of the cylinder Q for $t=0$, respectively.*

Our main results regarding the existence, uniqueness and regularity of solutions to problem (8) (the well-posedness of the solutions to the non-linear second-order boundary value problems (1) or (3)) are presented below.

Theorem 1. *Suppose $(U(t,x), \zeta(t,x)) \in C^{1,2}(Q) \times C^{1,2}(\Sigma)$ is a classical solution to problem (8), and for positive numbers M, M_0, m_1, M_1, M_2, M_3, M_4 and M_5 one has*

$\mathbf{I_1}$. $|U(t,x)| < M$ *for any $(t,x) \in Q$ and for any $z(t,x)$, the map $K(t,x,z)$ is continuous, differentiable in x, where its x-derivatives are bounded, satisfy (6), and*

$$0 < K_{min} \leq K(t,x,U(t,x)) < K_{max}, \quad \text{for } (t,x) \in Q, \quad (9)$$

$$\sum_{i=1}^n \left[|a_i(t,x,U(t,x),z(t,x))| + \left| \dfrac{\partial}{\partial U} a_i(t,x,U(t,x),z(t,x)) \right| \right](1+|z|)$$
$$+ \sum_{i,j=1}^n \left| \dfrac{\partial}{\partial x_j} a_i(t,x,U(t,x),z(t,x)) \right| + |U(t,x)| \leq M_0(1+|z|)^2. \quad (10)$$

$\mathbf{I_2}$. *For any sufficiently small $\varepsilon > 0$, the functions $U(t,x)$ and $K(t,x,U(t,x))$ satisfy the relations*

$$\|U\|_{L^s(Q)} \leq M_2, \quad \|K(t,x,U(t,x))U_{x_i}\|_{L^r(Q)} < M_3, \quad i=1,\ldots,n,$$

where

$$r = \begin{cases} \max\{p,4\} & p \neq 4 \\ 4+\varepsilon & p = 4, \end{cases} \quad s = \begin{cases} \max\{p,2\} & p \neq 2 \\ 2+\varepsilon & p = 2. \end{cases}$$

Then, when $\forall g_d \in L^p(Q)$, $U_0 \in W_\infty^{2-\frac{2}{p}}(\Omega)$, $\zeta_0(x) \in W_\infty^{2-\frac{2}{p}}(\Gamma)$, $g_{fr} \in W_p^{1-\frac{1}{2p}, 2-\frac{1}{p}}(\Sigma)$, with $p \neq \frac{3}{2}$, there exists a unique solution $(U,\zeta) \in W_p^{1,2}(Q) \times W_p^{1,2}(\Sigma)$ to (8) which satisfies

$$\|U\|_{W_p^{1,2}(Q)} + \|\zeta\|_{W_p^{1,2}(\Sigma)}$$

$$\leq C\left\{1 + \|U_0\|_{W_\infty^{2-\frac{2}{p}}(\Omega)} + \|\zeta_0\|_{W_\infty^{2-\frac{2}{p}}(\Gamma)} + \|U_0\|_{L^{3p-2}(\Omega)}^{\frac{3p-2}{p}} + \|\zeta_0\|_{L^{3p-2}(\Gamma)}^{\frac{3p-2}{p}} \right. \tag{11}$$

$$\left. + \|g_d\|_{L^{3p-2}(Q)}^{\frac{3p-2}{p}} + \|g_{f^r}\|_{L^{3p-2}(\Sigma)}^{\frac{3p-2}{p}} + \|g_{fr}\|_{W_p^{1-\frac{1}{2p},2-\frac{1}{p}}(\Sigma)} \right\},$$

where $C > 0$ does not depend on U, ζ, g_d, or g_{fr}.

If (U^1, ζ^1) and (U^2, ζ^2) are solutions to (8) which correspond to (U_0^1, ζ_0^1), $(U_0^2, \zeta_0^2) \in W_\infty^{2-\frac{2}{p}}(\Omega) \times W_\infty^{2-\frac{2}{p}}(\Gamma)$, g_d^1, g_d^2, g_{fr}^1 and g_{fr}^2, respectively, then

$$\|U^1\|_{W_p^{1,2}(Q)}, \quad \|U^2\|_{W_p^{1,2}(Q)} \leq M_4, \tag{12}$$

$$\|\zeta^1\|_{W_p^{1,2}(\Sigma)}, \quad \|\zeta^2\|_{W_p^{1,2}(\Sigma)} \leq M_5, \tag{13}$$

and the following holds

$$\max_{(t,x)\in Q} |U^1 - U^2| + \max_{(t,x)\in \Sigma} |\zeta^1 - \zeta^2|$$
$$\leq C_1 e^{CT} \max\left\{ \max_{(t,x)\in \Omega} |U_0^1 - U_0^2|, \max_{(t,x)\in \Gamma} |\zeta_0^1 - \zeta_0^2|, \right. \tag{14}$$
$$\left. \max_{(t,x)\in Q} |g_d^1 - g_d^2|, \max_{(t,x)\in \Sigma} |g_{fr}^1 - g_{fr}^2| \right\},$$

where $C_1 > 0$ and $C > 0$, do not depend on $\{U^1, \zeta^1, g_d^1, g_{fr}^1, U_0^1, \zeta_0^1\}$ and $\{U^2, \zeta^2, g_d^2, g_{fr}^2, U_0^2, \zeta_0^2\}$. In particular, the uniqueness of the solution to (8) holds.

As far as the techniques used in this paper are concerned, it should be noted that we derive the a priori estimates for $L^p(Q)$ and $L^p(\Sigma)$. Moreover, basic tools in our approach are:

- the Leray–Schauder degree theory (see [15] (p. 221) and reference therein);
- the L^p theory of linear and quasi-linear parabolic equations [10];
- Green's first identity

$$-\int_\Omega y \operatorname{div} z \, dx = \int_\Omega \nabla y \cdot z \, dx - \int_{\partial\Omega} y \frac{\partial}{\partial \mathbf{n}} z \, d\gamma,$$
$$-\int_\Omega y \Delta z \, dx = \int_\Omega \nabla y \cdot \nabla z \, dx - \int_{\partial\Omega} y \frac{\partial}{\partial \mathbf{n}} z \, d\gamma, \tag{15}$$

for any scalar-valued function y and z in a continuously differentiable vector field in n dimensional space;

- the Lions and Peetre embedding theorem [1] (p. 100) to ensure the existence of a continuous embedding $W_p^{1,2}(Q) \subset L^\mu(Q)$, where the number μ is defined as follows (see (2))

$$\mu = \begin{cases} \text{any positive number } \geq 3p & \text{if } \frac{1}{p} - \frac{2}{n+2} \leq 0, \\ \frac{p(n+2)}{n+2-2p} & \text{if } \frac{1}{p} - \frac{2}{n+2} > 0. \end{cases} \tag{16}$$

For a given positive integer k and $1 \leq p \leq \infty$, we denote by $W_p^{k,2k}(Q)$ the Sobolev space on Q:

$$W_p^{k,2k}(Q) = \left\{ y \in L^p(Q) : \frac{\partial^i}{\partial t^i} \frac{\partial^j}{\partial x^j} y \in L^p(Q), \text{ for } 2i + j \leq 2k \right\},$$

i.e., the spaces of functions whose t- and x-derivatives up to the order k and $2k$, respectively, belong to $L^p(Q)$. Furthermore, we use the Sobolev spaces $W_p^i(\Omega)$ and $W_p^{\frac{i}{2},i}(\Sigma)$ with the non-integral i for the initial and boundary conditions, respectively, (see [10] (p. 70 and 81)).

Furthermore, we use the set $C^{1,2}(\bar{D})$ ($C^{1,2}(D)$) of all continuous functions in $\bar{D}$ (in D) with continuous derivatives u_t, u_x, and u_{xx} in $\bar{D}$ (in D) ($D = Q$ or $D = \Sigma$), as well as the Sobolev spaces $W_p^\ell(\Omega)$, and $W_p^{\ell,\ell/2}(\Sigma)$ with non-integral ℓ for the initial and boundary conditions, respectively (see [10] (p. 8, p. 70 and p. 81)).

In the following we will denote by C some positive constants.

3. Proof of the Main Result — Theorem 1

We consider $B = W_p^{0,1}(Q) \cap L^{3p}(Q) \times L^p(\Sigma)$ as a suitable Banach space, with the norm $\|\cdot\|_B$ expressed by

$$\|(\varphi, \bar{\varphi})\|_B = \|\varphi\|_{L^p(Q)} + \|\varphi_x\|_{L^p(Q)} + \|\bar{\varphi}\|_{L^p(\Sigma)},$$

and a non-linear operator $H : B \times [0,1] \to B$ defined by

$$(U, \zeta) = H(\varphi, \bar{\varphi}, \lambda) = (U(\varphi, \bar{\varphi}, \lambda), \zeta(\varphi, \bar{\varphi}, \lambda)) \quad \forall (\varphi, \bar{\varphi}) \in B, \ \forall \lambda \in [0,1], \tag{17}$$

where $(U(\varphi, \bar{\varphi}, \lambda), \zeta(\varphi, \bar{\varphi}, \lambda)$ is a unique solution to the following linear second-order boundary value problem

$$\begin{cases} p_1 \dfrac{\partial}{\partial t} U - p_2 \left[\lambda \dfrac{\partial}{\partial \varphi_{x_j}} (K(t, x, \varphi) \varphi_{x_i}) - (1-\lambda) \delta_i^j \right] U_{x_i x_j} \\ \qquad = \lambda \left\{ A(t, x, \varphi, \varphi_{x_i}) + p_r [\varphi(t,x) - \varphi^3(t,x)] + p_s g_d(t,x) \right\} & \text{in } Q \\ U(t,x) = \zeta(t,x) & \text{on } \Sigma \\ U(0,x) = \lambda U_0(x) & \text{on } \Omega \\ p_2 \dfrac{\partial}{\partial \mathbf{n}} U + p_1 \dfrac{\partial}{\partial t} \zeta - \Delta_\Gamma \zeta + p_t \zeta = \lambda g_{fr}(t,x) & \text{on } \Sigma \\ \zeta(0,x) = \lambda \zeta_0(x) & x \in \Gamma. \end{cases} \tag{18}$$

Remark 2. *The non-linear operator H in (17) depends on $\lambda \in [0,1]$ and its fixed point for $\lambda = 1$ is a solution to problem (18).*

Proof. We now prove that the non-linear operator H, defined in (17), is well-defined, continuous and compact.

From the right-hand side of $(17)_1$, it follows that, $\forall (\varphi, \bar{\varphi}) \in B$, then $\varphi^3 \in L^p(Q)$ and thus $A(t, x, \varphi, \varphi_{x_i}) + p_r[\varphi(t,x) - \varphi^3(t,x)] + p_s g_d(t,x) \in L^p(Q)$. Using the L^p theory of linear parabolic equations (see [10]), the solution (U, ζ) to problem (18) exists and it is unique with

$$(U, \zeta) = (U(\varphi, \bar{\varphi}, \lambda), \zeta(\varphi, \bar{\varphi}, \lambda)) \in B, \quad \forall (\varphi, \bar{\varphi}) \in B, \ \forall \lambda \in [0,1]. \tag{19}$$

Using the continuous inclusions (see [6])

$$\begin{cases} W_p^{1,2}(Q) \subset B \subset L^p(Q) \\ W_p^{1,2}(\Sigma) \subset L^p(\Sigma), \end{cases} \quad (20)$$

we obtain $H(\varphi, \bar{\varphi}, \lambda) = (U, \zeta) \in B$ for all $(\varphi, \bar{\varphi}) \in B$ and $\forall \lambda \in [0,1]$, meaning the non-linear operator H is well defined.

Now, using the ideas from [1–7,9,16,20], let $\varphi^n \to \varphi$ in $W_p^{0,1}(Q) \cap L^{3p}(Q)$, $\bar{\varphi}^n \to \bar{\varphi}$ in $L^p(\Sigma)$ and $\lambda^n \to \lambda$ in $[0,1]$. Using the notations

$$(U^{n,\lambda_n}, \zeta^{n,\lambda_n}) = H(\varphi^n, \bar{\varphi}^n, \lambda^n),$$
$$(U^{n,\lambda}, \zeta^{n,\lambda}) = H(\varphi^n, \bar{\varphi}^n, \lambda),$$
$$(U^\lambda, \zeta^\lambda) = H(\varphi, \bar{\varphi}, \lambda),$$

we obtain

$$\|u^{n,\lambda_n} - u^{n,\lambda}\|_{W_p^{1,2}(Q)} + \|\zeta^{n,\lambda_n} - \zeta^{n,\lambda}\|_{W_p^{1,2}(\Sigma)} \to 0 \quad \text{for } n \to \infty \quad (21)$$

and

$$\|u^{n,\lambda} - u^\lambda\|_{W_p^{1,2}(Q)} + \|\zeta^{n,\lambda} - \zeta^\lambda\|_{W_p^{1,2}(\Sigma)} \to 0 \quad \text{for } n \to \infty. \quad (22)$$

The continuous embedding of (20), (21), and (22) allows us to derive the continuity of the non-linear operator H, introduced in (17). Furthermore, H is compact, easily written as

$$B \times [0,1] \to W_p^{1,2}(Q) \times W_p^{1,2}(\Sigma) \hookrightarrow B = W_p^{0,1}(Q) \cap L^{3p}(Q) \times L^p(\Sigma),$$

where the second map is a compact inclusion (see [1] (p. 100)).

Next, we look at a positive number R, such that (see (17))

$$(U, \zeta, \lambda) \in B \times [0,1] \text{ with } (U, \zeta) = H(U, \zeta, \lambda) \implies \|(U, \zeta)\|_B < R. \quad (23)$$

The above expression $(U, \zeta) = H(U, \zeta, \lambda)$ can be written as (see (1), (8) and (18))

$$\begin{cases} p_1 \dfrac{\partial}{\partial t} U - \lambda p_2 \mathrm{div}\left(K(t,x,U)\nabla U\right) - (1-\lambda)p_2 \Delta U \\ \qquad = \lambda \left[p_r \left[U(t,x) - U^3(t,x)\right] + p_s g_d(t,x)\right] & \text{in } Q \\ U(t,x) = \zeta(t,x) & \text{on } \Sigma \\ U(0,x) = \lambda U_0(x) & \text{on } \Omega \\ p_2 \dfrac{\partial}{\partial n} U + p_1 \dfrac{\partial}{\partial t}\zeta - \Delta_\Gamma \zeta + p_t \zeta = \lambda g_{fr}(t,x)] & \text{on } \Sigma \\ \zeta(0,x) = \lambda \zeta_0(x) & x \in \Gamma. \end{cases} \quad (24)$$

Multiplying (24)$_1$ by $|U|^{3p-4}U$ and integrating over $Q_s := (0,s) \times \Omega$, $s \in (0,T]$, we obtain

$$\frac{p_1}{3p-2} \int_\Omega |U(s,x)|^{3p-2}\,dx$$
$$-\lambda p_2 \int_{Q_s} \mathrm{div}\left(K(\tau,x,U)\nabla U\right)|U|^{3p-4}U\,d\tau dx$$
$$-(1-\lambda)p_2 \int_{Q_s} \Delta U\,|U|^{3p-4}U\,d\tau dx \qquad (25)$$
$$= \lambda p_r \int_{Q_s} [U(\tau,x) - U^3(\tau,x)]|U|^{3p-4}U\,d\tau dx + \lambda p_s \int_{Q_s} g_d(\tau,x)|U|^{3p-4}U\,d\tau dx.$$

To process the terms

$$\int_{Q_s} \mathrm{div}\left(K(\tau,x,U)\nabla U\right)|U|^{3p-4}U d\tau dx$$

and

$$\int_{Q_s} \Delta U\,|U|^{3p-4}U d\tau dx, \text{ in (25)}$$

we use Green's first identity (15)$_1$ and (15)$_2$, respectively, to obtain

$$-\lambda p_2 \int_{Q_s} \mathrm{div}\left(K(\tau,x,U)\nabla U\right)|U|^{3p-4}U\,d\tau dx$$
$$= \lambda p_2 \int_{Q_s} K(\tau,x,U)\nabla U \cdot \nabla\left(|U|^{3p-4}U\right)d\tau dx + \lambda \int_{\Sigma_s} |U|^{3p-4}U\left(-p_2\frac{\partial}{\partial \mathbf{n}}U\right)d\tau d\gamma, \qquad (26)$$

$$-(1-\lambda)p_2 \int_{Q_s} \Delta U\,|U|^{3p-4}U\,d\tau dx$$
$$= (1-\lambda)3(p-1)p_2 \int_{Q_s} |\nabla U|^2|U|^{3p-4}d\tau dx + (1-\lambda)\int_{\Sigma_s} |U|^{3p-4}U\left(-p_2\frac{\partial}{\partial \mathbf{n}}U\right)d\tau d\gamma, \qquad (27)$$

where $\Sigma_s = (0,s) \times \partial\Omega$, $s \in (0,T]$ and

$$-p_2 \frac{\partial}{\partial \mathbf{n}}U = p_1\frac{\partial}{\partial t}\zeta - \Delta_\Gamma \zeta + p_t\zeta - \lambda g_{fr}$$

(see (24)$_4$).

Combining the above equality with the boundary condition in (24)$_2$, the left inequality in (9), and the relations (26), (27), and (25) leads us to the following inequality

$$\frac{p_1}{3p-2}\int_\Omega |U(s,x)|^{3p-2}dx+\lambda\frac{p_1}{3p-2}\int_\Gamma |\zeta(s,x)|^{3p-2}d\gamma+(1-\lambda)\frac{p_1}{3p-2}\int_\Gamma |\zeta(s,x)|^{3p-2}d\gamma$$

$$+\lambda p_2\int_{Q_s}K(\tau,x,U)\nabla U\cdot\nabla\left(|U|^{3p-4}U\right)d\tau dx+(1-\lambda)3(p-1)p_2\int_{Q_s}|\nabla U|^2|U|^{3p-4}d\tau dx$$

$$+\lambda p_t\int_{\Sigma_s}|\zeta(\tau,x)|^{3p-2}\,d\tau d\gamma+(1-\lambda)p_t\int_{\Sigma_s}|\zeta(\tau,x)|^{3p-2}\,d\tau d\gamma$$

$$+\lambda\int_{\Sigma_s}\nabla_\Gamma\left(|\zeta|^{3p-3}\right)\cdot\nabla_\Gamma\zeta\,d\tau d\gamma+(1-\lambda)\int_{\Sigma_s}\nabla_\Gamma\left(|\zeta|^{3p-3}\right)\cdot\nabla_\Gamma\zeta\,d\tau d\gamma \qquad(28)$$

$$\leq\lambda\frac{p_1}{3p-2}\int_\Omega |U_0(x)|^{3p-2}\,dx+\frac{p_1}{3p-2}\int_\Gamma |\zeta_0(x)|^{3p-2}d\gamma$$

$$+\lambda p_r\int_{Q_s}\left[U(\tau,x)-U^3(\tau,x)\right]|U|^{3p-4}U\,d\tau dx$$

$$+\lambda p_s\int_{Q_s}g_d(\tau,x)|U|^{3p-4}U\,d\tau dx+\lambda\int_{\Sigma_t}g_{fr}(\tau,x)|U|^{3p-4}U\,d\tau d\gamma$$

for all $s\in(0,T]$. The last two terms in the above inequalities can be manipulated via Hölder and Cauchy's inequality giving us the following estimates

a. $\lambda p_s\int_{Q_s}g_d(\tau,x)|U|^{3p-4}Ud\tau dx$

$$\leq\frac{(3p-2)-1}{3p-2}\varepsilon^{\frac{3p-2}{3p-3}}\int_{Q_s}|U|^{3p-2}d\tau dx+\lambda p_s\frac{1}{3p-2}\varepsilon^{-(3p-2)}\int_{Q_s}|g_d|^{3p-2}d\tau dx,$$

b. $\lambda\int_{\Sigma_s}g_{fr}(\tau,x)|U|^{3p-4}Ud\tau d\gamma$

$$\leq\frac{(3p-2)-1}{3p-2}\varepsilon^{\frac{3p-2}{3p-3}}\int_{\Sigma_s}|U|^{3p-2}d\tau d\gamma+\lambda\frac{1}{3p-2}\varepsilon^{-(3p-2)}\int_{\Sigma_t}|g_{fr}|^{3p-2}d\tau d\gamma.$$

Due to the inequalities **a.** and **b.**, from (28) we obtain

$$\frac{p_1}{3p-2}\left[\int_\Omega |U(s,x)|^{3p-2}dx + \int_\Gamma |\zeta(s,x)|^{3p-2}d\gamma\right]$$

$$+\lambda p_2\int_{Q_s} K(\tau,x,U)\nabla U \cdot \nabla\left(|U|^{3p-4}U\right)d\tau dx + (1-\lambda)3(p-1)p_2\int_{Q_s}|\nabla U|^2|U|^{3p-4}d\tau dx$$

$$+\lambda p_r \int_{Q_s} |U(\tau,x)|^{3p}\, d\tau dx$$

$$+p_t\int_{\Sigma_s} |\zeta(\tau,x)|^{3p-2}\, d\tau d\gamma + \int_{\Sigma_s} \nabla_\Gamma\left(|\zeta|^{3p-3}\right)\cdot\nabla_\Gamma\zeta\, d\tau d\gamma$$

$$\leq \frac{p_1}{3p-2}\left[\int_\Omega |U_0(x)|^{3p-2}\, dx + \int_\Gamma |\zeta_0(x)|^{3p-2}d\gamma\right]$$

$$+\left[\lambda p_r + \frac{(3p-2)-1}{3p-2}\varepsilon^{\frac{3p-2}{3p-3}}\right]\int_{Q_s}|U(\tau,x)|^{3p-2}d\tau dx$$

$$+\frac{(3p-2)-1}{3p-2}\varepsilon^{\frac{3p-2}{3p-3}}\int_{\Sigma_s}|U(\tau,x)|^{3p-2}\, d\tau dx$$

$$+p_s\frac{1}{3p-2}\varepsilon^{-(3p-2)}\|g_d\|_{L^{3p-2}(Q_s)}^{3p-2} + \frac{1}{3p-2}\varepsilon^{-(3p-2)}\|g_{f^r}\|_{L^{3p-2}(\Sigma_s)}^{3p-2} \quad (29)$$

for all $s \in (0,T]$.

In particular, it follows that from (29) we obtain

$$\int_\Omega |U(s,x)|^{3p-2}dx + \int_\Gamma |\zeta(s,x)|^{3p-2}d\gamma$$

$$\leq C_0\left[\|U_0(x)\|_{L^{3p-2}(\Omega)}^{3p-2} + \|\zeta_0(x)\|_{L^{3p-2}(\Gamma)}^{3p-2} + \|g_d\|_{L^{3p-2}(Q_s)}^{3p-2} + \|g_{f^r}\|_{L^{3p-2}(\Sigma_s)}^{3p-2}\right] \quad (30)$$

$$+C_0\int_0^t\left[\int_\Omega |U(\tau,x)|^{3p-2}d\tau dx + \int_\Gamma |\zeta(\tau,x)|^{3p-2}d\gamma\right]d\tau$$

where $C_0 = C(|\Omega|, |\Gamma|, p, p_1, p_2, p_r, p_t, p_s)$, in conjuction with $(24)_2$.

By Gronwall's lemma and owing to $L^{3p-2}(Q) \subset L^p(Q)$, from (30) we obtain

$$\|U\|_{L^p(Q)}^p + \|\zeta\|_{L^p(\Sigma)}^p$$

$$\leq C(T,C_0)\left[\|U\|_{L^{3p-2}(Q)}^{3p-2} + \|\zeta\|_{L^{3p-2}(\Sigma)}^{3p-2}\right] \quad (31)$$

$$\leq C(T,C_0)\left[\|U_0(x)\|_{L^{3p-2}(\Omega)}^{3p-2} + \|\zeta_0(x)\|_{L^{3p-2}(\Gamma)}^{3p-2} + \|g_d\|_{L^{3p-2}(Q)}^{3p-2} + \|g_{f^r}\|_{L^{3p-2}(\Sigma)}^{3p-2}\right].$$

Having established an estimate for $\|U\|_{L^{3p-2}(Q)}^{3p-2} + \|\zeta\|_{L^{3p-2}(\Sigma)}^{3p-2}$ (see (31)), we now return to the relation in (29) to derive the following estimate:

$$\lambda p_r \| |U|^3 \|_{L^p(Q)}^p$$
$$\leq C(T, C_0) \Big[\|U_0(x)\|_{L^{3p-2}(\Omega)}^{3p-2} + \|\zeta_0(x)\|_{L^{3p-2}(\Gamma)}^{3p-2} + \|g_d\|_{L^{3p-2}(Q)}^{3p-2} + \|g_{f^r}\|_{L^{3p-2}(\Sigma)}^{3p-2} \Big], \quad (32)$$

where the boundary condition in $(24)_2$ is also used.

Applying Lemma 7.4 in Choban and Moroşanu [1] (p. 114) to the linear inhomogeneous problem (24) with

$$f_3 = \lambda \{ p_r [U(t,x) - U^3(t,x)] + p_s g_d(t,x) \} \in L^p(Q) \text{ and}$$
$$g_3 = \lambda g_{f_r}(t,x) \in L^p(\Sigma),$$

we obtain

$$\|U\|_{W_p^{1,2}(Q)} + \|\zeta\|_{W_p^{1,2}(\Sigma)}$$
$$\leq C_1 \Big\{ \|U_0\|_{W_\infty^{2-\frac{2}{p}}(\Omega)} + \|\zeta_0\|_{W_\infty^{2-\frac{2}{p}}(\Gamma)} + \|g_d\|_{L^p(Q)} + \|g_{f^r}\|_{L^p(\Sigma)} \quad (33)$$
$$+ \lambda p_r \Big[\|U\|_{L^p(\Omega)} + \| |U|^3 \|_{L^p(\Omega)} \Big] \Big\},$$

for a constant $C_1 = C(n, C(T, C_0)) > 0$.

Now using (31) and (32), (33) then becomes

$$\|U\|_{W_p^{1,2}(Q)} + \|\zeta\|_{W_p^{1,2}(\Sigma)}$$
$$\leq C_1 \Big\{ 1 + \|U_0\|_{W_\infty^{2-\frac{2}{p}}(\Omega)} + \|\zeta_0\|_{W_\infty^{2-\frac{2}{p}}(\Gamma)} + \|U_0\|_{L^{3p-2}(\Omega)}^{\frac{3p-2}{p}} + \|\zeta_0\|_{L^{3p-2}(\Gamma)}^{\frac{3p-2}{p}} \quad (34)$$
$$+ \|g_d\|_{L^{3p-2}(Q)}^{\frac{3p-2}{p}} + \|g_{f^r}\|_{L^{3p-2}(\Sigma)}^{\frac{3p-2}{p}} + \|g_d\|_{L^p(Q)} + \|g_{f^r}\|_{L^p(\Sigma)} \Big\},$$

The inclusions in (20) guarantee that

$$\|U\|_{L^p(Q)} + \|\zeta\|_{L^p(\Sigma)} \leq C \Big(\|U\|_{W_p^{1,2}(Q)} + \|\zeta\|_{W_p^{1,2}(\Sigma)} \Big)$$

where, thanks to (34), we may conclude that a constant $R > 0$ exists such that the property in (23) is true.

Denoting $B_R^H := \{ (U, \zeta) \in B : \|(U, \zeta)\|_B < R \}$, relation (23) implies that

$$(U, \zeta, \lambda) \neq (U, \zeta) \quad \forall (U, \zeta) \in \partial B_R^H, \ \forall \lambda \in [0,1],$$

provided that $R > 0$ is sufficiently large. Furthermore, following the same ideas in [1,3–7,16,20], we can conclude that problem (8) has the solution $(U, \zeta) \in W_p^{1,2}(Q) \times W_p^{1,2}(\Sigma)$.

Making use of the embedded $L^{3p-2}(Q) \subset L^p(Q)$ and the estimate (34), it follows that (11) and this completes the proof of the first part in Theorem 1.

Proof of Theorem 1 Continued

In this subsection we demonstrate the second part of Theorem 1 which entails checking (14) and thus the uniqueness of the solution to (1) (or (3)). We consider (U^1, ζ^1) and (U^2, ζ^2) as in the statement of Theorem 1. From the first part we know that $U^1, U^2 \in W_p^{1,2}(Q)$ and $\zeta^1, \zeta^2 \in W_p^{1,2}(\Sigma)$. Therefore, $U = U^1 - U^2 \in W_p^{1,2}(Q)$ and $Z = \zeta^1 - \zeta^2 \in W_p^{1,2}(\Sigma)$.

Following [1–3,5–7,16,20], the increments of a_{ij} and A (see (4)) can be written in the following form

$$a_{ij}(s, x, U^1, U_x^1) - a_{ij}(s, x, U^2, U_x^2) = \int_0^1 \frac{d}{d\lambda} a_{i,j}\left(s, x, U^\lambda, U_x^\lambda\right) d\lambda,$$

$$A(s, x, U^1, U_x^1) - A(s, x, U^2, U_x^2) = \int_0^1 \frac{d}{d\lambda} A\left(s, x, U^\lambda, U_x^\lambda\right) d\lambda$$

and so

$$a_{ij}(s, x, U^1, U_x^1)U_{x_i x_j}^1 - a_{ij}(s, x, U^2, U_x^2)U_{x_i x_j}^2$$

$$= a_{ij}(s, x, U^1, U_x^1)U_{x_i x_j} + \left\{ U_{x_i x_j}^2 \int_0^1 \frac{\partial}{\partial U_{x_j}^\lambda} a_{i,j}\left(s, x, U^\lambda, U_x^\lambda\right) d\lambda \right\} U_{x_i}, \quad (35)$$

$$A(s, x, U^1, U_x^1) - A(s, x, U^2, U_x^2) = \left\{ \int_0^1 \frac{\partial}{\partial U_{x_j}^\lambda} A\left(s, x, U^\lambda, U_x^\lambda\right) d\lambda \right\} U_{x_i}, \quad (36)$$

where

$$a_{i,j}(s, x, U_x^\lambda, U_x^\lambda) = \frac{\partial}{\partial U_{x_j}^\lambda}\left[K(s, x, U^\lambda)U_{x_i}^\lambda\right],$$

$$A(s, x, U^\lambda, U_x^\lambda) = a_i(s, x, U^\lambda, U_x^\lambda), \quad a_i\left(s, x, U^\lambda, U_x^\lambda\right) = \frac{\partial}{\partial x_i}\left[K(s, x, U^\lambda)U_{x_i}^\lambda\right],$$

$$U^\lambda(s, x) = \lambda U^1(s, x) + (1 - \lambda)U^2(s, x) \text{ and}$$

$$U_x^\lambda(s, x) = \lambda U_x^1(s, x) + (1 - \lambda)U_x^2(s, x).$$

Subtracting (3) for $U^2(s, x)$ from (3) for $U^1(s, x)$ and using (35) and (36), we obtain the following linear parabolic problem with inhomogeneous dynamic boundary conditions, i.e.,

$$\begin{cases} p_1 \dfrac{\partial}{\partial t} U - \hat{a}_{ij}(s, x)\Delta U = -\hat{a}_i(s, x)\nabla U - p_2 U + p_s(g_d^1 - g_d^2) & \text{in } Q \\[4pt] U(s, x) = Z(s, x) & \text{on } \Sigma \\[4pt] U(0, x) = (U_0^1 - U_0^2)(x) & \text{in } \Omega \\[4pt] p_1 \dfrac{\partial}{\partial \mathbf{n}} U + p_2 \dfrac{\partial}{\partial t} Z - \Delta_\Gamma Z + p_t Z = g_{f^r}^1 - g_{f^r}^2 & \text{on } \Sigma \\[4pt] Z(0, x) = (\zeta_0^1 - \zeta_0^2)(x) & \text{on } \Gamma, \end{cases} \quad (37)$$

where

$$\hat{a}_{ij}(s,x) = a_{ij}(s,x,U^1,U_x^1),$$

$$\hat{a}_i(s,x) = -U_{x_ix_j}^2 \int_0^1 \frac{\partial}{\partial U_{x_j}^\lambda} a_{i,j}\left(s,x,U^\lambda,U_x^\lambda\right) d\lambda + \int_0^1 \frac{\partial}{\partial U_{x_j}^\lambda} \frac{\partial}{\partial x_i}\left[K(s,x,U^\lambda)U_{x_i}^\lambda\right] d\lambda.$$

Next, following the work of A. Miranville and C. Moroşanu [3], we easily deduce the validity of the estimate in (14); thus, the uniqueness of the solution to (1) or (3) is true. □

Corollary 1. *Corresponding to $U_0^1 = U_0^2$ and $\zeta_0^1 = \zeta_0^2$, the problem* (1) *possesses a unique classical solution.*

4. Approximating Scheme—Convergence and Error Estimate

Here we use the fractional steps method in order to approximate the unique solution to problem (8) with inhomogeneous dynamic boundary conditions (see Corollary 1). Precisely, $\forall \varepsilon > 0$, let $M_\varepsilon = \left[\frac{T}{\varepsilon}\right]$ and

$$Q_i^\varepsilon = [i\varepsilon, (i+1)\varepsilon] \times \Omega, \quad \Sigma_i^\varepsilon = [i\varepsilon, (i+1)\varepsilon] \times \partial\Omega \quad i = 0, 1, \cdots, M_\varepsilon - 1,$$

with $Q_{M_\varepsilon-1}^\varepsilon = [(M_\varepsilon - 1)\varepsilon, T] \times \Omega$, $\Sigma_{M_\varepsilon-1}^\varepsilon = [(M_\varepsilon - 1)\varepsilon, T] \times \partial\Omega$. Correspondingly, we link the following numerical scheme with problem (8)

$$\begin{cases} p_1 \frac{\partial}{\partial t} U^\varepsilon - p_2 \text{div}\left(K(t,x,U^\varepsilon) \nabla U^\varepsilon\right) = p_r U^\varepsilon + p_s g_a(t,x) & \text{in } Q_i^\varepsilon \\ p_2 \frac{\partial}{\partial \mathbf{n}} U^\varepsilon + p_1 \frac{\partial}{\partial t} \zeta^\varepsilon - \Delta_\Gamma \zeta^\varepsilon + p_t \zeta^\varepsilon = g_{fr}(t,x) & \text{on } \Sigma_i^\varepsilon \\ U^\varepsilon(i\varepsilon, x) = z(\varepsilon, U_-^\varepsilon(i\varepsilon, x)) & \text{on } \Omega \\ \zeta^\varepsilon(i\varepsilon, x) = U^\varepsilon(i\varepsilon, x) & \text{on } \partial\Omega, \end{cases} \quad (38)$$

with $z(\varepsilon, U_-^\varepsilon(i\varepsilon, x))$ being the solution of Cauchy problem:

$$\begin{cases} z'(s) + p_r z^3(s) = 0 & s \in [0, \varepsilon] \\ z(0) = U_-^\varepsilon(i\varepsilon, x) & \text{on } \Omega \\ U_-^\varepsilon(0, x) = U_0(x) & \text{on } \Omega \\ U_-^\varepsilon(0, x) = \zeta_0(x) & \text{on } \partial\Omega, \end{cases} \quad (39)$$

where U_-^ε stands for the left-hand limit of U^ε.

For a detailed discussion regarding the importance of the above numerical scheme we direct the reader to the works [5,9,11–14,17–19,22,23].

The main question of this work concerns the convergence as $\varepsilon \to 0$ of the sequence $(U^\varepsilon, \zeta^\varepsilon)$ of the solutions to problems (38) and (39), and to the solution (U, ζ) of problem (8) (see [11] for more details).

For simplicity, we note:

$$W_Q = L^2([0,T]; H^1(\Omega)) \cap L^\infty(Q) \quad \text{and} \quad W_\Sigma = L^2([0,T]; H^1(\partial\Omega)) \cap L^\infty(\Sigma).$$

Definition 2. By a weak solution to problem (8) we refer to a pair of functions $(U, \zeta) \in W_Q \times W_\Sigma$ and $U = \zeta$ on Σ, which satisfy (8) in the following sense:

$$p_1 \int_Q \left(\frac{\partial}{\partial t} U, \phi_1\right) dt\, dx + p_2 \int_Q K(t, x, U) \nabla U \cdot \nabla \phi_1 \, dt\, dx$$

$$+ p_2 \int_\Sigma \left(\frac{\partial}{\partial t} \zeta, \phi_2\right) dt\, d\gamma + \int_\Sigma \nabla \zeta \nabla \phi_2 \, dt\, d\gamma + p_t \int_\Sigma \zeta \phi_2 \, dt d\gamma \qquad (40)$$

$$= p_r \int_Q (U - U^3) \phi_1 \, dt\, dx + p_s \int_Q g_d \phi_1 \, dt\, dx + \int_\Sigma g_{fr} \phi_2 \, dt d\gamma$$

$$\forall (\phi_1, \phi_2) \in L^2([0, T]; H^1(\Omega)) \times L^2([0, T]; H^1(\Gamma)),$$

where $\phi_1 = \phi_2$ on Σ, and $U(0, x) = U_0(x)$ on Ω.

Definition 3. By a weak solution to problems (38) and (39) we refer to a pair of functions $(U^\varepsilon, \zeta^\varepsilon) \in W_{Q_i^\varepsilon} \times W_{\Sigma_i^\varepsilon}$, and $U_i^\varepsilon = \zeta_i^\varepsilon$ on Σ_i^ε, $i \in \{0, 1, \ldots, M_\varepsilon - 1\}$, which satisfy (38) and (39) in the following sense:

$$p_1 \int_Q \left(\frac{\partial}{\partial t} U^\varepsilon, \xi_1\right) dt\, dx + p_2 \int_Q K(t, x, U^\varepsilon) \nabla U^\varepsilon \cdot \nabla \xi_1 \, dt\, dx$$

$$+ p_2 \int_\Sigma \left(\frac{\partial}{\partial t} \zeta^\varepsilon, \xi_2\right) dt\, d\gamma + \int_\Sigma \nabla \zeta^\varepsilon \nabla \xi_2 \, dt\, d\gamma + p_t \int_\Sigma \zeta^\varepsilon \xi_2 \, dt d\gamma \qquad (41)$$

$$= p_r \int_Q U^\varepsilon \xi_1 \, dt\, dx + p_s \int_Q g_d \xi_1 \, dt\, dx + \int_\Sigma g_{fr} \xi_2 \, dt d\gamma$$

$$\forall (\xi_1, \xi_2) \in L^2([0, T]; H^1(\Omega)) \times L^2([0, T]; H^1(\partial \Omega)),$$

where $U_-^\varepsilon(0, x) = U_0(x)$ on Ω, and $U_-^\varepsilon(0, x) = \zeta_0(x)$ on $\partial \Omega$.

In (40) and (41) the symbols $\int_Q$ and $\int_\Sigma$ denote the duality between $L^2([0, T]; H^1(\Omega))$ and $L^2([0, T]; H^1(\Omega)')$ as well as $L^2([0, T]; H^1(\partial \Omega))$ and $L^2([0, T]; H^1(\partial \Omega)')$, respectively.

Convergence of the Numerical Schemes (38) *and* (39)

The purpose of this subsection is to prove the convergence of the solution to the numerical scheme associated with the non-linear problem (8). Therefore,

Theorem 2. Assume that $U_0(x) \in W_\infty^{2-\frac{2}{p}}(\Omega)$, satisfying $p_2 \frac{\partial}{\partial \nu} U_0 - \Delta_\Gamma U_0 + p_t U_0 = g_{fr}(0, x)$ on $\partial \Omega$ and $g_{fr}(s, x) \in W_p^{1-\frac{1}{2p}, 2-\frac{1}{p}}(\Sigma)$. Let $(U^\varepsilon, \zeta^\varepsilon)$ be the solution to the numerical schemes (38) and (39). As $\varepsilon \to 0$, one has

$$(U^\varepsilon, \zeta^\varepsilon) \to (U^\star, \zeta^\star) \quad \text{strongly in } L^2(\Omega) \times L^2(\partial \Omega) \text{ for any } s \in (0, T], \qquad (42)$$

where $(U^\star, \zeta^\star) \in L^2([0, T]; H^1(\Omega)) \times L^2([0, T]; H^1(\partial \Omega))$ is a weak solution to problem (8).

The following lemmas, which involve the Cauchy problem (39), are very useful in the proof of Theorem 2. These were proven for the first time in [11]. Here, we reproduce them as well as sketch out the proof when pertinent.

Lemma 1. Assume $U_-^\varepsilon(i\varepsilon, x) \in L^\infty(\Omega)$, $i = 0, 1, \ldots, M_\varepsilon - 1$. Then, $U^\varepsilon(i\varepsilon, x) \in L^\infty(\Omega)$ and

$$\|U^\varepsilon(i\varepsilon, x)\|_{L^2(\Omega)}^2 \leq \|U_-^\varepsilon(i\varepsilon, x)\|_{L^2(\Omega)}^2. \tag{43}$$

Proof. We write $(39)_1$ in the form $\left(\dfrac{1}{z^2}\right)' = p_r$, and following the same reasoning as in [11] we obtain

$$z^2(\varepsilon, U_-^\varepsilon(i\varepsilon, x)) \leq U_-^\varepsilon(i\varepsilon, x)^2, \quad a.e \ x \in \Omega. \tag{44}$$

Owing to $(38)_3$ and (44), we can easily conclude the inequality complete in (43). □

Lemma 2. For $i = 0, 1, \ldots, M_\varepsilon - 1$, the estimate below holds

$$\|\nabla U^\varepsilon(i\varepsilon, x)\|_{L^2(\Omega)} \leq \|\nabla U_-^\varepsilon(i\varepsilon, x)\|_{L^2(\Omega)}. \tag{45}$$

Lemma 3. The following estimate holds

$$\|z(\varepsilon, x) - U_-^\varepsilon(i\varepsilon, x)\|_{L^2(\Omega)} \leq \varepsilon L \tag{46}$$

where $L > 0$ depends on $|\Omega|$, $\|U_-^\varepsilon\|_{L^\infty(\Omega)}$ and p_2.

Now, we are in a position to give the proof of Theorem 2. Following the same steps as in [11], we obtain the solution to problem (38) as $(U^\varepsilon, \zeta^\varepsilon) \in W_p^{1,2}(Q_i^\varepsilon) \cap L^\infty(Q_i^\varepsilon) \times W_p^{1,2}(\Sigma_i^\varepsilon) \cap L^\infty(\Sigma_i^\varepsilon)$, $\forall i \in \{0, 1, \ldots, M_\varepsilon - 1\}$.

Next, we give a priori estimates to Q_i^ε, $\forall i \in \{0, 1, \ldots, M_\varepsilon - 1\}$. Firstly, we multiply $(38)_1$ by U_t^ε and obtain

$$p_1 \int_\Omega |U_t^\varepsilon|^2 dx + p_1 \int_\Gamma |\zeta_t^\varepsilon|^2 d\gamma$$

$$+ \frac{p_2}{2} \int_\Omega K(t, x, U^\varepsilon) \frac{d}{dt} |\nabla U^\varepsilon|^2 dx + \frac{1}{2} \frac{d}{dt} \int_\Gamma |\nabla_\Gamma \zeta^\varepsilon|^2 d\gamma + \frac{p_t}{2} \frac{d}{dt} \int_\Gamma |\zeta^\varepsilon|^2 d\gamma \tag{47}$$

$$= \frac{p_2}{2} \frac{d}{dt} \int_\Omega |U^\varepsilon|^2 dx + \int_\Gamma g_{fr} \zeta_t^\varepsilon d\gamma + p_s \int_\Omega g_d U_t^\varepsilon dx.$$

Using Hölder's inequality for the right-hand terms $\int_\Gamma g_{fr} \zeta_t^\varepsilon d\gamma$ and $\int_\Omega g_d U_t^\varepsilon dx$, we have

$$\int_\Gamma g_{fr} \zeta_t^\varepsilon d\gamma \leq \frac{p_1}{2} \int_\Gamma |\zeta_t^\varepsilon|^2 d\gamma + \frac{1}{2p_1} \int_\Gamma |g_{fr}|^2 d\gamma,$$

$$p_s \int_\Omega g_d U_t^\varepsilon dx \leq \frac{p_1}{2} \int_\Omega |U_t^\varepsilon|^2 dx + \frac{p_s}{2p_1} \int_\Omega |g_d|^2 dx,$$

and substituting them in (47), we derive

$$\frac{p_1}{2}\int_\Omega |U_t^\varepsilon|^2 dx + \frac{p_1}{2}\int_\Gamma |\zeta_t^\varepsilon|^2 d\gamma$$

$$+\frac{p_2}{2}K_{min}\frac{d}{dt}\int_\Omega |\nabla U^\varepsilon|^2 dx + \frac{1}{2}\frac{d}{dt}\int_\Gamma |\nabla_\Gamma \zeta^\varepsilon|^2 d\gamma + \frac{p_t}{2}\frac{d}{dt}\int_\Gamma |\zeta^\varepsilon|^2 d\gamma \qquad (48)$$

$$\leq \frac{p_2}{2}\frac{d}{dt}\int_\Omega |U^\varepsilon|^2 dx + \frac{1}{2p_1}\int_\Gamma |g_{fr}|^2 d\gamma + \frac{p_s}{2p_1}\int_\Omega |g_d|^2 dx,$$

where the inequality (9) is also used.

Multiplying (38)$_1$ by $\frac{1}{p_1 p_2}U^\varepsilon$ as shown above, we obtain

$$\frac{1}{2p_2}\frac{d}{dt}\int_\Omega |U^\varepsilon|^2 dx + \frac{1}{2p_2}\frac{d}{dt}\int_\Gamma |\zeta^\varepsilon|^2 d\gamma$$

$$+\frac{1}{p_1}\int_\Omega K(t,x,U^\varepsilon)|\nabla U^\varepsilon|^2 dx + \frac{1}{p_1}\int_\Gamma |\nabla_\Gamma \zeta^\varepsilon|^2 d\gamma + \frac{p_t}{p_1 p_2}\int_\Gamma |\zeta^\varepsilon|^2 d\gamma \qquad (49)$$

$$= \frac{1}{p_1 p_2 p_r}\int_\Omega |U^\varepsilon|^2 dx + \frac{1}{p_1 p_2}\int_\Gamma g_{fr}\zeta^\varepsilon d\gamma + \frac{p_s}{p_1 p_2}\int_\Omega g_d U^\varepsilon dx.$$

In addition, using Hölder's inequality for the right-hand terms $\int_\Gamma g_{fr}\zeta^\varepsilon d\gamma$ and $\int_\Omega g_d U^\varepsilon dx$, we have

$$\frac{1}{p_1 p_2}\int_\Gamma g_{fr}\zeta^\varepsilon d\gamma \leq \frac{2p_t}{p_1 p_2}\int_\Gamma |\zeta^\varepsilon|^2 d\gamma + \frac{1}{2p_t p_1 p_2}\int_\Gamma |g_{fr}|^2 d\gamma,$$

$$\frac{p_s}{p_1 p_2}\int_\Omega g_d U^\varepsilon dx \leq \frac{1}{p_1 p_2}\int_\Omega |U^\varepsilon|^2 dx + \frac{p_s}{p_1 p_2}\int_\Omega |g_d|^2 dx,$$

and then from (49) we obtain

$$\frac{1}{2p_2}\frac{d}{dt}\int_\Omega |U^\varepsilon|^2 dx + \frac{1}{2p_2}\frac{d}{dt}\int_\Gamma |\zeta^\varepsilon|^2 d\gamma$$

$$+\frac{1}{p_1}K_{min}\int_\Omega |\nabla U^\varepsilon|^2 dx + \frac{1}{p_1}\int_\Gamma |\nabla_\Gamma \zeta^\varepsilon|^2 d\gamma \qquad (50)$$

$$\leq C(p_s,p_t,p_1,p_2)\left[\int_\Omega |U^\varepsilon|^2 dx + \int_\Gamma |\zeta^\varepsilon|^2 d\gamma + \int_\Gamma |g_{fr}|^2 d\gamma + \int_\Omega |g_d|^2 dx\right],$$

where the inequality (9) is also used.

Adding (48) and (50), we obtain

$$\frac{\partial}{\partial t}\left[\frac{1}{2p_2}\int_\Omega |U^\varepsilon|^2 dx + \left(\frac{p_t}{2}+\frac{1}{2p_2}\right)\int_\Gamma |\zeta^\varepsilon|^2 d\gamma + \frac{p_2}{2}K_{min}\int_\Omega |\nabla U^\varepsilon|^2 dx + \frac{1}{2}\int_\Gamma |\nabla_\Gamma \zeta^\varepsilon|^2 dx\right]$$

$$+\frac{p_1}{2}\int_\Omega |U_t^\varepsilon|^2 dx + \frac{p_1}{2}\int_\Gamma |\zeta_t^\varepsilon|^2 d\gamma + \frac{K_{min}}{p_1}\int_\Omega |\nabla U^\varepsilon|^2 dx + \frac{1}{p_1}\int_\Gamma |\nabla_\Gamma \zeta^\varepsilon|^2 d\gamma$$

$$\leq C(p_s,p_t,p_1,p_2)\left[\int_\Omega |U^\varepsilon|^2 dx + \int_\Gamma |\zeta^\varepsilon|^2 d\gamma + \int_\Gamma |g_{f_r}|^2 d\gamma + \int_\Omega |g_d|^2 dx\right].$$

Integrating the preceding on Q_0^ε, we derive

$$\frac{1}{2p_2}\|U_-^\varepsilon(\varepsilon,x)\|_{L^2(\Omega)}^2 + \left(\frac{p_t}{2}+\frac{1}{2p_2}\right)\|\zeta_-^\varepsilon(\varepsilon,x)\|_{L^2(\Gamma)}^2$$

$$+\frac{p_2}{2}K_{min}\|\nabla U_-^\varepsilon(\varepsilon,x)\|_{L^2(\Omega)}^2 + \frac{1}{2}\|\nabla_\Gamma \zeta_-^\varepsilon(\varepsilon,x)\|_{L^2(\Gamma)}^2$$

$$+\int_0^\varepsilon \left[\frac{p_1}{2}\int_\Omega |U_t^\varepsilon|^2 dx + \frac{p_1}{2}\int_\Gamma |\zeta_t^\varepsilon|^2 d\gamma + \frac{K_{min}}{p_1}\int_\Omega |\nabla U^\varepsilon|^2 dx + \frac{1}{p_1}\int_\Gamma |\nabla_\Gamma \zeta^\varepsilon|^2 d\gamma\right] ds \quad (51)$$

$$\leq \frac{1}{2p_2}\|U_0\|_{L^2(\Omega)}^2 + \left(\frac{p_t}{2}+\frac{1}{2p_2}\right)\|\zeta_0\|_{L^2(\Gamma)}^2 + \frac{p_2}{2}K_{min}\|\nabla U_0\|_{L^2(\Omega)}^2 + \frac{1}{2}\|\nabla_\Gamma \zeta_0\|_{L^2(\Gamma)}^2$$

$$+C(p_s,p_t,p_1,p_2)\left\{\int_0^\varepsilon \left[\|U^\varepsilon\|_{L^2(\Omega)}^2 + \|\zeta^\varepsilon\|_{L^2(\Gamma)}^2\right] ds + \|g_{f_r}\|_{L^2(\Sigma_0^\varepsilon)}^2 + \|g_d\|_{L^2(Q_0^\varepsilon)}^2\right\}.$$

It is relatively easy to observe that the estimate above refers to Q_0^ε and Σ_0^ε ($i=0$). Proceeding in a similar way for $i=1,2,\ldots,M_\varepsilon-2$, we obtain

$$\frac{1}{2p_2}\|U_-^\varepsilon((i+1)\varepsilon,x)\|_{L^2(\Omega)}^2 + \left(\frac{p_t}{2}+\frac{1}{2p_2}\right)\|\zeta_-^\varepsilon((i+1)\varepsilon,x)\|_{L^2(\Gamma)}^2$$

$$+\frac{p_2}{2}K_{min}\|\nabla U_-^\varepsilon((i+1)\varepsilon,x)\|_{L^2(\Omega)}^2 + \frac{1}{2}\|\nabla_\Gamma \zeta_-^\varepsilon((i+1)\varepsilon,x)\|_{L^2(\Gamma)}^2$$

$$+\int_{i\varepsilon}^{(i+1)\varepsilon}\left[\frac{p_1}{2}\|U_t^\varepsilon\|_{L^2(\Omega)}^2 + \frac{p_1}{2}\|\zeta_t^\varepsilon\|_{L^2(\Gamma)}^2 + \frac{K_{min}}{p_1}\|\nabla U^\varepsilon\|_{L^2(\Omega)}^2 + \frac{1}{p_1}\|\nabla_\Gamma \zeta^\varepsilon\|_{L^2(\Gamma)}^2\right] ds \quad (52)$$

$$\leq \frac{1}{2p_2}\|U^\varepsilon(i\varepsilon,x)\|_{L^2(\Omega)}^2 + \left(\frac{p_t}{2}+\frac{1}{2p_2}\right)\|\zeta^\varepsilon(i\varepsilon,x)\|_{L^2(\Gamma)}^2$$

$$+\frac{p_2}{2}\|\nabla U^\varepsilon(i\varepsilon,x)\|_{L^2(\Omega)}^2 + \frac{1}{2}\|\nabla_\Gamma \zeta^\varepsilon(i\varepsilon,x)\|_{L^2(\Gamma)}^2$$

$$+C(p_s,p_t,p_1,p_2)\left\{\int_{i\varepsilon}^{(i+1)\varepsilon}\left[\|U^\varepsilon\|_{L^2(\Omega)}^2 + \|\zeta^\varepsilon\|_{L^2(\Gamma)}^2\right] ds + \|g_{f_r}\|_{L^2(\Sigma_i^\varepsilon)}^2 + \|g_d\|_{L^2(Q_i^\varepsilon)}^2\right\},$$

while for $i = M_\varepsilon - 1$ we have

$$\frac{1}{2p_2}\|U_-^\varepsilon(T,x)\|_{L^2(\Omega)}^2 + \left(\frac{p_t}{2} + \frac{1}{2p_2}\right)\|\zeta_-^\varepsilon(T,x)\|_{L^2(\Gamma)}^2$$

$$+\frac{p_2}{2}K_{min}\|\nabla U_-^\varepsilon(T,x)\|_{L^2(\Omega)}^2 + \frac{1}{2}\|\nabla_\Gamma \zeta_-^\varepsilon(T,x)\|_{L^2(\Gamma)}^2$$

$$+ \int_{M_\varepsilon-1}^T \left[\frac{p_1}{2}\|U_t^\varepsilon\|_{L^2(\Omega)}^2 + \frac{p_1}{2}\|\zeta_t^\varepsilon\|_{L^2(\Gamma)}^2 + \frac{1}{p_1}\|\nabla U^\varepsilon\|_{L^2(\Omega)}^2 + \frac{1}{p_1}\|\nabla_\Gamma \zeta^\varepsilon\|_{L^2(\Gamma)}^2\right]ds \quad (53)$$

$$\leq \frac{1}{2p_2}\|U^\varepsilon(T,x)\|_{L^2(\Omega)}^2 + \left(\frac{p_t}{2} + \frac{1}{2p_2}\right)\|\zeta^\varepsilon(T,x)\|_{L^2(\Gamma)}^2$$

$$+\frac{p_2}{2}\|\nabla U^\varepsilon(T,x)\|_{L^2(\Omega)}^2 + \frac{1}{2}\|\nabla_\Gamma \zeta^\varepsilon(T,x)\|_{L^2(\Gamma)}^2$$

$$+C(p_s,p_t,p_1,p_2)\left\{\int_{M_\varepsilon-1}^T \left[\|U^\varepsilon\|_{L^2(\Omega)}^2 + \|\zeta^\varepsilon\|_{L^2(\Gamma)}^2\right]ds + \|g_{fr}\|_{L^2(\Sigma_{M_\varepsilon-1}^\varepsilon)}^2 + \|g_d\|_{L^2(Q_{M_\varepsilon-1}^\varepsilon)}^2\right\}.$$

Adding (51)–(53) and owing to the inequalities (43) and (45), we obtain

$$\frac{1}{2p_2}\|U_-^\varepsilon(T,x)\|_{L^2(\Omega)}^2 + \left(\frac{p_t}{2} + \frac{1}{2p_2}\right)\|\zeta_-^\varepsilon(T,x)\|_{L^2(\Gamma)}^2$$

$$+ \frac{p_2}{2}\|\nabla U_-^\varepsilon(T,x)\|_{L^2(\Omega)}^2 + \frac{1}{2}\|\nabla_\Gamma \zeta_-^\varepsilon(T,x)\|_{L^2(\Gamma)}^2$$

$$+ \int_0^T \left[\frac{p_1}{2}\|U_t^\varepsilon\|_{L^2(\Omega)}^2 + \frac{p_1}{2}\|\zeta_t^\varepsilon\|_{L^2(\Gamma)}^2 + \frac{1}{p_1}\|\nabla U^\varepsilon\|_{L^2(\Omega)}^2 + \frac{1}{p_1}\|\nabla_\Gamma \zeta^\varepsilon\|_{L^2(\Gamma)}^2\right]dt$$

$$\leq \frac{1}{2p_2}\|U_0\|_{L^2(\Omega)}^2 + \left(\frac{p_t}{2} + \frac{1}{2p_2}\right)\|\psi_0\|_{L^2(\Gamma)}^2 + \frac{p_2}{2}\|\nabla U_0\|_{L^2(\Omega)}^2 + \frac{1}{2}\|\nabla_\Gamma \zeta_0\|_{L^2(\Gamma)}^2$$

$$+ C(p_s,p_t,p_1,p_2)\left\{\int_0^T \left[\|U^\varepsilon\|_{L^2(\Omega)}^2 + \|\zeta^\varepsilon\|_{L^2(\Gamma)}^2\right]dt + \|g_{fr}\|_{L^2(\Sigma)}^2 + \|g_d\|_{L^2(Q)}^2\right\}.$$

Applying the Gronwall inequality to the above inequalities, we finally deduce

$$\int_0^T \left\{\|U_t^\varepsilon\|_{L^2(\Omega)}^2 + \|\zeta_t^\varepsilon\|_{L^2(\Gamma)}^2 + \|\nabla U^\varepsilon\|_{L^2(\Omega)}^2 + \|\nabla_\Gamma \zeta^\varepsilon\|_{L^2(\Gamma)}^2\right\}dt \leq C, \quad (54)$$

where $C > 0$ is independent of ε and M_ε.

Owing to $(38)_3$, $(38)_4$ and (46), we obtain

$$\sum_{i=0}^{M_\varepsilon-1} \|U^\varepsilon(i\varepsilon,x) - U_-^\varepsilon(i\varepsilon,x)\|_{L^2(\Omega)} \leq TL = C_1, \quad (55)$$

$$\sum_{i=0}^{M_\varepsilon-1} \|\zeta^\varepsilon(i\varepsilon,x) - \zeta^\varepsilon_-(i\varepsilon,x)\|_{L^2(\Gamma)} \leq C_2, \tag{56}$$

where $C_1 > 0$ and $C_2 > 0$ are independent of M_ε and ε. Summing (54)–(56), we derive

$$\bigvee_0^T U^\varepsilon + \bigvee_0^T \zeta^\varepsilon + \int_0^T \left[\|U^\varepsilon_t\|^2_{L^2(\Omega)} + \|\zeta^\varepsilon_t\|^2_{L^2(\Gamma)} + \|\nabla U^\varepsilon\|^2_{L^2(\Omega)} + \|\nabla_\Gamma \zeta^\varepsilon\|^2_{L^2(\Gamma)} \right] ds \leq C, \tag{57}$$

where the positive constant C is independent of M_ε and ε, while $\bigvee_0^T U^\varepsilon$ and $\bigvee_0^T \zeta^\varepsilon$ stand for the variation of $U^\varepsilon : [0, T] \to L^2(\Omega)$ and $\zeta^\varepsilon : [0, T] \to L^2(\Gamma)$, respectively.

Since the introduction of $L^2(\Omega)$ into $H^{-1}(\Omega)$ is compact and $\{U^\varepsilon_s(s)\}$ is bounded in $L^2(\Omega)$ $\forall s \in [0, T]$, we conclude that there exists a bounded variation function $U^*(s) \in BV([0, T]; H^{-1}(\Omega))$ and subsequent $U^\varepsilon(s)$ (see [11]), such that

$$U^\varepsilon(s) \to U^*(s) \quad \text{strongly in} \quad H^{-1}(\Omega) \quad \forall s \in [0, T], \tag{58}$$

$$\zeta^\varepsilon(s) \to \zeta^*(s) \quad \text{strongly in} \quad H^{-1}(\Gamma) \quad \forall s \in [0, T]. \tag{59}$$

Further, from (57) we deduce that

$$\begin{cases} U^\varepsilon \to U^* & \text{weakly in } L^2(0, T; H^1(\Omega)) \\ \zeta^\varepsilon \to \zeta^* & \text{weakly in } L^2(0, T; H^1(\Gamma)). \end{cases} \tag{60}$$

By the well-known embeddings $H^1(\Omega) \subset L^2(\Omega) \subset H^{-1}(\Omega)$, and $H^1(\partial\Omega) \subset L^2(\partial\Omega) \subset H^{-1}(\partial\Omega)$, standard interpolation inequalities (see [11] p. 17) yield that $\forall \ell > 0$, $\exists C(\ell) > 0$ such that

$$\begin{cases} \|U^\varepsilon(s) - U^*(s)\|_{L^2(\Omega)} \leq \ell \|U^\varepsilon(s) - U^*(s)\|_{H^1(\Omega)} + C(\ell)\|U^\varepsilon(s) - U^*(s)\|_{H^{-1}(\Omega)}, \\ \|\zeta^\varepsilon(s) - \zeta^*(s)\|_{L^2(\partial\Omega)} \leq \ell \|\zeta^\varepsilon(s) - \zeta^*(s)\|_{H^1(\partial\Omega)} + C(\ell)\|\zeta^\varepsilon(s) - \zeta^*(s)\|_{H^{-1}(\partial\Omega)}, \end{cases} \tag{61}$$

$\forall \varepsilon > 0$ and $\forall s \in [0, T]$, where $C(\ell) \to 0$ as $\ell \to 0$.

Finally, relations (58)–(61) permit us to conclude that the assertion conducted in (42) holds true, ending the proof of Theorem 2.

Corollary 2. *Assume* $U_0 \in W_\infty^{2-\frac{2}{p}}(\Omega)$, $p_2 \frac{\partial}{\partial \nu} U_0(x) - \Delta_\Gamma U_0 + p_t U_0(x) = g_{fr}(0, x)$ *on* $\partial\Omega$ *and* $g_{fr} \in W_p^{1-\frac{1}{2p}, 2-\frac{1}{p}}(\Sigma)$. *Then* $U^\star \in W_Q$ *is a weak solution to the non-linear problem in* (1).

Now we search the error of the numerical schemes (38) and (39) relative to g_d and g_{fr}.

From Theorem 1 we know that $\forall g_d \in L^p(Q)$ and $g_{fr} \in W_p^{1-\frac{1}{2p}, 2-\frac{1}{p}}(\Sigma)$, the problem (8) has a unique solution $(U, \zeta) \in W_p^{1,2}(Q) \times W_p^{1,2}(\Sigma)$. Moreover, (see (11))

$$\|U\|_{W_p^{1,2}(Q)} + \|\zeta\|_{W_p^{1,2}(\Sigma)}$$
$$\leq C \left[1 + \|U_0\|_{W_\infty^{2-\frac{2}{p}}(\Omega)}^{3-\frac{2}{p}} + \|\zeta_0\|_{W_\infty^{2-\frac{2}{p}}(\Gamma)}^{3-\frac{2}{p}} + \|g_d\|_{L^{3p-2}(Q)}^{\frac{3p-2}{p}} + \|g_{fr}\|_{W_p^{1-\frac{1}{2p}, 2-\frac{1}{p}}(\Sigma)} \right], \tag{62}$$

with a fixed $\zeta_0 \in W_\infty^{2-\frac{2}{p}}(\Gamma)$ and $U_0 \in W_\infty^{2-\frac{2}{p}}(\Omega)$ verifying $p_2 \frac{\partial}{\partial \nu} U_0 - \Delta_\Gamma U_0 + p_t U_0 = g_{fr}(0, x)$. Thus, we have

Theorem 3. Let $g_d \in L^p(Q)$ and $g_{fr} \in W_p^{1-\frac{1}{2p}, 2-\frac{1}{p}}(\Sigma)$. Let $g_d^k \subset L^p(Q)$ and $g_{fr}^k \subset W_p^{1-\frac{1}{2p}, 2-\frac{1}{p}}(\Sigma)$ be two sequences such that $g_d^k \longrightarrow g_d$ in $L^p(Q)$ and $g_{fr}^k \longrightarrow g_{fr}$ in $W_p^{1-\frac{1}{2p}, 2-\frac{1}{p}}(\Sigma)$ as $k \longrightarrow \infty$. Denoted by $(U_m, \zeta_m) \subset W_p^{1,2}(Q) \times W_p^{1,2}(\Sigma)$ and $(U_{m,k}, \zeta_{m,k}) \subset W_p^{1,2}(Q) \times W_p^{1,2}(\Sigma)$, the approximating sequences are given in (38) and ((39), for (g_d, g_{fr}) and (g_d^k, g_{fr}^k), respectively, with $U_0 \in W_\infty^{2-\frac{2}{p}}(\Omega)$ fixed. Then,

$$\limsup_{m \longrightarrow \infty} \left[\|U_{m,k} - U\|_{L^2(Q)} + \|\zeta_{m,k} - \zeta\|_{L^2(\Sigma)} \right]$$

$$\leq C e^{CT} \max \left\{ \max_{(t,x) \in Q} |g_d^k - g_d|, \max_{(t,x) \in \Sigma} |g_{fr}^k - g_{fr}| \right\} \quad (63)$$

$\forall k \geq 1$, where $C > 0$ depends on $|\Omega|$, T, n, p, p_1, p_2, p_t, p_r, p_s, $\|U_0\|_{W_\infty^{2-\frac{2}{p}}(\Omega)}$, $\|g_d\|_{L^p(Q)}$ and $\|g_{fr}\|_{W_p^{1-\frac{1}{2p}, 2-\frac{1}{p}}(\Sigma)}$.

In particular, $\exists (U_{m,k}, \zeta_{m,k})$, denoted by (U_{m_k}, ζ_{m_k}), such that $(U_{m_k}, \zeta_{m_k}) \longrightarrow (U, \zeta)$ in $L^p(Q) \times L^p(\Sigma)$ and in $Q \times \Sigma$ as $k \longrightarrow \infty$.

Proof. Owing to (62) we assume that

$$\|U_k\|_{W_p^{1,2}(Q)} + \|\zeta_k\|_{W_p^{1,2}(\Sigma)}$$

$$\leq C \left\{ 1 + \|U_0\|_{W_\infty^{2-\frac{2}{p}}(\Omega)}^{3-\frac{2}{p}} + \|\zeta_0\|_{W_\infty^{2-\frac{2}{p}}(\Gamma)}^{3-\frac{2}{p}} + \|g_d^k\|_{L^{3p-2}(Q)}^{\frac{3p-2}{p}} + \|g_{fr}^k\|_{W_p^{1-\frac{1}{2p}, 2-\frac{1}{p}}(\Sigma)} \right\}$$

$$\leq C \left\{ 1 + \|U_0\|_{W_\infty^{2-\frac{2}{p}}(\Omega)}^{3-\frac{2}{p}} + \|\zeta_0\|_{W_\infty^{2-\frac{2}{p}}(\Gamma)}^{3-\frac{2}{p}} + \|g_d\|_{L^{3p-2}(Q)}^{\frac{3p-2}{p}} + \|g_{fr}\|_{W_p^{1-\frac{1}{2p}, 2-\frac{1}{p}}(\Sigma)} \right\},$$

where $C > 0$ is interpreted as M_4 in (12). This ensures the applicability of (14) in Theorem 1 with $U_0^1 = U_0^2$ and $\zeta_0^1 = \zeta_0^2$ obtains

$$\|U_k - U\|_{W_p^{1,2}(Q)} + \|\zeta_k - \zeta\|_{W_p^{1,2}(\Sigma)}$$

$$\leq C_1 e^{CT} \max \left\{ \max_{(t,x) \in Q} |g_d^k - g_d|, \max_{(t,x) \in \Sigma} |g_{fr}^k - g_{fr}| \right\}, \quad \forall k \geq 1, \quad (64)$$

where $C_1 > 0$. For $k \geq 1$, Theorem 2 gives

$$(U_{m,k}(s, \cdot), \zeta_{m,k}(s, \cdot)) \longrightarrow (U_k(s, \cdot), \zeta_k(s, \cdot)) \quad in \quad L^2(\Omega) \times L^2(\partial \Omega),$$

uniformly for $s \in [0, T]$, as $m \longrightarrow \infty$. In particular, $\forall k \geq 1$ we have

$$(U_{m,k}, \zeta_{m,k}) \longrightarrow (U_k, \zeta_k), \quad in \quad L^2(Q) \times L^2(\Sigma), \quad as \quad m \longrightarrow \infty. \quad (65)$$

On the base of the relation in (64) and owing to (20), we obtain

$$\|U_{m,k} - U\|_{L^2(Q)} + \|\zeta_{m,k} - \zeta\|_{L^2(\Sigma)}$$

$$\leq \|U_{m,k} - U_k\|_{L^2(Q)} + \|\zeta_{m,k} - \zeta_k\|_{L^2(\Sigma)} + \|U_k - U\|_{L^2(Q)} + \|\zeta_k - \zeta\|_{L^2(\Sigma)}$$

$$\leq \|U_{m,k} - U_k\|_{L^2(Q)} + \|\zeta_{m,k} - \zeta_k\|_{L^2(\Sigma)}$$

$$+ C_1 e^{CT} \max\left\{\max_{(t,x) \in Q} |g_d^k - g_d|, \max_{(t,x) \in \Sigma} |g_{fr}^k - g_{fr}|\right\}, \quad \forall m, k \geq 1.$$

Using (65) we can substitute the above inequality into the superior limit as $m \longrightarrow \infty$ to prove that (63) is correct.

The last statement in Theorem 3 follows directly on from (63). □

The general framework of the numerical algorithm to compute the approximate solution to problem (1) via the fractional steps scheme may be demonstrated as follows:

Begin **alg-frac_sec-ord_dbc**
$i = 0 \rightarrow U_0$ from (39)$_3$;
For $i = 0$ perform $M_\varepsilon - 1$
Compute $z(\varepsilon, \cdot)$ from (39);
$U^\varepsilon(i\varepsilon, \cdot) = z(\varepsilon, \cdot)$;
$\zeta^\varepsilon(i\varepsilon, \cdot) = U^\varepsilon(i\varepsilon, \cdot)$;
Compute $(U^\varepsilon((i+1)\varepsilon, \cdot), \zeta^\varepsilon((i+1)\varepsilon, \cdot))$ solving the linear system (38);
End-for;
End.

5. Conclusions

The main problem addressed in this work concerns the non-linear second-order reaction–diffusion equation with its principal part in divergence form with inhomogeneous dynamic boundary conditions. Provided that the initial and boundary data meet the appropriate regularity and compatibility conditions, the well-posedness of a classical solution to the non-linear problem is proven in this new formulation (Theorem 1). Precisely, the Leray–Schauder principle and L^p theory of linear and quasi-linear parabolic equations, via Lemma 7.4 (see [1]), were applied to prove the qualitative properties of solution $(U(t,x), \zeta(t,x))$. More precisely, we cannot directly apply the L^p theory to problem (1) (or (3)). Thus, this makes the result of Lemma 7.4 in Choban and Moroşanu [1] (p. 114) very important. Moreover, the a priori estimates were made in $L^p(Q)$ and $L^p(\Sigma)$ which permit the derivation of higher-order regularity properties, that is, $\left(U(t,x), \zeta(t,x)\right) \in W_p^{1,2}(Q) \times W_p^{1,2}(\Sigma)$. Thus, the classical method of bootstrapping (see Moroşanu and Motreanu [20]) can be avoided.

Let us note that, due to the presence of the terms $K(t, x, U(t, x))$, the non-linear operator H (see (17)) does not represent the gradient of the energy functional. Therefore, the new proposed second-order non-linear problem cannot be obtained from the minimisation of any energy cost functional, i.e., (1) is not a variational PDE model.

Furthermore, an iterative fractional step-type scheme was introduced to approximate problem (8). The convergence and error estimates were established for the proposed numerical scheme and a conceptual numerical algorithm was formulated. In this regards, we want to underline the solutions dependence in Theorem 2 on the physical parameters, which could be useful in future investigations regarding error analysis and numerical simulations.

The qualitative results obtained here could be later used in quantitative approaches to the mathematical model (1) (or (3)) as well as in the study of distributed and/or non-linear optimal boundary control problems governed by such a non-linear problem.

Numerical implementation of the conceptual algorithm, **alg-frac_sec-ord_dbc**, as well as various simulations regarding the physical phenomena described by the non-linear parabolic problem (1) represent a matter for further investigation.

Author Contributions: Conceptualization, C.F. and C.M.; methodology, C.M.; validation, C.F. and C.M.; writing—original draft preparation, C.M.; writing—review and editing, C.F.; visualization, C.F.; funding acquisition, C.F. All authors have read and agreed to the published version of the manuscript.

Funding: This research received no external funding.

Data Availability Statement: Not applicable.

Conflicts of Interest: The authors declare no conflict of interest.

References

1. Choban, M.; Moroşanu, C. Well-posedness of a nonlinear second-order anisotropic reaction-diffusion problem with nonlinear and inhomogeneous dynamic boundary conditions. *Carpathian J. Math.* **2022**, *38*, 95–116. [CrossRef]
2. Croitoru, A.; Moroşanu, C.; Tănase, G. Well-posedness and numerical simulations of an anisotropic reaction-diffusion model in case 2D. *J. Appl. Anal. Comput.* **2021**, *11*, 2258–2278. http://www.jaac-online.com/article/doi/10.11948/20200359 (accessed on 1 January 2021). [CrossRef] [PubMed]
3. Miranville, A.; Moroşanu, C. A Qualitative Analysis of a Nonlinear Second-Order Anisotropic Diffusion Problem with Non-homogeneous Cauchy-Stefan-Boltzmann Boundary Conditions. *Appl. Math. Optim.* **2021**, *84*, 227–244. [CrossRef]
4. Moroşanu, C.; Pavăl, S. Rigorous Mathematical Investigation of a Nonlocal and Nonlinear Second-Order Anisotropic Reaction-Diffusion Model: Applications on Image Segmentation. *Mathematics* **2021**, *9*, 91. [CrossRef]
5. Miranville, A.; Moroşanu, C. *Qualitative and Quantitative Analysis for the Mathematical Models of Phase Separation and Transition. Aplications*; Differential Equations & Dynamical Systems; AIMS—American Institute of Mathematical Sciences: Springfield, MO, USA, 2020; Volume 7. Available online: www.aimsciences.org/fileAIMS/cms/news/info/28df2b3d-ffac-4598-a89b-9494392d1394.pdf (accessed on 11 January 2023).
6. Moroşanu, C. Well-posedness for a phase-field transition system endowed with a polynomial nonlinearity and a general class of nonlinear dynamic boundary conditions. *J. Fixed Point Theory Appl.* **2016**, *18*, 225–250. [CrossRef]
7. Berinde, V.; Miranville, A.; Moroşanu, C. A qualitative analysis of a second-order anisotropic phase-field transition system endowed with a general class of nonlinear dynamic boundary conditions. *Discret. Contin. Dyn. Syst. Ser. S* **2023**, *16*, 148–186. [CrossRef]
8. Conti, M.; Gatti, S.; Miranville, A. Asymptotic behavior of the Caginalp phase-field system with coupled dynamic boundary conditions. *Discret. Contin. Dyn. Syst. Ser. S* **2012**, *5*, 485–505. [CrossRef]
9. Miranville, A.; Moroşanu, C. Analysis of an iterative scheme of fractional steps type associated with the nonlinear phase-field equation with non-homogeneous dynamic boundary conditions. *Discret. Contin. Dyn. Syst. Ser. S* **2016**, *9*, 537–556. [CrossRef]
10. Ladyzenskaja, O.A.; Solonnikov, V.A.; Uralceva, N.N. *Linear and Quasi-Linear Equations of Parabolic Type*; Translations of Mathematical Monographs; American Mathematical Society: 201 Charles Street, Providence, RI, USA, 1968; Volume 23.
11. Moroşanu, C. *Analysis and Optimal Control of Phase-Field Transition System: Fractional Steps Methods*; Bentham Science Publishers: Sharjah, United Arab Emirates, 2012. [CrossRef]
12. Arnăutu, V.; Moroşanu, C. Numerical approximation for the phase-field transition system. *Int. J. Comput. Math.* **1996**, *62*, 209–221. [CrossRef]
13. Benincasa, T.; Moroşanu, C. Fractional steps scheme to approximate the phase-field transition system with non-homogeneous Cauchy-Neumann boundary conditions. *Numer. Funct. Anal. Optimiz.* **2009**, *30*, 199–213. [CrossRef]
14. Benincasa, T.; Favini, A.; Moroşanu, C. A Product Formula Approach to a Non-homogeneous Boundary Optimal Control Problem Governed by Nonlinear Phase-field Transition System. PART I: A Phase-field Model. *J. Optim. Theory Appl.* **2011**, *148*, 14–30. [CrossRef]
15. Gatti, S.; Miranville, A. Asymptotic behavior of a phase-field system with dynamic boundary conditions. *Differential Equations: Inverse and Direct Problems*; Lecture Notes Pure Applied Mathematics; Chapman & Hall/CRC: Boca Raton, FL, USA, 2006; Volume 251, pp. 149–170.
16. Miranville, A.; Moroşanu, C. On the existence, uniqueness and regularity of solutions to the phase-field transition system with non-homogeneous Cauchy-Neumann and nonlinear dynamic boundary conditions. *Appl. Math. Model.* **2016**, *40*, 192–207. [CrossRef]
17. Moroşanu, C. Modeling of the continuous casting process of steel via phase-field transition system. Fractional steps method. *AIMS Math.* **2019**, *4*, 648–662. [CrossRef]

18. Moroşanu, C. Stability and errors analysis of two iterative schemes of fractional steps type associated with a nonlinear reaction-diffusion equation. *Discret. Contin. Dyn. Syst. Ser. S* **2020**, *13*, 1567–1587. [CrossRef]
19. Moroşanu, C.; Croitoru, A. Analysis of an iterative scheme of fractional steps type associated with the phase-field equation endowed with a general nonlinearity and Cauchy-Neumann boundary conditions. *J. Math. Anal. Appl.* **2015**, *425*, 1225–1239. [CrossRef]
20. Moroşanu, C.; Motreanu, D. The phase field system with a general nonlinearity. *Int. J. Differ. Equations Appl.* **2000**, *1*, 187–204.
21. Moroşanu, C.; Pavăl, S. On the numerical approximation of a nonlinear reaction-diffusion equation with non-homogeneous Neumann boundary conditions. Case 1D. *ROMAI J.* **2019**, *15*, 43–60. Available online: https://rj.romai.ro/arhiva/2019/2/Morosanu-Paval.pdf (accessed on 13 January 2023).
22. Moroşanu, C.; Pavăl, S.; Trenchea, C. Analysis of stability and errors of three methods associated with the nonlinear reaction-diffusion equation supplied with homogeneous Neumann boundary conditions. *J. Appl. Anal. Comput.* **2017**, *7*, 1–19. [CrossRef]
23. Ovono, A.A. Numerical approximation of the phase-field transition system with non-homogeneous Cauchy-Neumann boundary conditions in both unknown functions via fractional steps methods. *J. Appl. Anal. Comput.* **2013**, *3*, 377–397. [CrossRef]

Disclaimer/Publisher's Note: The statements, opinions and data contained in all publications are solely those of the individual author(s) and contributor(s) and not of MDPI and/or the editor(s). MDPI and/or the editor(s) disclaim responsibility for any injury to people or property resulting from any ideas, methods, instructions or products referred to in the content.

Article

Some New Jensen–Mercer Type Integral Inequalities via Fractional Operators

Bahtiyar Bayraktar [1,†], Péter Kórus [2,*,†] and Juan Eduardo Nápoles Valdés [3,†]

1. Faculty of Education, Bursa Uludag University, Gorukle Campus, 16059 Bursa, Turkey; bbayraktar@uludag.edu.tr
2. Department of Mathematics, Juhász Gyula Faculty of Education, University of Szeged, Hattyas utca 10, H-6725 Szeged, Hungary
3. Facultad de Ciencias Exactas y Naturales y Agrimensura, Universidad Nacional del Nordeste, Ave. Libertad 5450, Corrientes 3400, Argentina; jnapoles@exa.unne.edu.ar
* Correspondence: korus.peter@szte.hu
† These authors contributed equally to this work.

Abstract: In this study, we present new variants of the Hermite–Hadamard inequality via non-conformable fractional integrals. These inequalities are proven for convex functions and differentiable functions whose derivatives in absolute value are generally convex. Our main results are established using the classical Jensen–Mercer inequality and its variants for (h, m)-convex modified functions proven in this paper. In addition to showing that our results support previously known results from the literature, we provide examples of their application.

Keywords: convex functions; (h, m)-convex functions; Jensen–Mercer inequality; Hermite–Hadamard inequality; Hölder inequality, power mean inequality; non-conformable fractional operators

MSC: 26A33; 26A51; 26D15

Citation: Bayraktar, B.; Kórus, P.; Nápoles Valdés, J.E. Some New Jensen–Mercer Type Integral Inequalities via Fractional Operators. *Axioms* **2023**, *12*, 517. https://doi.org/10.3390/axioms12060517

Academic Editor: Hari Mohan Srivastava

Received: 28 April 2023
Revised: 19 May 2023
Accepted: 24 May 2023
Published: 25 May 2023

Copyright: © 2023 by the authors. Licensee MDPI, Basel, Switzerland. This article is an open access article distributed under the terms and conditions of the Creative Commons Attribution (CC BY) license (https://creativecommons.org/licenses/by/4.0/).

1. Introduction

Jensen's inequality is one of the most studied results in the literature. In the last few decades, quite a few researchers have been interested in refining and generalizing this inequality (see, e.g., [1–6]).

Let $0 < x_1 \leq x_2 \leq \ldots \leq x_n$ and let w_k $(1 \leq k \leq n)$ be positive weights associated with these x_k and let their sum demonstrate unity. Then, Jensen's inequality

$$\Phi\left(\sum_{k=1}^{n} w_k x_k\right) \leq \sum_{k=1}^{n} w_k \Phi(x_k) \qquad (1)$$

holds (see [7]).

Mercer investigated a generalized form of Jensen's inequality, which is famously known as the Jensen–Mercer inequality (see [8]): if Φ is a convex function on $[\rho, \sigma]$, then

$$\Phi\left(\rho + \sigma - \sum_{k=1}^{n} w_k x_k\right) \leq \Phi(\rho) + \Phi(\sigma) - \sum_{k=1}^{n} w_k \Phi(x_k) \qquad (2)$$

is fulfilled for $x_k \in [\rho, \sigma]$, $w_k \in [0, 1]$ with $\sum_{k=1}^{n} w_k = 1$. In case of $n = 1$, inequality (2) reads as

$$\Phi(\sigma - x + \rho) \leq \Phi(\rho) + \Phi(\sigma) - \Phi(x) \qquad (3)$$

for $x \in [\rho, \sigma]$. Extensions of this result can be found in e.g., [9–11].

The well-known refinement of Jensen's inequality, the Hermite–Hadamard inequality

$$\Phi\left(\frac{\rho+\sigma}{2}\right) \leq \frac{1}{\sigma-\rho}\int_\rho^\sigma \Phi(x)dx \leq \frac{\Phi(\rho)+\Phi(\sigma)}{2} \qquad (4)$$

for convex functions, was proved by Hermite in 1883 and independently by Hadamard in 1893; see, e.g., [12]. This inequality has been generalized by many researchers, taking into account various aspects such as general convexity and fractional operators. For Hermite–Hadamard–Mercer type results, see [13–18].

In general, the concept of convex and general convex functions plays a major role in the theory of integral inequalities. So far, many general convex classes have been described in the literature. A summary of many of these classes was given in [19].

Definition 1. *Let* $h : [0,1] \to [0,\infty)$, $h \neq 0$ *and* $\Phi : I = [0,\infty) \to \mathbb{R}$. *If inequality*

$$\Phi(\lambda x + m(1-\lambda)y) \leq h(\lambda)\Phi(x) + mh(1-\lambda)\Phi(y) \qquad (5)$$

is fulfilled $\forall \lambda \in [0,1]$ *and* $x, y \in I$, *where* $m \in [0,1]$, *then function* Φ *is called* (h,m)-*convex on* I.

In [20,21], the following definitions were presented.

Definition 2. *Let* $h : [0,1] \to (0,1]$ *and* $\Phi : I = [0,\infty) \to \mathbb{R}$. *If inequality*

$$\Phi(\lambda x + m(1-\lambda)y) \leq h^s(\lambda)\Phi(x) + m(1-h^s(\lambda))\Phi(y) \qquad (6)$$

is fulfilled $\forall \lambda \in [0,1]$ *and* $x, y \in I$, *where* $m \in [0,1]$, $s \in [-1,1]$, *then function* Φ *is called* (h,m)-*convex modified of the first type on* I *and this set of functions will be denoted as* $K_{h,m}^{1,s}(I)$.

Definition 3. *Let* $h : [0,1] \to (0,1]$ *and* $\Phi : I = [0,\infty) \to \mathbb{R}$. *If inequality*

$$\Phi(\lambda x + m(1-\lambda)y) \leq h^s(\lambda)\Phi(x) + m(1-h(\lambda))^s\Phi(y) \qquad (7)$$

is fulfilled $\forall \lambda \in [0,1]$ *and* $x, y \in I$, *where* $m \in [0,1]$, $s \in [-1,1]$, *then function* Φ *is called* (h,m)-*convex modified of the second type on* I *and this set of functions will be denoted as* $K_{h,m}^{2,s}(I)$.

Throughout the paper, for (h,m)-convex modified functions of the first or, of the second type, we assume that $m \in [0,1]$ and $s \in [-1,1]$.

The following results are extended versions of Jensen–Mercer inequality (3).

Theorem 1. *Let* $\Phi : I = [\rho, \sigma] \subset \mathbb{R} \to \mathbb{R}$ *be an integrable and* (h,m)-*convex function. Then, the following Mercer's type inequality holds:*

$$\Phi(x_1 + mx_n - x_k) \leq (h(\lambda) + h(1-\lambda))[\Phi(x_1) + m\Phi(x_n)] - \Phi(x_k) \qquad (8)$$

for $x_1 \leq mx_n$, $x_k \in [x_1, mx_n] \subseteq I$ *and* $\lambda \in [0,1]$, *such that* $x_k = \lambda x_1 + m(1-\lambda)x_n$.

Proof. Putting $x_k = \lambda x_1 + m(1-\lambda)x_n$ and $y_k = (1-\lambda)x_1 + m\lambda x_n$, we have $y_k + x_k = x_1 + mx_n$. Now, using the (h,m)-convexity of Φ, we have

$$\Phi(y_k) \leq h(1-\lambda)\Phi(x_1) + mh(\lambda)\Phi(x_n),$$
$$\Phi(x_k) \leq h(\lambda)\Phi(x_1) + mh(1-\lambda)\Phi(x_n).$$

By adding the corresponding sides of the inequalities, we obtain

$$\Phi(y_k) + \Phi(x_k) \leq (h(\lambda) + h(1-\lambda))[\Phi(x_1) + m\Phi(x_n)].$$

From the above, the desired inequality (8) is easily obtained. □

Corollary 1. Let $\Phi : I = [\rho, \sigma] \subset \mathbb{R} \to \mathbb{R}$ be an integrable (h,m)-convex function. Then, from (8), we have

$$\Phi(x_1 + mx_n - x_k) \leq \mathbf{A}_0[\Phi(x_1) + m\Phi(x_n)] - \Phi(x_k) \qquad (9)$$

for $x_1 \leq mx_n$, $x_k \in [x_1, mx_n] \subseteq I$ and $\mathbf{A}_0 = \sup\limits_{\lambda \in [0,1]} (h(\lambda) + h(1-\lambda))$.

Remark 1. For $m = 1$, Corollary 1 leads to a correct version of Lemma 3.1 of [11].

Theorem 2. Let $\Phi : I = [\rho, \sigma] \subset \mathbb{R} \to \mathbb{R}$ be an integrable and $\Phi \in K_{h,m}^{1,s}([\rho, \frac{\sigma}{m}])$. Then, the following Mercer's-type inequality holds:

$$\Phi(x_1 + mx_n - x_k) \leq (h^s(\lambda) + h^s(1-\lambda))\Phi(x_1) + (2 - h^s(\lambda) - h^s(1-\lambda))m\Phi(x_n) - \Phi(x_k) \qquad (10)$$

for $x_1 \leq mx_n$, $x_k \in [x_1, mx_n] \subseteq I$ and $\lambda \in [0,1]$ such that $x_k = \lambda x_1 + m(1-\lambda)x_n$.

Proof. The proof is analogous to that of Theorem 1. Taking $x_k = \lambda x_1 + m(1-\lambda)x_n$, $y_k = (1-\lambda)x_1 + m\lambda x_n$ and combining inequalities

$$\Phi(y_k) \leq h^s(1-\lambda)\Phi(x_1) + m(1 - h^s(1-\lambda))\Phi(x_n),$$
$$\Phi(x_k) \leq h^s(\lambda)\Phi(x_1) + m(1 - h^s(\lambda))\Phi(x_n)$$

results in inequality (10). □

Corollary 2. Let $\Phi : I = [\rho, \sigma] \subset \mathbb{R} \to \mathbb{R}$ be an integrable and $\Phi \in K_{h,m}^{1,s}([\rho, \frac{\sigma}{m}])$. Then, from (10), we have

$$\Phi(x_1 + mx_n - x_k) \leq \mathbf{A}_1[\Phi(x_1) + m\Phi(x_n)] - \Phi(x_k)$$

for $x_1 \leq mx_n$, $x_k \in [x_1, mx_n] \subseteq I$ and

$$\mathbf{A}_1 = \max\left\{\sup_{\lambda \in [0,1]} (h^s(\lambda) + h^s(1-\lambda)), \sup_{\lambda \in [0,1]} (2 - h^s(\lambda) - h^s(1-\lambda))\right\}.$$

Theorem 3. Let $\Phi : I = [\rho, \sigma] \subset \mathbb{R} \to \mathbb{R}$ be an integrable and $\Phi \in K_{h,m}^{2,s}([\rho, \frac{\sigma}{m}])$. Then, the following Mercer's type inequality holds:

$$\Phi(x_1 + mx_n - x_k) \leq (h^s(\lambda) + h^s(1-\lambda))\Phi(x_1) \\ + ((1 - h(\lambda))^s + (1 - h(1-\lambda))^s)m\Phi(x_n) - \Phi(x_k) \qquad (11)$$

for $x_1 \leq mx_n$, $x_k \in [x_1, mx_n] \subseteq I$ and $\lambda \in [0,1]$, such that $x_k = \lambda x_1 + m(1-\lambda)x_n$.

Proof. The proof is analogous to that of Theorem 1. Taking $x_k = \lambda x_1 + m(1-\lambda)x_n$, $y_k = (1-\lambda)x_1 + m\lambda x_n$ and combining inequalities

$$\Phi(y_k) \leq h^s(1-\lambda)\Phi(x_1) + m(1 - h(1-\lambda))^s\Phi(x_n),$$
$$\Phi(x_k) \leq h^s(\lambda)\Phi(x_1) + m(1 - h(\lambda))^s\Phi(x_n)$$

yields inequality (11). □

Corollary 3. Let $\Phi : I = [\rho, \sigma] \subset \mathbb{R} \to \mathbb{R}$ be an integrable and $\Phi \in K_{h,m}^{2,s}([\rho, \frac{\sigma}{m}])$. Then, from Theorem 3, we have

$$\Phi(x_1 + mx_n - x_k) \leq \mathbf{A}_2[\Phi(x_1) + m\Phi(x_n)] - \Phi(x_k) \qquad (12)$$

for $x_1 \leq mx_n$, $x_k \in [x_1, mx_n] \subseteq I$ and

$$A_2 = \max\left\{\sup_{\lambda \in [0,1]} (h^s(\lambda) + h^s(1-\lambda)), \sup_{\lambda \in [0,1]} ((1-h(\lambda))^s + (1-h(1-\lambda))^s)\right\}.$$

Remark 2. *For $m = s = 1$ and $h(t) = t$, we have $A_1 = A_2 = 1$, moreover, Theorems 2 and 3 (or, Corollaries 2 and 3) become the Jensen–Mercer inequality for convex functions (3).*

Remark 3. *Other variants of the Jensen–Mercer inequality (2), for different notions of convexity, can be found in [16,22–25].*

In the remainder of this paper, we aim to give generalizations of Hermite–Hadamard inequality (4) via non-conformable fractional integrals defined by Nápoles et al. in [26].

Definition 4. *Let $\alpha \in \mathbb{R}$ and $0 < \rho < \sigma$. For each function $\Phi \in L[\rho, \sigma]$, we define*

$$_{N_3}J_u^\alpha \Phi(x) = \int_u^x t^{-\alpha} \Phi(t) dt$$

for every $x, u \in [\rho, \sigma]$.

Definition 5. *Let $\alpha \in \mathbb{R}$ and $\rho < \sigma$. For each function $\Phi \in L_\alpha[\rho, \sigma]$, that is the linear space*

$$L_\alpha[\rho, \sigma] = \left\{\Phi : [\rho, \sigma] \to \mathbb{R} : (t-\rho)^{-\alpha} \Phi(t), (\sigma-t)^{-\alpha} \Phi(t) \in L[\rho, \sigma]\right\},$$

let us define the fractional integrals

$$_{N_3}J_{\rho^+}^\alpha \Phi(x) = \int_\rho^x (x-t)^{-\alpha} \Phi(t) dt \quad \text{and} \quad _{N_3}J_{\sigma^-}^\alpha \Phi(x) = \int_x^\sigma (t-x)^{-\alpha} \Phi(t) dt \quad (13)$$

for every $x \in [\rho, \sigma]$. Here, for $\alpha = 0$, we have $_{N_3}J_{\rho^+}^\alpha \Phi(x) = {}_{N_3}J_{\sigma^-}^\alpha \Phi(x) = \int_\rho^\sigma \Phi(t) dt$.

Definition 6. *More details on the fractional integral and the corresponding fractional derivative N_3^α can be read in [26].*

Fractional differential and integral computations have been widely used in many fields of applied sciences. The interested reader can read about the role of fractional calculus in the study of biological models and chemical processes in [27–29].

2. Inequalities for Convex Functions

In this section, we obtain analogues of Hermite–Hadamard inequality (4) for non-conformable fractional operators (13) using Jensen–Mercer inequalities.

Remark 4. *If in (2), we take $n = 2$ and $w_1 = w_2 = \frac{1}{2}$, then we have*

$$\Phi\left(\sigma - \frac{y_1}{2} + \rho - \frac{x_1}{2}\right) \leq \Phi(\rho) + \Phi(\sigma) - \frac{\Phi(x_1) + \Phi(y_1)}{2}. \quad (14)$$

Theorem 4. *Let $\Phi : [\rho, \sigma] \to \mathbb{R}$. If $\Phi \in L_\alpha[\rho, \sigma]$ and Φ is convex on $[\rho, \sigma]$, then*

$$\Phi\left(\sigma - \frac{y}{2} + \rho - \frac{x}{2}\right) \leq \Phi(\rho) + \Phi(\sigma) - \frac{1-\alpha}{2(y-x)^{1-\alpha}}\left[{}_{N_3}J_{y^-}^\alpha \Phi(x) + {}_{N_3}J_{x^+}^\alpha \Phi(y)\right]$$
$$\leq \Phi(\rho) + \Phi(\sigma) - \Phi\left(\frac{x+y}{2}\right), \quad (15)$$

where $x, y \in [\rho, \sigma]$ and $\alpha < 1$.

Proof. If in (14), we choose $x_1 = tx + (1-t)y$ and $y_1 = (1-t)x + ty$, and multiply by $t^{-\alpha}$, then we can write the inequality

$$2\Phi\left(\sigma - \frac{y}{2} + \rho - \frac{x}{2}\right) t^{-\alpha} \leq 2t^{-\alpha}[\Phi(\rho) + \Phi(\sigma)] - t^{-\alpha}\Phi(tx + (1-t)y) - t^{-\alpha}\Phi((1-t)x + ty).$$

Now, by integrating the resulting inequality with respect to t on $[0,1]$ and changing the variable, we obtain

$$\frac{2}{1-\alpha} \Phi\left(\sigma - \frac{y}{2} + \rho - \frac{x}{2}\right)$$

$$\leq 2[\Phi(\rho) + \Phi(\sigma)] \int_0^1 t^{-\alpha} dt - \left[\int_0^1 t^{-\alpha}\Phi(tx + (1-t)y)dt + \int_0^1 t^{-\alpha}\Phi((1-t)x + ty)dt\right]$$

$$= \frac{2[\Phi(\rho) + \Phi(\sigma)]}{1-\alpha} - \frac{1}{(y-x)^{1-\alpha}}\left[\int_x^y (y-z)^{-\alpha}\Phi(z)dz + \int_x^y (z-x)^{-\alpha}\Phi(z)dz\right]$$

$$= \frac{2[\Phi(\rho) + \Phi(\sigma)]}{1-\alpha} - \frac{1}{(y-x)^{1-\alpha}}\left[{}_{N_3}J^\alpha_{y^-}\Phi(x) + {}_{N_3}J^\alpha_{x^+}\Phi(y)\right].$$

After dividing both sides of the last inequality by $\frac{2}{1-\alpha}$, we get the left inequality in (15).

For the proof of the second inequality of (15), keeping in mind that Φ is convex, one can write

$$\Phi\left(\frac{x+y}{2}\right) = \Phi\left(\frac{tx + (1-t)y + ty + (1-t)x}{2}\right)$$

$$\leq \frac{\Phi(tx + (1-t)y) + \Phi(ty + (1-t)x)}{2}.$$

By multiplying both sides of last inequality by $t^{-\alpha}$ and by integrating with respect to t on $[0,1]$ and changing the variables, we obtain

$$\frac{1}{1-\alpha}\Phi\left(\frac{x+y}{2}\right) \leq \frac{1}{2(y-x)^{1-\alpha}}\left[\int_x^y (y-z)^{-\alpha}\Phi(z)dz + \int_x^y (z-x)^{-\alpha}\Phi(z)dz\right].$$

By multiplying the last inequality by $(\alpha - 1)$ and adding $\Phi(\rho) + \Phi(\sigma)$ to both sides, we get the right-hand side of (15):

$$\Phi(\rho) + \Phi(\sigma) - \Phi\left(\frac{x+y}{2}\right)$$

$$\geq \Phi(\rho) + \Phi(\sigma) - \frac{1-\alpha}{2(y-x)^{1-\alpha}}\left[\int_x^y (y-z)^{-\alpha}\Phi(z)dz + \int_x^y (z-x)^{-\alpha}\Phi(z)dz\right]$$

$$= \Phi(\rho) + \Phi(\sigma) - \frac{1-\alpha}{2(y-x)^{1-\alpha}}\left[{}_{N_3}J^\alpha_{y^-}\Phi(x) + {}_{N_3}J^\alpha_{x^+}\Phi(y)\right].$$

Thus, inequality (15) is proved. □

Corollary 4. *For $\alpha = 0$, under the assumptions of Theorem 4, we get*

$$\Phi\left(\sigma - \frac{y}{2} + \rho - \frac{x}{2}\right) \leq \Phi(\rho) + \Phi(\sigma) - \frac{1}{y-x}\int_x^y \Phi(t)dt \leq \Phi(\rho) + \Phi(\sigma) - \Phi\left(\frac{x+y}{2}\right)$$

for all $x, y \in [\rho, \sigma]$. This inequality was obtained by Kian and Moslehian in ([30], Theorem 2.1), and by Ögülmüs and Sarikaya in ([17], Remark 2.2).

Theorem 5. Let $\Phi : [\rho, \sigma] \to \mathbb{R}$. If $\Phi \in L_\alpha[\rho, \sigma]$ and Φ is convex on $[\rho, \sigma]$, then we have

$$\Phi\left(\sigma - \frac{y}{2} + \rho - \frac{x}{2}\right)$$
$$\leq \frac{1-\alpha}{2(y-x)^{1-\alpha}}\left[{}_{N_3}J^\alpha_{(\sigma-y+\rho)^+}\Phi(\sigma-x+\rho) + {}_{N_3}J^\alpha_{(\sigma-x+\rho)^-}\Phi(\sigma-y+\rho)\right] \quad (16)$$
$$\leq \frac{\Phi(\sigma-x+\rho) + \Phi(\sigma-y+\rho)}{2} \leq \Phi(\rho) + \Phi(\sigma) - \frac{\Phi(x) + \Phi(y)}{2},$$

where $x, y \in [\rho, \sigma]$ and $\alpha < 1$.

Proof. To prove inequality (16), we use the left-hand side of (14) and choose $x_1 = tx + (1-t)y$, $y_1 = (1-t)x + ty$ to obtain the auxiliary inequality

$$\Phi\left(\sigma - \frac{y_1}{2} + \rho - \frac{x_1}{2}\right)$$
$$= \Phi\left(\frac{\sigma - x_1 + \rho + \sigma - y_1 + \rho}{2}\right) \leq \frac{\Phi(\sigma - x_1 + \rho)}{2} + \frac{\Phi(\sigma - y_1 + \rho)}{2}$$
$$= \frac{\Phi(\rho + \sigma - tx - (1-t)y)}{2} + \frac{\Phi(\rho + \sigma - ty - (1-t)x)}{2}.$$

More precisely, we use the equivalent inequality

$$\Phi\left(\sigma - \frac{y}{2} + \rho - \frac{x}{2}\right) \leq \frac{\Phi(\rho + \sigma - tx - (1-t)y)}{2} + \frac{\Phi(\rho + \sigma - (1-t)x - ty)}{2}. \quad (17)$$

Multiplying both sides of (17) by $t^{-\alpha}$, integrating with respect to t on $[0, 1]$ and changing the variables yields

$$\frac{1}{1-\alpha}\Phi\left(\sigma - \frac{y}{2} + \rho - \frac{x}{2}\right)$$
$$\leq \frac{1}{2(y-x)^{1-\alpha}}\left[\int_{\sigma-y+\rho}^{\sigma-x+\rho}(z-(\sigma-y+\rho))^{-\alpha}\Phi(z)dz + \int_{\sigma-y+\rho}^{\sigma-x+\rho}((\sigma-x+\rho)-z)^{-\alpha}\Phi(z)dz\right]$$
$$= \frac{1}{2(y-x)^{1-\alpha}}\left[{}_{N_3}J^\alpha_{(\sigma-y+\rho)^+}\Phi(\sigma-x+\rho) + {}_{N_3}J^\alpha_{(\sigma-x+\rho)^-}\Phi(\sigma-y+\rho)\right].$$

It is easy to see that left-hand side of (16) is proved. To prove the remaining part of (16), we need the following inequalities:

$$\Phi(\rho + \sigma - (tx + (1-t)y)) = \Phi(\rho + \sigma + (\rho+\sigma)t - (\rho+\sigma)t - (tx + (1-t)y))$$
$$= \Phi(t(\sigma - x + \rho) + (1-t)(\sigma - y + \rho))$$
$$\leq t\Phi(\sigma - x + \rho) + (1-t)\Phi(\sigma - y + \rho)$$

and
$$\Phi(\rho + \sigma - (ty + (1-t)x)) \leq t\Phi(\sigma - y + \rho) + (1-t)\Phi(\sigma - x + \rho).$$

By summing the above inequalities, we have

$$\Phi(\rho + \sigma - (tx + (1-t)y)) + \Phi(\rho + \sigma - (ty + (1-t)x)) \leq \Phi(\sigma - x + \rho) + \Phi(\sigma - y + \rho).$$

By multiplying both sides (17) by $t^{-\alpha}$, integrating with respect to t on $[0, 1]$ and changing the variables, we obtain

$$\frac{1}{(y-x)^{1-\alpha}}\left[{}_{N_3}J^\alpha_{(\sigma-y+\rho)^+}\Phi(\sigma-x+\rho) + {}_{N_3}J^\alpha_{(\sigma-x+\rho)^-}\Phi(\sigma-y+\rho)\right]$$
$$\leq \frac{1}{1-\alpha}[\Phi(\sigma - x + \rho) + \Phi(\sigma - y + \rho)].$$

This inequality implies the remaining part of (16) by keeping (3) in mind. The proof is complete. □

Corollary 5. *For $\alpha = 0$, under the assumptions of Theorem 5, we have*

$$\Phi\left(\sigma - \frac{y}{2} + \rho - \frac{x}{2}\right) \leq \frac{1}{y-x} \int_{\sigma-y+\rho}^{\sigma-x+\rho} \Phi(t)dt \leq \Phi(\rho) + \Phi(\sigma) - \frac{\Phi(x) + \Phi(y)}{2} \quad (18)$$

for all $x, y \in [\rho, \sigma]$. This inequality was obtained by Kian and Moslehian in ([30], Theorem 2.1), and by Öğülmüş and Sarikaya in ([17], Remark 2.2).

Remark 5. *If in (18), we choose $x = \rho$ and $y = \sigma$, then we get the Hermite–Hadamard inequality (4).*

3. Inequalities for General Convex Functions

By considering (h, m)-convexity modified in the first and the second sense, we give analogues of Hermite–Hadamard inequality (4) for fractional operators (13) using Jensen–Mercer inequalities proven for these classes. Before that, we recall the following identity obtained by Nápoles et al. in [26] (see Lemma 1).

Lemma 1. *Let $\Phi : [\rho, \sigma] \to \mathbb{R}$ be a differentiable function. If $\Phi' \in L_{\alpha-1}[\rho, \sigma]$, then we have*

$$\frac{\Phi(\rho) + \Phi(\sigma)}{2} - \frac{1-\alpha}{2(\sigma-\rho)^{1-\alpha}} \left[{}_{N_3}J^\alpha_{\sigma-}\Phi(\rho) + {}_{N_3}J^\alpha_{\rho+}\Phi(\sigma) \right] = \frac{\sigma-\rho}{2}(I_{01} - I_{02}),$$

where $\alpha < 1$ and

$$I_{01} = \int_0^1 t^{1-\alpha} \Phi'((1-t)\rho + t\sigma)dt, \quad I_{02} = \int_0^1 (1-t)^{1-\alpha} \Phi'((1-t)\rho + t\sigma)dt.$$

If in Lemma 1, we substitute $\sigma - y + \rho$ in place of ρ and $\sigma - x + \rho$ in place of σ, we get the next equation.

Corollary 6. *Under the assumptions of Lemma 1, we have*

$$\frac{\Phi(\sigma-y+\rho) + \Phi(\sigma-x+\rho)}{2}$$
$$- \frac{1-\alpha}{2(y-x)^{1-\alpha}} \left[{}_{N_3}J^\alpha_{(\sigma-x+\rho)-}\Phi(\sigma-y+\rho) + {}_{N_3}J^\alpha_{(\sigma-y+\rho)+}\Phi(\sigma-x+\rho) \right] \quad (19)$$
$$= \frac{y-x}{2}(I_1 - I_2),$$

where $x, y \in [\rho, \sigma]$, $\alpha < 1$ and

$$I_1 = \int_0^1 t^{1-\alpha} \Phi'(\sigma - x + \rho t - (1-t)y)dt,$$
$$I_2 = \int_0^1 (1-t)^{1-\alpha} \Phi'(\sigma - x + \rho t - (1-t)y)dt.$$

Theorem 6. *Let* $\Phi : [\rho, \frac{\sigma}{m}] \to \mathbb{R}$ *be a differentiable function. If* $\Phi' \in L_{\alpha-1}[\rho, \sigma]$ *and* $|\Phi'| \in K_{h,m}^{1,s}([\rho, \frac{\sigma}{m}])$, *then the following inequality holds for all* $x, y \in [\rho, \sigma], \alpha < 1$:

$$\left| \frac{\Phi(\sigma - y + \rho) + \Phi(\sigma - x + \rho)}{2} \right.$$
$$\left. - \frac{1 - \alpha}{2(y-x)^{1-\alpha}} \left[{}_{N_3}J^{\alpha}_{(\sigma-x+\rho)^-} \Phi(\sigma - y + \rho) + {}_{N_3}J^{\alpha}_{(\sigma-y+\rho)^+} \Phi(\sigma - x + \rho) \right] \right| \quad (20)$$
$$\leq \frac{y-x}{2} \left\{ \frac{2\mathbf{A}_1 |\Phi'(\rho)| + 2\mathbf{A}_1 m |\Phi'(\frac{\sigma}{m})| - m(|\Phi'(\frac{x}{m})| + |\Phi'(\frac{y}{m})|)}{2 - \alpha} \right.$$
$$\left. - \left[|\Phi'(x)| + |\Phi'(y)| - m \left(\left|\Phi'\left(\frac{x}{m}\right)\right| + \left|\Phi'\left(\frac{y}{m}\right)\right| \right) \right] \int_0^1 t^{1-\alpha} h^s(t) dt \right\},$$

where $\mathbf{A}_1$ *is from Corollary 2.*

Proof. From Corollary 6 and modulus properties, we can write

$$\left| \frac{\Phi(\sigma - y + \rho) + \Phi(\sigma - x + \rho)}{2} \right.$$
$$\left. - \frac{1 - \alpha}{2(y-x)^{1-\alpha}} \left[{}_{N_3}J^{\alpha}_{(\sigma-x+\rho)^-} \Phi(\sigma - y + \rho) + {}_{N_3}J^{\alpha}_{(\sigma-y+\rho)^+} \Phi(\sigma - x + \rho) \right] \right| \quad (21)$$
$$= \frac{y-x}{2} |I_1 - I_2| \leq \frac{y-x}{2} (|I_1| + |I_2|).$$

Using (h, m)-convexity of the first sense of function $|\Phi'|$ and Corollary 2, for integral I_1, we get

$$|I_1| \leq \int_0^1 t^{1-\alpha} |\Phi'(\rho + \sigma - (xt + (1-t)y))| dt$$
$$\leq \int_0^1 t^{1-\alpha} \left[\mathbf{A}_1 |\Phi'(\rho)| + \mathbf{A}_1 m \left|\Phi'\left(\frac{\sigma}{m}\right)\right| - \left(h^s(t) |\Phi'(x)| + m(1 - h^s(t)) \left|\Phi'\left(\frac{y}{m}\right)\right|\right) \right] dt$$
$$= \frac{\mathbf{A}_1 [|\Phi'(\rho)| + m|\Phi'(\frac{\sigma}{m})|]}{2 - \alpha} - |\Phi'(x)| \int_0^1 t^{1-\alpha} h^s(t) dt - m \left|\Phi'\left(\frac{y}{m}\right)\right| \int_0^1 t^{1-\alpha} [1 - h^s(t)] dt$$
$$= \frac{\mathbf{A}_1 |\Phi'(\rho)| + \mathbf{A}_1 m |\Phi'(\frac{\sigma}{m})| - m|\Phi'(\frac{y}{m})|}{2 - \alpha} - \left[|\Phi'(x)| - m\left|\Phi'\left(\frac{y}{m}\right)\right| \right] \int_0^1 t^{1-\alpha} h^s(t) dt.$$

One can write for the second integral I_2 similarly

$$|I_2| \leq \int_0^1 (1-t)^{1-\alpha} |\Phi'(\sigma - x + \rho t - (1-t)y)| dt = \int_0^1 t^{1-\alpha} |\Phi'(\rho + \sigma - (1-t)x - ty)| dt$$
$$\leq \frac{\mathbf{A}_1 |\Phi'(\rho)| + \mathbf{A}_1 m |\Phi'(\frac{\sigma}{m})| - m|\Phi'(\frac{x}{m})|}{2 - \alpha} - \left[|\Phi'(y)| - m\left|\Phi'\left(\frac{x}{m}\right)\right| \right] \int_0^1 t^{1-\alpha} h^s(t) dt.$$

Thus, we have

$$|I_1| + |I_2| \leq \frac{2\mathbf{A}_1 (|\Phi'(\rho)| + m|\Phi'(\frac{\sigma}{m})|) - m(|\Phi'(\frac{x}{m})| + |\Phi'(\frac{y}{m})|)}{2 - \alpha}$$
$$- \left[|\Phi'(x)| + |\Phi'(y)| - m \left(\left|\Phi'\left(\frac{x}{m}\right)\right| + \left|\Phi'\left(\frac{y}{m}\right)\right| \right) \right] \int_0^1 t^{1-\alpha} h^s(t) dt.$$

By multiplying the last inequality by $\frac{y-x}{2}$ and taking into account (21), we obtain (20). □

Corollary 7. *If in Theorem 6, we choose $x = \rho$ and $y = \sigma$, then we have*

$$\left| \frac{\Phi(\rho) + \Phi(\sigma)}{2} - \frac{1-\alpha}{2(\sigma-\rho)^{1-\alpha}} \left[{}_{N_3}J^\alpha_{\sigma^-}\Phi(\rho) + {}_{N_3}J^\alpha_{\rho^+}\Phi(\sigma) \right] \right|$$

$$\leq \frac{\sigma - \rho}{2} \left\{ \frac{2\mathbf{A}_1 |\Phi'(\rho)| - m \left|\Phi'\left(\frac{\rho}{m}\right)\right| + (2\mathbf{A}_1 - 1)m\left|\Phi'\left(\frac{\sigma}{m}\right)\right|}{2-\alpha} \right.$$

$$\left. - \left[|\Phi'(\rho)| + |\Phi'(\sigma)| - m\left(\left|\Phi'\left(\frac{\rho}{m}\right)\right| + \left|\Phi'\left(\frac{\sigma}{m}\right)\right|\right) \right] \int_0^1 t^{1-\alpha} h^s(t) dt \right\}.$$

If, in addition, $m = 1$, then

$$\left| \frac{\Phi(\rho) + \Phi(\sigma)}{2} - \frac{1-\alpha}{2(\sigma-\rho)^{1-\alpha}} \left[{}_{N_3}J^\alpha_{\sigma^-}\Phi(\rho) + {}_{N_3}J^\alpha_{\rho^+}\Phi(\sigma) \right] \right| \qquad (22)$$

$$\leq \frac{(\sigma - \rho)(2\mathbf{A}_1 - 1)(|\Phi'(\rho)| + |\Phi'(\sigma)|)}{2(2-\alpha)}.$$

Theorem 7. *Let $\Phi : [\rho, \frac{\sigma}{m}] \to \mathbb{R}$ be a differentiable function. If $\Phi' \in L_{\alpha-1}[\rho, \sigma]$ and $|\Phi'| \in K^{2,s}_{h,m}([\rho, \frac{\sigma}{m}])$, then the following inequality holds for all $x, y \in [\rho, \sigma]$, $\alpha < 1$:*

$$\left| \frac{\Phi(\sigma - y + \rho) + \Phi(\sigma - x + \rho)}{2} \right.$$

$$\left. - \frac{1-\alpha}{2(y-x)^{1-\alpha}} \left[{}_{N_3}J^\alpha_{(\sigma-x+\rho)^-}\Phi(\sigma-y+\rho) + {}_{N_3}J^\alpha_{(\sigma-y+\rho)^+}\Phi(\sigma-x+\rho) \right] \right|$$

$$\leq \frac{(y-x)\mathbf{A}_2 \left(|\Phi'(\rho)| + m\left|\Phi'\left(\frac{\sigma}{m}\right)\right|\right)}{2-\alpha} - \frac{y-x}{2} \left\{ (|\Phi'(x)| + |\Phi'(y)|) \int_0^1 t^{1-\alpha} h^s(t) dt \right.$$

$$\left. + m\left(\left|\Phi'\left(\frac{y}{m}\right)\right| + \left|\Phi'\left(\frac{x}{m}\right)\right| \right) \int_0^1 t^{1-\alpha}(1 - h(t))^s dt \right\},$$

where $\mathbf{A}_2$ is from Corollary 3.

Proof. The proof is analogous to that of Theorem 7, but with the use of Corollary 3 instead of Corollary 2. □

Corollary 8. *If in Theorem 7, we choose $x = \rho$, $y = \sigma$ and $m = 1$, then we have*

$$\left| \frac{\Phi(\rho) + \Phi(\sigma)}{2} - \frac{1-\alpha}{2(\sigma-\rho)^{1-\alpha}} \left[{}_{N_3}J^\alpha_{\sigma^-}\Phi(\rho) + {}_{N_3}J^\alpha_{\rho^+}\Phi(\sigma) \right] \right| \qquad (23)$$

$$\leq \frac{\sigma - \rho}{2} (|\Phi'(\rho)| + |\Phi'(\sigma)|) \left\{ \frac{2\mathbf{A}_2}{2-\alpha} - \int_0^1 t^{1-\alpha} [h^s(t) + (1-h(t))^s] dt \right\}.$$

Theorem 8. *Let $\Phi : [\rho, \frac{\sigma}{m}] \to \mathbb{R}$ be a differentiable function. If $\Phi' \in L_{\alpha-1}[\rho, \sigma]$ and $|\Phi'|^q \in K^{1,s}_{h,m}([\rho, \frac{\sigma}{m}])$, then for all $x, y \in [\rho, \sigma]$, $\alpha < 1$, $q > 1$ with $\frac{1}{p} + \frac{1}{q} = 1$, the following inequality holds:*

$$\left| \frac{\Phi(\sigma - y + \rho) + \Phi(\sigma - x + \rho)}{2} \right.$$
$$\left. - \frac{1-\alpha}{2(y-x)^{1-\alpha}} \left[{}_{N_3}J^{\alpha}_{(\sigma-x+\rho)^-} \Phi(\sigma - y + \rho) + {}_{N_3}J^{\alpha}_{(\sigma-y+\rho)^+} \Phi(\sigma - x + \rho) \right] \right| \quad (24)$$
$$\leq \frac{y-x}{2} \left(\frac{1}{p - \alpha p + 1} \right)^{\frac{1}{p}} (\mathbf{B}_1 + \mathbf{C}_1),$$

where

$$\mathbf{B}_1 = \left\{ \mathbf{A}_1 |\Phi'(\rho)|^q + \mathbf{A}_1 m \left|\Phi'\left(\frac{\sigma}{m}\right)\right|^q - m\left|\Phi'\left(\frac{y}{m}\right)\right|^q \right.$$
$$\left. - \left[|\Phi'(x)|^q - m\left|\Phi'\left(\frac{y}{m}\right)\right|^q \right] \int_0^1 h^s(t) dt \right\}^{\frac{1}{q}},$$

$$\mathbf{C}_1 = \left\{ \mathbf{A}_1 |\Phi'(\rho)|^q + \mathbf{A}_1 m \left|\Phi'\left(\frac{\sigma}{m}\right)\right|^q - m\left|\Phi'\left(\frac{x}{m}\right)\right|^q \right.$$
$$\left. - \left[|\Phi'(y)|^q - m\left|\Phi'\left(\frac{x}{m}\right)\right|^q \right] \int_0^1 h^s(t) dt \right\}^{\frac{1}{q}}.$$

Proof. From Lemma 6 and modulus properties, we can write (21). Using the well-known Hölder integral inequality and Corollary 2, since $|\Phi'|^q \in K^{1,s}_{h,m}([\rho, \frac{\sigma}{m}])$, we get

$$|I_1| \leq \int_0^1 t^{1-\alpha} |\Phi'(\rho + \sigma - (xt + (1-t)y))| dt$$
$$\leq \left(\int_0^1 t^{(1-\alpha)p} dt \right)^{\frac{1}{p}} \left\{ \mathbf{A}_1 \int_0^1 \left(|\Phi'(\rho)|^q + m\left|\Phi'\left(\frac{\sigma}{m}\right)\right|^q \right) dt \right.$$
$$\left. - \int_0^1 \left[\left(h^s(t) |\Phi'(x)|^q + m(1 - h^s(t)) \left|\Phi'\left(\frac{y}{m}\right)\right|^q \right) \right] dt \right\}^{\frac{1}{q}} \quad (25)$$
$$= \left(\frac{1}{p - \alpha p + 1} \right)^{\frac{1}{p}} \left\{ \mathbf{A}_1 |\Phi'(\rho)|^q + \mathbf{A}_1 m \left|\Phi'\left(\frac{\sigma}{m}\right)\right|^q - m\left|\Phi'\left(\frac{y}{m}\right)\right|^q \right.$$
$$\left. - \left[|\Phi'(x)|^q - m\left|\Phi'\left(\frac{y}{m}\right)\right|^q \right] \int_0^1 h^s(t) dt \right\}^{\frac{1}{q}}.$$

Since

$$\int_0^1 (1-t)^{1-\alpha} |\Phi'(\sigma - x + \rho t - (1-t)y)| dt = \int_0^1 t^{1-\alpha} |\Phi'(\rho + \sigma - (1-t)x - ty)| dt,$$

we can write similarly for the second integral

$$|I_2| \leq \int_0^1 t^{1-\alpha} |\Phi'(\rho + \sigma - (1-t)x - ty)| dt$$
$$\leq \left(\frac{1}{p - \alpha p + 1} \right)^{\frac{1}{p}} \left\{ \mathbf{A}_1 |\Phi'(\rho)|^q + \mathbf{A}_1 m \left|\Phi'\left(\frac{\sigma}{m}\right)\right|^q - m\left|\Phi'\left(\frac{x}{m}\right)\right|^q \right. \quad (26)$$
$$\left. - \left[|\Phi'(y)|^q - m\left|\Phi'\left(\frac{x}{m}\right)\right|^q \right] \int_0^1 h^s(t) dt \right\}^{\frac{1}{q}}.$$

By adding inequalities (25) and (26), we get

$$|I_1| + |I_2| \leq \left(\frac{1}{p - \alpha p + 1} \right)^{\frac{1}{p}} (\mathbf{B}_1 + \mathbf{C}_1).$$

Multiplying both sides of the last inequality by the expression $\frac{y-x}{2}$ and keeping (21) in mind yields (24). The proof is complete. $\square$

Corollary 9. *If in Theorem 8, we choose $x = \rho$, $y = \sigma$ and $m = 1$, then we have*

$$\left| \frac{\Phi(\rho) + \Phi(\sigma)}{2} - \frac{1-\alpha}{2(\sigma-\rho)^{1-\alpha}} \left[{}_{N_3}J^{\alpha}_{\sigma-}\Phi(\rho) + {}_{N_3}J^{\alpha}_{\rho+}\Phi(\sigma) \right] \right|$$

$$\leq \frac{\sigma-\rho}{2} \left(\frac{1}{p-\alpha p+1} \right)^{\frac{1}{p}}$$

$$\times \left[\left\{ \mathbf{A}_1 |\Phi'(\rho)|^q + (\mathbf{A}_1 - 1)|\Phi'(\sigma)|^q - \left[|\Phi'(\rho)|^q - |\Phi'(\sigma)|^q \right] \int_0^1 h^s(t) dt \right\}^{\frac{1}{q}} \right.$$

$$\left. + \left\{ (\mathbf{A}_1 - 1)|\Phi'(\rho)|^q + \mathbf{A}_1 |\Phi'(\sigma)|^q - \left[|\Phi'(\sigma)|^q - |\Phi'(\rho)|^q \right] \int_0^1 h^s(t) dt \right\}^{\frac{1}{q}} \right].$$

Theorem 9. *Let $\Phi : [\rho, \frac{\sigma}{m}] \to \mathbb{R}$ be a differentiable function. If $\Phi' \in L_{\alpha-1}[\rho, \sigma]$ and $|\Phi'|^q \in K^{2,s}_{h,m}([\rho, \frac{\sigma}{m}])$, then for all $x, y \in [\rho, \sigma]$, $\alpha < 1$, $q > 1$ with $\frac{1}{p} + \frac{1}{q} = 1$, the following inequality holds:*

$$\left| \frac{\Phi(\sigma - y + \rho) + \Phi(\sigma - x + \rho)}{2} \right.$$

$$\left. - \frac{1-\alpha}{2(y-x)^{1-\alpha}} \left[{}_{N_3}J^{\alpha}_{(\sigma-x+\rho)-}\Phi(\sigma-y+\rho) + {}_{N_3}J^{\alpha}_{(\sigma-y+\rho)+}\Phi(\sigma-x+\rho) \right] \right|$$

$$\leq \frac{y-x}{2} \left(\frac{1}{p-\alpha p+1} \right)^{\frac{1}{p}} (\mathbf{B}_2 + \mathbf{C}_2),$$

where

$$\mathbf{B}_2 = \left\{ \mathbf{A}_2 |\Phi'(\rho)|^q + \mathbf{A}_2 m \left| \Phi'\left(\frac{\sigma}{m}\right) \right|^q \right.$$

$$\left. - |\Phi'(x)|^q \int_0^1 h^s(t) dt - m \left| \Phi'\left(\frac{y}{m}\right) \right|^q \int_0^1 (1-h(t))^s dt \right\}^{\frac{1}{q}},$$

$$\mathbf{C}_2 = \left\{ \mathbf{A}_2 |\Phi'(\rho)|^q + \mathbf{A}_2 m \left| \Phi'\left(\frac{\sigma}{m}\right) \right|^q \right.$$

$$\left. - |\Phi'(y)|^q \int_0^1 h^s(t) dt - m \left| \Phi'\left(\frac{x}{m}\right) \right|^q \int_0^1 (1-h(t))^s dt \right\}^{\frac{1}{q}}.$$

Proof. The proof is analogous to that of Theorem 8, but with the use of Corollary 3 instead of Corollary 2. $\square$

Corollary 10. *If in Theorem 9, we choose* $x = \rho$, $y = \sigma$ *and* $m = 1$, *then we have*

$$\left| \frac{\Phi(\rho) + \Phi(\sigma)}{2} - \frac{1-\alpha}{2(\sigma-\rho)^{1-\alpha}} \left[{}_{N_3}J_{\sigma^-}^{\alpha} \Phi(\rho) + {}_{N_3}J_{\rho^+}^{\alpha} \Phi(\sigma) \right] \right|$$

$$\leq \frac{\sigma - \rho}{2} \left(\frac{1}{p - \alpha p + 1} \right)^{\frac{1}{p}}$$

$$\times \left[\left\{ |\mathbf{A}_2 \Phi'(\rho)|^q + \mathbf{A}_2 |\Phi'(\sigma)|^q - |\Phi'(\rho)|^q \int_0^1 h^s(t)dt - |\Phi'(\sigma)|^q \int_0^1 (1-h(t))^s dt \right\}^{\frac{1}{q}} \right.$$

$$\left. + \left\{ \mathbf{A}_2 |\Phi'(\rho)|^q + \mathbf{A}_2 |\Phi'(\sigma)|^q - |\Phi'(\sigma)|^q \int_0^1 h^s(t)dt - |\Phi'(\rho)|^q \int_0^1 (1-h(t))^s dt \right\}^{\frac{1}{q}} \right].$$

Theorem 10. *Let* $\Phi : [\rho, \frac{\sigma}{m}] \to \mathbb{R}$ *be a differentiable function. If* $\Phi' \in L_{\alpha-1}[\rho, \sigma]$ *and* $|\Phi'|^q \in K_{h,m}^{1,s}([\rho, \frac{\sigma}{m}])$, *then for all* $x, y \in [\rho, \sigma]$, $\alpha < 1$, $q \geq 1$, *we have*

$$\left| \frac{\Phi(\sigma - y + \rho) + \Phi(\sigma - x + \rho)}{2} \right.$$

$$\left. - \frac{1-\alpha}{2(y-x)^{1-\alpha}} \left[{}_{N_3}J_{(\sigma-x+\rho)^-}^{\alpha} \Phi(\sigma - y + \rho) + {}_{N_3}J_{(\sigma-y+\rho)^+}^{\alpha} \Phi(\sigma - x + \rho) \right] \right| \quad (27)$$

$$\leq \frac{y-x}{2} \left(\frac{1}{2-\alpha} \right)^{1-\frac{1}{q}} (\mathbf{D}_1 + \mathbf{E}_1),$$

where

$$\mathbf{D}_1 = \left\{ \frac{\mathbf{A}_1 |\Phi'(\rho)|^q + \mathbf{A}_1 m |\Phi'(\frac{\sigma}{m})|^q - m|\Phi'(\frac{y}{m})|^q}{2-\alpha} \right.$$

$$\left. - \left[|\Phi'(x)|^q - m \left| \Phi'\left(\frac{y}{m}\right) \right|^q \right] \int_0^1 t^{1-\alpha} h^s(t) dt \right\}^{\frac{1}{q}},$$

$$\mathbf{E}_1 = \left\{ \frac{\mathbf{A}_1 |\Phi'(\rho)|^q + \mathbf{A}_1 m |\Phi'(\frac{\sigma}{m})|^q - m|\Phi'(\frac{x}{m})|^q}{2-\alpha} \right.$$

$$\left. - \left[|\Phi'(y)|^q - m \left| \Phi'\left(\frac{x}{m}\right) \right|^q \right] \int_0^1 t^{1-\alpha} h^s(t) dt \right\}^{\frac{1}{q}}.$$

Proof. We first write (21). Then, using the well-known power–mean integral inequality and Corollary 2, since $|\Phi'|^q \in K_{h,m}^{1,s}([\rho, \frac{\sigma}{m}])$, for the integral I_1, we obtain

$$|I_1| \leq \int_0^1 t^{1-\alpha} |\Phi'(\rho + \sigma - (xt + (1-t)y))| dt$$

$$\leq \left(\int_0^1 t^{1-\alpha} dt\right)^{1-\frac{1}{q}} \left\{ \left(\mathbf{A}_1 |\Phi'(\rho)|^q + \mathbf{A}_1 m \left|\Phi'\left(\frac{\sigma}{m}\right)\right|^q\right) \int_0^1 t^{1-\alpha} dt \right.$$

$$\left. - \int_0^1 t^{1-\alpha} \left[\left(h^s(t)|\Phi'(x)|^q + m(1-h^s(t))\left|\Phi'\left(\frac{y}{m}\right)\right|^q\right)\right] dt \right\}^{\frac{1}{q}}$$

$$= \left(\frac{1}{2-\alpha}\right)^{1-\frac{1}{q}} \left\{ \frac{\mathbf{A}_1 |\Phi'(\rho)|^q + \mathbf{A}_1 m \left|\Phi'\left(\frac{\sigma}{m}\right)\right|^q}{2-\alpha} - |\Phi'(x)|^q \int_0^1 t^{1-\alpha} h^s(t) dt \right.$$ (28)

$$\left. - m\left|\Phi'\left(\frac{y}{m}\right)\right|^q \int_0^1 t^{1-\alpha}(1-h^s(t)) dt \right\}^{\frac{1}{q}}$$

$$= \left(\frac{1}{2-\alpha}\right)^{1-\frac{1}{q}} \left\{ \frac{\mathbf{A}_1 |\Phi'(\rho)|^q + \mathbf{A}_1 m \left|\Phi'\left(\frac{\sigma}{m}\right)\right|^q - m\left|\Phi'\left(\frac{y}{m}\right)\right|^q}{2-\alpha} \right.$$

$$\left. - \left[|\Phi'(x)|^q - m\left|\Phi'\left(\frac{y}{m}\right)\right|^q\right] \int_0^1 t^{1-\alpha} h^s(t) dt \right\}^{\frac{1}{q}}.$$

One can write for the second integral similarly

$$|I_2| \leq \int_0^1 t^{1-\alpha} |\Phi'(\rho + \sigma - (1-t)x - ty)| dt$$

$$\leq \left(\frac{1}{2-\alpha}\right)^{1-\frac{1}{q}} \left\{ \frac{\mathbf{A}_1 |\Phi'(\rho)|^q + \mathbf{A}_1 m \left|\Phi'\left(\frac{\sigma}{m}\right)\right|^q - m\left|\Phi'\left(\frac{x}{m}\right)\right|^q}{2-\alpha} \right.$$ (29)

$$\left. - \left[|\Phi'(y)|^q - m\left|\Phi'\left(\frac{x}{m}\right)\right|^q\right] \int_0^1 t^{1-\alpha} h^s(t) dt \right\}^{\frac{1}{q}}.$$

By adding inequalities (28) and (29), we obtain

$$|I_1| + |I_2| \leq \left(\frac{1}{2-\alpha}\right)^{1-\frac{1}{q}} (\mathbf{D}_1 + \mathbf{E}_1).$$

Multiplying both sides of the last inequality by the expression $\frac{y-x}{2}$ and keeping (21) in mind, we get (27). The proof is complete. □

Corollary 11. *If in Theorem 10, we choose $x = \rho$, $y = \sigma$ and $m = 1$, then we have*

$$\left| \frac{\Phi(\rho) + \Phi(\sigma)}{2} - \frac{1-\alpha}{2(\sigma-\rho)^{1-\alpha}} \left[{}_{N_3}J^\alpha_{\sigma^-} \Phi(\rho) + {}_{N_3}J^\alpha_{\rho^+} \Phi(\sigma) \right] \right|$$

$$\leq \frac{\sigma - \rho}{2} \left(\frac{1}{2-\alpha}\right)^{1-\frac{1}{q}}$$

$$\times \left[\left\{ \frac{\mathbf{A}_1 |\Phi'(\rho)|^q + (\mathbf{A}_1 - 1)|\Phi'(\sigma)|^q}{2-\alpha} - \left[|\Phi'(\rho)|^q - |\Phi'(\sigma)|^q\right] \int_0^1 t^{1-\alpha} h^s(t) dt \right\}^{\frac{1}{q}} \right.$$

$$\left. + \left\{ \frac{(\mathbf{A}_1 - 1)|\Phi'(\rho)|^q + \mathbf{A}_1 |\Phi'(\sigma)|^q}{2-\alpha} - \left[|\Phi'(\sigma)|^q - |\Phi'(\rho)|^q\right] \int_0^1 t^{1-\alpha} h^s(t) dt \right\}^{\frac{1}{q}} \right].$$

If, in addition, we suppose $q = 1$, then we get (22).

Theorem 11. Let $\Phi : [\rho, \frac{\sigma}{m}] \to \mathbb{R}$ be a differentiable function. If $\Phi' \in L_{\alpha-1}[\rho, \sigma]$ and $|\Phi'|^q \in K_{h,m}^{2,s}([\rho, \frac{\sigma}{m}])$, then for all $x, y \in [\rho, \sigma]$, $\alpha < 1$, $q \geq 1$, we have

$$\left| \frac{\Phi(\sigma - y + \rho) + \Phi(\sigma - x + \rho)}{2} \right.$$

$$\left. - \frac{1-\alpha}{2(y-x)^{1-\alpha}} \left[{}_{N_3}J^\alpha_{(\sigma-x+\rho)^-} \Phi(\sigma - y + \rho) + {}_{N_3}J^\alpha_{(\sigma-y+\rho)^+} \Phi(\sigma - x + \rho) \right] \right|$$

$$\leq \frac{y-x}{2} \left(\frac{1}{2-\alpha} \right)^{1 - \frac{1}{q}} (\mathbf{D}_2 + \mathbf{E}_2),$$

where

$$\mathbf{D}_2 = \left\{ \frac{\mathbf{A}_2 |\Phi'(\rho)|^q + \mathbf{A}_2 m |\Phi'(\frac{\sigma}{m})|^q}{2-\alpha} \right.$$

$$\left. - \left[|\Phi'(x)|^q \int_0^1 t^{1-\alpha} h^s(t) dt + m \left| \Phi'\left(\frac{y}{m}\right) \right|^q \int_0^1 t^{1-\alpha} (1-h(t))^s dt \right] \right\}^{\frac{1}{q}},$$

$$\mathbf{E}_2 = \left\{ \frac{\mathbf{A}_2 |\Phi'(\rho)|^q + \mathbf{A}_2 m |\Phi'(\frac{\sigma}{m})|^q}{2-\alpha} \right.$$

$$\left. - \left[|\Phi'(y)|^q \int_0^1 t^{1-\alpha} h^s(t) dt + m \left| \Phi'\left(\frac{x}{m}\right) \right|^q \int_0^1 t^{1-\alpha} (1-h(t))^s dt \right] \right\}^{\frac{1}{q}}.$$

Proof. The proof is analogous to that of Theorem 10, but with the use of Corollary 3 instead of Corollary 2. □

Corollary 12. If in Theorem 11, we choose $x = \rho$, $y = \sigma$ and $m = 1$, then we have

$$\left| \frac{\Phi(\rho) + \Phi(\sigma)}{2} - \frac{1-\alpha}{2(\sigma-\rho)^{1-\alpha}} \left[{}_{N_3}J^\alpha_{\sigma^-} \Phi(\rho) + {}_{N_3}J^\alpha_{\rho^+} \Phi(\sigma) \right] \right|$$

$$\leq \frac{\sigma - \rho}{2} \left(\frac{1}{2-\alpha} \right)^{1-\frac{1}{q}}$$

$$\times \left[\left\{ \frac{\mathbf{A}_2 |\Phi'(\rho)|^q + \mathbf{A}_2 |\Phi'(\sigma)|^q}{2-\alpha} - |\Phi'(\rho)|^q \int_0^1 t^{1-\alpha} h^s(t) dt \right.\right.$$

$$\left. - |\Phi'(\sigma)|^q \int_0^1 t^{1-\alpha}(1-h(t))^s dt \right\}^{\frac{1}{q}} + \left\{ \frac{\mathbf{A}_2 |\Phi'(\rho)|^q + \mathbf{A}_2 |\Phi'(\sigma)|^q}{2-\alpha} \right.$$

$$\left.\left. - |\Phi'(\sigma)|^q \int_0^1 t^{1-\alpha} h^s(t) dt - |\Phi'(\rho)|^q \int_0^1 t^{1-\alpha}(1-h(t))^s dt \right\}^{\frac{1}{q}} \right].$$

If, in addition, we suppose $q = 1$, then we get (23).

4. Applications

Throughout the paper, we examined the fractional integral sums

$${}_{N_3}J^\alpha_{y^-} \Phi(x) + {}_{N_3}J^\alpha_{x^+} \Phi(y) = \int_x^y (t-x)^{-\alpha} \Phi(t) dt + \int_x^y (y-t)^{-\alpha} \Phi(t) dt,$$

for $x, y \in [\rho, \sigma] \subset \mathbb{R}$.

We demonstrate the scope and strength of our results through three examples, two related to trigonometric functions and one to arithmetic means.

First, consider a convex function. Let $\Phi : [\rho, \sigma] = [\pi, 2\pi] \to \mathbb{R}$, $\Phi(t) = \sin t$, which is convex on $[\pi, 2\pi]$, and fix $\alpha = \frac{1}{2}$. Then, according to Theorem 4, we have the inequality

$$\sin\left(\frac{x+y}{2}\right) \leq -\frac{1}{4\sqrt{y-x}}\left[\int_x^y \frac{\sin t}{\sqrt{t-x}}dt + \int_x^y \frac{\sin t}{\sqrt{y-t}}dt\right] \leq -\sin\left(\frac{x+y}{2}\right)$$

for all $x, y \in [\pi, 2\pi]$.

Second, we consider a non-convex function that has a convex derivative in absolute value. Let $\Phi : [\pi, 2\pi] \to \mathbb{R}$, $\Phi(t) = t - \cos t$, which has a convex derivative $\Phi'(t) = 1 + \sin t$ on $[\pi, 2\pi]$, and fix $\alpha = \frac{1}{2}$. Keeping Remark 2 in mind, applying Corollary 7 or Corollary 8 (with x in place of ρ and y in place of σ) yields

$$\left| x + y - \cos x - \cos y - \frac{1}{2\sqrt{y-x}}\left[\int_x^y \frac{t - \cos t}{\sqrt{t-x}}dt + \int_x^y \frac{t - \cos t}{\sqrt{y-t}}dt\right]\right|$$
$$\leq \frac{2(y-x)(2 + \sin x + \sin y)}{3}$$

for all $x, y \in [\pi, 2\pi]$.

Finally, consider the convex function $\Phi : [\rho, \sigma] \subset [0, \infty) \to \mathbb{R}$, $\Phi(t) = t^n$ with $n \geq 1$, and fix $\alpha < 1$. Then, according to Theorem 4, we have

$$\left[\sigma - \frac{y}{2} + \rho - \frac{x}{2}\right]^n \leq \rho^n + \sigma^n - \frac{1 - \alpha}{2(y-x)^{1-\alpha}}\left[\int_x^y \frac{t^n}{(t-x)^\alpha}dt + \int_x^y \frac{t^n}{(y-t)^\alpha}dt\right]$$
$$\leq \rho^n + \sigma^n - \left(\frac{x+y}{2}\right)^n$$

for $x, y \in [\rho, \sigma]$, from which we obtain an inequality of arithmetic means:

$$[2A(\rho, \sigma) - A(x, y)]^n \leq 2A(\rho^n, \sigma^n) - \frac{1 - \alpha}{2(y-x)^{1-\alpha}}\left[\int_x^y \frac{t^n}{(t-x)^\alpha}dt + \int_x^y \frac{t^n}{(y-t)^\alpha}dt\right]$$
$$\leq 2A(\rho^n, \sigma^n) - A^n(x, y),$$

where $A(u, v)$ denotes the arithmetic mean $A(u, v) = \frac{u+v}{2}$.

5. Conclusions

In the present work, we obtained interesting results pertaining to the Jensen–Mercer-type Hermite–Hadamard inequalities via non-conformable integrals, using the classical convex, (h, m)-convex, and (h, m)-convex modified functions. Thus, we presented various relevant fractional inequalities related to convex functions and differentiable functions of general convex derivative in absolute value.

As applications, we gave examples of functions for which our main inequalities can be applied, and we presented the resulting inequalities.

Our results are expected to provide motivation to generate further research on inequalities that includes other notions of convexity, such as new variants of the Hermite–Hadamard–Mercer inequalities obtained in this work. For example, instead of working with the operators of [26], one can consider the following more general fractional integral:

Definition 7 ([31]). *Let $\Phi : [0, \infty) \to [0, \infty)$, such that $\Phi \in L[0, \infty)$. Generalized fractional Riemann–Liouville integral of order $\alpha \in \mathbb{R}$ and $\beta \in \mathbb{R}$, $\beta \neq -1$, is given as follows:*

$$^\beta J^{\frac{\alpha}{k}}_{\Phi, u}\Phi(x) = \frac{1}{k\Gamma_k(\alpha)}\int_u^x \frac{\Phi(t)dt}{[\Phi(x,t)]^{1-\frac{\alpha}{k}}\Phi(t,\beta)}$$

with $\Phi(t, \beta) > 0$, $\Phi(t, 0) = 1$ and $\Phi(x, t) = \int_t^x \frac{d\theta}{\Phi(\theta, \beta)}$. Obviously $\Phi(x, t) = -\Phi(t, x)$.

By considering the kernel $\Phi(t, \beta) = t^{-\beta}$, we have

$$\Phi(x,t) = \frac{x^{\beta+1} - t^{\beta+1}}{\beta + 1} \quad \text{and} \quad [\Phi(x,t)]^{1-\frac{\alpha}{k}} = \left[\frac{x^{\beta+1} - t^{\beta+1}}{\beta + 1}\right]^{1-\frac{\alpha}{k}},$$

and we get the (k, β)–Riemann–Liouville fractional integral in Definition 2.1 of [32]. Furthermore, by setting $k = 1$, we obtain the Katugampola fractional integral (see [33]).

Author Contributions: Writing—original draft preparation, B.B., P.K. and J.E.N.V. All authors have read and agreed to the published version of the manuscript.

Funding: This research received no external funding.

Institutional Review Board Statement: Not applicable.

Informed Consent Statement: Not applicable.

Data Availability Statement: Not applicable.

Conflicts of Interest: The authors declare no conflict of interest.

References

1. Butt, S.I.; Agarwal, P.; Yousaf, S.; Guirao, J.L.G. Generalized fractal Jensen and Jensen–Mercer inequalities for harmonic convex function with applications. *J. Inequal. Appl.* **2022**, *2022*, 1. [CrossRef]
2. Deng, Y.; Ullah, H.; Khan, M.A.; Iqbal, S.; Wu, S. Refinements of Jensen's Inequality via Majorization Results with Applications in the Information Theory. *J. Math.* **2021**, *2021*, 1951799. [CrossRef]
3. Dragomir, S.S. Some reverses of the Jensen inequality with applications. *Bull. Aust. Math. Soc.* **2013**, *87*, 177–194. [CrossRef]
4. Duc, D.T.; Hue, N.N. Jensen-type inequalities and their applications. *J. Math. Inequal.* **2020**, *14*, 319–327. [CrossRef]
5. Lu, G. New refinements of Jensen's inequality and entropy upper bounds. *J. Math. Inequal.* **2018**, *12*, 403–421. [CrossRef]
6. Varosanec, S. On h-convexity. *J. Math. Anal. Appl.* **2007**, *326*, 303–311. [CrossRef]
7. Mitrinovic, D.S.; Pecaric, J.E.; Fink, A.M. *Classical and New Inequalities in Analysis*; Springer Science+Business Media: Dordrecht, The Netherlands, 1993. [CrossRef]
8. Mercer, A.M. A variant of Jensen's inequality. *J. Inequal. Pure Appl. Math.* **2003**, *4*, 73.
9. Khan, A.R.; Pecaric, J.; Praljak, M. A Note on Generalized Mercer's Inequality. *Bull. Malays. Math. Sci. Soc.* **2017**, *40*, 881–889. [CrossRef]
10. Moradi, H.R.; Furuichi, S. Improvement and generalization of some Jensen-Mercer-type inequalities. *J. Math. Inequal.* **2020**, *14*, 377–383. [CrossRef]
11. Vivas Cortez, M.J.; Hernández Hernández, J.E. Una Variante de la desigualdad de Jensen-Mercer para funciones $h-$convexas y funciones de operadores $h-$convexas. *Revista MATUA* **2017**, *4*, 62–76.
12. Dragomir, S.S.; Pearce, C. Selected Topics on Hermite-Hadamard Inequalities and Applications, Science Direct Working Paper No S1574-0358(04)70845-X. Available online: https://ssrn.com/abstract=3158351 (accessed on 24 May 2023).
13. Abdeljawad, T.; Ali, M.A.; Mohammed, P.O.; Kashuri, A. On inequalities of Hermite-Hadamard-Mercer type involving Riemann-Liouville fractional integrals. *AIMS Math.* **2021**, *6*, 712–725. [CrossRef]
14. Aljaaidi, T.A.; Pachpatte, D.B. The Hermite–Hadamard–Mercer Type Inequalities via Generalized Proportional Fractional Integral Concerning Another Function. *Int. J. Math. Math. Sci.* **2022**, *2022*, 6716830. [CrossRef]
15. Butt, S.I.; Yousaf, S.; Asghar, A.; Khan, K.A.; Moradi, H.R. New Fractional Hermite–Hadamard–Mercer Inequalities for Harmonically Convex Function. *J. Funct. Spaces* **2021**, *2021*, 5868326. [CrossRef]
16. Iscan, I. Jensen–Mercer inequality for GA-convex functions and some related inequalities. *J. Inequal. Appl.* **2020**, *2020*, 212. [CrossRef]
17. Ögülmüs, H.; Sarikaya, M.Z. Hermite-Hadamard-Mercer Type Inequalities for Fractional Integrals. *Filomat* **2021**, *35*, 2425–2436. [CrossRef]
18. Zhao, J.; Butt, S.I.; Nasir, J.; Wang, Z.; Tlili, I. Hermite–Jensen–Mercer Type Inequalities for Caputo Fractional Derivatives. *J. Funct. Spaces* **2020**, *2020*, 7061549. [CrossRef]
19. Nápoles Valdés, J.E.; Rabossi, F.; Samaniego, A.D. Convex functions: Ariadne's thread or Charlotte's Spiderweb? *Adv. Math. Model. Appl.* **2020**, *5*, 176–191.
20. Bayraktar, B.; Nápoles, J.E. Hermite–Hadamard weighted integral inequalities for (h, m)-convex modified functions. *Fract. Differ. Calc.* **2022**, *12*, 235–248. [CrossRef]
21. Bayraktar, B.; Nápoles, J.E. New generalized integral inequalities via (h, m)-convex modified functions. *Izv. Inst. Mat. Inform.* **2022**, *60*, 3–15. [CrossRef]
22. Alomari, M.W. Mercer's inequality for h-convex functions. *Turkish J. Ineq.* **2018**, *2*, 38–41.

23. Butt, S.I.; Nasir, J.; Qaisar, S.; Abualnaja, K.M. k-Fractional Variants of Hermite-Mercer-Type Inequalities via s-Convexity with Applications. *J. Funct. Spaces* **2021**, *2021*, 5566360. [CrossRef]
24. Khan, M.A.; Khan, A.R.; Pecaric, J. On the refinements of Jensen-Mercer's inequality. *Rev. Anal. Numér. Théor. Approx.* **2012**, *41*, 62–81. [CrossRef]
25. Niezgoda, M. A generalization of Mercer's result on convex functions. *Nonlinear Anal.* **2009**, *71*, 2771–2779. [CrossRef]
26. Nápoles Valdés, J.E.; Rodriguez, J.M.; Sigarreta, J.M. New Hermite–Hadamard Type Inequalities Involving Non-Conformable Integral Operators. *Symmetry* **2019**, *11*, 1108. [CrossRef]
27. Akgül, A.; Khoshnaw, S.H.A. Application of fractional derivative on non-linear biochemical reaction models. *Int. J. Intell. Netw.* **2020**, *1*, 52–58. [CrossRef]
28. Rezapour, S.; Deressa, C.T.; Hussain, A.; Etemad, S.; George, R.; Ahmad, B. A Theoretical Analysis of a Fractional Multi-Dimensional System of Boundary Value Problems on the Methylpropane Graph via Fixed Point Technique. *Mathematics* **2022**, *10*, 568. [CrossRef]
29. Sintunavarat, W.; Turab, A. A unified fixed point approach to study the existence of solutions for a class of fractional boundary value problems arising in a chemical graph theory. *PLoS ONE* **2022**, *17*, e0270148. [CrossRef]
30. Kian, M.; Moslehian, M.S. Refinements of the operator Jensen–Mercer inequality. *Electron. J. Linear Algebra* **2013**, *26*, 742–753. [CrossRef]
31. Bayraktar, B.; Nápoles Valdes, J.E. Generalized Fractional Integral Inequalities for (h, m, s)-convex modified functions of second type. *Sahand Commun. Math. Anal.* **2023**, submitted.
32. Sarikaya, M.Z.; Dahmani, Z.; Kiris, M.E.; Ahmad, F. (k, s)-Riemann-Liouville fractional integral and applications. *Hacet. J. Math. Stat.* **2016**, *45*, 77–89. [CrossRef]
33. Katugampola, U.N. New approach to a generalized fractional integral. *Appl. Math. Comput.* **2011**, *218*, 860–865. [CrossRef]

Disclaimer/Publisher's Note: The statements, opinions and data contained in all publications are solely those of the individual author(s) and contributor(s) and not of MDPI and/or the editor(s). MDPI and/or the editor(s) disclaim responsibility for any injury to people or property resulting from any ideas, methods, instructions or products referred to in the content.

Article

New Applications of Faber Polynomials and q-Fractional Calculus for a New Subclass of m-Fold Symmetric bi-Close-to-Convex Functions

Mohammad Faisal Khan [1], Suha B. Al-Shaikh [2,*], Ahmad A. Abubaker [2] and Khaled Matarneh [2]

[1] Department of Basic Sciences, College of Science and Theoretical Studies, Saudi Electronic University, Riyadh 11673, Saudi Arabia; f.khan@seu.edu.sa
[2] Faculty of Computer Studies, Arab Open University, Riyadh 11681, Saudi Arabia; a.abubaker@arabou.edu.sa (A.A.A.); k.matarneh@arabou.edu.sa (K.M.)
* Correspondence: s.alshaikh@arabou.edu.sa

Abstract: Using the concepts of q-fractional calculus operator theory, we first define a (λ, q)-differintegral operator, and we then use m-fold symmetric functions to discover a new family of bi-close-to-convex functions. First, we estimate the general Taylor–Maclaurin coefficient bounds for a newly established class using the Faber polynomial expansion method. In addition, the Faber polynomial method is used to examine the Fekete–Szegö problem and the unpredictable behavior of the initial coefficient bounds of the functions that belong to the newly established class of m-fold symmetric bi-close-to-convex functions. Our key results are both novel and consistent with prior research, so we highlight a few of their important corollaries for a comparison.

Keywords: analytic functions; quantum (or q-) calculus; q-fractional derivative; close-to-convex functions; m-fold symmetric functions; Faber polynomial expansion

Citation: Khan, M.F.; Al-Shaikh, S.B.; Abubaker, A.A.; Matarneh, K. New Applications of Faber Polynomials and q-Fractional Calculus for a New Subclass of m-Fold Symmetric bi-Close-to-Convex Functions. *Axioms* **2023**, *12*, 600. https://doi.org/10.3390/axioms12060600

Academic Editors: Péter Kórus and Juan Eduardo Nápoles Valdes

Received: 14 May 2023
Revised: 7 June 2023
Accepted: 8 June 2023
Published: 16 June 2023

Copyright: © 2023 by the authors. Licensee MDPI, Basel, Switzerland. This article is an open access article distributed under the terms and conditions of the Creative Commons Attribution (CC BY) license (https://creativecommons.org/licenses/by/4.0/).

MSC: 05A30; 30C45; 11B65; 47B38

1. Introduction

Let $\mathcal{A}$ stand for the family of analytic functions in $E = \{z \in \mathbb{C} : |z| < 1\}$ that are normalized when $\eta(0) = 0$ and $\eta'(0) = 1$ and express every $\eta \in \mathcal{A}$ that has the following series in the form shown below:

$$\eta(z) = z + \sum_{j=2}^{\infty} a_j z^j.$$

In addition, $\mathcal{S}$ is a subclass of $\mathcal{A}$, and members of $\mathcal{S}$ are univalent in E. The function $\eta \in \mathcal{S}$ is called a starlike $(\mathcal{S}^*)$ function in E (see [1]) if

$$Re\left(\frac{z\eta'(z)}{\eta(z)}\right) > 0, \ z \in E$$

and the function $\eta \in \mathcal{S}$ is called a convex $(\mathcal{C})$ function in E (see [2]) if

$$1 + Re\left(\frac{z\eta''(z)}{\eta'(z)}\right) > 0, \ z \in E.$$

The function $\eta \in \mathcal{S}$ is called a close-to-convex $(\mathcal{K})$ function in E (see [3]) if and only if $g \in \mathcal{S}^*$, such that

$$Re\left(\frac{z\eta'(z)}{g(z)}\right) > 0.$$

In [4], Noor introduced the class of functions $\eta \in \mathcal{S}$ that are called quasi-close-to-convex ($\mathcal{Q}$) functions in E if and only if $g \in \mathcal{K}$ exists, such that

$$Re\left(\frac{(z\eta'(z))'}{g'(z)}\right) > 0.$$

Among the subclasses of $\mathcal{S}$, the starlike ($\mathcal{S}^*$) convex ($\mathcal{C}$) and close-to-convex ($\mathcal{K}$) functions are the most well known. To learn more about the well-known and extensive research of the starlike and convex function subclasses $\mathcal{S}$ and $\mathcal{C}$, see [5–7].

The idea of starlike and convex functions of order α was first presented by Robertson [8] in 1936 as follows:

For $0 \leq \alpha < 1$, the function $\eta \in \mathcal{S}$ is called a starlike ($\mathcal{S}^*(\alpha)$) function of order α in E (see [8]) if

$$Re\left(\frac{z\eta'(z)}{\eta(z)}\right) > \alpha$$

and for $0 \leq \alpha < 1$, the function $\eta \in \mathcal{S}$ is called a convex ($\mathcal{C}(\alpha)$) function of order α in E (see [8]) if

$$Re\left(\frac{(z\eta'(z))'}{\eta'(z)}\right) > \alpha.$$

For $\alpha = 0$,
$$\mathcal{S}^*(\alpha) = \mathcal{S}^*$$

and
$$\mathcal{C}(\alpha) = \mathcal{C}.$$

Let $0 \leq \alpha < 1$; the function $\eta \in \mathcal{S}$ is called a close-to-convex ($\mathcal{K}(\alpha)$) function of order α in E (see [3]) if and only if $g \in \mathcal{S}^*(\alpha) = \mathcal{S}^*$, such that

$$Re\left(\frac{z\eta'(z)}{g(z)}\right) > \alpha.$$

For more details, see [5].

Let $0 \leq \alpha < 1$; the function $\eta \in \mathcal{S}$ is said to be in the class of quasi-close-to-convex ($\mathcal{Q}(\alpha)$) functions if and only if $g \in \mathcal{K}$ exists, such that

$$Re\left(\frac{(z\eta'(z))'}{g'(z)}\right) > \alpha.$$

For $\alpha = 0$,
$$\mathcal{K}(\alpha) = \mathcal{K}$$

and
$$\mathcal{Q}(\alpha) = \mathcal{Q}.$$

We present the well-known class $\mathcal{P}$ (see [6]) of analytic functions p in E, which satisfy the following conditions:
$$Re(p(z)) > 0$$

and
$$p(0) = 1.$$

For $\eta_1, \eta_2 \in \mathcal{A}$, and η_1 subordinate to η_2 in E, denoted by (see [9])

$$\eta_1(z) \prec \eta_2(z), \quad z \in E,$$

suppose that an analytic function w_0, such that $|w_0(z)| < 1$ and $w_0(0) = 0$, and

$$\eta(z) = \eta_2(w_0(z)), \ z \in E.$$

Each function $\eta \in S$ has an inverse $\eta^{-1} = F$ that may be written as

$$F(\eta(z)) = z, \ z \in E$$

and

$$\eta(F(w)) = w, \ |w| < r_0(\eta), \ r_0(\eta) \geq \frac{1}{4}.$$

The series of the inverse function is given by

$$F(w) = w - a_2 w^2 + (2a_2^2 - a_3)w^3 - (5a_2^3 - 5a_2 a_3 + a_4)w^4 + \ldots. \tag{1}$$

An analytic function η is called bi-univalent in E if η and η^{-1} are univalent in E, and Σ stands for the class of all bi-univalent functions. Here, we give some examples of bi-univalent functions below:

$$\eta_1(z) = \frac{z}{1-z}, \ \eta_2(z) = -\log(1-z), \ \eta_3(z) = \frac{1}{2}\log\left(\frac{1+z}{1-z}\right), \ z \in E.$$

The famous Koebe function

$$k(z) = z(1-z)^{-2}, \quad \text{for all } z \in E,$$

is not in class Σ.

Lewin [10] introduced the concept of class Σ and established $|a_2| < 1.51$ for every $\eta \in \Sigma$. Following that, Brannan and Clunie [11] demonstrated that $|a_2| \leq \sqrt{2}$. Subsequently, Netanyahu [12] showed that $\max |a_2| = \frac{4}{3}$, and Styer and Wright [13] showed the existence of $\eta \in \Sigma$, for which $|a_2| < \frac{4}{3}$. Furthermore, Tan [14] demonstrated that, for functions in Σ, $|a_2| < 1.485$. Since class Σ was first introduced, many scholars have attempted to establish the connection between the geometric features of the functions inside it and the coefficient bounds. As a matter of fact, authors Lewin [10], Brannan and Taha [11], Srivastava et al. [15], and others [16–20] built a solid framework for the study of bi-univalent functions. In these more recent publications, the initial coefficients were only estimated using non-sharp methods, and the coefficient estimates for the general class of analytic bi-univalent functions were also discovered in [21]; however, Atshan [22] utilized the quasi-subordination characteristics and obtained some results for new bi-univalent function subclasses. A new subclass of m-fold bi-univalent functions was defined by Oros and Cotirla [23], who also found the coefficient estimates of the Fekete–Szegö problem. More recently, the integral operator based on the Lucas polynomial was used to estimate coefficients for general subclasses of analytic bi-univalent functions [24]. Numerous authors looked into the bounds for various m-fold bi-univalent function subclasses [25–30]. The sharp coefficient bound for $|a_m|$, $(m = 3, 4, 5, \ldots)$ is still an unsolved problem.

Gong [31] discussed the uses and significance of the Faber polynomial methods that Faber [32] introduced. The coefficient bounds $|a_j|$ for $j \geq 3$ were recently determined by Hamidi and Jahangiri [33,34] using the Faber polynomial expansion method. The Faber polynomial expansion approach has been used to introduce and study a number of new bi-univalent function subclasses. Bult introduced a few new subclasses of bi-univalent functions in References [35–37], and she implemented the Faber polynomial method to discover the general coefficient bounds $|a_j|$ for $j \geq 3$. She also discussed how the initial coefficient bounds have unpredictable behavior. In [38,39], new subclasses of meromorphic bi-univalent functions were studied using the Faber polynomial. Recently, the subordination features and the method of generating Faber polynomials were also used to derive the general coefficient bounds $|a_j|$ for $j \geq 3$ of analytic bi-univalent functions [40]. Altinkaya and Yalcin [41] addressed the unusual behavior of coefficient bounds for novel subclasses of bi-univalent functions using a similar methodology. Additionally, numerous authors used the Faber polynomial technique and obtained some intriguing findings for bi-univalent functions (see [42–47] for additional information).

Let $m \in \mathbb{N}$. If a rotation of a domain E with an angle of $2\pi/m$ at its origin maps that domain onto itself, then the domain is said to be m-fold symmetric.

Following that, it is demonstrated that an analytic η in E, being m-fold symmetric, satisfies the following requirement:

$$\eta\left(e^{\frac{2\pi i}{m}}z\right) = e^{\frac{2\pi i}{m}}\eta(z)$$

and $\mathcal{S}_m$ in E represents m-fold symmetric univalent functions. The function $\eta \in \mathcal{S}_m$ has the following form:

$$\eta(z) = z + \sum_{j=1}^{\infty} a_{mj+1} z^{mj+1}. \tag{2}$$

Srivastava et al. [48,49] gave an additional boost to the study of the family Σ_m, which has led to a large number of works on subclasses of Σ_m. Then, for a new subclass of Σ_m, Srivastava et al. [50] explored the initial coefficient bounds. Note that $\Sigma_1 = \Sigma$. Sakar and Tasar [51] developed further subclasses of m-fold bi-univalent functions and derived the initial coefficient bounds for the functions belonging to these families. In [52], coefficient bounds were established for new subclasses of analytic and m-fold symmetric bi-univalent functions. Recently, Swamy et al. [29] defined a new family of m-fold symmetric bi-univalent functions by ensuring that they satisfied the subordination requirement. References [53–58] presented interesting results on the initial coefficient bounds and the Fekete–Szegö functional problem for some subfamilies of Σ_m.

Recent work by Srivastava et al. [59] shows the series expansion for η^{-1} to be as follows:

$$F(w) = \eta^{-1}(w) = w - a_{m+1}w^{m+1} + A_m w^{2m+1} - B_m w^{3m+1}, \tag{3}$$

where

$$A_m = (m+1)a_{m+1}^2 - a_{2m+1},$$
$$B_m = \frac{1}{2}(m+1)(3m+2)a_{m+1}^3 - (3m+2)a_{m+1}a_{2m+1} + a_{3m+1}$$

For $m = 1$, Equation (3) coincides with Equation (1). Here, we provide examples of an insignificant number of m-fold symmetric bi-univalent functions:

$$\eta_4(z) = \left(\frac{z^m}{1-z^m}\right)^m, \eta_5(z) = [\log(1-z^m)]^{\frac{-1}{m}},$$

$$\eta_6(z) = \log\sqrt{\frac{1+z^m}{1-z^m}}, \quad z \in E$$

and their inverse functions are

$$F_7(z) = \left(\frac{w^m}{1+w^m}\right)^{\frac{1}{m}}, F_8(z) = \left(\frac{e^{2w^m}-1}{e^{2w^m}+1}\right)^{\frac{1}{m}},$$

$$F_9(z) = \left(\frac{e^{w^m}-1}{e^{w^m}}\right)^{\frac{1}{m}}.$$

Many new classes of analytic functions have been built and studied by scholars in the field of Geometric Function Theory (GFT) using q-calculus and fractional q-calculus. In 1909, Jackson [60] developed the q-calculus (D_q) operator, and in [61], Ismail et al. utilized this operator for the first time to build a class of q-starlike functions in E. See [62–65] for more reading on q-calculus and analytic functions.

The Faber polynomial is one such subject, and it has become more important in mathematics and other sciences in recent years. This article is divided into three parts. In Section 1, we quickly review some elementary concepts from the theory of geometric functions since they are essential to our primary discovery. These elements are all standard fare, and we appropriately reference them. In Section 2, we introduce the Faber polynomial method, give a few illustrations, define some key terms, and present some preliminary lemmas. In Section 3, we present the new (λ, q)-differintegral operator for m-fold symmetric functions, and, considering this operator, we define a new class of close-to-convex functions and investigate the main results. Section 4 offers some final remarks.

2. Preliminaries

Addressing the basic definitions and notions of q-fractional calculus is now necessary in order to construct some new subclasses of m-fold symmetric bi-univalent functions.

Definition 1 ([66]). *Let us define the q-shifted factorial $(\gamma, q)_j$ as*

$$(\gamma, q)_j = \prod_{j=0}^{j-1}\left(1 - \gamma q^j\right), \quad (j \in \mathbb{N}, \; \gamma, q \in \mathbb{C}). \tag{4}$$

If $\gamma \neq q^{-m}$, ($m \in \mathbb{N}_0 = \{0, 1, 2, \dots\}$), then it can be written as

$$(\gamma, q)_\infty = \prod_{j=0}^{\infty}\left(1 - \gamma q^j\right), \quad (\gamma \in \mathbb{C} \text{ and } |q| < 1). \tag{5}$$

Remark 1. *When $\gamma \neq 0$ and $q \geq 1$, $(\gamma, q)_\infty$ diverges. Thus, if and when this occurs $(\gamma, q)_\infty$, then we will assume $|q| < 1$.*

Remark 2. *When $q \to 1-$ in (4), then we obtain the Pochhammer symbol $(\gamma)_j$ defined as*

$$(\gamma)_j = \prod_{l=0}^{j-1}(\gamma + l), \; \text{if } j \in \mathbb{N}.$$

If $j = 0$, then $(\gamma)_j = 1$.

Definition 2 ([60]). *The expression for the q-factorial $[j]_q$ is*

$$[j]_q! = \prod_{l=1}^{j}[l]_q, \quad (l \in \mathbb{N}), \tag{6}$$

where

$$[j]_q = \frac{1 - q^j}{1 - q}.$$

If $j = 0$, then

$$[j]_q! = 1.$$

Definition 3 ([66]). *$(\gamma, q)_j$ in (4) can be precise in terms of the q-Gamma function as follows:*

$$F_q(\gamma) = \frac{(1-q)^{1-\gamma}(q, q)_\infty}{(q^\gamma, q)_\infty}, \quad (0 < q < 1),$$

or

$$(q^\gamma, q)_j = \frac{(1 - q^j) F_q(\gamma + j)}{F_q(\gamma)}, \quad (j \in \mathbb{N}).$$

For analytic functions, Jackson [60] presented the q-difference operator as follows:

Definition 4 ([60])**.** For $\eta \in \mathcal{A}$, the q-difference operator is defined as

$$D_q\eta(z) = \frac{\eta(z) - \eta(qz)}{z(1-q)}, \quad z \in E.$$

Note that

$$D_q(z^j) = [j]_q z^{j-1}, \quad D_q\left(\sum_{j=1}^{\infty} a_j z^j\right) = \sum_{j=1}^{\infty} [j]_q a_j z^{j-1}.$$

Definition 5. Pochhammer's generalized symbol for q is denoted by

$$[\gamma]_{q,j} = \frac{\Gamma_q(\gamma+j)}{\Gamma_q(\gamma)}, \quad j \in \mathbb{N}, \ \gamma \in \mathbb{C}.$$

Remark 3. When $q \to 1-$, $[\gamma]_{q,j}$ simplifies to $(\gamma)_j = \frac{\Gamma(\gamma+j)}{\Gamma(\gamma)}$.

Definition 6 ([67])**.** For $\lambda > 0$, the fractional q-integral operator is defined by

$$I_q^\lambda \eta(z) = \frac{1}{\Gamma_q(\lambda)} \int_0^z (z-tq)_{\lambda-1} \eta(t) d_q(t), \qquad (7)$$

where the definition of the q-binomial function $(z-tq)_{\lambda-1}$ is

$$(z-tq)_{\lambda-1} = z^{\lambda-1} {}_1\Phi_0\left(q^{-\lambda+1}, -, q, tq^\lambda/z\right).$$

The series ${}_1\Phi_0$ is given by

$${}_1\Phi_0(a,-,q,z) = 1 + \sum_{j=1}^{\infty} \frac{(a,q)_j}{(q,q)_j} z^j, \quad (|q|<1, |z|<1).$$

This final equivalence is known as the q-binomial theorem (for reference, see [68]). For more details, see [67,69].

Definition 7 ([68,70])**.** For an analytic function η, the fractional q-derivative operator D_q^λ is defined by

$$\begin{aligned} D_q^\lambda \eta(z) &= D_q I_q^{1-\lambda} \eta(z) \\ &= \frac{1}{\Gamma_q(1-\lambda)} D_q \int_0^z (z-tq)_{-\lambda} \eta(t) d_q(t), \quad (0 \le \lambda < 1). \end{aligned}$$

Definition 8 ([67,68])**.** For k to be the smallest integer, the extended fractional q-derivative D_q^λ of order λ is defined by

$$D_q^\lambda \eta(z) = D_q^k\left(I_q^{k-\lambda} \eta(z)\right). \qquad (8)$$

We find from (8) that

$$D_q^\lambda z^j = \frac{\Gamma_q(j+1)}{\Gamma_q(j+1-\lambda)} z^{j-\lambda}, \quad (0 \le \lambda, \ j > -1).$$

Note that D_q^λ represents the fractional q-integral of order λ when $-\infty < \lambda < 0$ and the fractional q-derivative of order λ when $0 \le \lambda < 2$.

Definition 9 ([71]). *Selvakumaran et al. defined the (λ, q)-differintegral operator $\Omega_q^\lambda : \mathcal{A} \to \mathcal{A}$ as follows:*

$$\Omega_q^\lambda \eta(z) = \frac{F_q(2-\lambda)}{F_q(2)} z^\lambda D_q^\lambda \eta(z)$$

$$= z + \sum_{j=2}^{\infty} \frac{F_q(2-\lambda) F_q(j+1)}{F_q(2) F_q(j+1-\lambda)} a_j z^j, \quad z \in E,$$

where

$$0 \leq \lambda < 2, \text{ and } 0 < q < 1.$$

Consider the following:

$$\lim_{\lambda \to 1} \Omega_q^\lambda \eta(z) = \Omega_q \eta(z) = z D_q \eta(z).$$

Definition 10. *For k to be the smallest integer, the extended fractional q-derivative $D_q^{\lambda,m}$ of order λ is defined for m-fold symmetric functions as follows:*

$$D_q^{\lambda,m} \eta(z) = D_q^k \left(I_q^{k-\lambda} \eta(z) \right); \tag{9}$$

we find from (9) that

$$D_q^{\lambda,m} z^j = \frac{F_q(mj+2)}{F_q(mj+2-\lambda)} z^{mj+1-\lambda}, \quad (0 \leq \lambda, \ j > -1, \ m \in \mathbb{N}).$$

The Faber Polynomial Expansion Method and Its Applications

The coefficients of the inverse map F may be expressed using the Faber polynomial method applied to the analytic functions (see [72,73]).

$$F(w) = \eta^{-1}(w) = w + \sum_{j=2}^{\infty} \frac{1}{j} Q_{j-1}^j (a_2, a_3, \ldots, a_j) w^j,$$

where

$$Q_{j-1}^{-j} = \frac{(-j)!}{(-2j+1)!(j-1)!} a_2^{j-1} + \frac{(-j)!}{[2(-j+1)]!(j-3)!} a_2^{j-3} a_3$$

$$+ \frac{(-j)!}{(-2j+3)!(j-4)!} a_2^{j-4} a_4$$

$$+ \frac{(-j)!}{[2(-j+2)]!(j-5)!} a_2^{j-5} \left[a_5 + (-j+2) a_3^2 \right]$$

$$+ \frac{(-j)!}{(-2j+5)!(j-6)!} a_2^{j-6} [a_6 + (-2j+5) a_3 a_4]$$

$$+ \sum_{i \geq 7} a_2^{j-i} Q_i,$$

and for $7 \leq i \leq j$, Q_i is a homogeneous polynomial in $a_2, a_3, \ldots a_j$. To be more specific, the first three terms of Q_{j-1}^{-j} are

$$\frac{1}{2}Q_1^{-2} = -a_2, \quad \frac{1}{3}Q_2^{-3} = 2a_2^2 - a_3,$$

$$\frac{1}{4}Q_3^{-4} = -(5a_2^3 - 5a_2a_3 + a_4).$$

The usual form of the expansion of Q_j^r for $r \in \mathbb{Z}$ ($\mathbb{Z} := 0, \pm 1, \pm 2, \ldots$ and $j \geq 2$ is

$$Q_j^r = ra_j + \frac{r(r-1)}{2}\mathcal{V}_j^2 + \frac{r!}{(r-3)!3!}\mathcal{V}_j^3 + \cdots + \frac{r!}{(r-j)!(j)!}\mathcal{V}_j^j,$$

where

$$\mathcal{V}_j^r = \mathcal{V}_j^r(a_2, a_3, \ldots)$$

and according to [72], we have

$$\mathcal{V}_j^v(a_2, \ldots, a_j) = \sum_{j=1}^{\infty} \frac{v!(a_2)^{\mu_1} \ldots (a_j)^{\mu_j}}{\mu_1!, \ldots, \mu_j!}, \quad \text{for } a_1 = 1 \text{ and } v \leq j.$$

The sum takes over all non-negative integers $\mu_1, \ldots, \mu_j$, which satisfies

$$\mu_1 + \mu_2 + \cdots + \mu_j = v,$$
$$\mu_1 + 2\mu_2 + \cdots + j\mu_j = j.$$

Clearly,

$$\mathcal{V}_j^j(a_1, \ldots, a_j) = \mathcal{V}_1^j$$

and the first and last polynomials are

$$\mathcal{V}_j^j = a_1^j, \text{ and } \mathcal{V}_j^1 = a_j.$$

Lemma 1 ([5]). *If* $p(z) = 1 + \sum_{j=1}^{\infty} c_j z^j \in \mathcal{P}$ *and* $Re(p(z)) > 0$, *then*

$$|c_j| \leq 2.$$

In this section, we define the (λ, q)-differintegral operator for m-fold symmetric functions, consider this operator, and define a new class of close-to-convex functions. Then, we obtain our main results by using the technique of Faber polynomial expansion.

3. Main Results

By using the same technique as Selvakumaran et al. [71], we define the (λ, q)-differintegral operator for m-fold symmetric functions as follows:

Definition 11. *For* $m \in \mathbb{N}$, *the* (λ, q)-*differintegral operator for m-fold symmetric functions* $\Omega_q^{\lambda,m} : \mathcal{S}_m \to \mathcal{S}_m$ *is defined as follows:*

$$\Omega_q^{\lambda,m}\eta(z) = \frac{F_q(2-\lambda)}{F_q(2)}z^\lambda D_q^{\lambda,m}\eta(z)$$

$$= z + \sum_{j=1}^{\infty} \frac{F_q(2-\lambda)F_q(mj+2)}{F_q(2)F_q(mj+2-\lambda)}a_{mj+1}z^{mj+1}, \quad z \in E,$$

where

$$0 \leq \lambda < 2, \text{ and } 0 < q < 1.$$

Taking motivation from [33] and considering the (λ, q)-differintegral operator, we define a new class of close-to-convex bi-univalent functions of class Σ_m.

Definition 12. *The function $f \in \Sigma_m$ belongs to class $C_\Sigma^{\lambda,q}(\alpha, m)$ if and only if there exists a function $g \in \mathcal{S}^*$ satisfying*

$$\text{Re}\left(\frac{D_q\left(\Omega_q^{\lambda,m}\eta(z)\right)}{g(z)}\right) > \alpha$$

and

$$\text{Re}\left(\frac{D_q\left(\Omega_q^{\lambda,m}F(w)\right)}{G(w)}\right) > \alpha,$$

where $0 \leq \alpha < 1, 0 \leq \lambda < 1, m \in \mathbb{N}, z, w \in E$ and $F = \eta^{-1}$.

The Faber polynomial method is applied to Definition 12 in order to derive the jth coefficient bounds, $|a_{mj+1}|$, and the initial coefficient bounds, $|a_{m+1}|, |a_{2m+1}|$, as well as the Feketo–Szegö problem $|a_{2m+1} - \mu a_{m+1}^2|$.

Theorem 1. *Let $\eta \in C_\Sigma^{\lambda,q}(\alpha, m)$ be given by (2) if $a_{mk+1} = 0$, and $1 \leq k \leq j-1$. Then,*

$$|a_{mj+1}| \leq \frac{F_q(2)F_q(mj+2-\lambda)(3-2\alpha+mj)}{[mj+1]_q F_q(2-\lambda)F_q(mj+2)}, \text{ for } j \geq 2.$$

Proof. Since $\eta \in C_\Sigma^{\lambda,q}(\alpha, m)$, then, by definition and using the Faber polynomial,

$$\frac{D_q\left(\Omega_q^\lambda \eta(z)\right)}{g(z)}$$
$$= 1 + \sum_{j=1}^{\infty}\left[K_1(q,m,j,\lambda)\sum_{l=1}^{j-1}Q_l^{-1}(b_{m+1}, b_{m+2}, \ldots b_{ml+1}) \times K_2(q,m,j,\lambda)\right]z^{mj}, \quad (10)$$

where

$$K_1(q,m,j,\lambda)$$
$$= \left([mj+1]_q \frac{F_q(2-\lambda)F_q(mj+2)}{F_q(2)F_q(mj+2-\lambda)}a_{mj+1} - b_{mj+1}\right)$$
$$K_2(q,m,j,\lambda)$$
$$= \left(([mj+1]_q - ml)\frac{F_q(2-\lambda)F_q(mj-ml+2)}{F_q(2)F_q(mj-ml+2-\lambda)}a_{mj+1-ml} - b_{mj+1-ml}\right).$$

For the inverse map $F = \eta^{-1}$ and $G = g^{-1}$, we obtain

$$\frac{D_q\left(\Omega_q^\lambda F(w)\right)}{G(w)}$$
$$= 1 + \sum_{j=2}^{\infty}\left[K_3(q,m,j,\lambda)\sum_{l=1}^{j-1}Q_l^{-1}(B_{m+1}, B_{m+2}, \ldots B_{ml+1}) \times K_4(q,m,j,\lambda)\right]w^{mj}, \quad (11)$$

where

$$K_3(q, m, j, \lambda) = \left([mj+1]_q \frac{F_q(2-\lambda)F_q(mj+2)}{F_q(2)F_q(mj+2-\lambda)} A_{mj+1} - B_{mj+1}\right)$$

$$K_4(q, m, j, \lambda) = \left(([mj+1]_q - ml) \frac{F_q(2-\lambda)F_q(mj-ml+2)}{F_q(2)F_q(mj-ml+2-\lambda)} A_{mj+1-ml} - B_{mj+1-ml}\right).$$

As opposed to that, $Re \frac{D_q(\Omega_q^\lambda \eta(z))}{g(z)} > \alpha$ in E, and

$$p(z) = 1 + \sum_{j=1}^{\infty} c_{mj} z^{mj};$$

therefore,

$$\frac{D_q\left(\Omega_q^\lambda \eta(z)\right)}{g(z)} = 1 + (1-\alpha)p(z)$$

$$= 1 + (1-\alpha) \sum_{j=1}^{\infty} c_{mj} z^{mj}. \quad (12)$$

Similarly, $Re \frac{D_q(\Omega_q^\lambda F(w))}{G(w)} > \alpha$ in E, and there exists the function

$$s(w) = 1 + \sum_{j=1}^{\infty} d_{mj} w^{mj}$$

so that

$$\frac{D_q\left(\Omega_q^\lambda F(w)\right)}{G(w)} = 1 + (1-\alpha)s(w)$$

$$= 1 + (1-\alpha) \sum_{j=1}^{\infty} d_{mj} w^{mj}. \quad (13)$$

Evaluating the coefficients of Equations (10) and (12), for any $j \geq 2$, yields

$$\left\{K_1(q, m, j, \lambda) Q_l^{-1}(b_{m+1}, b_{m+2}, \ldots b_{ml+1}) \times K_2(q, m, j, \lambda)\right\} = (1-\alpha)c_{mj}. \quad (14)$$

Evaluating the coefficients of Equations (11) and (13), for any $j \geq 2$, yields

$$K_3(q, m, j, \lambda) \sum_{l=1}^{j-1} Q_l^{-1}(B_{m+1}, B_{m+2}, \ldots B_{ml+1}) \times K_4(q, m, j, \lambda) = (1-\alpha)d_{mj}. \quad (15)$$

For the special case $j = 1$, from Equations (14) and (15), we obtain

$$\frac{[m+1]_q F_q(2-\lambda)F_q(m+2)}{F_q(2)F_q(m+2-\lambda)} a_{m+1} - b_{m+1} = (1-\alpha)c_m$$

and

$$\frac{[m+1]_q F_q(2-\lambda)F_q(m+2)}{F_q(2)F_q(m+2-\lambda)} A_{m+1} - B_{m+1} = (1-\alpha)d_m.$$

By utilizing Lemma 1 and solving a_{m+1} in absolute values, we achieve

$$|a_{m+1}| \leq \frac{F_q(2)F_q(m+2-\lambda)}{[m+1]_q F_q(2-\lambda)F_q(m+2)}(3-2\alpha+m).$$

However, under this assumption, $a_{mk+1} = 0$ and $1 \leq k \leq j-1$ both yield

$$A_j = -a_j.$$

Therefore,

$$[mj+1]_q \frac{F_q(2-\lambda)F_q(mj+2)}{F_q(2)F_q(mj+2-\lambda)} a_{mj+1} - b_{mj+1} = (1-\alpha)c_{mj} \qquad (16)$$

and

$$-[mj+1]_q \frac{F_q(2-\lambda)F_q(mj+2)}{F_q(2)F_q(mj+2-\lambda)} a_{mj+1} - B_{mj+1} = (1-\alpha)d_{mj}. \qquad (17)$$

By solving Equations (16) and (17) for a_j and determining the absolute values, and by using Lemma 1, we obtain

$$|a_{mj+1}| \leq \frac{F_q(2)F_q(mj+2-\lambda)(3-2\alpha+mj)}{[mj+1]_q F_q(2-\lambda)F_q(mj+2)},$$

upon noticing that

$$|b_{mj+1}| \leq mj+1 \text{ and } |B_{mj+1}| \leq mj+1.$$

This completes Theorem 1. □

Corollary 1. *Let $\eta \in C_\Sigma^{\lambda,q}(\alpha, 1)$ be given by (2) if $a_{k+1} = 0$, and $1 \leq k \leq j-1$. Then,*

$$|a_{j+1}| \leq \frac{F_q(2)F_q(j+2-\lambda)(3-2\alpha+j)}{[j+1]_q F_q(2-\lambda)F_q(j+2)}, \text{ for } j \geq 2.$$

Corollary 2. *Let $\eta \in C_\Sigma^{0,q}(\alpha, m)$ be given by (2) if $a_{mk+1} = 0$, and $1 \leq k \leq j-1$. Then,*

$$|a_{mj+1}| \leq \frac{(3-2\alpha+mj)}{[mj+1]_q}, \text{ for } j \geq 2.$$

Corollary 3. *Let $\eta \in C_\Sigma^{\lambda,1}(\alpha, m)$ be given by (2) if $a_{mk+1} = 0$, and $1 \leq k \leq j-1$. Then,*

$$|a_{mj+1}| \leq \frac{F(mj+2-\lambda)(3-2\alpha+mj)}{[mj+1]F(2-\lambda)F(mj+2)}, \text{ for } j \geq 2.$$

Corollary 4. *Let $\eta \in C_\Sigma^{0,1}(\alpha, m)$ be given by (2) if $a_{mk+1} = 0$, and $1 \leq k \leq j-1$. Then,*

$$|a_{mj+1}| \leq \frac{(3-2\alpha+mj)}{[mj+1]_q}, \text{ for } j \geq 2.$$

When we set $\lambda = 0$, $m = 1$, and $q \to 1-$, we have a well-established corollary, which is proven in [33].

Corollary 5 ([33])**.** *Let $\eta \in C_\Sigma(\alpha)$ if $a_{k+1} = 0$, $1 \leq k \leq j$. Then,*

$$|a_j| \leq 1 + \frac{2(1-\alpha)}{j}, \text{ for } j \geq 3.$$

The following theorem is obtained given the initial coefficients $|a_{m+1}|$ and $|a_{2m+1}|$, as well as the Feketo–Szegö problem $|a_{2m+1} - a_{m+1}^2|$ in $C_\Sigma(m, \alpha, q)$.

Theorem 2. Let $\eta \in C_\Sigma^{\lambda,q}(\alpha, m)$ be given by (2). Then,

$$|a_{m+1}| \leq \sqrt{\frac{2F_q(2)F_q(m+2-\lambda)F_q(2m+2)(1-\alpha)}{F_q(2-\lambda)\{K_5(q,m,j,\lambda) - K_6(q,m,j,\lambda)\}}}$$

for $0 \leq \alpha < 1 - \phi(q,\lambda)$.

$$|a_{m+1}| \leq \frac{2F_q(2)F_q(m+2-\lambda)(1-\alpha)}{[m+1]_q F_q(2-\lambda)F_q(m+2) - F_q(2)F_q(m+2-\lambda)},$$

for $1 - \phi(q,\lambda) \leq \alpha < 1$

$$|a_{2m+1}| \leq \frac{2F_q(2)F_q(2m+2-\lambda)(1-\alpha)}{[2m+1]_q F_q(2m+2)F_q(2-\lambda) - F_q(2)F_q(2m+2-\lambda)} \times K_7(q,m,j,\lambda),$$

where

$$\phi(q,\lambda) = K_9(q,m,j,\lambda) \times \left(F_q(2)F_q(2m+2-\lambda)\{Q_1(q,m,\lambda)\}^2\right)$$

and

$$K_9(q,m,j,\lambda) = \frac{1}{2F_q(m+1-\lambda)F_q(2)Q_2(q,m,\lambda)}$$
$$Q_1(q,m,\lambda) = [m+1]_q F_q(2-\lambda)F_q(m+2) - F_q(2)F_q(m+2-\lambda)$$
$$Q_2(q,m,\lambda) = \{K_5(q,m,j,\lambda)F_q(m+1-\lambda) - K_6(q,m,j,\lambda)F_q(2-\lambda)\}.$$

Now,

$$\left|a_{2m+1} - a_{m+1}^2\right| \leq \frac{2F_q(2)F_q(2m+2-\lambda)(1-\alpha)}{[2m+1]_q F_q(2-\lambda)F_q(2m+2) - F_q(2)F_q(2m+2-\lambda)}.$$

where $K_5(q,m,j,\lambda)$, $K_6(q,m,j,\lambda)$, and $K_7(q,m,j,\lambda)$ are given by (18)–(20).

Proof. In the proof of Theorem 1, we obtain $a_{mj} = -b_{mj}$ for the function $g(z) = \Omega_q^\lambda \eta(z)$. For $j = 1$, (14) and (15) respectively yield

$$a_{m+1}\left(\frac{[m+1]_q F_q(2-\lambda)F_q(m+2)}{F_q(2)F_q(m+2-\lambda)} - 1\right) = (1-\alpha)c_m$$

$$a_{m+1}\left(-\frac{[m+1]_q F_q(2-\lambda)F_q(m+2)}{F_q(2)F_q(m+2-\lambda)} + 1\right) = (1-\alpha)d_m.$$

Any one of these two equations, when taken at its absolute value, gives

$$|a_{m+1}| \leq \frac{2F_q(2)F_q(m+2-\lambda)(1-\alpha)}{[m+1]_q F_q(2-\lambda)F_q(m+2) - F_q(2)F_q(m+2-\lambda)}.$$

For $j = 2$, Equations (14) and (15) respectively yield

$$\left(\frac{[2m+1]_q F_q(2-\lambda) F_q(2m+2)}{F_q(2) F_q(2m+2-\lambda)} - 1\right) a_{2m+1}$$
$$-\left(\frac{[m+1]_q F_q(2-\lambda) F_q(m+2)}{F_q(2) F_q(m+2-\lambda)} - 1\right) a_{m+1}^2$$
$$= (1-\alpha) c_{2m}$$

and

$$\left(2a_{m+1}^2 - a_{2m+1}\right)\left(\frac{[2m+1]_q F_q(2-\lambda) F_q(2m+2)}{F_q(2) F_q(2m+2-\lambda)} - 1\right)$$
$$-\left(\frac{[m+1]_q F_q(2-\lambda) F_q(m+2)}{F_q(2) F_q(m+2-\lambda)} - 1\right) a_{m+1}^2$$
$$= (1-\alpha) d_{2m}.$$

Combining the two equations and solving $|a_{m+1}|$ yield

$$\left|a_{m+1}^2\right| = \frac{F_q(2) F_q(m+2-\lambda) F_q(2m+2)(1-\alpha)|d_{2m}+c_{2m}|}{2F_q(2-\lambda)\{K_5(q,m,j,\lambda) - K_6(q,m,j,\lambda)\}},$$

where

$$K_5(q,m,j,\lambda) = [2m+1]_q F_q(2m+2) F_q(m+2-\lambda) \tag{18}$$

$$K_6(q,m,j,\lambda) = [m+1]_q F_q(m+2) F_q(2m+2-\lambda). \tag{19}$$

By applying Carathéodory's Lemma 1, we obtain

$$|a_{m+1}| \leq \sqrt{\frac{2F_q(2) F_q(m+2-\lambda) F_q(2m+2)(1-\alpha)}{F_q(2-\lambda)\{K_5(q,m,j,\lambda) - K_6(q,m,j,\lambda)\}}}.$$

As a result, we obtain the estimate

$$\sqrt{\frac{2F_q(2) F_q(m+2-\lambda) F_q(2m+2)(1-\alpha)}{F_q(2-\lambda)\{K_5(q,m,j,\lambda) - K_6(q,m,j,\lambda)\}}}$$
$$< \frac{2F_q(2) F_q(m+2-\lambda) F_q(2m+2)(1-\alpha)}{F_q(2-\lambda)\{K_5(q,m,j,\lambda) - K_6(q,m,j,\lambda)\}}.$$

By substituting

$$a_{m+1} = \frac{c_m(1-\alpha) F_q(2) F_q(m+2-\lambda)}{[m+1]_q F_q(2-\lambda) F_q(m+2) - F_q(2) F_q(m+2-\lambda)}$$

in (4), we obtain

$$a_{2m+1} = \frac{F_q(2) F_q(2m+2-\lambda)(1-\alpha)}{[2m+1]_q F_q(2m+2) F_q(2-\lambda) - F_q(2) F_q(2m+2-\lambda)}$$
$$\times \left\{ c_{2m} + \frac{(1-\alpha) F_q(2) F_q(m+2-\lambda)}{[m+1]_q F_q(2-\lambda) F_q(m+2) - F_q(2) F_q(m+2-\lambda)} c_m^2 \right\}.$$

Using the modulus and Carathéodory's Lemma 1, we may prove the following:

$$|a_{2m+1}| \leq K_7(q,m,j,\lambda) \left(\frac{2F_q(2)F_q(2m+2-\lambda)(1-\alpha)}{[2m+1]_q F_q(2m+2)F_q(2-\lambda) - F_q(2)F_q(2m+2-\lambda)} \right),$$

where

$$\begin{aligned} K_7(q,m,j,\lambda) &= K_8(q,m,j,\lambda)\left([m+1]_q F_q(2-\lambda)F_q(m+2) - W(q,m,\lambda)\right), \end{aligned} \qquad (20)$$

$$W(q,m,\lambda) = F_q(2)F_q(m+2-\lambda) + 2(1-\alpha)F_q(2)F_q(m+2-\lambda)$$

and

$$K_8(q,m,j,\lambda) = \frac{1}{[m+1]_q F_q(2-\lambda)F_q(m+2) - F_q(2)F_q(m+2-\lambda)}.$$

Lastly, by subtracting Equation (4) from Equation (5), we obtain

$$\left| a_{2m+1} - a_{m+1}^2 \right| \leq \frac{2F_q(2)F_q(2m+2-\lambda)(1-\alpha)}{[2m+1]_q F_q(2-\lambda)F_q(2m+2) - F_q(2)F_q(2m+2-\lambda)}.$$

□

Corollary 6. *Let* $\eta \in C_\Sigma^{\lambda,q}(\alpha,1)$ *be given by (2). Then,*

$$|a_2| \leq \sqrt{\frac{2F_q(2)F_q(3-\lambda)F_q(4)(1-\alpha)}{F_q(2-\lambda)\left\{[3]_q F_q(4)F_q(3-\lambda) - [2]_q F_q(3)F_q(4-\lambda)\right\}}}$$

for $0 \leq \alpha < 1 - \phi(q,\lambda)$ *and*

$$|a_2| \leq \frac{2F_q(2)F_q(3-\lambda)(1-\alpha)}{[2]_q F_q(2-\lambda)F_q(3) - F_q(2)F_q(3-\lambda)}$$

for $1 - \phi(q,\lambda) \leq \alpha < 1$ *and*

$$\begin{aligned} |a_3| &\leq \frac{2F_q(2)F_q(4-\lambda)(1-\alpha)}{[3]_q F_q(4)F_q(2-\lambda) - F_q(2)F_q(4-\lambda)} \\ &\quad \times \left\{ \frac{[2]_q F_q(2-\lambda)F_q(3) - F_q(2)F_q(3-\lambda) + 2(1-\alpha)F_q(2)F_q(3-\lambda)}{[2]_q F_q(2-\lambda)F_q(3) - F_q(2)F_q(3-\lambda)} \right\} \end{aligned}$$

and

$$\left|a_3 - a_2^2\right| \leq \frac{2F_q(2)F_q(4-\lambda)(1-\alpha)}{[3]_q F_q(2-\lambda)F_q(4) - F_q(2)F_q(4-\lambda)},$$

where

$$\begin{aligned} \phi(q,\lambda) &= \\ &= \frac{F_q(4-\lambda)\left\{[2]_q F_q(2-\lambda)F_q(3) - F_q(2)F_q(3-\lambda)\right\}^2}{2F_q(2-\lambda)W_1(q,\lambda)} \end{aligned}$$

and
$$W_1(q,\lambda) = \left([3]_q F_q(4) F_q(2-\lambda) F_q(3-\lambda) - [2]_q F_q(3) F_q(2-\lambda) F_q(4-\lambda)\right).$$

Corollary 7. *Let $\eta \in C_\Sigma^{0,q}(\alpha,m)$ be given by (2). Then,*
$$|a_{m+1}| \leq \sqrt{\frac{2(1-\alpha)}{\left\{[2m+1]_q - [m+1]_q\right\}}}$$

for $0 \leq \alpha < 1 - \phi(q,0)$. Now,
$$|a_{m+1}| \leq \frac{2(1-\alpha)}{[m+1]_q - 1}$$

for $1 - \phi(q,0) \leq \alpha < 1$.

$$|a_{2m+1}| \leq \frac{2(1-\alpha)}{[2m+1]_q - 1} \left\{ \frac{[m+1]_q - 1 + 2(1-\alpha)}{[m+1]_q - 1} \right\}$$

and
$$\left|a_{2m+1} - a_{m+1}^2\right| \leq \frac{2(1-\alpha)}{[2m+1]_q - 1},$$

where
$$\phi(q,0) = \frac{F_q(m+2)\{[m+1]_q F_q(2) - F_q(2)\}^2}{2F_q(m+1)\{[2m+1]_q F_q(m+1) - [m+1]_q F_q(2)\}}.$$

Corollary 8. *Let $\eta \in C_\Sigma^{0,1}(\alpha,m)$ be given by (2). Then,*
$$|a_{m+1}| \leq \sqrt{\frac{2(1-\alpha)}{m}}$$

for $0 \leq \alpha < 1 - \phi(1,0)$. Now,
$$|a_{m+1}| \leq \frac{2(1-\alpha)}{m}$$

for $1 - \phi(1,0) \leq \alpha < 1$.

$$|a_{2m+1}| \leq \frac{1-\alpha}{m} \times \left\{\frac{m + 2(1-\alpha)}{m}\right\}$$

and
$$\left|a_{2m+1} - a_{m+1}^2\right| \leq \frac{1-\alpha}{m},$$

where
$$\phi(1,0) = \frac{m}{2}.$$

The well-known corollary for $\lambda = 0$, $m = 1$, and $q \to 1-$ is proven in [33].

Corollary 9 ([33]). *Let $\eta \in C_\Sigma(\alpha)$ be given by (2). Then,*
$$|a_2| \leq \begin{cases} \sqrt{2(1-\alpha)} & \text{if } 0 \leq \alpha < \frac{1}{2}, \\ 2(1-\alpha) & \text{if } \frac{1}{2} \leq \alpha < 1, \end{cases}$$

and
$$|a_3| \leq \begin{cases} 2(1-\alpha) & \text{if } 0 \leq \alpha < \frac{1}{2}, \\ (1-\alpha)(3-2\alpha) & \text{if } \frac{1}{2} \leq \alpha < 1. \end{cases}$$

4. Conclusions

In this paper, we introduced the (λ, q)-differintegral operator for m-fold symmetric functions given in (11) and discussed its applications for a class of m-fold symmetric bi-close-to-convex functions that is defined in (12). We applied the Faber polynomial technique and investigated the jth coefficient bounds, the initial coefficients, and the Fekete–Szegö functional for this newly defined class of m-fold symmetric functions. This research also shows how current discoveries and other improvements may be made via careful parameter specialization.

This article has three parts. Since the basics of geometric function theory are necessary to understand our major discovery, we briefly cover them in Section 1. These elements are all well recognized, and we appropriately reference them. The Faber polynomial method, several related applications, and some preliminary lemmas are presented in Section 2. In Section 3, we discuss our results. Researchers may create many other classes of m-fold symmetric bi-univalent functions by using different extended q-operators in place of the (λ, q)-differintegral operator in their future investigations. Researchers may also explore the behavior of coefficient estimations for newly defined subclasses of m-fold symmetric bi-univalent functions using the Faber polynomial approach.

Author Contributions: Supervision, S.B.A.-S.; Methodology, A.A.A. and M.F.K.; Formal analysis, A.A.A. and K.M.; Writing—review and editing original draft, S.B.A.-S.; Funding acquisition, S.B.A.-S. All authors have read and agreed to the published version of the manuscript.

Funding: This research received no external funding.

Data Availability Statement: Not applicable.

Acknowledgments: The authors would like to thank Arab Open University for supporting this work.

Conflicts of Interest: The authors state that they have no competing interest.

References

1. Nevalinna, R. Uber Uber die Konforme Abbildung Sterngebieten. *Oversiktav-Fin. Vetenskaps Soc. Forh.* **1920**, *63*, 1–21.
2. Study, E. *Konforme Abbildung Einfachzusammenhangender Bereiche*; B. C. Teubner: Leipzig/Berlin, Germany, 1913.
3. Kaplan, W. Close-to-convex schlicht functions. *Mich. Math. J.* **1952**, *1*, 169–185. [CrossRef]
4. Noor, K.I. On quasi-convex functions and related topics. *Int. J. Math. Math. Sci.* **1987**, *10*, 241–258. [CrossRef]
5. Duren, P.L. Univalent functions. In *Grundehren der Math. Wiss.*; Springer: New York, NY, USA, 1983; Volume 259.
6. Goodman, A.W. *Univalent Functions*; Mariner: Tampa, FL, USA, 1983; Volume I, II.
7. Hayman, W.K. *Multivalent Functions*; Cambridge University Press: Cambridge, UK, 1967.
8. Robertson, M.S. On the theory of univalent functions. *Ann. Math.* **1936**, *37*, 1374–1408. [CrossRef]
9. Lindelöf, E. Mémoire sur certaines inégalitis dans la théorie des functions monogénses et sur quelques propriété s nouvelles de ces fonctions dans levoisinage dun point singulier essentiel. *Ann. Soc. Sci. Fenn.* **1909**, *35*, 1–35.
10. Lewin, M. On a coefficient problem for bi-univalent functions. *Proc. Am. Math. Soc.* **1967**, *18*, 63–68. [CrossRef]
11. Brannan, D.A.; Cluni, J. Aspects of contemporary complex analysis. In *Proceedings of the NATO Advanced Study Institute Held at University of Durham*; Academic Press: New York, NY, USA, 1979.
12. Netanyahu, E. The minimal distance of the image boundary from the origin and the second coefficient of a univalent function in $|z| < 1$. *Arch. Ration. March. Anal.* **1967**, *32*, 100–112.
13. Styer, D.; Wright, D.J. Results on bi-univalent functions. *Proc. Am. Math. Soc.* **1981**, *82*, 243–248. [CrossRef]
14. Tan, D.L. Coefficient estimates for bi-univalent functions. *Chin. Ann. Math. Ser. A* **1984**, *5*, 559–568.
15. Srivastava, H.M.; Mishra, A.K.; Gochhayat, P. Certain subclasses of analytic and bi-univalent functions. *Appl. Math. Lett.* **2010**, *23*, 1188–1192. [CrossRef]
16. Brannan, D.A.; Taha, T.S. On some classes of bi-univalent function. *Study. Univ. Babes Bolyai Math.* **1986**, *31*, 70–77.
17. Hayami, T.; Owa, S. Coefficient bounds for bi-univalent functions. *Pan Am. Math. J.* **2012**, *22*, 15–26.
18. Khan, S.; Khan, N.; Hussain, S.; Ahmad, Q.Z.; Zaighum, M.A. Some classes of bi-univalent functions associated with Srivastava-Attiya operator. *Bull. Math. Anal. Appl.* **2017**, *9*, 37–44.
19. Srivastava, H.M.; Bulut, S.; Caglar, M.; Yagmur, N. Coefficient estimates for a general subclass of analytic and bi-univalent functions. *Filomat* **2013**, *27*, 831–842. [CrossRef]
20. Xu, Q.H.; Xiao, H.G.; Srivastava, H.M. A certain general subclass of analytic and bi-univalent functions and associated coefficient estimate problems. *Appl. Math. Comput.* **2012**, *218*, 11461–11465. [CrossRef]

21. Srivastava, H.M.; Gaboury, S.; Ghanim, F. Coefficient estimates for some general subclasses of analytic and bi-univalent functions. *Afr. Mat.* **2017**, *28*, 693–706. [CrossRef]
22. Atshan, W.G.; Rahman, I.A.R.; Alb Lupas, A. Some results of new subclasses for bi-univalent functions using quasi subordination. *Symmetry* **2021**, *13*, 1653. [CrossRef]
23. Oros, G.I.; Cotirla, L.I. Coefficient estimates and the Fekete-Szegö problem for new classes of m-fold symmetric bi-univalent functions. *Mathematics* **2022**, *10*, 129. [CrossRef]
24. Alb Lupas, A.; El-Deeb, S.M. Subclasses of bi-univalent functions connected with integral operator based upon Lucas polynomial. *Symmetry* **2022**, *14*, 622. [CrossRef]
25. Al Amoush, A.G.; Murugusundaramoorthy, G. Certain subclasses of λ-pseudo bi-univalent functions with respect to symmetric points associated with the Gegenbauer polynomial. *Afr. Mat.* **2023**, *34*, 11. [CrossRef]
26. Khan, B.; Liu, Z.G.; Shaba, T.G.; Araci, S.; Khan, N.; Khan, M.G. Applications of q-derivative operator to the subclass of bi-univalent functions involving q-Chebyshev polynomials. *J. Math.* **2022**, *7*, 8162182
27. Amini, E.; Al-Omari, S.; Nonlaopon, K.; Baleanu, D. Estimates for coefficients of bi-univalent functions associated with a fractional q-difference operator. *Symmetry* **2022**, *14*, 879. [CrossRef]
28. Amourah, A.; Frasin, B.A.; Swamy, S.R.; Sailaja, Y. Coefficient bounds for Al-Oboudi type bi-univalent functions connected with a modified sigmoid activated function and k-Fibonacci numbers. *J. Math. Comput. Sci.* **2022**, *27*, 105–117. [CrossRef]
29. Swamy, S.R.; Bulut, S.; Sailaja, Y. Some special families of holomorphic and Salagean type bi-univalent functions associated with Horadam polynomials involving modified sigmoid activation function. *Hacet. J. Math. Stat.* **2021**, *50*, 710–720. [CrossRef]
30. Amourah, A.; Frasin, B.A.; Ahmad, M.; Yousef, F. Exploiting the Pascal distribution series and Gegenbauer polynomials to construct and study a new subclass of analytic bi-univalent functions. *Symmetry* **2022**, *14*, 147. [CrossRef]
31. Gong, S. The Bieberbach conjecture, translated from the 1989 Chinese original and revised by the author. *AMS/IP Stud. Adv. Math.* **1999**, *12*, MR1699322.
32. Faber, G. Uber polynomische Entwickelungen. *Math. Ann.* **1903**, *57*, 1569–1573. [CrossRef]
33. Hamidi, S.G.; Jahangiri, J.M. Faber polynomials coefficient estimates for analytic bi-close-to-convex functions. *Comptes Rendus Math.* **2014**, *352*, 17–20. [CrossRef]
34. Hamidi, S.G.; Jahangiri, J.M. Faber polynomial coefficient estimates for bi-univalent functions defined by subordinations. *Bull. Iran. Math. Soc.* **2015**, *41*, 1103–1119.
35. Bulut, S. Faber polynomial coefficient estimates for a comprehensive subclass of m-fold symmetric analytic bi-univalent functions. *J. Fract. Calc. Appl.* **2017**, *8*, 108–117.
36. Bulut, S. Faber polynomial coefficients estimates for a comprehensive subclass of analytic bi-univalent functions. *Comptes Rendus Math.* **2014**, *352*, 479–484. [CrossRef]
37. Bulut, S. Faber polynomial coefficient estimates for certain subclasses of meromorphic bi-univalent functions. *Comptes Rendus Math.* **2015**, *353*, 113–116. [CrossRef]
38. Hamidi, S.G.; Halim, S.A.; Jahangiri, J.M. Faber polynomial coefficient estimates for meromorphic bi-starlike functions. *Int. J. Math. Math. Sci.* **2013**, *2013*, 498159. [CrossRef]
39. Hamidi, S.G.; Halim, S.A.; Jahangiri, J.M. Coefficient estimates for a class of meromorphic bi-univalent functions. *Comptes Rendus Math.* **2013**, *351*, 349–352. [CrossRef]
40. Hamidi, S.G.; Jahangiri, J.M. Faber polynomial coefficients of bi-subordinate functions. *Comptes Rendus Math.* **2016**, *354*, 365–370. [CrossRef]
41. Altinkaya, S.; Yalcin, S. Faber polynomial coefficient bounds for a subclass of bi-univalent functions. *Comptes Rendus Math.* **2015**, *353*, 1075–1080. [CrossRef]
42. Attiya, A.A.; Yassen, M.F. A Family of analytic and bi-univalent functions associated with Srivastava-Attiya Operator. *Symmetry* **2022**, *14*, 2006. [CrossRef]
43. Srivastava, H.M.; Eker, S.S.; Ali, R.M. Coefficient bounds for a certain class of analytic and bi-univalent functions. *Filomat* **2015**, *29*, 1839–1845. [CrossRef]
44. Wang, R.; Singh, M.; Khan, S.; Tang, H.; Khan, M.f.; Kamal, M. New applications of Faber polynomial expansion for analytical bi-close-to-convex functions defined by using q-calculus. *Mathematics* **2023**, *11*, 1217. [CrossRef]
45. Khan, M.F.; Khan, S.; Hussain, S.; Darus, M.; Matarneh, K. Certain new class of analytic functions defined by using a fractional derivative and Mittag-Leffler functions. *Axioms* **2022**, *11*, 655. [CrossRef]
46. Khan, N.; Khan, S.; Xin, Q.; Tchier, F.; Malik, S.N.; Javed, U. Some applications of analytic functions associated with q-fractional operator. *Mathematics* **2023**, *11*, 930. [CrossRef]
47. Khan, S.; Altınkaya, S.; Xin, Q.; Tchier, F.; Malik, S.N.; Khan, N. Faber polynomial coefficient estimates for Janowski type bi-close-to-convex and bi-quasi-convex functions. *Symmetry* **2023**, *15*, 604. [CrossRef]
48. Srivastava, H.M.; Gaboury, S.; Ghanim, F. Coefficients estimate for some subclasses of m-fold symmetric bi-univalent functions. *Acta Univ. Apulensis Math. Inform.* **2015**, *41*, 153–164.
49. Srivastava, H.M.; Gaboury, S.; Ghanim, F. Initial coefficients estimate for some subclasses of m-fold symmetric bi-univalent functions. *Acta Math. Sci.* **2016**, *36*, 863–971. [CrossRef]
50. Srivastava, H.M.; Zireh, A.; Hajiparvaneh, S. Coefficients estimate for some subclasses of m-fold symmetric bi-univalent functions. *Filomat* **2018**, *32*, 3143–3153. [CrossRef]

51. Sakar, F.M.; Tasar, N. Coefficients bounds for certain subclasses of m-fold symmetric bi-univalent functions. *New Trends Math. Sci.* **2019**, *7*, 62–70. [CrossRef]
52. Wanas, A.K.; Páll-Szabó, A.O. Coefficient bounds for new subclasses of analytic and m-fold symmetric bi-univalent functions. *Stud. Univ. Babeș Bolyai Math.* **2021**, *66*, 659–666. [CrossRef]
53. Motamednezhad, A.; Salehian, S.; Magesh, N. Coefficint estimates for subclass of m-fold symmetric bi-univalent functioms. *Kragujev. J. Math.* **2022**, *46*, 395–406. [CrossRef]
54. Aldawish, I.; Swamy, S.R.; Frasin, B.A. A special family of m -fold symmetric bi-univalent functions satisfying subordination condition. *Fractal Fract.* **2022**, *6*, 271. [CrossRef]
55. Breaz, D.; Cotîrlă, L.I. The study of coefficient estimates and Fekete–Szegö inequalities for the new classes of m-fold symmetric bi-univalent functions defined using an operator. *J. Inequalities Appl.* **2023**, *2023*, 15. [CrossRef]
56. Tang, H.; Srivastava, H.M.; Sivasubramanian, S.; Gurusamy, P. Fekete–Szegö functional problems of m-fold symmetric bi-univalent functions. *J. Math. Ineq.* **2016**, *10*, 1063–1092. [CrossRef]
57. Motamednezhad, A.; Salehian, S. Certain class of m-fold functions by applying Faber polynomial expansions. *Stud. Univ. Babe s-Bolyai Math.* **2021**, *66*, 491–505. [CrossRef]
58. Al-shbeil, I.; Khan, N.; Tchier, F.; Xin, Q.; Malik, S.N.; Khan, S. Coefficient bounds for a family of m-fold symmetric bi-univalent functions. *Axioms* **2023**, *12*, 317. [CrossRef]
59. Srivastava, H.M.; Sivasubramanian, S.; Sivakumar, R. Initial coefficient bounds for a subclass of m-fold symmetric bi-univalent functions. *Tbilisi Math. J.* **2014**, *7*, 1–10. [CrossRef]
60. Jackson, F.H. On q-functions and a certain difference operator. *Earth Environ. Sci. Trans. R. Soc. Edinb.* **1909**, *46* , 253–281. [CrossRef]
61. Ismail, M.E.H.; Merkes, E.; Styer, D. A generalization of starlike functions. *Complex Var. Theory Appl. Int. J.* **1990**, *14*, 77–84. [CrossRef]
62. Aldweby, H.; Darus, M. Some subordination results on q -analogue of Ruscheweyh differential operator. *Abstr. Appl. Anal.* **2014**, *2014*, 1–6. [CrossRef]
63. Kanas, S.; Raducanu, D. Some class of analytic functions related to conic domains. *Math. Slovaca* **2014**, *64*, 1183–1196. [CrossRef]
64. Mahmood, S.; Sokol, J. New subclass of analytic functions in conical domain associated with ruscheweyh q-differential operator. *Results Math.* **2017**, *71*, 1–13. [CrossRef]
65. Srivastava, H.M. Univalent functions, fractional calculus, and associated generalized hypergeometric functions, in univalent functions. In *Fractional Calculus; and Their Applications*; Srivastava, H.M., Owa, S., Eds.; Halsted Press: Chichester, UK; John Wiley and Sons: New York, NY, USA, 1989; pp. 329–354.
66. Gasper, G.; Rahman, M. Basic hypergeometric series (with a Foreword by Richard Askey). In *Encyclopedia of Mathematics and Its Applications*; Cambridge University Press: Cambridge, UK, 1990; Volume 35.
67. Purohit, S.D.; Raina, R.K. Certain subclasses of analytic functions associated with fractional q-calculus operators. *Math. Scand.* **2011**, *109*, 55–70. [CrossRef]
68. Srivastava, H.M.; Choi, J. *Zeta and q-Zeta Functions and Associated Series and Integrals*; Elsevier Science Publishers: Amsterdam, The Netherlands; London, UK; New York, NY, USA, 2012.
69. Srivastava, H.M. Operators of basic (or q-) calculus and fractional q-calculus and their applications in geometric function theory of complex analysis. *Iran. J. Sci. Tech. Tran. A Sci.* **2020**, *44*, 327–344. [CrossRef]
70. Srivastava, H.M. Some parametric and argument variations of the operators of fractional calculus and related special functions and integral transformations. *J. Nonlinear Convex Anal.* **2021**, *22*, 1501–1520.
71. Selvakumaran, K.A.; Choi, J.; Purohit, S.D. Certain subclasses of analytic functions defined by fractional q-calculus operators. *Appl. Math. E-Notes* **2021**, *21*, 72–80.
72. Airault, H. Symmetric sums associated to the factorizations of Grunsky coefficients. In *Groups and Symmetries: From Neolithic Scots to John McKay*; American Mathematical Society: Washington, DC, USA, 2007; Volume 47, p. 3.
73. Airault, H.; Bouali, H. Differential calculus on the Faber polynomials. *Bull. Sci. Math.* **2006**, *130*, 179–222. [CrossRef]

Disclaimer/Publisher's Note: The statements, opinions and data contained in all publications are solely those of the individual author(s) and contributor(s) and not of MDPI and/or the editor(s). MDPI and/or the editor(s) disclaim responsibility for any injury to people or property resulting from any ideas, methods, instructions or products referred to in the content.

Article

Some New Bullen-Type Inequalities Obtained via Fractional Integral Operators

Asfand Fahad [1,2], Saad Ihsaan Butt [3], Bahtiyar Bayraktar [4], Mehran Anwar [3] and Yuanheng Wang [1,*]

[1] School of Mathematical Sciences, Zhejiang Normal University, Jinhua 321004, China; asfandfahad1@zjnu.edu.cn or asfandfahad1@bzu.edu.pk
[2] Centre for Advanced Studies in Pure and Applied Mathematics, Bahauddin Zakariya University Multan, Multan 60800, Pakistan
[3] Department of Mathematics, COMSATS University Islamabad, Lahore Campus, Lahore 54000, Pakistan; saadihsanbutt@gmail.com (S.I.B.); mehrananwar140@gmail.com (M.A.)
[4] Department of Mathematics and Science Education, Uludag University, Bursa 16059, Türkiye; bbayraktar@uludag.edu.tr
* Correspondence: yhwang@zjnu.cn

Abstract: In this paper, we establish a new auxiliary identity of the Bullen type for twice-differentiable functions in terms of fractional integral operators. Based on this new identity, some generalized Bullen-type inequalities are obtained by employing convexity properties. Concrete examples are given to illustrate the results, and the correctness is confirmed by graphical analysis. An analysis is provided on the estimations of bounds. According to calculations, improved Hölder and power mean inequalities give better upper-bound results than classical inequalities. Lastly, some applications to quadrature rules, modified Bessel functions and digamma functions are provided as well.

Keywords: convex functions; Bullen's inequality; Hadamard inequality; Hölder inequality; power mean; fractional integral operators

MSC: 26A51; 26D15

Citation: Fahad, A.; Butt, S.I.; Bayraktar, B.; Anwar, M.; Wang, Y. Some New Bullen-Type Inequalities Obtained via Fractional Integral Operators. *Axioms* **2023**, *12*, 691. https://doi.org/10.3390/axioms12070691

Academic Editor: Chris Goodrich

Received: 10 June 2023
Revised: 6 July 2023
Accepted: 12 July 2023
Published: 16 July 2023

Copyright: © 2023 by the authors. Licensee MDPI, Basel, Switzerland. This article is an open access article distributed under the terms and conditions of the Creative Commons Attribution (CC BY) license (https://creativecommons.org/licenses/by/4.0/).

1. Introduction

Convexity (concavity) has many applications in several fields, which include mathematics, economics, finance, engineering and computer science. Numerous noteworthy inequalities and properties can be found in various categories of mathematics employing convexity (concavity) theory (see [1–4]). The unique global minimum in convex optimization problems can be efficiently located by applying a variety of optimization methods, including gradient descent, Newton's method and interior-point approaches. In applied problems, especially in optimization problems, the role of the concept of convexity is well-known. This concept, along with the functions derived from it, has a special place in the theory of integral inequalities; for example the inequalities of Jensen, Hermite, Simpson, Bullen, etc. (see [5–7]). Here, we first recall some necessary definitions and inequalities (see [8] and references therein).

Definition 1. *The function $\psi : [\vartheta^*, \varrho^*] \to \mathbb{R}$ is said to be convex if we have*

$$\psi(\varepsilon \rho + (1-\varepsilon)y) \leq \varepsilon \psi(\rho) + (1-\varepsilon)\psi(y),$$

for all $\rho, y \in [\vartheta^*, \varrho^*]$ and $\varepsilon \in [0,1]$. If $-\psi$ is convex, then ψ is concave.

The double Hermite–Hadamard inequality (hereinafter the Hadamard inequality), widely known in the theory of inequalities, is closely related to convex functions. This inequality is formulated in the literature as follows:

Let $\psi:[\vartheta^*, \varrho^*] \to \mathbb{R}$ be a convex function. Then, we have the following double inequality:

$$\psi\left(\frac{\vartheta^* + \varrho^*}{2}\right) \leq \frac{1}{\varrho^* - \vartheta^*} \int_{\vartheta^*}^{\varrho^*} \psi(\varepsilon)d\varepsilon \leq \frac{\psi(\vartheta^*) + \psi(\varrho^*)}{2}. \tag{1}$$

Many important inequalities have been established in the literature for various classes of convex functions and classes derived from them (for example, see [2,9–11]).

In [12], Bullen proved the following inequality, which is known as Bullen's inequality, for the convex function ψ:

$$\frac{1}{\varrho^* - \vartheta^*} \int_{\vartheta^*}^{\varrho^*} \psi(\varepsilon)d\varepsilon \leq \frac{1}{2}\left[\psi\left(\frac{\vartheta^* + \varrho^*}{2}\right) + \frac{\psi(\vartheta^*) + \psi(\varrho^*)}{2}\right]. \tag{2}$$

The well-known Bullen's inequality was first presented by Bullen in 1978 [12]. Due to their outstanding uses, Bullen-type inequalities have garnered a lot of interest. Bullen's inequality is a topic that many scientists and mathematicians are very interested in and concerned about because of its importance in many different domains. Bullen's inequality has drawn a lot of interest from scholars, who have worked hard over the years to enhance and generalize it. Numerous researchers have generalized the well-known Bullen's inequality in its conventional form for various subcategories of convex functions. Recently, there have been many interesting and attention-grabbing studies in the literature devoted to improving and generalizing Bullen-type inequalities. For example, some of these works are listed below.

In [13], Cakmak established some inequalities of the Hadmard and Bullen types for Lipschitzian functions. In [14], Çakmak presented Bullen-type inequalities via fractional integral operators for differentiable convex and $h-$convex functions and gave good examples. In [15] (see also [16]), Erden and Sarikaya established generalized Bullen-type inequalities using local fractional integrals and some applications for special means were given. In [17], Işcan et al. obtained some generalized Hadamard- and Bullen-type inequalities for convex functions and described some applications and error estimates for the left and right Hadamard inequalities. In [18], Hussain and Mehboob, using the generalized fractional integral identity, derived new estimates for the Bullen-type functional for $(s, p)-$convex functions. In [19], Yaşar et al. presented the Bullen-, midpoint-, trapezoid- and Simpson-type inequalities for s-convex functions in the fourth sense. In [20], Boulares et al. presented fractional multiplicative Bullen-type inequalities, along with some applications, using multiplicative calculus. Recently, in [21], Bahtiyar et al. gave a uniform treatment of fractional Bullen-type inequalities to provide a concrete estimation analysis of bounds using Lipschitz functions, mean value theorem and convexity theory.

It was inevitable that fractional calculus would arise using arbitrary-order integrals and derivatives. Due to its applicability in numerous fields of science and engineering, this topic has gained considerable prominence. The fact that researchers have over time suggested more efficient solutions to physical phenomena attuned to new operators with dominant kernels is a significant difference in this subject. Fractional derivatives play an important role in a number of mathematical problems and the corresponding practical consequences [22,23]. The fractional calculus approach has recently been employed to define the intricate dynamics of problems in real-life scenarios in several branches of applied science domains. There are numerous uses in the literature [24,25]. Fractional calculus has been widely employed to achieve novel results in the theory of inequality, connecting fractional operators through the idea of convexity (see [26–30]). We need the following definition of classical integral operators:

Definition 2 ([23]). *Let $\psi \in L[\vartheta^*, \varrho^*]$. The Riemann–Liouville integrals $J_{\vartheta^*+}^{\alpha}\psi$ and $J_{\varrho^*-}^{\alpha}\psi$ of order $\alpha > 0$ with $\vartheta^* \geq 0$ are defined by*

$$J_{\vartheta^*+}^{\alpha}\psi(\rho) = \frac{1}{\Gamma(\alpha)} \int_{\vartheta^*}^{\rho} (\rho - \varepsilon)^{\alpha-1} \psi(\varepsilon)d\varepsilon, \qquad \rho > \vartheta^*$$

and
$$J^{\alpha}_{\varrho^*-}\psi(\rho) = \frac{1}{\Gamma(\alpha)}\int_{\rho}^{\varrho^*}(\varepsilon-\rho)^{\alpha-1}\psi(\varepsilon)d\varepsilon, \qquad \rho < \varrho^*,$$

respectively, where $\Gamma(\alpha) = \int_0^{\infty} e^{-u}u^{\alpha-1}du$. Here we have $J^0_{a^+}\psi(x) = J^0_{b^-}\psi(\rho) = \psi(\rho)$. In the case of $\alpha = 1$, the fractional integral reduces to the classical integral.

Two classical inequalities—namely, the Hölder inequality and its other form—and the power mean inequalities have been used frequently in the development of the theory of integral inequalities.

Theorem 1 (Hölder inequality). Let $p > 1$, $\frac{1}{p} + \frac{1}{q} = 1$ and $\psi(\varepsilon), g(\varepsilon) : [\vartheta^*, \varrho^*] \longrightarrow \mathbb{R}$. If $|\psi|^p, |g|^q \in L[\vartheta^*, \varrho^*]$, then

$$\int_{\vartheta^*}^{\varrho^*}|\psi(\varepsilon)g(\varepsilon)|d\varepsilon \leq \left(\int_{\vartheta^*}^{\varrho^*}|\psi(\varepsilon)|^p d\varepsilon\right)^{\frac{1}{p}}\left(\int_{\vartheta^*}^{\varrho^*}|g(\varepsilon)|^q d\varepsilon\right)^{\frac{1}{q}}, \qquad (3)$$

for which equality holds if and only if $A|\psi(\varepsilon)|^p = B|g(\varepsilon)|^q$ almost everywhere, where A and B are constants.

Theorem 2 (Improved Hölder integral inequality [31]). Let $p > 1$, $\frac{1}{p} + \frac{1}{q} = 1$ and $\psi(\varepsilon), g(\varepsilon):[\vartheta^*, \varrho^*] \longrightarrow \mathbb{R}$. If $|\psi|^p, |g|^q \in L[\vartheta^*, \varrho^*]$, then

$$\int_{\vartheta^*}^{\varrho^*}|\psi(\varepsilon)g(\varepsilon)|d\varepsilon \qquad (4)$$
$$\leq \frac{1}{\varrho^* - \vartheta^*}\left(\int_{\vartheta^*}^{\varrho^*}(\varrho^*-\varepsilon)|\psi(\varepsilon)|^p d\varepsilon\right)^{\frac{1}{p}}\left(\int_{\vartheta^*}^{\varrho^*}(\varrho^*-\varepsilon)|g(\varepsilon)|^q d\varepsilon\right)^{\frac{1}{q}}$$
$$+ \frac{1}{\varrho^* - \vartheta^*}\left(\int_{\vartheta^*}^{\varrho^*}(\varepsilon-\vartheta^*)|\psi(\varepsilon)|^p d\varepsilon\right)^{\frac{1}{p}}\left(\int_{\vartheta^*}^{\varrho^*}(\varepsilon-\vartheta^*)|g(\varepsilon)|^q d\varepsilon\right)^{\frac{1}{q}}.$$

Theorem 3 (Power mean inequality). Let $q \geq 1$, $\frac{1}{p} + \frac{1}{q} = 1$ and $\psi(\varepsilon), g(\varepsilon) : [\vartheta^*, \varrho^*] \longrightarrow \mathbb{R}$. If $|\psi|^p, |g|^q \in L[\vartheta^*, \varrho^*]$, then

$$\int_{\vartheta^*}^{\varrho^*}|\psi(\varepsilon)g(\varepsilon)|d\varepsilon \leq \left(\int_{\vartheta^*}^{\varrho^*}|\psi(\varepsilon)|d\varepsilon\right)^{1-\frac{1}{q}}\left(\int_{\vartheta^*}^{\varrho^*}|\psi(\varepsilon)||g(\varepsilon)|^q d\varepsilon\right)^{\frac{1}{q}}. \qquad (5)$$

Theorem 4. *[Improved power mean integral inequality [32]] Let $q \geq 1$ and $\psi(\varepsilon), g(\varepsilon):[\vartheta^*, \varrho^*] \longrightarrow \mathbb{R}$. If $|\psi|, |g|^q \in L[\vartheta^*, \varrho^*]$ are the integrable functions on $[\vartheta^*, \varrho^*]$, then*

$$\int_{\vartheta^*}^{\varrho^*}|\psi(\varepsilon)g(\varepsilon)|d\varepsilon \qquad (6)$$
$$\leq \frac{1}{\varrho^*-\vartheta^*}\left(\int_{\vartheta^*}^{\varrho^*}(\varrho^*-\varepsilon)|\psi(\varepsilon)|d\varepsilon\right)^{1-\frac{1}{q}}\left(\int_{\vartheta^*}^{\varrho^*}(\varrho^*-\varepsilon)|\psi(\varepsilon)||g(\varepsilon)|^q d\varepsilon\right)^{\frac{1}{q}}$$
$$+ \frac{1}{\varrho^*-\vartheta^*}\left(\int_{\vartheta^*}^{\varrho^*}(\varepsilon-\vartheta^*)|\psi(\varepsilon)|d\varepsilon\right)^{1-\frac{1}{q}}\left(\int_{\vartheta^*}^{\varrho^*}(\varepsilon-\vartheta^*)|\psi(\varepsilon)||g(\varepsilon)|^q d\varepsilon\right)^{\frac{1}{q}}.$$

In [33], U. Kırmacı proved the following lemma.

Lemma 1. *Let $\psi : [\vartheta^*, \varrho^*] \to \mathbb{R}$ and $\psi \in C^2(\vartheta^*, \varrho^*)$ with $\psi'' \in L[\vartheta^*, \varrho^*]$. Then, we have*

$$\frac{(\varrho^*-\vartheta^*)^2}{2}(I_1+I_2) = \frac{1}{\varrho^*-\vartheta^*}\int_{\vartheta^*}^{\varrho^*}\psi(\varepsilon)d\varepsilon - \frac{1}{2}\left[\frac{\psi(\vartheta^*)+\psi(\varrho^*)}{2} + \psi\left(\frac{\vartheta^*+\varrho^*}{2}\right)\right], \qquad (7)$$

where

$$I_1 = \int_0^{1/2} \varepsilon(\varepsilon - 0.5)\psi''(\vartheta^*\varepsilon + \varrho^*(1-\varepsilon))d\varepsilon,$$

$$I_2 = \int_{1/2}^1 (\varepsilon - 0.5)(\varepsilon - 1)\psi''(\vartheta^*\varepsilon + \varrho^*(1-\varepsilon))d\varepsilon.$$

The main objective of this paper is to obtain some generalized Bullen-type inequalities for continuously differentiable functions. We first establish an identity of the Bullen type for twice-differentiable functions in terms of fractional integral operators. Based on this new identity, some generalized Bullen-type inequalities are obtained by employing convexity properties. Concrete examples are constructed to illustrate the results, and the correctness is verified by graphical analysis. An analysis is provided on the estimations of bounds. According to calculations, improved Hölder and power mean inequalities give better upper-bound results than classical inequalities. Lastly, some applications to quadrature rules, modified Bessel functions and digamma functions are provided as well.

2. Main Results

We start the results in this section by proving the following lemma.

Lemma 2. Let $\psi:[\vartheta^*, \varrho^*] \to \mathbb{R}$ and $\psi \in C^2(\vartheta^*, \varrho^*)$ with $\psi'' \in L[\vartheta^*, \varrho^*]$. When $\forall \varkappa \in [0,1]$, the equality holds:

$$\psi(c) - \mathbf{F}\left\{\frac{\alpha+1}{\varrho^* - \vartheta^*}\left[J_{c^+}^\alpha \psi(\varrho^*) + J_{c^-}^\alpha \psi(\vartheta^*)\right] - \left[\varkappa J_{c^+}^{\alpha-1}\psi(\varrho^*) + (1-\varkappa)J_{c^-}^{\alpha-1}\psi(\vartheta^*)\right]\right\}$$
$$= \frac{(\varrho^* - \vartheta^*)^2}{\varkappa^\alpha + (1-\varkappa)^\alpha}(I_1 + I_2), \tag{8}$$

where $c = \varkappa\vartheta^* + (1-\varkappa)\varrho^*$, $\alpha > 1$, $\mathbf{F} = \frac{\Gamma(\alpha+1)}{[\varkappa^\alpha + (1-\varkappa)^\alpha](\varrho^* - \vartheta^*)^{\alpha-1}}$,

$$I_1 = \int_0^\varkappa \varepsilon^\alpha (\varkappa - \varepsilon)\psi''(\vartheta^*\varepsilon + \varrho^*(1-\varepsilon))d\varepsilon,$$

$$I_2 = \int_\varkappa^1 (\varepsilon - \varkappa)(1-\varepsilon)^\alpha \psi''(\vartheta^*\varepsilon + \varrho^*(1-\varepsilon))d\varepsilon.$$

Proof. By integrating the first integral by parts twice, we get

$$I_1 = -\frac{1}{\vartheta^* - \varrho^*}\int_0^\varkappa \left[\varkappa\alpha\varepsilon^{\alpha-1} - (\alpha+1)\varepsilon^\alpha\right]\psi'(\vartheta^*\varepsilon + \varrho^*(1-\varepsilon))d\varepsilon$$

$$= -\frac{1}{\vartheta^* - \varrho^*}\left[\frac{\varkappa\alpha\varepsilon^{\alpha-1} - (\alpha+1)\varepsilon^\alpha}{\vartheta^* - \varrho^*}\psi(\varepsilon\vartheta^* + (1-\varepsilon)\varrho^*)\bigg|_0^\varkappa\right.$$
$$\left. - \frac{1}{\vartheta^* - \varrho^*}\int_0^\varkappa \left[\varkappa\alpha(\alpha-1)\varepsilon^{\alpha-2} - (\alpha+1)\alpha\varepsilon^{\alpha-1}\right]\psi(\vartheta^*\varepsilon + \varrho^*(1-\varepsilon))d\varepsilon\right]$$

$$= \frac{\varkappa^\alpha}{(\vartheta^* - \varrho^*)^2}\psi(c) + \frac{\varkappa\alpha(\alpha-1)}{(\vartheta^* - \varrho^*)^2}\int_0^\varkappa \varepsilon^{\alpha-2}\psi(\varepsilon\vartheta^* + (1-\varepsilon)\varrho^*)d\varepsilon$$
$$- \frac{(\alpha+1)\alpha}{(\vartheta^* - \varrho^*)^2}\int_0^\varkappa \varepsilon^{\alpha-1}\psi(\vartheta^*\varepsilon + \varrho^*(1-\varepsilon))d\varepsilon.$$

After changing the variable $\vartheta^*\varepsilon + \varrho^*(1-\varepsilon) = z$, we get

$$I_1 = \int_0^\varkappa \varepsilon^\alpha (\varepsilon - \varkappa)\psi''(\vartheta^*\varepsilon + \varrho^*(1-\varepsilon))d\varepsilon$$

$$= \frac{\varkappa^\alpha}{(\varrho^* - \vartheta^*)^2}\psi(c) + \frac{\varkappa\alpha(\alpha-1)}{(\varrho^* - \vartheta^*)^2}\int_{\varrho^*}^c \left(\frac{\varrho^* - z}{\varrho^* - \vartheta^*}\right)^{\alpha-2}\psi(z)d\left(\frac{z - \varrho^*}{\vartheta^* - \varrho^*}\right)$$
$$- \frac{(1+\alpha)\alpha}{(\varrho^* - \vartheta^*)^2}\int_{\varrho^*}^c \left(\frac{\varrho^* - z}{\varrho^* - \vartheta^*}\right)^{\alpha-1}\psi(z)d\left(\frac{z - \varrho^*}{\vartheta^* - \varrho^*}\right)$$

145

$$= \frac{\varkappa^\alpha}{(\varrho^* - \vartheta^*)^2}\psi(c) + \frac{\varkappa\alpha(\alpha-1)}{(\varrho^* - \vartheta^*)^3}\int_c^{\varrho^*}\left(\frac{\varrho^* - z}{\varrho^* - \vartheta^*}\right)^{\alpha-2}\psi(z)dz$$
$$- \frac{(1+\alpha)\alpha}{(\varrho^* - \vartheta^*)^3}\int_c^{\varrho^*}\left(\frac{\varrho^* - z}{\varrho^* - \vartheta^*}\right)^{\alpha-1}\psi(z)dz$$
$$= \frac{\varkappa^\alpha}{(\varrho^* - \vartheta^*)^2}\psi(c) + \frac{\varkappa\Gamma(\alpha+1)}{(\varrho^* - \vartheta^*)^{\alpha+1}}J_{c+}^{\alpha-1}\psi(\varrho^*) - \frac{\Gamma(\alpha+2)}{(\varrho^* - \vartheta^*)^{\alpha+2}}J_{c+}^{\alpha}\psi(\varrho^*).$$

For the I_2, we can write

$$I_2 = \int_\varkappa^1 (\varepsilon - \varkappa)(1-\varepsilon)^\alpha \psi''(\vartheta^*\varepsilon + \varrho^*(1-\varepsilon))d\varepsilon$$
$$= (1-\varkappa)\int_\varkappa^1 (1-\varepsilon)^\alpha \psi''(\vartheta^*\varepsilon + \varrho^*(1-\varepsilon))d\varepsilon$$
$$- \int_\varkappa^1 (1-\varkappa)^{\alpha+1}\psi''(\vartheta^*\varepsilon + \varrho^*(1-\varepsilon))d\varepsilon,$$

and, similarly to the first integral, we obtain

$$I_2 = \frac{(1-\varkappa)^\alpha}{(\varrho^* - \vartheta^*)^2}\psi(c) + \frac{(1-\varkappa)\Gamma(\alpha+1)}{(\varrho^* - \vartheta^*)^{\alpha+1}}J_{c-}^{\alpha-1}\psi(\vartheta^*) - \frac{\Gamma(\alpha+2)}{(\varrho^* - \vartheta^*)^{\alpha+2}}J_{c-}^{\alpha}\psi(\vartheta^*),$$

and

$$I_1 + I_2 = \frac{\varkappa^\alpha}{(\varrho^* - \vartheta^*)^2}\psi(c) + \frac{\varkappa\Gamma(\alpha+1)}{(\varrho^* - \vartheta^*)^{\alpha+1}}J_{c+}^{\alpha-1}\psi(\varrho^*) - \frac{\Gamma(\alpha+2)}{(\varrho^* - \vartheta^*)^{\alpha+2}}J_{c+}^{\alpha}\psi(\varrho^*) \qquad (9)$$
$$+ \frac{(1-\varkappa)^\alpha}{(\varrho^* - \vartheta^*)^2}\psi(c) + \frac{(1-\varkappa)\Gamma(\alpha+1)}{(\varrho^* - \vartheta^*)^{\alpha+1}}J_{c-}^{\alpha-1}\psi(\vartheta^*) - \frac{\Gamma(\alpha+2)}{(\varrho^* - \vartheta^*)^{\alpha+2}}J_{c-}^{\alpha}\psi(\vartheta^*)$$
$$= \frac{\varkappa^\alpha + (1-\varkappa)^\alpha}{(\varrho^* - \vartheta^*)^2}\psi(c) - \left\{\frac{\Gamma(\alpha+2)}{(\varrho^* - \vartheta^*)^{\alpha+2}}\left[J_{c+}^\alpha\psi(\varrho^*) + J_{c-}^\alpha\psi(\vartheta^*)\right]\right.$$
$$\left. - \frac{\Gamma(\alpha+1)}{(\varrho^* - \vartheta^*)^{\alpha+1}}\left[\varkappa J_{c+}^{\alpha-1}\psi(\varrho^*) + (1-\varkappa)J_{c-}^{\alpha-1}\psi(\vartheta^*)\right]\right\}.$$

Multiplying both sides of Equation (9) by $\frac{(\varrho^* - \vartheta^*)^2}{\varkappa^\alpha + (1-\varkappa)^\alpha}$, we complete the proof. □

Remark 1. *From Equation (8), for $\varkappa = \frac{1}{2}$ and $\alpha = 1$, we have Equation (7).*

Theorem 5. *Let $\psi:[\vartheta^*, \varrho^*] \to \mathbb{R}$ and $\psi \in C^2(\vartheta^*, \varrho^*)$. If $\psi'' \in L[\vartheta^*, \varrho^*]$ and $|\psi''|$ is a convex function, then the inequality*

$$\left|\psi(c) - \mathbf{F}\left\{\frac{\alpha+1}{\varrho^* - \vartheta^*}\left[J_{c+}^\alpha\psi(\varrho^*) + J_{c-}^\alpha\psi(\vartheta^*)\right] - \left[\varkappa J_{c+}^{\alpha-1}\psi(\varrho^*) + (1-\varkappa)J_{c-}^{\alpha-1}\psi(\vartheta^*)\right]\right\}\right|$$
$$\leq \frac{(\varrho^* - \vartheta^*)^2}{\varkappa^\alpha + (1-\varkappa)^\alpha}\left[\mu|\psi''(\vartheta^*)| + \varepsilon|\psi''(\varrho^*)|\right], \qquad (10)$$

holds $\forall \alpha > 1$. Here,

$$\mu = \frac{(\alpha+1)\varkappa^{\alpha+3} + (\alpha+3)\varkappa(1-\varkappa)^{\alpha+2} + 2(1-\varkappa^{\alpha+3})}{(\alpha+1)(\alpha+2)(\alpha+3)},$$

$$\varepsilon = \frac{(\alpha+3)\varkappa^{\alpha+2} - (\alpha+1)\varkappa^{\alpha+3} + (\alpha+1)(1-\varkappa)^{\alpha+3}}{(\alpha+1)(\alpha+2)(\alpha+3)},$$

and $\mathbf{F}$ and c are defined above in Lemma 2.

Proof. From Lemma 2, taking into account that $|\psi''|$ is convex, we obtain

$$\left|\psi(c) - \mathbf{F}\left\{\frac{\alpha+1}{\varrho^* - \vartheta^*}\left[J_{c^+}^\alpha \psi(\varrho^*) + J_{c^-}^\alpha \psi(\vartheta^*)\right] - \left[\varkappa J_{c^+}^{\alpha-1}\psi(\varrho^*) + (1-\varkappa)J_{c^-}^{\alpha-1}\psi(\vartheta^*)\right]\right\}\right|$$

$$\leq \frac{(\varrho^* - \vartheta^*)^2}{\varkappa^\alpha + (1-\varkappa)^\alpha}\left[\int_0^\varkappa |\varepsilon^\alpha(\varkappa - \varepsilon)\psi''(\varepsilon\vartheta^* + (1-\varepsilon)\varrho^*)|d\varepsilon\right.$$

$$\left.+ \int_\varkappa^1 |(\varepsilon - \varkappa)(1-\varepsilon)^\alpha \psi''(\vartheta^*\varepsilon + \varrho^*(1-\varepsilon))|d\varepsilon\right]$$

$$= \frac{(\varrho^* - \vartheta^*)^2}{\varkappa^\alpha + (1-\varkappa)^\alpha}\left[|\psi''(\vartheta^*)|\left(\int_0^\varkappa \varepsilon^\alpha(\varkappa-\varepsilon)\varepsilon + \int_\varkappa^1 (\varepsilon-\varkappa)(1-\varepsilon)^\alpha \varepsilon\right)d\varepsilon\right.$$

$$\left.+|\psi''(\varrho^*)|\left(\int_0^\varkappa \varepsilon^\alpha(\varkappa-\varepsilon)(1-\varepsilon) + \int_\varkappa^1 (\varepsilon-\varkappa)(1-\varepsilon)^\alpha(1-\varepsilon)\right)d\varepsilon\right].$$

By solving the integrals and taking into account notations, we get

$$\leq \frac{(\varrho^* - \vartheta^*)^2}{\varkappa^\alpha + (1-\varkappa)^\alpha}[\mu|\psi''(\vartheta^*)| + \varepsilon|\psi''(\varrho^*)|].$$

The proof is completed. □

Corollary 1. *If we choose $\varkappa = \frac{1}{2}$ and $\alpha = 1$, then, from Equation (10), we obtain*

$$\left|\frac{1}{2}\left[\psi\left(\frac{\vartheta^* + \varrho^*}{2}\right) + \frac{\psi(\varrho^*) + \psi(\vartheta^*)}{2}\right] - \frac{1}{\varrho^* - \vartheta^*}\int_{\vartheta^*}^{\varrho^*} \psi(\varepsilon)d\varepsilon\right|$$

$$\leq \frac{(\varrho^* - \vartheta^*)^2}{96}[|\psi''(\vartheta^*)| + |\psi''(\varrho^*)|],$$

and if $\|\psi''\|_\infty = \sup_{\varepsilon \in [\vartheta^*, \varrho^*]}|\psi''(\varepsilon)|$, *then*

$$\left|\frac{1}{2}\left[\psi\left(\frac{\vartheta^* + \varrho^*}{2}\right) + \frac{\psi(\varrho^*) + \psi(\vartheta^*)}{2}\right] - \frac{1}{\varrho^* - \vartheta^*}\int_{\vartheta^*}^{\varrho^*} \psi(\varepsilon)d\varepsilon\right| \leq \frac{(\varrho^* - \vartheta^*)^2}{48}\|\psi''\|_\infty.$$

This inequality was obtained by Kırmacı in [33] (see Corollary 1 for $m = 1$, Remarks 1 and 3) and by Dragomir and Pearse in [2] (see Corollary 13).

Theorem 6. *Let $\psi:[\vartheta^*, \varrho^*] \to \mathbb{R}$ and $\psi \in C^2(\vartheta^*, \varrho^*)$. If $\psi'' \in L[\vartheta^*, \varrho^*]$ and $|\psi''|^q$ is a convex function, then inequality*

$$\left|\psi(c) - \mathbf{F}\left\{\frac{\alpha+1}{\varrho^* - \vartheta^*}\left[J_{c^+}^\alpha \psi(\varrho^*) + J_{c^-}^\alpha \psi(\vartheta^*)\right] - \left[\varkappa J_{c^+}^{\alpha-1}\psi(\varrho^*) + (1-\varkappa)J_{c^-}^{\alpha-1}\psi(\vartheta^*)\right]\right\}\right|$$

$$\leq \frac{(\varrho^* - \vartheta^*)^2}{\varkappa^\alpha + (1-\varkappa)^\alpha}\mathbf{A}^{\frac{1}{p}}\left\{\varkappa^{\frac{1+\alpha p+p}{p}}\left[\varkappa^2|\psi''(\vartheta^*)|^q + \varkappa(2-\varkappa)|\psi''(\varrho^*)|^q\right]^{\frac{1}{q}}\right. \quad (11)$$

$$\left.+(1-\varkappa)^{\frac{1+\alpha p+p}{p}}\left[(1-\varkappa^2)|\psi''(\vartheta^*)|^q + (1-\varkappa)^2|\psi''(\varrho^*)|^q\right]^{\frac{1}{q}}\right\},$$

holds $\forall \alpha > 1$, $q > 1$. $\mathbf{F}$ and c are defined above in Lemma 2, and $\mathbf{A} = \frac{2+2\alpha p+p}{(1+\alpha p)(1+\alpha p+p)}$.

Proof. From Lemma 2, taking into account the properties of the modulus, we obtain

$$\left|\psi(c) - \mathbf{F}\left\{\frac{\alpha+1}{\varrho^* - \vartheta^*}\left[J_{c^+}^\alpha \psi(\varrho^*) + J_{c^-}^\alpha \psi(\vartheta^*)\right] - \left[\varkappa J_{c^+}^{\alpha-1}\psi(\varrho^*) + (1-\varkappa)J_{c^-}^{\alpha-1}\psi(\vartheta^*)\right]\right\}\right|$$

$$\leq \frac{(\varrho^* - \vartheta^*)^2}{\varkappa^\alpha + (1-\varkappa)^\alpha}(|I_1| + |I_2|). \quad (12)$$

By using the Hölder inequality (Equation (3)), and since $|\psi''|^q$ is a convex function for the first integral $|I_1|$, we have

$$|I_1| \leq \int_0^{\varkappa} \varepsilon^{\alpha}(\varkappa - \varepsilon)|\psi''(\vartheta^*\varepsilon + \varrho^*(1-\varepsilon))|d\varepsilon$$

$$\leq \left(\int_0^{\varkappa} \varepsilon^{\alpha p}(\varkappa - \varepsilon)^p d\varepsilon\right)^{\frac{1}{p}} \left(\int_0^{\varkappa} \left[\varepsilon|\psi''(\vartheta^*)|^q + (1-\varepsilon)|\psi''(\varrho^*)|^q\right] d\varepsilon\right)^{\frac{1}{q}}.$$

Let us calculate the integrals.

Considering that $|x+y|^p \leq 2^{p-1}(|x|^p + |y|^p)$ for $p \geq 0$ and $x, y \in \mathbb{R}$, we have:

$$\int_0^{\varkappa} \varepsilon^{\alpha p}(\varkappa - \varepsilon)^p d\varepsilon = \int_0^{\varkappa} |\varepsilon^{\alpha p}(\varkappa - \varepsilon)^p| d\varepsilon \leq \int_0^{\varkappa} |\varepsilon^{\alpha p}|(|\varkappa| + |\varepsilon|)^p d\varepsilon$$

$$\leq 2^{p-1} \int_0^{\varkappa} |\varepsilon^{\alpha p}|(|\varkappa|^p + |\varepsilon|^p) d\varepsilon$$

$$= \frac{2^{p-1} \varkappa^{1+\alpha p+p}(2 + 2\alpha p + p)}{(1+\alpha p)(1+\alpha p+p)},$$

and

$$\int_0^{\varkappa} \left[\varepsilon|\psi''(\vartheta^*)|^q + (1-\varepsilon)|\psi''(\varrho^*)|^q\right] d\varepsilon = \frac{\varkappa^2}{2}|\psi''(\vartheta^*)|^q + \frac{\varkappa(2-\varkappa)}{2}|\psi''(\varrho^*)|^q.$$

Thus, for first integral, we get

$$|I_1| \leq \left[\frac{2^{p-1} \varkappa^{1+\alpha p+p}(2+2\alpha p+p)}{(1+\alpha p)(1+\alpha p+p)}\right]^{\frac{1}{p}} \left[\frac{\varkappa^2}{2}|\psi''(\vartheta^*)|^q + \frac{\varkappa(2-\varkappa)}{2}|\psi''(\varrho^*)|^q\right]^{\frac{1}{q}}$$

$$= \left[\frac{\varkappa^{1+\alpha p+p}(2+2\alpha p+p)}{(1+\alpha p)(1+\alpha p+p)}\right]^{\frac{1}{p}} \left[\varkappa^2|\psi''(\vartheta^*)|^q + \varkappa(2-\varkappa)|\psi''(\varrho^*)|^q\right]^{\frac{1}{q}}. \quad (13)$$

Similarly, for the second integral, we can write

$$|I_2| = \int_{\varkappa}^1 (\varepsilon - \varkappa)(1-\varepsilon)^{\alpha}|\psi''(\vartheta^*\varepsilon + \varrho^*(1-\varepsilon))|d\varepsilon$$

$$\leq \left(\int_{\varkappa}^1 [(\varepsilon - \varkappa)(1-\varepsilon)^{\alpha}]^p d\varepsilon\right)^{\frac{1}{p}} \left(\int_{\varkappa}^1 |\psi''(\vartheta^*\varepsilon + \varrho^*(1-\varepsilon))|^q d\varepsilon\right)^{\frac{1}{q}},$$

and, after solving the integrals, we have

$$\int_{\varkappa}^1 [(\varepsilon - \varkappa)(1-\varepsilon)^{\alpha}]^p d\varepsilon = \int_0^{1-\varkappa} (1 - \varkappa - z)^p z^{\alpha p} dz$$

$$\leq 2^{p-1} \int_0^{1-\varkappa} [(1-\varkappa)^p + z^p] z^{\alpha p} dz$$

$$= 2^{p-1}(1-\varkappa)^{p+\alpha p+1} \frac{2+2\alpha p+p}{(1+\alpha p)(1+\alpha p+p)},$$

and

$$\int_{\varkappa}^1 \left[\varepsilon|\psi''(\vartheta^*)|^q + (1-\varepsilon)|\psi''(\varrho^*)|^q\right] d\varepsilon = \frac{1-\varkappa^2}{2}|\psi''(\vartheta^*)|^q + \frac{(1-\varkappa)^2}{2}|\psi''(\varrho^*)|^q.$$

In this way, for the second integral, we get

$$|I_2| \leq \left[2^{p-1}(1-\varkappa)^{1+\alpha p+p} \frac{2+2\alpha p+p}{(1+\alpha p)(1+\alpha p+p)}\right]^{\frac{1}{p}}$$

$$\times \left[\frac{1-\varkappa^2}{2}|\psi''(\vartheta^*)|^q + \frac{(1-\varkappa)^2}{2}|\psi''(\varrho^*)|^q\right]^{\frac{1}{q}}$$

$$= \left[(1-\varkappa)^{1+\alpha p+p} \frac{2+2\alpha p+p}{(1+\alpha p)(1+\alpha p+p)}\right]^{\frac{1}{p}} \left[\left(1-\varkappa^2\right)|\psi''(\vartheta^*)|^q + (1-\varkappa)^2|\psi''(\varrho^*)|^q\right]^{\frac{1}{q}}.$$

By summing I_1 and I_2 and taking into account Equation (12) and the notations, we get Equation (11). The proof is completed. □

Corollary 2. *If we choose $\varkappa = \frac{1}{2}$ and $\alpha = 1$, from Equation (11), we get*

$$\left| \frac{1}{2}\left[\psi\left(\frac{\vartheta^* + \varrho^*}{2} \right) + \frac{\psi(\varrho^*) + \psi(\vartheta^*)}{2} \right] - \frac{1}{\varrho^* - \vartheta^*} \int_{\vartheta^*}^{\varrho^*} \psi(\varepsilon) d\varepsilon \right| \quad (14)$$

$$\leq \frac{(\varrho^* - \vartheta^*)^2}{8} \mathbf{S}^{\frac{1}{p}} \left\{ \left[\frac{|\psi''(\vartheta^*)|^q}{2} + \frac{3|\psi''(\varrho^*)|^q}{2} \right]^{\frac{1}{q}} \right.$$

$$\left. + \left[\frac{3|\psi''(\vartheta^*)|^q}{2} + \frac{|\psi''(\varrho^*)|^q}{2} \right]^{\frac{1}{q}} \right\},$$

where $\mathbf{S} = \frac{2+3p}{(1+p)(1+2p)}$.

Theorem 7. *Let $\psi:[\vartheta^*, \varrho^*] \to \mathbb{R}$ and $\psi \in C^2(\vartheta^*, \varrho^*)$. If $\psi'' \in L[\vartheta^*, \varrho^*]$ and $|\psi''|^q$ is a convex function, then inequality*

$$\left| \psi(c) - \mathbf{F}\left\{ \frac{\alpha + 1}{\varrho^* - \vartheta^*} [J_{c^+}^\alpha \psi(\varrho^*) + J_{c^-}^\alpha \psi(\vartheta^*)] - \left[\varkappa J_{c^+}^{\alpha-1} \psi(\varrho^*) + (1 - \varkappa) J_{c^-}^{\alpha-1} \psi(\vartheta^*) \right] \right\} \right|$$

$$\leq \frac{(\varrho^* - \vartheta^*)^2}{\varkappa^\alpha + (1 - \varkappa)^\alpha} \left\{ B^{\frac{1}{p}}(1 + \alpha p, 2 + p) \left[\varkappa^{\alpha+2} \mathbf{M}_1 + (1 - \varkappa)^{\alpha+2} \mathbf{M}_3 \right] \right. \quad (15)$$

$$\left. + B^{\frac{1}{p}}(\alpha p + 2, 1 + p) \left[\varkappa^{\alpha+2} \mathbf{M}_2 + (1 - \varkappa)^{\alpha+2} \mathbf{M}_4 \right] \right\},$$

holds $\forall \alpha > 1$, $q > 1$. $\mathbf{F}$ and c are defined above in Lemma 2, and $B(.,.)$ is the Euler beta function,

$$\mathbf{M}_1 = \left[\frac{\varkappa}{6} |\psi''(\vartheta^*)|^q + \left(\frac{1}{2} - \frac{\varkappa}{6} \right) |f''(\varrho^*)|^q \right]^{\frac{1}{q}},$$

$$\mathbf{M}_2 = \left[\frac{\varkappa}{3} |\psi''(\vartheta^*)|^q + \left(\frac{1}{2} - \frac{\varkappa}{3} \right) |\psi''(\varrho^*)|^q \right]^{\frac{1}{q}},$$

$$\mathbf{M}_3 = \left[\frac{1 - \varkappa}{6} |\psi''(\varrho^*)|^q + \left(\frac{1}{2} - \frac{1 - \varkappa}{6} \right) |\psi''(\vartheta^*)|^q \right]^{\frac{1}{q}},$$

$$\mathbf{M}_4 = \left[\frac{1 - \varkappa}{3} |\psi''(\varrho^*)|^q + \left(\frac{1}{2} - \frac{1 - \varkappa}{3} \right) |\psi''(\vartheta^*)|^q \right]^{\frac{1}{q}}.$$

Proof. By using the improved Hölder inequality (Equation (4)) for the I_1 from Equation (12), we get

$$|I_1| \leq \int_0^\varkappa |\varepsilon^\alpha(\varkappa - \varepsilon)| |\psi''(\vartheta^* \varepsilon + \varrho^*(1 - \varepsilon))| d\varepsilon$$

$$\leq \frac{1}{\varkappa} \left(\int_0^\varkappa (\varkappa - \varepsilon) |\varepsilon^\alpha(\varkappa - \varepsilon)|^p d\varepsilon \right)^{\frac{1}{p}} \left(\int_0^\varkappa (\varkappa - \varepsilon) |\psi''(\vartheta^* \varepsilon + \varrho^*(1 - \varepsilon))|^q d\varepsilon \right)^{\frac{1}{q}}$$

$$+ \frac{1}{\varkappa} \left(\int_0^\varkappa \varepsilon |\varepsilon^\alpha(\varkappa - \varepsilon)|^p d\varepsilon \right)^{\frac{1}{p}} \left(\int_0^\varkappa \varepsilon |\psi''(\vartheta^* \varepsilon + \varrho^*(1 - \varepsilon))|^q d\varepsilon \right)^{\frac{1}{q}}$$

$$= \frac{1}{\varkappa} \left(\int_0^\varkappa (\varkappa - \varepsilon)^{1+p} \varepsilon^{\alpha p} d\varepsilon \right)^{\frac{1}{p}} \left(\int_0^\varkappa (\varkappa - \varepsilon) |\psi''(\vartheta^* \varepsilon + \varrho^*(1 - \varepsilon))|^q d\varepsilon \right)^{\frac{1}{q}}$$

$$+ \frac{1}{\varkappa} \left(\int_0^\varkappa \varepsilon^{1+\alpha p} (\varkappa - \varepsilon)^p d\varepsilon \right)^{\frac{1}{p}} \left(\int_0^\varkappa \varepsilon |\psi''(\vartheta^* \varepsilon + \varrho^*(1 - \varepsilon))|^q d\varepsilon \right)^{\frac{1}{q}}.$$

Here,

$$\int_0^\varkappa (\varkappa-\varepsilon)^{1+p}\varepsilon^{\alpha p}d\varepsilon = \int_0^1 (\varkappa-\varkappa z)^{1+p}(\varkappa z)^{\alpha p}\varkappa dz$$

$$= \varkappa^{\alpha p+2+p}\int_0^1 z^{\alpha p}(1-z)^{1+p}dz = \varkappa^{\alpha p+2+p}B(1+\alpha p, 2+p)$$

$$\int_0^\varkappa \varepsilon^{1+\alpha p}(\varkappa-\varepsilon)^p d\varepsilon = \int_0^1 (\varkappa-\varkappa z)^p(\varkappa z)^{1+\alpha p}\varkappa dz$$

$$= \varkappa^{\alpha p+2+p}\int_0^1 z^{1+\alpha p}(1-z)^p dz = \varkappa^{\alpha p+2+p}B(\alpha p+2, 1+p),$$

Using the definition of convexity,

$$\int_0^\varkappa (\varkappa-\varepsilon)|\psi''(\varepsilon\vartheta^*+(1-\varepsilon t)\varrho^*)|^q d\varepsilon \leq |\psi''(\vartheta^*)|^q \int_0^\varkappa t(\varkappa-\varepsilon)d\varepsilon$$

$$+ |\psi''(\varrho^*)|^q \int_0^\varkappa (\varkappa-\varepsilon)(1-\varepsilon)d\varepsilon$$

$$= \frac{\varkappa^3}{6}|\psi''(\vartheta^*)|^q + \left(\frac{\varkappa^2}{2}-\frac{\varkappa^3}{6}\right)|\psi''(\varrho^*)|^q$$

$$\int_0^\varkappa \varepsilon|\psi''(\vartheta^*\varepsilon+\varrho^*(1-\varepsilon))|^q d\varepsilon \leq |\psi''(\vartheta^*)|^q \int_0^\varkappa \varepsilon^2 d\varepsilon + |\psi''(\varrho^*)|^q \int_0^\varkappa \varepsilon(1-\varepsilon)d\varepsilon$$

$$= \frac{\varkappa^3}{3}|\psi''(\vartheta^*)|^q + \left(\frac{\varkappa^2}{2}-\frac{\varkappa^3}{3}\right)|\psi''(\varrho^*)|^q.$$

Thus, we have

$$|I_1| \leq \varkappa^{\frac{\alpha p+2+p}{p}-1}B^{\frac{1}{p}}(1+\alpha p, 2+p)\left[\frac{\varkappa^3}{6}|\psi''(\vartheta^*)|^q + \left(\frac{\varkappa^2}{2}-\frac{\varkappa^3}{6}\right)|\psi''(\varrho^*)|^q\right]^{\frac{1}{q}}$$

$$+ \varkappa^{\frac{\alpha p+2+p}{p}-1}B^{\frac{1}{p}}(\alpha p+2, 1+p)\left[\frac{\varkappa^3}{3}|\psi''(a)|^q + \left(\frac{\varkappa^2}{2}-\frac{\varkappa^3}{3}\right)|\psi''(\varrho^*)|^q\right]^{\frac{1}{q}}$$

$$= \varkappa^{\alpha+2}B^{\frac{1}{p}}(1+\alpha p, 2+p)\left[\frac{\varkappa}{6}|\psi''(\vartheta^*)|^q + \left(\frac{1}{2}-\frac{\varkappa}{6}\right)|\psi''(\varrho^*)|^q\right]^{\frac{1}{q}}$$

$$+ \varkappa^{\alpha+2}B^{\frac{1}{p}}(\alpha p+2, 1+p)\left[\frac{\varkappa}{3}|\psi''(\vartheta^*)|^q + \left(\frac{1}{2}-\frac{\varkappa}{3}\right)|\psi''(\varrho^*)|^q\right]^{\frac{1}{q}}.$$

First, in I_2, replace ε with $1-\varepsilon$; then, by using the improved Hölder inequality (Equation (4)), we can write

$$|I_2| \leq \int_\varkappa^1 |(\varepsilon-\varkappa)(1-\varepsilon)^\alpha||\psi''(\vartheta^*\varepsilon+\varrho^*(1-\varepsilon))|d\varepsilon$$

$$= \int_0^{1-\varkappa} |(1-\varkappa-\varepsilon)\varepsilon^\alpha||\psi''((1-\varepsilon)\vartheta^*+\varepsilon\varrho^*)|d\varepsilon$$

$$= \int_0^\tau |(\tau-\varepsilon)\varepsilon^\alpha||\psi''((1-\varepsilon)\vartheta^*+\varepsilon\varrho^*)|d\varepsilon, \text{ here } (\tau = 1-\varkappa)$$

$$\leq \frac{1}{\tau}\left(\int_0^\tau (\tau-\varepsilon)^{1+p}\varepsilon^{\alpha p}d\varepsilon\right)^{\frac{1}{p}}\left(\int_0^\tau (\tau-\varepsilon)|\psi''(\varepsilon\varrho^*+(1-\varepsilon)\vartheta^*)|^q d\varepsilon\right)^{\frac{1}{q}}$$

$$+ \frac{1}{\tau}\left(\int_0^\tau \varepsilon^{1+\alpha p}(\tau-\varepsilon)^p d\varepsilon\right)^{\frac{1}{p}}\left(\int_0^\tau \varepsilon|\psi''(\varepsilon\varrho^*+(1-\varepsilon)\vartheta^*)|^q d\varepsilon\right)^{\frac{1}{q}}.$$

Similarly, for I_2, we get

$$|I_2| \leq (1-\varkappa)^{\alpha+2}B^{\frac{1}{p}}(1+\alpha p, 2+p)\left[\frac{1-\varkappa}{6}|\psi''(\varrho^*)|^q + \left(\frac{1}{2}-\frac{1-\varkappa}{6}\right)|\psi''(\vartheta^*)|^q\right]^{\frac{1}{q}}$$

$$+ (1-\varkappa)^{\alpha+2}B^{\frac{1}{p}}(\alpha p+2, 1+p)\left[\frac{1-\varkappa}{3}|\psi''(\varrho^*)|^q + \left(\frac{1}{2}-\frac{1-\varkappa}{3}\right)|\psi''(\vartheta^*)|^q\right]^{\frac{1}{q}}.$$

After summing the integrals and groupings, taking into account the accepted notation, we get

$$|I_1| + |I_2| \leq B^{\frac{1}{p}}(1+\alpha p, 2+p)\left[\varkappa^{\alpha+2}\mathbf{M}_1 + (1-\varkappa)^{\alpha+2}\mathbf{M}_3\right]$$
$$+ B^{\frac{1}{p}}(\alpha p + 2, 1+p)\left[\varkappa^{\alpha+2}\mathbf{M}_2 + (1-\varkappa)^{\alpha+2}\mathbf{M}_4\right].$$

Taking into account the last inequality, from Equation (12), we obtain Equation (15). The proof is completed. □

Corollary 3. *If we choose $\varkappa = \frac{1}{2}$ and $\alpha = 1$, then, from Equation (15), we obtain*

$$\left|\frac{1}{2}\left[\psi\left(\frac{\vartheta^* + \varrho^*}{2}\right) + \frac{\psi(\varrho^*) + \psi(\vartheta^*)}{2}\right] - \frac{1}{\varrho^* - \vartheta^*}\int_{\vartheta^*}^{\varrho^*} \psi(\varepsilon)d\varepsilon\right| \qquad (16)$$
$$\leq \frac{(\varrho^* - \vartheta^*)^2}{16} B^{\frac{1}{p}}(1+p, 2+p)(\tilde{\mathbf{M}}_1 + \tilde{\mathbf{M}}_2 + \tilde{\mathbf{M}}_3 + \tilde{\mathbf{M}}_4),$$

where

$$\tilde{\mathbf{M}}_1 = \left(\frac{|\psi''(\vartheta^*)|^q}{12} + \frac{5|\psi''(\varrho^*)|^q}{12}\right)^{\frac{1}{q}}, \tilde{\mathbf{M}}_2 = \left(\frac{|\psi''(\vartheta^*)|^q}{6} + \frac{|\psi''(\varrho^*)|^q}{3}\right)^{\frac{1}{q}},$$
$$\tilde{\mathbf{M}}_3 = \left(\frac{|\psi''(\varrho^*)|^q}{12} + \frac{5|\psi''(\vartheta^*)|^q}{12}\right)^{\frac{1}{q}}, \tilde{\mathbf{M}}_4 = \left(\frac{|\psi''(\varrho^*)|^q}{6} + \frac{|\psi''(\vartheta^*)|^q}{3}\right)^{\frac{1}{q}}.$$

Remark 2. *If we use the inequality $|x+y|^p \leq 2^{p-1}(|x|^p + |y|^p)$ for $p \geq 0$ and $x, y \in \mathbb{R}$, then we will have*

$$B^{\frac{1}{p}}(1+p, 2+p) = \left(\int_0^1 z^p(1-z)^{1+p}dz\right)^{\frac{1}{p}} \leq 2\left(\int_0^1 z^p\left(1+z^{1+p}\right)dz\right)^{\frac{1}{p}}$$
$$= 2\left(\frac{1}{1+p} + \frac{1}{2p+2}\right)^{\frac{1}{p}} = 2\left[\frac{3}{2(1+p)}\right]^{\frac{1}{p}};$$

i.e., the inequality in Equation (16) will take the form:

$$\left|\frac{1}{2}\left[\psi\left(\frac{\vartheta^* + \varrho^*}{2}\right) + \frac{\psi(\varrho^*) + \psi(\vartheta^*)}{2}\right] - \frac{1}{\varrho^* - \vartheta^*}\int_{\vartheta^*}^{\varrho^*} \psi(\varepsilon)d\varepsilon\right|$$
$$\leq \frac{(\varrho^* - \vartheta^*)^2}{8}\left[\frac{3}{2(1+p)}\right]^{\frac{1}{p}}(\tilde{\mathbf{M}}_1 + \tilde{\mathbf{M}}_2 + \tilde{\mathbf{M}}_3 + \tilde{\mathbf{M}}_4).$$

Theorem 8. *Let $\psi: [\vartheta^*, \varrho^*] \to \mathbb{R}$ and $\psi \in C^2(\vartheta^*, \varrho^*)$. If $\psi'' \in L[\vartheta^*, \varrho^*]$ and $|\psi''|^p$ is a convex function, then inequality*

$$\left|\psi(c) - \mathbf{F}\left\{\frac{\alpha+1}{\varrho^* - \vartheta^*}\left[J_{c^+}^\alpha \psi(\varrho^*) + J_{c^-}^\alpha \psi(\vartheta^*)\right] - \left[\varkappa J_{c^+}^{\alpha-1}\psi(\varrho^*) + (1-\varkappa)J_{c^-}^{\alpha-1}\psi(\vartheta^*)\right]\right\}\right|$$
$$\leq \frac{(\varrho^* - \vartheta^*)^2}{\varkappa^\alpha + (1-\varkappa)^\alpha} \cdot \mathbf{P}_1 \cdot (\mathbf{P}_2 + \mathbf{P}_3), \qquad (17)$$

holds $\forall \alpha > 1$, $p > 1$. $\mathbf{F}$ and c are defined above in Lemma 2 and

$$\mathbf{P}_1 = \frac{1}{(\alpha+1)(\alpha+2)}, \mathbf{P}_2 = \varkappa^{\alpha+2}\left[\varkappa|\psi''(\vartheta^*)|^p + \frac{(1-\varkappa)(\alpha+1)+2}{\alpha+1}|\psi''(\varrho^*)|^p\right]^{\frac{1}{p}},$$
$$\mathbf{P}_3 = (1-\varkappa)^{\alpha+2}\left[\frac{\varkappa(\alpha+1)+2}{\alpha+1}|\psi''(\vartheta^*)|^p + (1-\varkappa)|\psi''(\varrho^*)|^p\right]^{\frac{1}{p}}.$$

Proof. Since $|\psi''|^p$ is a convex function, using the power mean inequality (Equation (5)) for the I_1 from Equation (12), we have

$$|I_1| \leq \int_0^\varkappa \varepsilon^\alpha(\varkappa-\varepsilon)|\psi''(\vartheta^*\varepsilon+\varrho^*(1-\varepsilon))|d\varepsilon$$

$$= \int_0^\varkappa [\varepsilon^\alpha(\varkappa-\varepsilon)]^{\frac{1}{p}+\frac{1}{q}}|\psi''(\vartheta^*\varepsilon+\varrho^*(1-\varepsilon))|d\varepsilon$$

$$\leq \left(\int_0^\varkappa \varepsilon^\alpha(\varkappa-\varepsilon)d\varepsilon\right)^{1-\frac{1}{p}}\left(\int_0^\varkappa \varepsilon^\alpha(\varkappa-\varepsilon)|\psi''(\vartheta^*\varepsilon+\varrho^*(1-\varepsilon))|^p d\varepsilon\right)^{\frac{1}{p}}$$

$$\leq \left(\int_0^\varkappa \varepsilon^\alpha(\varkappa-\varepsilon)d\varepsilon\right)^{1-\frac{1}{p}}\left(\int_0^\varkappa \varepsilon^\alpha(\varkappa-\varepsilon)\left[\varepsilon|\psi''(\vartheta^*)|^p+(1-\varepsilon)|\psi''(\varrho^*)|^p\right]d\varepsilon\right)^{\frac{1}{q}}.$$

Let us calculate the integrals:

$$\int_0^\varkappa \varepsilon^\alpha(\varkappa-\varepsilon)d\varepsilon = \frac{\varkappa^{\alpha+2}}{(\alpha+1)(\alpha+2)};$$

$$\int_0^\varkappa \varepsilon^\alpha(\varkappa-\varepsilon)\left[\varepsilon|\psi''(\vartheta^*)|^p+(1-\varepsilon)|\psi''(\varrho^*)|^p\right]d\varepsilon$$

$$= |\psi''(\vartheta^*)|^p\int_0^\varkappa \varepsilon^{\alpha+1}(\varkappa-\varepsilon)d\varepsilon + |\psi''(\varrho^*)|^p\int_0^\varkappa \varepsilon^\alpha(\varkappa-\varepsilon)(1-\varepsilon)d\varepsilon$$

$$= \frac{\varkappa^{\alpha+3}|\psi''(\vartheta^*)|^p}{(\alpha+2)(\alpha+3)} + |\psi''(\varrho^*)|^p\left(\frac{\varkappa^{\alpha+2}}{\alpha+1}-\frac{\varkappa^{\alpha+3}}{\alpha+2}-\frac{\varkappa^{\alpha+2}}{\alpha+2}+\frac{\varkappa^{\alpha+3}}{\alpha+3}\right)$$

$$= \frac{\varkappa^{\alpha+3}|\psi''(\vartheta^*)|^p}{(\alpha+2)(\alpha+3)} + \frac{\varkappa^{\alpha+2}}{\alpha+2}\left(\frac{1}{\alpha+1}-\frac{\varkappa}{\alpha+3}\right)|\psi''(\varrho^*)|^p$$

$$= \frac{\varkappa^{\alpha+2}}{(\alpha+2)(\alpha+3)}\left[\varkappa|\psi''(\vartheta^*)|^p+\frac{(1-\varkappa)(\alpha+1)+2}{\alpha+1}|\psi''(\varrho^*)|^p\right].$$

Thus, for first integral, we get

$$|I_1| \leq \left[\frac{\varkappa^{\alpha+2}}{(\alpha+1)(\alpha+2)}\right]^{1-\frac{1}{p}}\left[\frac{\varkappa^{\alpha+2}}{(\alpha+2)(\alpha+3)}\right]^{\frac{1}{p}} \qquad (18)$$

$$\times \left[\varkappa|\psi''(\vartheta^*)|^p+\frac{(1-\varkappa)(\alpha+1)+2}{\alpha+1}|\psi''(\varrho^*)|^p\right]^{\frac{1}{p}}.$$

Similarly, for the second integral, we get

$$|I_2| = \int_\varkappa^1 (\varepsilon-\varkappa)(1-\varepsilon)^\alpha|\psi''(\vartheta^*\varepsilon+\varrho^*(1-\varepsilon))|d\varepsilon$$

$$\leq \left(\int_\varkappa^1 (\varepsilon-\varkappa)(1-\varepsilon)^\alpha d\varepsilon\right)^{1-\frac{1}{p}}\left(\int_\varkappa^1 (1-\varepsilon)^\alpha(\varepsilon-\varkappa)|\psi''(\vartheta^*\varepsilon+\varrho^*(1-\varepsilon))|^p d\varepsilon\right)^{\frac{1}{p}}$$

$$= \left(\int_0^{1-\varkappa}(1-z-\varkappa)z^\alpha dz\right)^{1-\frac{1}{p}}\left(\int_0^{1-\varkappa}z^\alpha(1-z-\varkappa)|\psi''((1-z)\vartheta^*+z\varrho^*)|^p dz\right)^{\frac{1}{p}}.$$

or

$$|I_2| \leq \left(\frac{(1-\varkappa)^{\alpha+2}}{(\alpha+1)(\alpha+2)}\right)^{1-\frac{1}{p}}\left(|\psi''(\vartheta^*)|^p\int_0^{1-\varkappa}z^\alpha(1-z-\varkappa)(1-z)dz\right.$$

$$\left.+|\psi''(\varrho^*)|^p\int_0^{1-\varkappa}z^{\alpha+1}(1-\varkappa-z)dz\right)^{\frac{1}{p}}$$

$$= \left(\frac{(1-\varkappa)^{\alpha+2}}{(\alpha+1)(\alpha+2)}\right)^{1-\frac{1}{p}}\left[\frac{(1-\varkappa)^{\alpha+2}}{\alpha+2}\left(\frac{1}{\alpha+1}-\frac{1-\varkappa}{\alpha+3}\right)|\psi''(\vartheta^*)|^p\right.$$

$$\left.+\frac{(1-\varkappa)^{\alpha+3}|\psi''(\varrho^*)|^p}{(\alpha+2)(\alpha+3)}\right]^{\frac{1}{p}}.$$

Thus, for the second integral, we have

$$|I_2| \leq \left[\frac{(1-\varkappa)^{\alpha+2}}{(\alpha+1)(\alpha+2)}\right]^{1-\frac{1}{p}} \left[\frac{(1-\varkappa)^{\alpha+2}}{(\alpha+2)(\alpha+3)}\right]^{\frac{1}{p}} \quad (19)$$

$$\times \left[\frac{\varkappa(\alpha+1)+2}{\alpha+1}|\psi''(\vartheta^*)|^p + (1-\varkappa)|\psi''(\varrho^*)|^p\right]^{\frac{1}{p}}.$$

By summing Equations (18) and (19), we get

$$|I_1| + |I_2| \leq \left[\frac{\varkappa^{\alpha+2}}{(\alpha+1)(\alpha+2)}\right]^{1-\frac{1}{p}} \left[\frac{\varkappa^{\alpha+2}}{(\alpha+2)(\alpha+3)}\right]^{\frac{1}{p}}$$

$$\times \left[\varkappa|\psi''(\vartheta^*)|^p + \frac{(1-\varkappa)(\alpha+1)+2}{\alpha+1}|\psi''(\varrho^*)|^p\right]^{\frac{1}{p}}$$

$$+ \left[\frac{(1-\varkappa)^{\alpha+2}}{(\alpha+1)(\alpha+2)}\right]^{1-\frac{1}{p}} \left[\frac{(1-\varkappa)^{\alpha+2}}{(\alpha+2)(\alpha+3)}\right]^{\frac{1}{p}}$$

$$\times \left[\frac{\varkappa(\alpha+1)+2}{\alpha+1}|\psi''(\vartheta^*)|^p + (1-\varkappa)|\psi''(\varrho^*)|^p\right]^{\frac{1}{p}}$$

$$= \frac{\varkappa^{\alpha+2}}{(\alpha+1)(\alpha+2)}\left[\varkappa|\psi''(\vartheta^*)|^p + \frac{(1-\varkappa)(\alpha+1)+2}{\alpha+1}|\psi''(\varrho^*)|^p\right]^{\frac{1}{p}}$$

$$+ \frac{(1-\varkappa)^{\alpha+2}}{(\alpha+1)(\alpha+2)}\left[\frac{\varkappa(\alpha+1)+2}{\alpha+1}|\psi''(\vartheta^*)|^p + (1-\varkappa)|\psi''(\varrho^*)|^p\right]^{\frac{1}{p}}.$$

Taking into account the introduced notation and the inequality from Equation (12), we obtain Equation (17). The proof is completed. □

Corollary 4. *If we choose $\varkappa = \frac{1}{2}$ and $\alpha = 1$, then, from Equation (17), we obtain*

$$\left|\frac{1}{2}\left[\psi\left(\frac{\vartheta^*+\varrho^*}{2}\right) + \frac{\psi(\varrho^*)+\psi(\vartheta^*)}{2}\right] - \frac{1}{\varrho^*-\vartheta^*}\int_{\vartheta^*}^{\varrho^*}\psi(\varepsilon)d\varepsilon\right| \quad (20)$$

$$\leq \frac{(\varrho^*-\vartheta^*)^2}{96 \cdot 2^{\frac{1}{p}}}\left\{\left[|\psi''(\vartheta^*)|^p + 3|\psi''(\varrho^*)|^p\right]^{\frac{1}{p}} + \left[3|\psi''(\vartheta^*)|^p + |\psi''(\varrho^*)|^p\right]^{\frac{1}{p}}\right\}.$$

Proof. For $\varkappa = \frac{1}{2}$ and $\alpha = 1$ for the components of the inequality in Equation (17), we have

$$F = \frac{1}{\varkappa^\alpha + (1-\varkappa)^\alpha} \cdot \frac{\Gamma(\alpha+1)}{(\varrho^*-\vartheta^*)^{\alpha-1}} = 1,$$

$$\psi(c) - \frac{\alpha+1}{\varrho^*-\vartheta^*}\left[J^\alpha_{c^+}\psi(\varrho^*) + J^\alpha_{c^-}\psi(\vartheta^*)\right] - \left[\varkappa \cdot J^{\alpha-1}_{c^+}\psi(\varrho^*) + (1-\varkappa) \cdot J^{\alpha-1}_{c^-}\psi(\vartheta^*)\right]$$

$$= \psi\left(\frac{\vartheta^*+\varrho^*}{2}\right) - \frac{2}{\varrho^*-\vartheta^*}\left[\int_{\frac{\vartheta^*+\varrho^*}{2}}^{b}\psi(\varepsilon)d\varepsilon + \int_{\vartheta^*}^{\frac{\vartheta^*+\varrho^*}{2}}\psi(\varepsilon)d\varepsilon\right] + \left[\frac{1}{2}\psi(\varrho^*) + \frac{1}{2}\psi(\vartheta^*)\right]$$

$$= \psi\left(\frac{\vartheta^*+\varrho^*}{2}\right) - \frac{2}{\varrho^*-\vartheta^*}\int_{\vartheta^*}^{\varrho^*}\psi(\varepsilon)d\varepsilon + \frac{\psi(\varrho^*)+\psi(\vartheta^*)}{2},$$

$$\mathbf{P}_1 = \frac{1}{(\alpha+1)(\alpha+2)} = \frac{1}{6},$$

$$\mathbf{P}_2 = \varkappa^{\alpha+2}\left[\varkappa|\psi''(\vartheta^*)|^p + \frac{(1-\varkappa)(\alpha+1)+2}{\alpha+1}|\psi''(\varrho^*)|^p\right]^{\frac{1}{p}}$$

$$= \frac{1}{8}\left(\frac{1}{2}\right)^{\frac{1}{p}}\left[|\psi''(\vartheta^*)|^p + 3|\psi''(\varrho^*)|^p\right]^{\frac{1}{p}},$$

$$\mathbf{P}_3 = (1-\varkappa)^{\alpha+2}\left[\frac{\varkappa(\alpha+1)+2}{\alpha+1}|\psi''(\vartheta^*)|^p + (1-\varkappa)|\psi''(\varrho^*)|^p\right]^{\frac{1}{p}}$$

$$= \frac{1}{8}\left(\frac{1}{2}\right)^{\frac{1}{p}}\left[3|\psi''(\vartheta^*)|^p + |\psi''(\varrho^*)|^p\right]^{\frac{1}{p}},$$

$$\frac{(\varrho^*-\vartheta^*)^2}{\varkappa^\alpha+(1-\varkappa)^\alpha}\cdot \mathbf{P}_1\cdot(\mathbf{P}_2+\mathbf{P}_3) = \frac{(\varrho^*-\vartheta^*)^2}{6\cdot 8\cdot 2^{\frac{1}{p}}}\left\{\left[|\psi''(\vartheta^*)|^p + 3|\psi''(\varrho^*)|^p\right]^{\frac{1}{p}}\right.$$

$$\left. + \left[3|\psi''(\vartheta^*)|^p + |\psi''(\varrho^*)|^p\right]^{\frac{1}{p}}\right\}.$$

Thus,

$$\left|\left[\psi\left(\frac{\vartheta^*+\varrho^*}{2}\right) + \frac{\psi(\varrho^*)+\psi(\vartheta^*)}{2}\right] - \frac{2}{\varrho^*-\vartheta^*}\int_{\vartheta^*}^{\varrho^*}\psi(\varepsilon)d\varepsilon\right|$$

$$\leq \frac{(\varrho^*-\vartheta^*)^2}{6\cdot 8\cdot 2^{\frac{1}{p}}}\left\{\left[|\psi''(\vartheta^*)|^p + 3|\psi''(\varrho^*)|^p\right]^{\frac{1}{p}} + \left[3|\psi''(\vartheta^*)|^p + |\psi''(\varrho^*)|^p\right]^{\frac{1}{p}}\right\}.$$

or

$$\left|\frac{1}{2}\left[\psi\left(\frac{\vartheta^*+\varrho^*}{2}\right) + \frac{\psi(\varrho^*)+\psi(\vartheta^*)}{2}\right] - \frac{1}{\varrho^*-\vartheta^*}\int_{\vartheta^*}^{\varrho^*}\psi(\varepsilon)d\varepsilon\right|$$

$$\leq \frac{(\varrho^*-\vartheta^*)^2}{96\cdot 2^{\frac{1}{p}}}\left\{\left[|\psi''(\vartheta^*)|^p + 3|\psi''(\varrho^*)|^p\right]^{\frac{1}{p}} + \left[3|\psi''(\vartheta^*)|^p + |\psi''(\varrho^*)|^p\right]^{\frac{1}{p}}\right\}.$$

□

Theorem 9. *Let $\psi:[\vartheta^*,\varrho^*]\to\mathbb{R}$ and $\psi\in C^2(\vartheta^*,\varrho^*)$. If $\psi''\in L[\vartheta^*,\varrho^*]$ and $|\psi''|^q$ is a convex function on $[\vartheta^*,\varrho^*]$, then the inequality*

$$\left|\psi(c) - \mathbf{F}\left\{\frac{\alpha+1}{\varrho^*-\vartheta^*}[J^\alpha_{c^+}\psi(\varrho^*)+J^\alpha_{c^-}\psi(\vartheta^*)] - \left[\varkappa J^{\alpha-1}_{c^+}\psi(\varrho^*) + (1-\varkappa)J^{\alpha-1}_{c^-}\psi(\vartheta^*)\right]\right\}\right|$$

$$\leq \frac{(\varrho^*-\vartheta^*)^2}{\varkappa^\alpha+(1-\varkappa)^\alpha}\left\{B^{\frac{1}{p}}(\alpha+1,3)\left[\varkappa^{\alpha+2}\mathbf{P}_1 + (1-\varkappa)^{\alpha+2}\mathbf{P}_3\right]\right. \quad (21)$$

$$\left. + B^{\frac{1}{p}}(\alpha+2,2)\left[\varkappa^{\alpha+2}\mathbf{P}_2 + (1-\varkappa)^{\alpha+2}\mathbf{P}_4\right]\right\},$$

holds $\forall \alpha > 1$, $q \geq 1$, $\frac{1}{p}+\frac{1}{q}=1$. $\mathbf{F}$ and c are defined above in Lemma 2, and $B(.,.)$ is the Euler beta function,

$$\mathbf{P}_1 = \left\{B(\alpha+1,3)|\psi''(\varrho^*)|^q + \varkappa B(\alpha+2,3)\left[|\psi''(\varrho^*)|^q - |\psi''(\vartheta^*)|^q\right]\right\}^{\frac{1}{q}},$$

$$\mathbf{P}_2 = \left\{B(\alpha+2,2)|\psi''(\varrho^*)|^q + \varkappa B(\alpha+3,2)\left[|\psi''(\varrho^*)|^q - |\psi''(\vartheta^*)|^q\right]\right\}^{\frac{1}{q}},$$

$$\mathbf{P}_3 = \left\{B(\alpha+1,3)|\psi''(\vartheta^*)|^q + (1-\varkappa)B(\alpha+2,3)\left[|\psi''(\varrho^*)|^q - |\psi''(\vartheta^*)|^q\right]\right\}^{\frac{1}{q}},$$

$$\mathbf{P}_4 = \left\{B(\alpha+2,2)|\psi''(\vartheta^*)|^q + (1-\varkappa)B(\alpha+3,2)\left[|\psi''(\varrho^*)|^q - |\psi''(\vartheta^*)|^q\right]\right\}^{\frac{1}{q}}.$$

Proof. By using the improved power mean inequality (Equation (6)) for the I_1 from Equation (12), we get

$$|I_1| \leq \int_0^\varkappa |\varepsilon^\alpha(\varkappa-\varepsilon)||\psi''(\vartheta^*\varepsilon + \varrho^*(1-\varepsilon))|d\varepsilon$$

$$\leq \frac{1}{\varkappa}\left(\int_0^\varkappa (\varkappa-\varepsilon)|\varepsilon^\alpha(\varkappa-\varepsilon)|d\varepsilon\right)^{1-\frac{1}{q}}\left(\int_0^\varkappa (\varkappa-\varepsilon)|\varepsilon^\alpha(\varkappa-\varepsilon)||\psi''(\psi\vartheta^* + (1-\varepsilon)\varrho^*)|^q d\varepsilon\right)^{\frac{1}{q}}$$

$$+ \frac{1}{\varkappa}\left(\int_0^\varkappa \varepsilon|\varepsilon^\alpha(\varkappa-\varepsilon)|d\varepsilon\right)^{1-\frac{1}{q}}\left(\int_0^\varkappa \varepsilon|\varepsilon^\alpha(\varkappa-\varepsilon)||\psi''(\vartheta^*\varepsilon + \varrho^*(1-\varepsilon))|^q d\varepsilon\right)^{\frac{1}{q}}$$

$$= \frac{1}{\varkappa}\left(\int_0^\varkappa \varepsilon^\alpha(\varkappa-\varepsilon)^2 d\varepsilon\right)^{1-\frac{1}{q}}\left(\int_0^\varkappa \varepsilon^\alpha(\varkappa-\varepsilon)^2|\psi''(\vartheta^*\varepsilon + \varrho^*(1-\varepsilon))|^q d\varepsilon\right)^{\frac{1}{q}}$$

$$+ \frac{1}{\varkappa}\left(\int_0^\varkappa \varepsilon^{\alpha+1}(\varkappa-\varepsilon)d\varepsilon\right)^{1-\frac{1}{q}}\left(\int_0^\varkappa \varepsilon^{\alpha+1}(\varkappa-t)|\psi''(\vartheta^*\varepsilon + \varrho^*(1-\varepsilon))|^q d\varepsilon\right)^{\frac{1}{q}}.$$

Here,

$$\int_0^\varkappa \varepsilon^\alpha(\varkappa-\varepsilon)^2 dt = \int_0^1 (\varkappa z)^\alpha(\varkappa-\varkappa z)^2 \varkappa dz$$

$$= \varkappa^{\alpha+3}\int_0^1 z^\alpha(1-z)^2 dz = \varkappa^{\alpha+3}B(\alpha+1,3),$$

$$\int_0^\varkappa \varepsilon^{\alpha+1}(\varkappa-\varepsilon)d\varepsilon = \int_0^1 (\varkappa z)^{\alpha+1}(\varkappa-\varkappa z)\varkappa dz$$

$$= \varkappa^{\alpha+3}\int_0^1 z^{\alpha+1}(1-z)dz = \varkappa^{\alpha+3}B(\alpha+2,2),$$

and, using the definition of convexity,

$$\int_0^\varkappa \varepsilon^\alpha(\varkappa-\varepsilon)^2|\psi''(\vartheta^*\varepsilon + \varrho^*(1-\varepsilon))|^q d\varepsilon$$

$$\leq |\psi''(\vartheta^*)|^q \int_0^\varkappa \varepsilon^{\alpha+1}(\varkappa-\varepsilon)^2 d\varepsilon + |\psi''(\varrho^*)|^q \int_0^\varkappa \varepsilon^\alpha(\varkappa-\varepsilon)^2(1-\varepsilon)d\varepsilon$$

$$= |\psi''(\vartheta^*)|^q \int_0^\varkappa \varepsilon^{\alpha+1}(\varkappa-\varepsilon)^2 d\varepsilon + |\psi''(\varrho^*)|^q \left[\int_0^\varkappa \varepsilon^\alpha(\varkappa-\varepsilon)^2 d\varepsilon - \int_0^\varkappa \varepsilon^{\alpha+1}(\varkappa-\varepsilon)^2 d\varepsilon\right]$$

$$= \varkappa^{\alpha+4}|\psi''(\vartheta^*)|^q B(\alpha+2,3) + \left[\varkappa^{\alpha+3}B(\alpha+1,3) - \varkappa^{\alpha+4}B(\alpha+2,3)\right]|\psi''(\varrho^*)|^q$$

$$= \varkappa^{\alpha+3}B(\alpha+1,3)|\psi''(\varrho^*)|^q + \varkappa^{\alpha+4}B(\alpha+2,3)\left[|\psi''(\varrho^*)|^q - |\psi''(\vartheta^*)|^q\right],$$

and

$$\int_0^\varkappa \varepsilon^{\alpha+1}(\varkappa-\varepsilon)|\psi''(\vartheta^*\varepsilon + \varrho^*(1-\varepsilon))|^q d\varepsilon$$

$$\leq |\psi''(\vartheta^*)|^q \int_0^\varkappa \varepsilon^{\alpha+2}(\varkappa-\varepsilon)d\varepsilon + |\psi''(\varrho^*)|^q \int_0^\varkappa \varepsilon^{\alpha+1}(\varkappa-\varepsilon)(1-\varepsilon)d\varepsilon$$

$$= \varkappa^{\alpha+4}B(\alpha+3,2)|\psi''(a)|^q + |\psi''(\varrho^*)|^q\left(\int_0^\varkappa \varepsilon^{\alpha+1}(\varkappa-\varepsilon)d\varepsilon - \int_0^\varkappa \varepsilon^{\alpha+2}(\varkappa-\varepsilon)d\varepsilon\right)$$

$$= \varkappa^{\alpha+4}B(\alpha+3,2)|\psi''(\vartheta^*)|^q + \left[\varkappa^{\alpha+3}B(\alpha+2,2) - \varkappa^{\alpha+4}B(\alpha+3,2)\right]|\psi''(\varrho^*)|^q$$

$$= \varkappa^{\alpha+3}B(\alpha+2,2)|\psi''(\varrho^*)|^q + \varkappa^{\alpha+4}B(\alpha+3,2)\left[|\psi''(\varrho^*)|^q - |\psi''(\vartheta^*)|^q\right].$$

Thus, we have

$$|I_1| \leq \varkappa^{\alpha+2} B^{1-\frac{1}{q}}(\alpha+1,3)\Big\{ B(\alpha+1,3)|\psi''(\varrho^*)|^q$$
$$+\varkappa B(\alpha+2,3)\Big[|\psi''(\varrho^*)|^q - |\psi''(\vartheta^*)|^q\Big]\Big\}^{\frac{1}{q}}$$
$$+ \varkappa^{\alpha+2} B^{1-\frac{1}{q}}(\alpha+2,2)\Big\{ B(\alpha+2,2)|\psi''(\varrho^*)|^q$$
$$+\varkappa B(\alpha+3,2)\Big[|\psi''(\varrho^*)|^q - |\psi''(\vartheta^*)|^q\Big]\Big\}^{\frac{1}{q}}.$$

First, in I_2, replace ε with $1-\varepsilon$; then, by using the improved power mean inequality (Equation (6)), we can write

$$|I_2| \leq \int_{\varkappa}^{1} |(\varepsilon-\varkappa)(1-\varepsilon)^{\alpha}||\psi''(\vartheta^*\varepsilon + \varrho^*(1-\varepsilon))|d\varepsilon$$
$$= \int_{0}^{1-\varkappa} |(1-\varkappa-\varepsilon)\varepsilon^{\alpha}||\psi''((1-\varepsilon)\vartheta^* + \varepsilon\varrho^*)|d\varepsilon$$
$$= \int_{0}^{\tau} |(\tau-\varepsilon)\varepsilon^{\alpha}||\psi''((1-\varepsilon)\vartheta^* + \varepsilon\varrho^*)|d\varepsilon, \text{ here } (\tau = 1-\varkappa)$$
$$\leq \frac{1}{\tau}\left(\int_{0}^{\tau}(\tau-\varepsilon)\varepsilon^{\alpha}|\tau-\varepsilon|d\varepsilon\right)^{1-\frac{1}{q}} \left(\int_{0}^{\tau}(\tau-\varepsilon)\varepsilon^{\alpha}|\tau-\varepsilon||\psi''(\varepsilon\varrho^* + (1-\varepsilon)\vartheta^*)|^q d\varepsilon\right)^{\frac{1}{q}}$$
$$+ \frac{1}{\tau}\left(\int_{0}^{\tau}\varepsilon|(\tau-\varepsilon)|\varepsilon^{\alpha}d\varepsilon\right)^{1-\frac{1}{q}}\left(\int_{0}^{\tau}\varepsilon|\tau-\varepsilon|\varepsilon^{\alpha}|\psi''(\varepsilon\varrho^* + (1-\varepsilon)\vartheta^*)|^q d\varepsilon\right)^{\frac{1}{q}}.$$
$$= \frac{1}{\tau}\left(\int_{0}^{\tau}\varepsilon^{\alpha}(\tau-\varepsilon)^2 d\varepsilon\right)^{1-\frac{1}{q}}\left(\int_{0}^{\tau}\varepsilon^{\alpha}(\tau-\varepsilon)^2|\psi''(\varepsilon\varrho^* + (1-\varepsilon)\vartheta^*)|^q d\varepsilon\right)^{\frac{1}{q}}$$
$$+ \frac{1}{\tau}\left(\int_{0}^{\tau}\varepsilon^{\alpha+1}(\tau-\varepsilon)d\varepsilon\right)^{1-\frac{1}{q}}\left(\int_{0}^{\tau}\varepsilon^{\alpha+1}(\tau-\varepsilon)|\psi''(\varepsilon\varrho^* + (1-\varepsilon)\vartheta^*)|^q d\varepsilon\right)^{\frac{1}{q}}.$$

Similarly, for the second integral, we get

$$|I_2| \leq (1-\varkappa)^{\alpha+2} B^{1-\frac{1}{q}}(\alpha+1,3)\Big\{ B(\alpha+1,3)|\psi''(\vartheta^*)|^q$$
$$+(1-\varkappa)B(\alpha+2,3)\Big[|\psi''(\varrho^*)|^q - |\psi''(\vartheta^*)|^q\Big]\Big\}^{\frac{1}{q}}$$
$$+ (1-\varkappa)^{\alpha+2} B^{1-\frac{1}{q}}(\alpha+2,2)\Big\{ B(\alpha+2,2)|\psi''(\vartheta^*)|^q$$
$$+(1-\varkappa)B(\alpha+3,2)\Big[|\psi''(\varrho^*)|^q - |\psi''(\vartheta^*)|^q\Big]\Big\}^{\frac{1}{q}}.$$

After summing the integrals and groupings, taking into account the accepted notation, we get

$$|I_1| + |I_2| \leq B^{1-\frac{1}{q}}(\alpha+1,3)\Big[\varkappa^{\alpha+2}\mathbf{P}_1 + (1-\varkappa)^{\alpha+2}\mathbf{P}_3\Big]$$
$$+ B^{1-\frac{1}{q}}(\alpha+2,2)\Big[\varkappa^{\alpha+2}\mathbf{P}_2 + (1-\varkappa)^{\alpha+2}\mathbf{P}_4\Big].$$

Taking into account the last inequality and Equation (12), we obtain Equation (21). The proof is completed. □

Corollary 5. *If we choose $\varkappa = \frac{1}{2}$ and $\alpha = 1$, then, from Equation (21), we obtain*

$$\left|\frac{1}{2}\left[\psi\left(\frac{\vartheta^*+\varrho^*}{2}\right)+\frac{\psi(\varrho^*)+\psi(\vartheta^*)}{2}\right]-\frac{1}{\varrho^*-\vartheta^*}\int_{\vartheta^*}^{\varrho^*}\psi(\varepsilon)d\varepsilon\right| \qquad (22)$$

$$\leq \frac{(\varrho^*-\vartheta^*)^2}{16}\left(\frac{1}{12}\right)^{1-\frac{1}{q}}\left[\left\{\frac{1}{10}|\psi''(\varrho^*)|^q-\frac{1}{60}|\psi''(\vartheta^*)|^q\right\}^{\frac{1}{q}}+\left\{\frac{1}{60}|\psi''(\varrho^*)|^q-\frac{1}{15}|\psi''(\vartheta^*)|^q\right\}^{\frac{1}{q}}\right.$$

$$\left.+\left\{\frac{13}{120}|\psi''(\varrho^*)|^q-\frac{1}{40}|\psi''(\vartheta^*)|^q\right\}^{\frac{1}{q}}+\left\{\frac{1}{40}|\psi''(\varrho^*)|^q-\frac{7}{120}|\psi''(\vartheta^*)|^q\right\}^{\frac{1}{q}}\right],$$

and for $q=1$, we get

$$\left|\frac{1}{2}\left[\psi\left(\frac{\vartheta^*+\varrho^*}{2}\right)+\frac{\psi(\varrho^*)+\psi(\vartheta^*)}{2}\right]-\frac{1}{\varrho^*-\vartheta^*}\int_{\vartheta^*}^{\varrho^*}\psi(\varepsilon)d\varepsilon\right|$$

$$\leq \frac{(\varrho^*-\vartheta^*)^2}{16}\left[\frac{7}{60}|\psi''(\varrho^*)|-\frac{1}{12}|\psi''(\vartheta^*)|+\frac{8}{60}|\psi''(\varrho^*)|-\frac{1}{12}|\psi''(\vartheta^*)|\right]$$

$$= \frac{(\varrho^*-\vartheta^*)^2}{16}\left[\frac{1}{4}|\psi''(\varrho^*)|-\frac{1}{6}|\psi''(\vartheta^*)|\right]$$

$$= \frac{(\varrho^*-\vartheta^*)^2}{192}\left[3|\psi''(\varrho^*)|-2|\psi''(\vartheta^*)|\right].$$

3. Examples

Let us demonstrate the obtained results with examples.

Example 1. *Case one: If we choose* $\psi(\varepsilon)=e^{2\varepsilon}, \varepsilon>0$. *If we attempt to take* $\vartheta^*=1, \varrho^*=2$ *and* $q\in[1.1,10]$, *then the mapping* $\psi''(\varepsilon)=4e^{2\varepsilon}$ *is convex for* $\varepsilon>0$, *and we can infer that the inequality in Equation (14) will convert to*

$$-\frac{1}{8}\cdot\left[\frac{2+3\left(\frac{q}{q-1}\right)}{\left(1+\frac{q}{q-1}\right)\left(1+\frac{2q}{q-1}\right)}\right]^{1-\frac{1}{q}}\left\{\left[\frac{|4e^2|^q+|4e^4|^q}{2}\right]^{\frac{1}{q}}+\left[\frac{|4e^2|^q+|4e^4|^q}{2}\right]^{\frac{1}{q}}\right\}$$

$$\leq \left\{\frac{e^3}{2}+\frac{e^4+e^2}{4}\right\}-\frac{e^4-e^2}{2} \qquad (23)$$

$$\leq \frac{1}{8}\cdot\left[\frac{2+3\left(\frac{q}{q-1}\right)}{\left(1+\frac{q}{q-1}\right)\left(1+\frac{2q}{q-1}\right)}\right]^{1-\frac{1}{q}}\left\{\left[\frac{|4e^2|^q+|4e^4|^q}{2}\right]^{\frac{1}{q}}+\left[\frac{|4e^2|^q+|4e^4|^q}{2}\right]^{\frac{1}{q}}\right\}.$$

Case two: Let $\psi(\varepsilon)=e^{2\varepsilon}, \varepsilon>0$. *If we consider taking* $q=2$ *and* $\vartheta^*\in[1,2], \varrho^*\in[3,4]$, *then we can infer that the inequality in Equation (14) will convert to*

$$-\frac{1}{8}\cdot\left(\frac{8}{15}\right)^{\frac{1}{2}}\left\{\left[\frac{\left|4e^{2\vartheta^*}\right|^2+\left|4e^{2\varrho^*}\right|^2}{2}\right]^{\frac{1}{2}}+\left[\frac{\left|4e^{2\vartheta^*}\right|^2+\left|4e^{2\varrho^*}\right|^2}{2}\right]^{\frac{1}{2}}\right\}$$

$$\leq \left\{\frac{e^{\vartheta^*+\varrho^*}}{2}+\frac{e^{2\varrho^*}+e^{2\vartheta^*}}{4}\right\}-\frac{e^{2\varrho^*}-e^{2\vartheta^*}}{2(\varrho^*-\vartheta^*)} \qquad (24)$$

$$\leq \frac{1}{8}\cdot\left(\frac{8}{15}\right)^{\frac{1}{2}}\left\{\left[\frac{\left|4e^{2\vartheta^*}\right|^2+\left|4e^{2\varrho^*}\right|^2}{2}\right]^{\frac{1}{2}}+\left[\frac{\left|4e^{2\vartheta^*}\right|^2+\left|4e^{2\varrho^*}\right|^2}{2}\right]^{\frac{1}{2}}\right\}.$$

The three mappings attained in the R_ψ, M_ψ and L_ψ in the inequalities in Equation (23) are drawn out in Figure 1 against $q \in [1.1, 10]$. The three mappings deduced from the R_ψ, M_ψ and L_ψ in the inequalities in Equation (24) are drawn out in Figure 2 against $\vartheta^* \in [1,2]$, $\varrho^* \in [3,4]$.

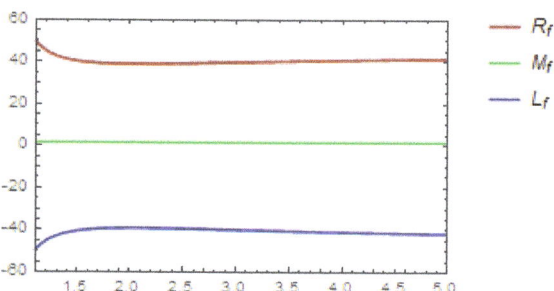

Figure 1. The graphical representation of Example 1 for $\vartheta^* = 1$, $\varrho^* = 2$ and $q \in [1.1, 10]$.

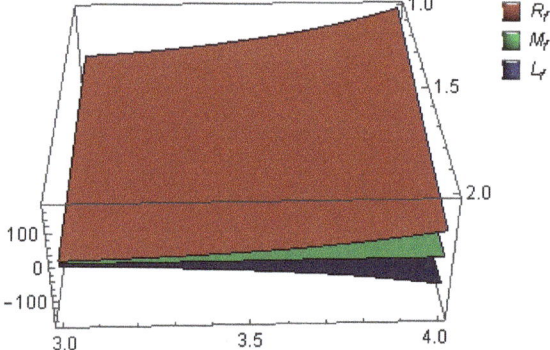

Figure 2. The graphical representation of Example 1 for $\vartheta^* \in [1,2]$, $\varrho^* \in [3,4]$.

Example 2. *Case one: We choose $\psi(\varepsilon) = \frac{1}{24}\varepsilon^3$, $\varepsilon > 0$. If we consider taking $\vartheta^* = 1$, $\varrho^* = 2$ and $q \in [1.1, 10]$, then the mapping $\psi''(\varepsilon) = \frac{1}{4}\varepsilon$ is convex for $\varepsilon > 0$ and we find that the inequality from Equation (20) will convert to*

$$-\frac{1}{96 \cdot 2^{1-\frac{1}{q}}} \cdot \left\{ \left[\left(\frac{1}{4}\right)^{\frac{q}{q-1}} + 3 \cdot \left(\frac{1}{2}\right)^{\frac{q}{q-1}} \right]^{1-\frac{1}{q}} + \left[3 \cdot \left(\frac{1}{4}\right)^{\frac{q}{q-1}} + \left(\frac{1}{2}\right)^{\frac{q}{q-1}} \right]^{1-\frac{1}{q}} \right\}$$

$$\leq \left\{ \frac{1}{48} \cdot \left(\frac{27}{8}\right) + \frac{9}{96} \right\} - \frac{15}{96} \approx \frac{1}{128} \quad (25)$$

$$\leq \frac{1}{96 \cdot 2^{1-\frac{1}{q}}} \cdot \left\{ \left[\left(\frac{1}{4}\right)^{\frac{q}{q-1}} + 3 \cdot \left(\frac{1}{2}\right)^{\frac{q}{q-1}} \right]^{1-\frac{1}{q}} + \left[3 \cdot \left(\frac{1}{4}\right)^{\frac{q}{q-1}} + \left(\frac{1}{2}\right)^{\frac{q}{q-1}} \right]^{1-\frac{1}{q}} \right\}.$$

Case two: Let $\psi(\varepsilon) = \frac{1}{24}\varepsilon^3$, $\varepsilon > 0$. If we consider taking $q = 2$ and $\vartheta^* \in [1,2]$, $\varrho^* \in [3,4]$, then we can infer that the inequality from Equation (20) will convert to

$$-\frac{(\varrho^* - \vartheta^*)^2}{96 \cdot 2^{\frac{1}{2}}} \cdot \left\{ \left[\left(\frac{\vartheta^*}{4}\right)^2 + 3 \cdot \left(\frac{\varrho^*}{4}\right)^2 \right]^{\frac{1}{2}} + \left[3 \cdot \left(\frac{\vartheta^*}{4}\right)^2 + \left(\frac{\varrho^*}{4}\right)^2 \right]^{\frac{1}{2}} \right\}$$

$$\leq \left\{ \frac{1}{48} \cdot \left(\frac{\vartheta^* + \varrho^*}{2}\right)^3 + \frac{\varrho^{*3} + \vartheta^{*3}}{96} \right\} - \frac{\varrho^{*4} - \vartheta^{*4}}{96(\varrho^* - \vartheta^*)} \quad (26)$$

$$\leq \frac{(\varrho^* - \vartheta^*)^2}{96 \cdot 2^{\frac{1}{2}}} \cdot \left\{ \left[\left(\frac{\vartheta^*}{4}\right)^2 + 3 \cdot \left(\frac{\varrho^*}{4}\right)^2 \right]^{\frac{1}{2}} + \left[3 \cdot \left(\frac{\vartheta^*}{4}\right)^2 + \left(\frac{\varrho^*}{4}\right)^2 \right]^{\frac{1}{2}} \right\}.$$

The three mappings attained from the R_ψ, M_ψ and L_ψ in the inequalities in Equation (25) are drawn out in Figure 3 against $q \in [1.1, 10]$. The three mappings deduced from the R_ψ, M_ψ and L_ψ in the inequalities in Equation (26) are drawn out in Figure 4 against $\vartheta^* \in [1,2], \varrho^* \in [3,4]$.

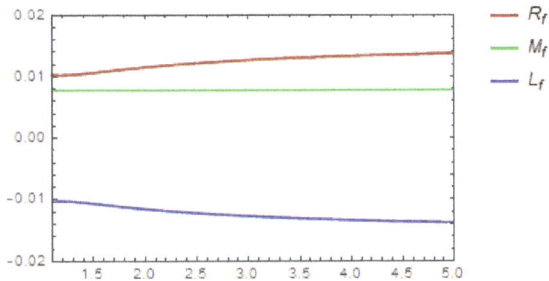

Figure 3. The graphical representation of Example 2 for $\vartheta^* = 1$, $\varrho^* = 2$ and $q \in [1.1, 10]$.

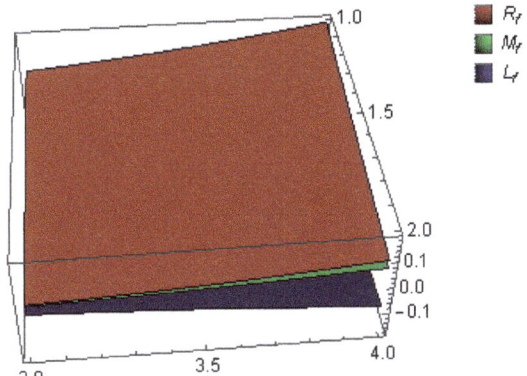

Figure 4. The graphical representation of Example 2 for $\vartheta^* \in [1,2], \varrho^* \in [3,4]$.

Comparative Analysis of Classical and Improved Bounds

Example 3. *If we choose $\psi(\varepsilon) = \frac{1}{12}\varepsilon^4, \varepsilon > 0$, then $|\psi''(\varepsilon)|^q = varepsilon^4$ for $q > 1$ and $\varepsilon > 0$ is a convex function. For the case where $\alpha = 1, \vartheta^* = 1, \varrho^* = 2$ and $q = 2$, let us find the right part of the inequalities from Equations (14) and (16).*

(a) *For Equation (14), we have*

$$\left|\frac{1}{2}\left[\psi\left(\frac{\vartheta^*+\varrho^*}{2}\right)+\frac{\psi(\varrho^*)+\psi(\vartheta^*)}{2}\right]-\frac{1}{\varrho^*-\vartheta^*}\int_{\vartheta^*}^{\varrho^*}\psi(t)dt\right|$$
$$\leq \frac{(\varrho^*-\vartheta^*)^2}{8}\mathbf{S}^{\frac{1}{p}}\left\{\left[\frac{|\psi''(\vartheta^*)|^q}{2}+\frac{3|\psi''(\varrho^*)|^q}{2}\right]^{\frac{1}{q}}\right.$$
$$\left.+\left[\frac{3|\psi''(\vartheta^*)|^q}{2}+\frac{|\psi''(\varrho^*)|^q}{2}\right]^{\frac{1}{q}}\right\}$$
$$=\frac{1}{8}\left(\frac{8}{15}\right)^{\frac{1}{2}}\left\{\left[\frac{1}{2}+24\right]^{\frac{1}{2}}+\left[\frac{3}{2}+8\right]^{\frac{1}{2}}\right\}$$
$$\approx 0.733214.$$

(b) For Equation (16), we have

$$\left|\frac{1}{2}\left[\psi\left(\frac{\vartheta^*+\varrho^*}{2}\right)+\frac{\psi(\varrho^*)+\psi(\vartheta^*)}{2}\right]-\frac{1}{\varrho^*-\vartheta^*}\int_{\vartheta^*}^{\varrho^*}\psi(t)dt\right|$$
$$\leq \frac{(\varrho^*-\vartheta^*)^2}{16}B^{\frac{1}{2}}(3,4)\{\tilde{\mathbf{M}}_1+\tilde{\mathbf{M}}_3+\tilde{\mathbf{M}}_2+\tilde{\mathbf{M}}_4\}$$
$$=\frac{1}{16}[0.12909\cdot\{2.598076+2.345208+1.322876+1.732051\}]$$
$$\approx 0.064530.$$

Since $0.733214 > 0.064530$, the extended Hölder inequality gives a better estimate than the classical Hölder inequality. The 2D and 3D graphical illustrations of Example 3 are mentioned in Figures 5 and 6, respectively.

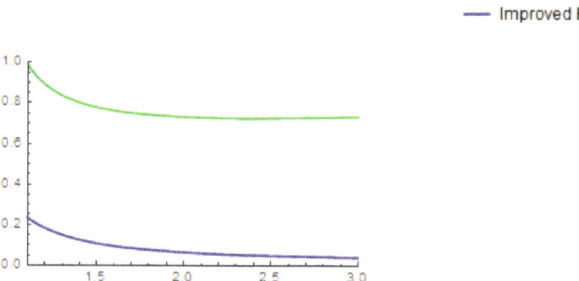

Figure 5. The graphical representation of Example 3 for $\vartheta^*=1$, $\varrho^*=2$ and $q\in[1.1,10]$.

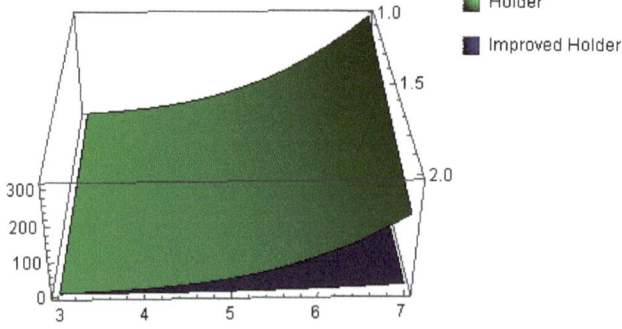

Figure 6. The graphical representation of Example 3 for $\vartheta^*\in[1,2]$, $\varrho^*\in[3,7]$.

Example 4. If we choose $\psi(\varepsilon) = e^\varepsilon, \varepsilon > 0$, then $|\psi''(\varepsilon)|^q = e^\varepsilon$ for $q > 1$ and $\varepsilon > 0$ is a convex function. For the case where $\alpha = 1, \vartheta^* = 1, \varrho^* = 2$ and $q = 2$, let us find the right part of the inequalities from Equations (20) and (22).

(a) For Equation (20), we have

$$\left| \frac{1}{2}\left[\psi\left(\frac{\vartheta^* + \varrho^*}{2}\right) + \frac{\psi(\varrho^*) + \psi(\vartheta^*)}{2}\right] - \frac{1}{\varrho^* - \vartheta^*}\int_{\vartheta^*}^{\varrho^*}\psi(\varepsilon)d\varepsilon \right|$$

$$\leq \frac{(\varrho^* - \vartheta^*)^2}{96 \cdot 2^{\frac{1}{p}}}\left\{\left[|\psi''(\vartheta^*)|^p + 3|\psi''(\varrho^*)|^p\right]^{\frac{1}{p}} + \left[3|\psi''(\vartheta^*)|^p + |\psi''(\varrho^*)|^p\right]^{\frac{1}{p}}\right\}$$

$$= \frac{1}{96 \cdot 2^{\frac{1}{2}}} \cdot \left[(7.3891 + 163.7944)^{\frac{1}{2}} + (22.16716 + 54.5981)^{\frac{1}{2}}\right]$$

$$\approx 0.1609.$$

(b) For Equation (22), we have

$$\left| \frac{1}{2}\left[\psi\left(\frac{\vartheta^* + \varrho^*}{2}\right) + \frac{\psi(\varrho^*) + \psi(\vartheta^*)}{2}\right] - \frac{1}{\varrho^* - \vartheta^*}\int_{\vartheta^*}^{\varrho^*}\psi(\varepsilon)d\varepsilon \right|$$

$$\leq \frac{(\varrho^* - \vartheta^*)^2}{16}\left(\frac{1}{12}\right)^{1-\frac{1}{q}}\left[\left\{\frac{|\psi''(\varrho^*)|^q}{10} - \frac{|\psi''(\vartheta^*)|^q}{60}\right\}^{\frac{1}{q}} + \left\{\frac{|\psi''(\varrho^*)|^q}{60} - \frac{|\psi''(\vartheta^*)|^q}{15}\right\}^{\frac{1}{q}}\right.$$

$$\left. + \left\{\frac{13|\psi''(\varrho^*)|^q}{120} - \frac{|\psi''(\vartheta^*)|^q}{40}\right\}^{\frac{1}{q}} + \left\{\frac{|\psi''(\varrho^*)|^q}{40} - \frac{7|\psi''(\vartheta^*)|^q}{120}\right\}^{\frac{1}{q}}\right].$$

$$= \frac{1}{16}0.2887 \cdot [2.310122 + 0.646038 + 2.393757 + 0.966398]$$

$$\approx 0.113958.$$

Since $0.1609 > 0.113958$, the extended power mean inequality gives a better estimate than the classical power mean inequality. The 2D and 3D graphical illustrations of Example 4 are mentioned in Figures 7 and 8, respectively.

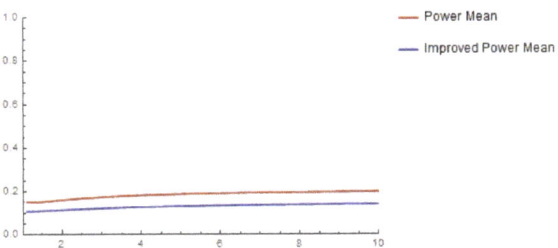

Figure 7. The graphical representation of Example 4 for $\vartheta^* = 1, \varrho^* = 2$ and $q \in [1.1, 10]$.

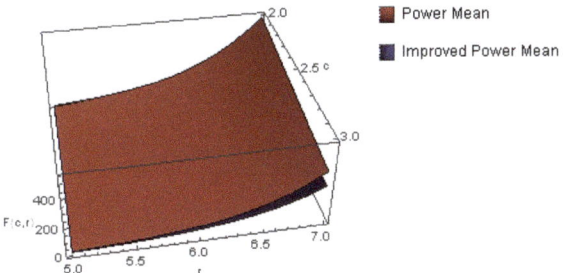

Figure 8. The graphical representation of Example 4 for $\vartheta^* \in [2,3], \varrho^* \in [5,7]$.

4. Applications

In this section, we employ our obtained results to derive some notable applications in terms of special means, the quadrature rule and estimations of inequalities in terms of special functions.

4.1. Special Means

We here consider the means for arbitrary real numbers ϑ^*, ϱ^* ($\vartheta^* \neq \varrho^*$). We use the following:

1. Arithmetic mean:
$$A(\vartheta^*, \varrho^*) = \frac{\vartheta^* + \varrho^*}{2}, \quad \vartheta^*, \varrho^* \in \mathbb{R}.$$

2. Logarithmic mean:
$$L(\vartheta^*, \varrho^*) = \frac{\vartheta^* - \varrho^*}{\ln|\vartheta^*| - \ln|\varrho^*|}, \quad |\vartheta^*| \neq |\varrho^*|, \ \vartheta^*, \varrho^* \neq 0, \ \vartheta^*, \varrho^* \in \mathbb{R}.$$

3. Generalized log-mean:
$$L_n(\vartheta^*, \varrho^*) = \left[\frac{(\varrho^*)^{n+1} - (\vartheta^*)^{n+1}}{(n+1)(\varrho^* - \vartheta^*)}\right]^{\frac{1}{n}}, \quad n \in \mathbb{Z}\setminus\{-1, 0\}, \vartheta^*, \varrho^* \in \mathbb{R}^+.$$

4. Harmonic mean:
$$H = H(\vartheta^*, \varrho^*) = \frac{2\vartheta^*\varrho^*}{\vartheta^* + \varrho^*}; \ \vartheta^*, \varrho^* > 0.$$

5. p-Logarithmic mean:
$$L_p(\vartheta^*, \varrho^*) = \left(\frac{(\varrho^*)^{1+p} - (\vartheta^*)^{1+p}}{(1+p)(\varrho^* - \vartheta^*)}\right)^{\frac{1}{p}}, \quad p \in \mathbb{R} - \{-1, 0\}, \ \vartheta^*, \ \varrho^* > 0.$$

Proposition 1. *Let* $\vartheta^*, \varrho^* \in [0, \infty)$, $\vartheta^* < \varrho^*$ *and* $n \in \mathbb{Z}^+, n \geq 2$. *Then, we have*

$$\left| L_n^n - \frac{1}{2}[A^n(\vartheta^*, \varrho^*) + A(\vartheta^{*n}, \varrho^{*n})] \right|$$
$$\leq \frac{n(n-1)(\varrho^* - \vartheta^*)^2}{8} S^{\frac{1}{p}} \left\{ A^{\frac{1}{q}}\left(|\vartheta^*|^{(n-2)q}, 3|\varrho^*|^{(n-2)q}\right) + A^{\frac{1}{q}}\left(3|\vartheta^*|^{(n-2)q}, |\varrho^*|^{(n-2)q}\right) \right\},$$

where
$$S = \frac{2 + 3p}{(1+p)(1+2p)}.$$

Proof. This follows from Corollary 2 applied to the convex function
$$\psi(\varepsilon) = \varepsilon^n, \psi : [0, \infty) \to \mathbb{R}.$$
□

Proposition 2. *Let* $\vartheta^*, \varrho^* \in \mathbb{R}$ *with* $0 < \vartheta^* < \varrho^*$. *Then,*

$$\left| L^{-1}(\vartheta^*, \varrho^*) - \frac{1}{2}\left[A^{-1}(\vartheta^*, \varrho^*) + H^{-1}(\vartheta^*, \varrho^*)\right] \right|$$
$$\leq \frac{(\varrho^* - \vartheta^*)^2}{2^{3-\frac{1}{q}}} S^{\frac{1}{p}} \left\{ A^{\frac{1}{q}}\left(|\vartheta^*|^{-3q}, 3|\varrho^*|^{-3q}\right) + A^{\frac{1}{q}}\left(3|\vartheta^*|^{-3q}, |\varrho^*|^{-3q}\right) \right\}.$$

Proof. This follows from Corollary 2 applied to the convex function
$$\psi(\varepsilon) = \frac{1}{\varepsilon}, \varepsilon \neq 0.$$

□

Proposition 3. *Let* $\vartheta^*, \varrho^* \in [0, \infty), \vartheta^* < \varrho^*, \forall\, q > 1$. *Then, we have*

$$\left| L(\vartheta^*, \varrho^*) - \frac{1}{2}\left[e^{A(\vartheta^*, \varrho^*)} + A\left(e^{\vartheta^*}, e^{\varrho^*}\right) \right] \right|$$
$$\leq \frac{(\varrho^* - \vartheta^*)^2}{8} S^{\frac{1}{p}} \left\{ A^{\frac{1}{q}}\left(|e|^{\vartheta^* q}, 3|e|^{\varrho^* q}\right) + A^{\frac{1}{q}}\left(3|e|^{\vartheta^* q}, |e|^{\varrho^* q}\right) \right\}.$$

Proof. This follows from Corollary 2 applied to the convex function

$$\psi(\varepsilon) = e^\varepsilon, \psi : [0, \infty) \to \mathbb{R}.$$

□

Proposition 4. *Let* $\vartheta^*, \varrho^* \in [0, \infty), \vartheta^* < \varrho^*$ *and* $n \in \mathbb{Z}^+, n \geq 2$. *Then, we have*

$$\left| L_n^n(\vartheta^*, \varrho^*) - \frac{1}{2}\left[A^n(\vartheta^*, \varrho^*) + A(\vartheta^{*n}, \varrho^{*n}) \right] \right|$$
$$\leq \frac{(\varrho^* - \vartheta^*)^2}{96} n(n-1) \left[A^{\frac{1}{p}}\left(|\vartheta^*|^{(n-2)p}, 3|\varrho^*|^{(n-2)p}\right) + A^{\frac{1}{p}}\left(3|\vartheta^*|^{(n-2)p}, |\varrho^*|^{(n-2)p}\right) \right].$$

Proof. This follows from Corollary 4 applied to the convex function

$$\psi(\varepsilon) = \varepsilon^n, \psi : [0, \infty) \to \mathbb{R}.$$

□

Proposition 5. *Let* $\vartheta^*, \varrho^* \in \mathbb{R}$ *with* $0 < \vartheta^* < \varrho^*$. *Then,*

$$\left| L^{-1}(\vartheta^*, \varrho^*) - \frac{1}{2}\left[A^{-1}(\vartheta^*, \varrho^*) + H^{-1}(\vartheta^*, \varrho^*) \right] \right|$$
$$\leq \frac{(\varrho^* - \vartheta^*)^2}{96} \left[A^{\frac{1}{p}}\left(|\vartheta^*|^{-3p}, 3|\varrho^*|^{-3p}\right) + A^{\frac{1}{p}}\left(3|\vartheta^*|^{-3p}, |\varrho^*|^{-3p}\right) \right].$$

Proof. This follows from Corollary 4 applied to the convex function

$$\psi(\varepsilon) = \frac{1}{\varepsilon}, \varepsilon \neq 0.$$

□

4.2. Quadrature Formula

Here, we present an application to a quadrature formula. Let d be a partition $\vartheta^* = \varepsilon_0 < \varepsilon_1 \ldots < \varepsilon_{m-1} < \varepsilon_m = \varrho^*$ of the interval $[\vartheta^*, \varrho^*]$ and consider the quadrature formula

$$\int_{\vartheta^*}^{\varrho^*} \psi(\varepsilon) d\varepsilon = T(\psi, d) + E(\psi, d),$$

where

$$T(\psi, d) = \sum_{i=0}^{m-1} \frac{(\varepsilon_{i+1} - \varepsilon_i)}{2} \left[\frac{\psi(\varepsilon_i) + \psi(\varepsilon_{i+1})}{2} + \psi\left(\frac{\varepsilon_i + \varepsilon_{i+1}}{2}\right) \right], \qquad (27)$$

is the quadrature version and $E(\psi, d)$ is the approximation error. Here, we present some error estimates for the quadrature formula.

Proposition 6. *Under the condition of Corollary 1, the following inequality is true:*

$$\left| \int_{\vartheta^*}^{\varrho^*} \psi(\varepsilon) d\varepsilon - T(\psi, d) \right| \leq \sum_{i=0}^{m-1} \frac{(\varepsilon_{i+1} - \varepsilon_i)^3}{96} \left[|\psi''(\varepsilon_{i+1})| + |\psi''(\varepsilon_i)| \right]. \tag{28}$$

Proof. Apply Corollary 1 and we get the desired result. □

Remark 3. *If the d-fragmentation of the interval $[\vartheta^*, \varrho^*]$ is uniform, then, from Equations (27) and (28), we get*

$$T(\psi, d) = \frac{h}{2} \sum_{i=0}^{m-1} \left[\frac{\psi(\varepsilon_i) + \psi(\varepsilon_{i+1})}{2} + \psi\left(\frac{\varepsilon_i + \varepsilon_{i+1}}{2} \right) \right],$$

and

$$\left| \int_{\vartheta^*}^{\varrho^*} \psi(\varepsilon) d\varepsilon - T(\psi, d) \right| \leq \frac{mh^3}{48} M_2 \leq \frac{m^3 h^3}{48} M_2 = \frac{(\varrho^* - \vartheta^*)^3}{48} M_2,$$

where $h = \varepsilon_{i+1} - \varepsilon_i$ and $M_2 = \max_{x \in [\vartheta^*, \varrho^*]}(|\psi''(x)|)$.

The resulting error is better than the errors expressed in terms of the second derivatives of the Newton–Cotes (midpoint or trapezoid formula) and Gauss quadrature formulas:

$$R_1(\psi) = \frac{M_2}{24}(\varrho^* - \vartheta^*)^3, \text{ or } R_2(\psi) = \frac{M_2}{12}(\varrho^* - \vartheta^*)^3,$$

and

$$R_{2n}(\psi) = \frac{M_{2n}(n!)^4}{((2n)!)^3(2n+1)}(\varrho^* - \vartheta^*)^3, M_{2n} = \max_{x \in [\vartheta^*, \varrho^*]}\left(|\psi^{(2n)}(x)|\right), \text{ for } n = 1$$

respectively.

Proposition 7. *Let $\psi: [\vartheta^*, \varrho^*] \to \mathbb{R}$ be the differentiable mapping on (ϑ^*, ϱ^*) with $\vartheta^* < \varrho^*$. Suppose that $|\psi''|^q, q \geq 1$ is a convex function; then, for every partition of $[\vartheta^*, \varrho^*]$, the midpoint error satisfies*

$$\left| \int_{\vartheta^*}^{\varrho^*} \psi(\varepsilon) d\varepsilon - T(\psi, d) \right| \leq \frac{B^{\frac{1}{p}}(1+p, 2+p)}{16}$$

$$\times \sum_{i=0}^{m-1} (\varepsilon_{i+1} - \varepsilon_i)^3 \left[\left(\frac{|\psi''(\varepsilon_i)|^q + 5|\psi''(\varepsilon_{i+1})|^q}{12} \right)^{\frac{1}{q}} + \left(\frac{|\psi''(\varepsilon_{i+1})|^q + 5|\psi''(\varepsilon_i)|^q}{12} \right)^{\frac{1}{q}} \right.$$

$$\left. + \left(\frac{|\psi''(\varepsilon_i)|^q + 2|\psi''(\varepsilon_{i+1})|^q}{6} \right)^{\frac{1}{q}} + \left(\frac{|\psi''(\varepsilon_{i+1})|^q + 2|\psi''(\varepsilon_i)|^q}{6} \right)^{\frac{1}{q}} \right].$$

Proof. Apply Corollary 3 and then we get the desired result. □

4.3. q̃-Digamma Function

The q̃-digamma mapping is determined by the expression below [34]:

$$\delta_{\tilde{q}}(\varepsilon) = -\ln(\tilde{q} - 1) + \ln(\tilde{q}) \left(\varepsilon - \frac{1}{2} - \sum_{j=1}^{\infty} \frac{\tilde{q}^{-j\varepsilon}}{1 - \tilde{q}^{-j\varepsilon}} \right),$$

with $\tilde{q} > 1$ and $\varepsilon > 0$.

Proposition 8. *For* $0 < \vartheta^* < \varrho^*$, *we get*

$$\left| \frac{1}{2} \left[\delta'_{\bar{q}} \left(\frac{\vartheta^* + \varrho^*}{2} \right) + \frac{\delta'_{\bar{q}}(\varrho^*) + \delta'_{\bar{q}}(\vartheta^*)}{2} \right] - \frac{\delta_{\bar{q}}(\varrho^*) - \delta_{\bar{q}}(\vartheta^*)}{\varrho^* - \vartheta^*} \right|$$

$$\leq \frac{(\varrho^* - \vartheta^*)^2}{96} \left[\left| \delta'''_{\bar{q}}(\vartheta^*) \right| + \left| \delta'''_{\bar{q}}(\varrho^*) \right| \right].$$

Proof. Applying $\psi(\varepsilon) = \delta'_{\bar{q}}(\varepsilon)$ for $\varepsilon > 0$ to Corollary 1, we obtain the desired result. □

Proposition 9. *For* $0 < \vartheta^* < \varrho^*, q > 1$ *and* $\frac{1}{p} + \frac{1}{q} = 1$, *we get that*

$$\left| \frac{1}{2} \left[\delta'_{\bar{q}} \left(\frac{\vartheta^* + \varrho^*}{2} \right) + \frac{\delta'_{\bar{q}}(\varrho^*) + \delta'_{\bar{q}}(\vartheta^*)}{2} \right] - \frac{\delta_{\bar{q}}(\varrho^*) - \delta_{\bar{q}}(\vartheta^*)}{\varrho^* - \vartheta^*} \right|$$

$$\leq \frac{(\varrho^* - \vartheta^*)^2}{96} \left[\left(\left| \delta'''_{\bar{q}}(\vartheta^*) \right|^p + 3 \left| \delta'''_{\bar{q}}(\varrho^*) \right|^p \right)^{\frac{1}{p}} + \left(3 \left| \delta'''_{\bar{q}}(\vartheta^*) \right|^p + \left| \delta'''_{\bar{q}}(\varrho^*) \right|^p \right)^{\frac{1}{p}} \right].$$

Proof. Applying $\psi(\varepsilon) = \delta'_{\bar{q}}(\varepsilon)$ for $\varepsilon > 0$ to Corollary 4, we obtain the desired result. □

4.4. Modified Bessel Function

Let the function $\mathcal{I}_p : \mathbb{R} \to [1,0)$ be defined by

$$\mathcal{I}_p(\varepsilon) = 2^p \Gamma(1+p) \varepsilon^{-\varrho^*} I_p(\varepsilon),$$

For this, we recall the modified Bessel function of the first kind I_p, which is defined as [35]:

$$I_p(\varepsilon) = \sum_{n \geq 0} \frac{(\frac{\varepsilon}{2})^{p+2n}}{n! \Gamma(p+n+1)}.$$

The first- and nth-order derivative formulas of $\mathcal{I}_p(\varepsilon)$ are, respectively [36]:

$$\mathcal{I}'_p(\varepsilon) = \frac{\varepsilon}{2(1+p)} \mathcal{I}_{1+p}(\varepsilon),$$

$$\frac{\partial^n \mathcal{I}_p(\varepsilon)}{\partial^n \varepsilon} = 2^{n-2p} \sqrt{\pi} \varepsilon^{p-n} \Gamma(1+p) {}_2F_3\left(\frac{1+p}{2}, \frac{2+p}{2}; \frac{1+p-n}{2}, 1+p; \frac{\varepsilon^2}{4} \right),$$

where ${}_2F_3(.,.,.,.)$ is the hypergeometric function defined by [36]:

$${}_2F_3\left(\frac{1+p}{2}, \frac{2+p}{2}; \frac{1+p-n}{2}, 1+p; \frac{\varepsilon^2}{4} \right) = \sum_{k=0}^{\infty} \frac{(\frac{1+p}{2})_k (\frac{1+p}{2})_k}{(\frac{p-2}{2})_k (\frac{p-1}{2})_k (1+p)_k} \frac{\varepsilon^{2k}}{4^k (k)!}.$$

Proposition 10. *Let* $\vartheta^*, \varrho^* \in \mathbb{R}$ *with* $0 < \vartheta^* < \varrho^*$; *then, for each* $p > -1$, *we have*

$$\left| \frac{1}{2} \left[\frac{\vartheta^* + \varrho^*}{4(1+p)} \mathcal{I}_{1+p}\left(\frac{\vartheta^* + \varrho^*}{2} \right) + \frac{\varrho^* \mathcal{I}_{1+p}(\varrho^*) + \vartheta^* \mathcal{I}_{1+p}(\vartheta^*)}{4(1+p)} \right] - \frac{\mathcal{I}_p(\varrho^*) - \mathcal{I}_p(\vartheta^*)}{\varrho^* - \vartheta^*} \right|$$

$$\leq \frac{(\varrho^* - \vartheta^*)^2}{96} 2^{3-2p} \sqrt{\pi} \Gamma(1+p) \times \left(|\vartheta^*|^{p-3} \left| {}_2F_3\left(\frac{1+p}{2}, \frac{2+p}{2}; \frac{p-2}{2}, \frac{p-1}{2}, 1+p; \frac{(\vartheta^*)^2}{4} \right) \right| \right.$$

$$+ |\varrho^*|^{p-3} \left| {}_2F_3\left(\frac{1+p}{2}, \frac{2+p}{2}; \frac{p-2}{2}, \frac{p-1}{2}, 1+p; \frac{(\varrho^*)^2}{4} \right) \right| \Bigg).$$

Proof. Applying $\psi(\varepsilon) = \mathcal{I}'_p(\varepsilon)$ to Corollary 1, we get the desired result. □

5. Concluding Remarks

In this study, we first developed a new fractional Bullen-type identity with a parameter. Thus employing the theory of convexity, we provided new estimations of fractional Bullen-type inequalities pertaining to twice-differentiable functions. An analysis of the improvement of the estimations was provided using several concrete examples with graphical visualizations. Finally, several applications were provided as well. This study could be used to explore for other general fractional integral operators with non-singular kernels. Also, one can think about studying such results for other classes of convex functions, especially coordinate convex functions.

Author Contributions: Conceptualization, A.F. and B.B.; methodology, B.B.; validation, S.I.B. and A.F.; investigation, B.B. and M.A.; writing—original draft preparation, B.B. and A.F.; writing—review and editing, A.F. and S.I.B.; visualization, Y.W.; supervision, Y.W.; project administration, A.F.; funding acquisition, A.F. and Y.W. All authors have read and agreed to the published version of the manuscript.

Funding: This research was funded by the National Natural Science Foundation of China (Grant no. 12171435).

Institutional Review Board Statement: Not applicable.

Informed Consent Statement: Not applicable.

Data Availability Statement: Not applicable.

Acknowledgments: All the authors are thankful to their respective institutes. In addition, Asfand Fahad also acknowledges the Grant No. YS304023966 to support his Postdoctoral Fellowship at Zhejiang Normal University, China.

Conflicts of Interest: The authors declare no conflict of interest.

References

1. Mitrinovic, D.S.; Pećarixcx, J.; Fink, A.M. *Classical and New Inequalities in Analysis*; Mathematics and Its Applications (East European Series); Kluwer Academic Publishers Group: Dordrecht, The Netherlands, 1993; Volume 61.
2. Dragomir, S.S.; Pearse, C.E.M. *Selected Topics on Hermite-Hadamard Inequalities and Applications*; RGMIA Monograps; Victoria University: Footscray, VIC, Australia, 2000.
3. Rasheed, T.; Butt, S.I.; Pečarić, D.; Pečarić, J. Generalized Cyclic Jensen and Information Inequalities. *Chaos Solitons Fractals* **2022**, *163*, 112602. [CrossRef]
4. Gasimov, Y.S.; Nápoles, J.E. Some refinements of Hermite-Hadamard inequality using k-fractional Caputo derivatives. *Fract. Differ. Calc.* **2022**, *12*, 209–221. [CrossRef]
5. Agarwal, P.; Dragomir, S.S.; Jleli, M.; Samet, B. (Eds.) *Advances in Mathematical Inequalities and Applications*; Springer: Singapore, 2018.
6. Qin, Y. *Integral and Discrete Inequalities and Their Applications*; Springer International Publishing: Basel, Switzerland, 2016.
7. Fahad, A.; Ayesha; Wang, Y.; Butt, S.I. Jensen-Mercer and Hermite-Hadamard-Mercer Type Inequalities for $GA-h$-Convex Functions and Its Subclasses with Applications. *Mathematics* **2023**, *11*, 278. [CrossRef]
8. Pečarić, J.; Tong, Y.L. *Convex Functions, Partial Orderings, and Statistical Applications*; Academic Press: Cambridge, MA, USA, 1992.
9. Tariq, M.; Ntouyas, S.K.; Shaikh, A.A. New Variant of Hermite-Hadamard, Fejér and Pachpatte-Type Inequality and Its Refinements Pertaining to Fractional Integral Operator. *Fractal Fract.* **2023**, *7*, 405. [CrossRef]
10. Nápoles, J.E.; Bayraktar, B. On the generalized inequalities of the Hermite-Hadamard type. *Filomat* **2021**, *35*, 4917–4924. [CrossRef]
11. Bayraktar, B.; Gürbüz, B. On some integral inequalities for (s,m)- convex functions. *TWMS J. Appl. Eng. Math.* **2020**, *10*, 288–295.
12. Bullen, P.S. *Error Estimates for Some Elementary Quadrature Rules*; No. 602/633; University of Belgrade: Belgrade, Serbia, 1978; pp. 97–103.
13. Tseng, K.-L.; Hwang, S.-R.; Hsua, K.-C. Hadamard-type and Bullen-type inequalities for Lipschitzian functions and their applications. *Comput. Math. Appl.* **2012**, *64*, 651–660. [CrossRef]
14. Çakmak, M. The differentiable h-convex functions involving the Bullen inequality. *Acta Univ. Apulensis* **2021**, *65*, 29–36.
15. Erden, S.; Sarikaya, M.Z. Generalized Bullen-type inequalities for local fractional integrals and its applications. *Palest. J. Math.* **2020**, *9*, 945–956.
16. Sarikaya, M.Z.; Tunc, T.; Budak, H. On generalized some integral inequalities for local fractional integrals. *Appl. Math. Comput.* **2016**, *276*, 316–323.
17. Işcan, T.; Toplu, T.; Yetgin, F. Some new inequalities on generalization of Hermite-Hadamard and Bullen type inequalities, applications to trapezoidal and midpoint formula. *Kragujev. J. Math.* **2021**, *45*, 647–657. [CrossRef]

18. Hussain, S.; Mehboob, S. On some generalized fractional integral Bullen type inequalities with applications. *J. Fract. Calc. Nonlinear Syst.* **2021**, *2*, 93–112. [CrossRef]
19. Yaşar, B.N.; Aktan, N.; Kizilkan, G.Ç. Generalization of Bullen type, trapezoid type, midpoint type and Simpson type inequalities for s-convex in the fourth sense. *Turk. J. Inequal.* **2022**, *6*, 40–51.
20. Boulares, H.; Meftah, B.; Moumen, A.; Shafqat, R.; Saber, H.; Alraqad, T.; Ali, E. Fractional multiplicative Bullen-type inequalities for multiplicative differentiable functions. *Symmetry* **2023**, *15*, 451. [CrossRef]
21. Bayraktar, B.; Butt, S.I.; Napoles, J.E.; Rabossi, F. Some New Estimates of Integral Inequalities and Their Applications. *Ukr. Math. J.* in press.
22. Adjabi, Y.; Jarad, F.; Baleanu, D.; Abdeljawad, T. On Cauchy problems with Caputo Hadamard fractional derivatives. *J. Comput. Anal. Appl.* **2016**, *21*, 661–681.
23. Kilbas, A.A.; Srivastava, H.M.; Trujillo, J.J. *Theory and Applications of Fractional Differential Equations*; Elsevier: Amsterdam, The Netherlands, 2006; Volume 204.
24. Cai, Z.; Huang, J.; Huang, L. Periodic orbit analysis for the delayed Filippov system. *Proc. Am. Math. Soc.* **2018**, *146*, 4667–4682. [CrossRef]
25. Chen, T.; Huang, L.; Yu, P.; Huang, W. *Bifurcation of Limit Cycles at Infinity in Piecewise Polynomial Systems. Nonlinear Anal. Real World Appl.* **2018**, *41*, 82–106. [CrossRef]
26. Liu, J.B.; Butt, S.I.; Nasir, J.; Aslam, A.; Fahad, A.; Soontharanon, J. Jensen-Mercer Variant of Hermite-Hadamard Type Inequalities via Atangana-Baleanu Fractional Operator. *AIMS Math.* **2022**, *7*, 2123–2141. [CrossRef]
27. Sarikaya, M.Z.; Set, E.; Yaldiz, H.; Budak, N. Hermite-Hadamards inequalities for fractional integrals and related fractional inequalities. *Math. Comput. Model.* **2013**, *57*, 2403–2407. [CrossRef]
28. Du, T.; Liu, J.; Yu, Y. Certain Error Bounds on the Parametrized Integral Inequalitiues in the Sense of Fractal Sets. *Chaos Solitons Fractals* **2022**, *161*, 112328.
29. Butt, S.I.; Yousaf, S.; Akdemir, A.O.; Dokuyucu, M.A. New Hadamard-type integral inequalities via a general form of fractionalintegral operators. *Chaos Solitons Fractals* **2021**, *148*, 111025. [CrossRef]
30. Vivas-Cortez, M.; Kórus, P.; Nápoles, J.E. Some generalized Hermite–Hadamard–Fejér inequality for convex functions. *Adv. Differ. Equ.* **2021**, *1*, 1–11. [CrossRef]
31. Iscan, I. New refinements for integral and sum forms of Hölder inequality. *J. Inequalities Appl.* **2019**, *2019*, 304.
32. Kadakal, M.; Iscan, I.; Kadakal, H.; Bekar, K. On improvements of some integral inequalities. *Honam Math. J.* **2021**, *43*, 441–452.
33. Kıramcı, U. On Some Hermite-Hadamard Type İnequlities for Twice Differentable (α, m)-convex functions and Applications. *RGMIA* **2017**, *20*.
34. Yuan, X.; Xu, L.; Du, T. Simpson-like inequalities for twice differentable (s, P)-convex mappings involving with AB-fractional integrals and their applications. *Fractals* **2023**, *31*, 2350024. [CrossRef]
35. Watson, G.N. *A Treatise on the Theory of Bessel Functions*; Cambridge University Press: Cambridge, UK, 1944.
36. Luke, Y.L. *The Special Functions and Their Approximations*; Academic Press: New York, NY, USA, 1969; Volume 1.

Disclaimer/Publisher's Note: The statements, opinions and data contained in all publications are solely those of the individual author(s) and contributor(s) and not of MDPI and/or the editor(s). MDPI and/or the editor(s) disclaim responsibility for any injury to people or property resulting from any ideas, methods, instructions or products referred to in the content.

Article

Hermite–Hadamard–Mercer Inequalities Associated with Twice-Differentiable Functions with Applications

Muhammad Aamir Ali [1], Thanin Sitthiwirattham [2,*], Elisabeth Köbis [3] and Asma Hanif [4]

[1] Jiangsu Key Laboratory for NSLSCS, School of Mathematical Sciences, Nanjing Normal University, Nanjing 210023, China
[2] Mathematics Department, Faculty of Science and Technology, Suan Dusit University, Bangkok 10300, Thailand
[3] Department of Mathematical Sciences, Norwegian University of Science and Technology, 7491 Trondheim, Norway
[4] Department of Mathematics, Government College University Lahore, Lahore 54000, Pakistan
* Correspondence: thanin_sit@dusit.ac.th

Abstract: In this work, we initially derive an integral identity that incorporates a twice-differentiable function. After establishing the recently created identity, we proceed to demonstrate some new Hermite–Hadamard–Mercer-type inequalities for twice-differentiable convex functions. Additionally, it demonstrates that the recently introduced inequalities have extended certain pre-existing inequalities found in the literature. Finally, we provide applications to the newly established inequalities to verify their usefulness.

Keywords: Hermite–Hadamard inequality; Jensen–Mercer inequality; convex functions

MSC: 26D10; 26D15; 26A51

Citation: Ali, M.A.; Sitthiwirattham, T.; Köbis, E.; Hanif, A. Hermite–Hadamard–Mercer Inequalities Associated with Twice-Differentiable Functions with Applications. *Axioms* **2024**, *13*, 114. https://doi.org/10.3390/axioms13020114

Academic Editor: Péter Kórus

Received: 20 September 2022
Revised: 12 October 2022
Accepted: 13 October 2022
Published: 8 February 2024

Copyright: © 2024 by the authors. Licensee MDPI, Basel, Switzerland. This article is an open access article distributed under the terms and conditions of the Creative Commons Attribution (CC BY) license (https://creativecommons.org/licenses/by/4.0/).

1. Introduction

The inequality commonly referred to as Hadamard's inequality, named after Charles Hermite and Jacques Hadamard, asserts that for a function $\varphi : [\sigma, \varsigma] \to \mathbb{R}$ is convex, the following double inequality is valid:

$$\varphi\left(\frac{\sigma+\varsigma}{2}\right) \leq \frac{1}{\varsigma-\sigma}\int_{\sigma}^{\varsigma}\varphi(\omega)d\omega \leq \frac{\varphi(\sigma)+\varphi(\varsigma)}{2}. \tag{1}$$

If φ is a concave mapping, the reverse of the inequality stated above is true. The proof of the inequality (1) can be established through the application of the Jensen inequality. Extensive research has been conducted exploring various forms of convexities in the context of Hermite–Hadamard. For example, in [1–4], the authors derived certain inequalities associated with midpoint, trapezoid, Simpson's, and other numerical integration formulas for convex functions.

In 2003, Mercer [5] established an alternative form of Jensen's inequality known as the Jensen–Mercer inequality, which is formulated as

Theorem 1. *For a convex mapping $\varphi : [\sigma, \varsigma] \to \mathbb{R}$, The subsequent inequality is valid for all values of $\omega_j \in [\sigma, \varsigma]$ $(j = 1, \ldots, n)$:*

$$\varphi\left(\sigma + \varsigma - \sum_{j=i}^{n} u_j \omega_j\right) \leq \varphi(\sigma) + \varphi(\varsigma) - \sum_{j=1}^{n} u_j \varphi(\omega_j),$$

where $u_j \in [0,1]$ $(j = 1, \ldots, n)$ and $\sum_{j=1}^{n} u_j = 1$.

In 2019, Moradi and Furuichi, as documented in [6], focused on enhancing and extending Jensen–Mercer-type inequalities. Then, in 2020, Adil Khan et al. [7] demonstrated the practical applications of the Jensen–Mercer inequality in information theory. Their work involved calculating novel estimates for Csiszár and associated divergences. Additionally, he established fresh limits for Zipf–Mandelbrot entropy using the Jensen–Mercer inequality.

Kian et al. [8] applied the recently introduced Jensen inequality to derive novel formulations of the Hermite–Hadamard inequality as follows:

Theorem 2. *For a convex mapping $\varphi : [\sigma, \varsigma] \to \mathbb{R}$, the subsequent inequalities are valid for every value of $\omega, y \in [\sigma, \varsigma]$ and $\omega < y$:*

$$\varphi\left(\sigma + \varsigma - \frac{\omega + y}{2}\right) \leq \varphi(\sigma) + \varphi(\varsigma) - \frac{1}{y - \omega}\int_\omega^y \varphi(u)du \leq \varphi(\sigma) + \varphi(\varsigma) - \varphi\left(\frac{\omega + y}{2}\right) \quad (2)$$

and

$$\begin{aligned}
\varphi\left(\sigma + \varsigma - \frac{\omega + y}{2}\right) &\leq \frac{1}{y - \omega}\int_{\sigma+\varsigma-y}^{\sigma+\varsigma-\omega} \varphi(u)du \\
&\leq \frac{\varphi(\sigma + \varsigma - \omega) + \varphi(\sigma + \varsigma - y)}{2} \\
&\leq \varphi(\sigma) + \varphi(\varsigma) - \frac{\varphi(\omega) + \varphi(y)}{2}.
\end{aligned} \quad (3)$$

Remark 1. *The transformation of the inequality (3) into the classical Hermite–Hadamard inequality (1) for convex functions is readily apparent by setting $\sigma = \omega$, $\varsigma = y$.*

After that, many researchers tended towards these useful inequalities and succeeded in proving different new variants of Hermite–Hadamard–Mercer inequalities. For example, in [9–11], the authors applied the Riemann–Liouville fractional integrals and established Hermite–Hadamard–Mercer-type inequalities with their estimates for differentiable convex functions. In [12], Set et al. demonstrated some new Hermite–Hadamard–Mercer-type inequalities for generalized fractional integrals, and each inequality demonstrated here is a family of inequalities for different fractional operators. Chu et al. [13] proved some new estimates of Hermite–Hadamard–Mercer inequalities for fractional integral and differentiable functions. Recently, Sial et al. [14] demonstrated Ostrowski's type inequalities using the Jensen–Mercer inequality for differentiable functions. Kara et al. [15] used the convexity for interval-valued functions and demonstrated fractional Hermite–Hadamard–Mercer-type inequalities. The authors applied the concept of harmonically convex functions and established Hermite–Hadamard–Mercer inequalities with their estimates in [16].

So far, the Hermite–Hadamard–Mercer inequalities for twice-differentiable functions have not been established as Hermite–Hadamard-type inequalities are proved. This is the reason we employ double differentiability and introduce novel midpoint approximations for the Hermite-Hadamard-Mercer inequality applicable to convex functions. These inequalities are new and a generalization of some inequalities existing in the literature. We also observe that the bounds proved here are better than the already established ones.

2. Main Results

In this section, we establish novel midpoint-type inequalities by employing the Jensen–Mercer inequality for convex functions.

Begin by considering the following lemma.

Lemma 1. *Let $\varphi : [\sigma, \varsigma] \to \mathbb{R}$ be a twice-differentiable mapping. If φ is integrable and continuous, then the following equality holds for all $\omega, y \in [\sigma, \varsigma]$ and $\omega < y$:*

$$\frac{1}{y-\omega}\int_{\sigma+\varsigma-y}^{\sigma+\varsigma-\omega}\varphi(w)dw - \varphi\left(\sigma+\varsigma-\left(\frac{\omega+y}{2}\right)\right) \tag{4}$$
$$= \frac{(y-\omega)^2}{16}\left[\int_0^1 \theta^2\left[\varphi''\left(\sigma+\varsigma-\left(\frac{\theta}{2}y+\frac{2-\theta}{2}\omega\right)\right) + \varphi''\left(\sigma+\varsigma-\left(\frac{\theta}{2}\omega+\frac{2-\theta}{2}y\right)\right)\right]d\theta\right].$$

Proof. From the right side of (4), we have

$$\int_0^1 \theta^2\left[\varphi''\left(\sigma+\varsigma-\left(\frac{\theta}{2}y+\frac{2-\theta}{2}\omega\right)\right) + \varphi''\left(\sigma+\varsigma-\left(\frac{\theta}{2}\omega+\frac{2-\theta}{2}y\right)\right)\right]d\theta \tag{5}$$
$$= \int_0^1 \theta^2 \varphi''\left(\sigma+\varsigma-\left(\frac{\theta}{2}y+\frac{2-\theta}{2}\omega\right)\right)d\theta + \int_0^1 \theta^2 \varphi''\left(\sigma+\varsigma-\left(\frac{\theta}{2}\omega+\frac{2-\theta}{2}y\right)\right)d\theta$$
$$= I_1 + I_2.$$

Using the fundamental rules for integration by parts, we have

$$I_1 = \int_0^1 \theta^2 \varphi''\left(\sigma+\varsigma-\left(\frac{\theta}{2}y+\frac{2-\theta}{2}\omega\right)\right)d\theta \tag{6}$$
$$= -\frac{2\theta^2}{y-\omega}\varphi'\left(\sigma+\varsigma-\left(\frac{\theta}{2}y+\frac{2-\theta}{2}\omega\right)\right)\bigg|_0^1 + \frac{4}{y-\omega}\int_0^1 \theta \varphi'\left(\sigma+\varsigma-\left(\frac{\theta}{2}y+\frac{2-\theta}{2}\omega\right)\right)d\theta$$
$$= -\frac{2}{y-\omega}\varphi'\left(\sigma+\varsigma-\left(\frac{\omega+y}{2}\right)\right) + \frac{4}{y-\omega}\left[-\frac{2\theta}{y-\omega}\varphi\left(\sigma+\varsigma-\left(\frac{\theta}{2}y+\frac{2-\theta}{2}\omega\right)\right)\bigg|_0^1\right.$$
$$\left. +\frac{2}{y-\omega}\int_0^1 \varphi\left(\sigma+\varsigma-\left(\frac{\theta}{2}y+\frac{2-\theta}{2}\omega\right)\right)d\theta\right]$$
$$= -\frac{2}{y-\omega}\varphi'\left(\sigma+\varsigma-\left(\frac{\omega+y}{2}\right)\right) - \frac{8}{(y-\omega)^2}\varphi\left(\sigma+\varsigma-\left(\frac{\omega+y}{2}\right)\right)$$
$$+\frac{8}{(y-\omega)^2}\int_0^1 \varphi\left(\sigma+\varsigma-\left(\frac{\theta}{2}y+\frac{2-\theta}{2}\omega\right)\right)d\theta$$
$$= -\frac{2}{y-\omega}\varphi'\left(\sigma+\varsigma-\left(\frac{\omega+y}{2}\right)\right) - \frac{8}{(y-\omega)^2}\varphi\left(\sigma+\varsigma-\left(\frac{\omega+y}{2}\right)\right) + \frac{16}{(y-\omega)^3}\int_{\sigma+\varsigma-\frac{\omega+y}{2}}^{\sigma+\varsigma-\omega}\varphi(w)dw.$$

Similarly, we have

$$\int_0^1 \theta^2 \varphi''\left(\sigma+\varsigma-\left(\frac{\theta}{2}\omega+\frac{2-\theta}{2}y\right)\right)d\theta \tag{7}$$
$$= \frac{2}{y-\omega}\varphi'\left(\sigma+\varsigma-\left(\frac{\omega+y}{2}\right)\right) - \frac{8}{(y-\omega)^2}\varphi\left(\sigma+\varsigma-\left(\frac{\omega+y}{2}\right)\right) + \frac{16}{(y-\omega)^3}\int_{\sigma+\varsigma-y}^{\sigma+\varsigma-\frac{\omega+y}{2}}\varphi(w)dw.$$

Thus, we obtain the required equality by using (6) and (7) in (5). □

Remark 2. *For $\omega = \sigma$ and $y = \varsigma$, we can express the equality as follows:*

$$\frac{1}{\varsigma-\sigma}\int_\sigma^\varsigma \varphi(w)dw - \varphi\left(\frac{\sigma+\varsigma}{2}\right) \tag{8}$$
$$= \frac{(\varsigma-\sigma)^2}{16}\left[\int_0^1 \theta^2\left[\varphi''\left(\frac{\theta}{2}\sigma+\frac{2-\theta}{2}\varsigma\right) + \varphi''\left(\frac{\theta}{2}\varsigma+\frac{2-\theta}{2}\sigma\right)\right]d\theta\right].$$

This reduces to a result by Sarikaya and Kiris in [17].

Theorem 3. *If conditions of Lemma 1 hold and $|\varphi''|$ is convex, then we have the following inequality:*

$$\left| \frac{1}{y-\omega} \int_{\sigma+\varsigma-y}^{\sigma+\varsigma-\omega} \varphi(w)dw - \varphi\left(\sigma+\varsigma - \left(\frac{\omega+y}{2}\right)\right) \right| \qquad (9)$$
$$\leq \frac{(y-\omega)^2}{16} \left[\frac{2}{3}(|\varphi''(\sigma)| + |\varphi''(\varsigma)|) - \frac{1}{3}(|\varphi''(\omega)| + |\varphi''(y)|) \right].$$

Proof. Using the equality (4) and the Jensen–Mercer inequality, we obtain

$$\left| \frac{1}{y-\omega} \int_{\sigma+\varsigma-y}^{\sigma+\varsigma-\omega} \varphi(w)dw - \varphi\left(\sigma+\varsigma - \left(\frac{\omega+y}{2}\right)\right) \right|$$
$$\leq \frac{(y-\omega)^2}{16} \left[\int_0^1 \theta^2 \left|\varphi''\left(\sigma+\varsigma - \left(\frac{\theta}{2}y + \frac{2-\theta}{2}\omega\right)\right)\right| d\theta \right.$$
$$\left. + \int_0^1 \theta^2 \left|\varphi''\left(\sigma+\varsigma - \left(\frac{\theta}{2}\omega + \frac{2-\theta}{2}y\right)\right)\right| d\theta \right]$$
$$\leq \frac{(y-\omega)^2}{16} \left[\int_0^1 \theta^2 \left(|\varphi''(\sigma)| + |\varphi''(\varsigma)| - \left(\frac{\theta}{2}|\varphi''(y)| + \frac{2-\theta}{2}|\varphi''(\omega)|\right)\right) d\theta \right.$$
$$\left. + \int_0^1 \theta^2 \left(|\varphi''(\sigma)| + |\varphi''(\varsigma)| - \left(\frac{\theta}{2}|\varphi''(\omega)| + \frac{2-\theta}{2}|\varphi''(y)|\right)\right) d\theta \right]$$
$$= \frac{(y-\omega)^2}{16} \left[\frac{2}{3}(|\varphi''(\sigma)| + |\varphi''(\varsigma)|) - \frac{1}{3}(|\varphi''(\omega)| + |\varphi''(y)|) \right]$$

which completes the proof. □

Remark 3. *For $\omega = \sigma$ and $y = \varsigma$, we get the following inequality:*

$$\left| \frac{1}{\varsigma-\sigma} \int_\sigma^\varsigma \varphi(w)dw - \varphi\left(\frac{\sigma+\varsigma}{2}\right) \right|$$
$$\leq \frac{(y-\omega)^2}{48} \left[|\varphi''(\sigma)| + |\varphi''(\varsigma)| \right].$$

This is established by Sarikaya and Kiris in [17] (Theorem 3 for $s = 1$).

Theorem 4. *If conditions of Lemma 1 hold and $|\varphi''|^q$, $q \geq 1$ is convex, then we have the following inequality:*

$$\left| \frac{1}{y-\omega} \int_{\sigma+\varsigma-y}^{\sigma+\varsigma-\omega} \varphi(w)dw - \varphi\left(\sigma+\varsigma - \left(\frac{\omega+y}{2}\right)\right) \right| \qquad (10)$$
$$\leq \frac{(y-\omega)^2}{16} \left(\frac{1}{3}\right)^{1-\frac{1}{q}} \left[\left(\frac{1}{3}(|\varphi''(\sigma)|^q + |\varphi''(\varsigma)|^q) - \frac{1}{8}\left(|\varphi''(\omega)|^q + \frac{5}{3}|\varphi''(y)|^q\right) \right)^{\frac{1}{q}} \right.$$
$$\left. + \left(\frac{1}{3}(|\varphi''(\sigma)|^q + |\varphi''(\varsigma)|^q) - \frac{1}{8}\left(|\varphi''(y)|^q + \frac{5}{3}|\varphi''(\omega)|^q\right) \right)^{\frac{1}{q}} \right].$$

Proof. From the equality (4) and employing the power mean inequality, we obtain:

$$\left| \frac{1}{y-\omega} \int_{\sigma+\varsigma-y}^{\sigma+\varsigma-\omega} \varphi(w)dw - \varphi\left(\sigma+\varsigma - \left(\frac{\omega+y}{2}\right)\right) \right|$$
$$\leq \frac{(y-\omega)^2}{16} \left[\int_0^1 \theta^2 \left|\varphi''\left(\sigma+\varsigma - \left(\frac{\theta}{2}y + \frac{2-\theta}{2}\omega\right)\right)\right| d\theta \right.$$
$$\left. + \int_0^1 \theta^2 \left|\varphi''\left(\sigma+\varsigma - \left(\frac{\theta}{2}\omega + \frac{2-\theta}{2}y\right)\right)\right| d\theta \right]$$

$$\leq \frac{(y-\omega)^2}{16} \left(\int_0^1 \theta^2 d\theta\right)^{1-\frac{1}{q}} \left[\left(\int_0^1 \theta^2 \left|\varphi''\left(\sigma+\varsigma-\left(\frac{\theta}{2}y+\frac{2-\theta}{2}\omega\right)\right)\right|^q d\theta\right)^{\frac{1}{q}}\right.$$
$$\left.+\left(\int_0^1 \theta^2 \left|\varphi''\left(\sigma+\varsigma-\left(\frac{\theta}{2}\omega+\frac{2-\theta}{2}y\right)\right)\right|^q d\theta\right)^{\frac{1}{q}}\right].$$

According to the Jensen–Mercer inequality, we can express it as

$$\left|\frac{1}{y-\omega}\int_{\sigma+\varsigma-y}^{\sigma+\varsigma-\omega}\varphi(w)dw - \varphi\left(\sigma+\varsigma-\left(\frac{\omega+y}{2}\right)\right)\right|$$
$$\leq \frac{(y-\omega)^2}{16}\left(\frac{1}{3}\right)^{1-\frac{1}{q}}\left[\left(\frac{1}{3}\left(|\varphi''(\sigma)|^q+|\varphi''(\varsigma)|^q\right)-\frac{1}{8}\left(|\varphi''(\omega)|^q+\frac{5}{3}|\varphi''(y)|^q\right)\right)^{\frac{1}{q}}\right.$$
$$\left.+\left(\frac{1}{3}\left(|\varphi''(\sigma)|^q+|\varphi''(\varsigma)|^q\right)-\frac{1}{8}\left(|\varphi''(y)|^q+\frac{5}{3}|\varphi''(\omega)|^q\right)\right)^{\frac{1}{q}}\right].$$

Hence, the proof is completed. □

Remark 4. *For $\omega = \sigma$ and $y = \varsigma$ in Theorem 4, we have the following inequality:*

$$\left|\frac{1}{\varsigma-\sigma}\int_\sigma^\varsigma \varphi(w)dw - \varphi\left(\frac{\sigma+\varsigma}{2}\right)\right|$$
$$\leq \frac{(\varsigma-\sigma)^2}{16}\left(\frac{1}{3}\right)^{1-\frac{1}{q}}\left[\left(\frac{5}{24}|\varphi''(\sigma)|^q+\frac{1}{8}|\varphi''(\varsigma)|^q\right)^{\frac{1}{q}}\right.$$
$$\left.+\left(\frac{1}{8}|\varphi''(\sigma)|^q+\frac{5}{24}|\varphi''(\varsigma)|^q\right)^{\frac{1}{q}}\right].$$

This is established by Sarikaya and Kiris in [17] (Theorem 5 for $s = 1$).

Theorem 5. *If conditions of Lemma 1 hold and $|\varphi''|^q$, $q > 1$ is convex, then we have the following inequality:*

$$\left|\frac{1}{y-\omega}\int_{\sigma+\varsigma-y}^{\sigma+\varsigma-\omega}\varphi(w)dw - \varphi\left(\sigma+\varsigma-\left(\frac{\omega+y}{2}\right)\right)\right|$$
$$\leq \frac{(y-\omega)^2}{16 \times 2^{p+1}}\left[\left(|\varphi''(\sigma)|^q+|\varphi''(\varsigma)|^q - \left(\frac{|\varphi''(y)|^q+3|\varphi''(\omega)|^q}{4}\right)\right)^{\frac{1}{q}}\right.$$
$$\left.+\left(|\varphi''(\sigma)|^q+|\varphi''(\varsigma)|^q - \left(\frac{3|\varphi''(y)|^q+|\varphi''(\omega)|^q}{4}\right)\right)^{\frac{1}{q}}\right].$$

Proof. From the equality (4) and Hölder inequality, we get

$$\left|\frac{1}{y-\omega}\int_{\sigma+\varsigma-y}^{\sigma+\varsigma-\omega}\varphi(w)dw - \varphi\left(\sigma+\varsigma-\left(\frac{\omega+y}{2}\right)\right)\right|$$
$$\leq \frac{(y-\omega)^2}{16}\left(\int_0^1 \theta^{2p}d\theta\right)^{\frac{1}{p}}\left[\left(\int_0^1 \left|\varphi''\left(\sigma+\varsigma-\left(\frac{\theta}{2}y+\frac{2-\theta}{2}\omega\right)\right)\right|^q d\theta\right)^{\frac{1}{q}}\right.$$
$$\left.+\left(\int_0^1 \left|\varphi''\left(\sigma+\varsigma-\left(\frac{\theta}{2}\omega+\frac{2-\theta}{2}y\right)\right)\right|^q d\theta\right)^{\frac{1}{q}}\right].$$

From the Jensen–Mercer inequality, we have

$$\left| \frac{1}{y-\omega} \int_{\sigma+\varsigma-y}^{\sigma+\varsigma-\omega} \varphi(w)dw - \varphi\left(\sigma+\varsigma-\left(\frac{\omega+y}{2}\right)\right)\right|$$
$$\leq \frac{(y-\omega)^2}{16 \times 2^{p+1}} \left[\left(|\varphi''(\sigma)|^q + |\varphi''(\varsigma)|^q - \left(\frac{|\varphi''(y)|^q + 3|\varphi''(\omega)|^q}{4}\right)\right)^{\frac{1}{q}} \right.$$
$$\left. + \left(|\varphi''(\sigma)|^q + |\varphi''(\varsigma)|^q - \left(\frac{3|\varphi''(y)|^q + |\varphi''(\omega)|^q}{4}\right)\right)^{\frac{1}{q}} \right].$$

Thus, the proof is completed. □

Remark 5. *For $\omega = \sigma$ and $y = \varsigma$ in Theorem 5, we obtain [17] (Theorem 4 for $s = 1$).*

3. Applications

In this section, we present practical uses for the specific mean of real numbers. For any given positive real numbers σ, ς ($\sigma \neq \varsigma$), we establish the following definitions for means:

(1) The arithmetic mean
$$A(\sigma, \varsigma) = \frac{\sigma + \varsigma}{2},$$

(2) The harmonic mean
$$H(\sigma, \varsigma) = \frac{2\sigma\varsigma}{\sigma + \varsigma},$$

(3) The logarithmic mean
$$L(\sigma, \varsigma) = \frac{\varsigma - \sigma}{\ln \varsigma - \ln \sigma},$$

(4) The p-logarithmic mean for $p \in \mathbb{R} - \{-1, 0\}$
$$L_p(\sigma, \varsigma) = \left[\frac{\varsigma^{p+1} - \sigma^{p+1}}{(p+1)(\varsigma - \sigma)}\right]^{\frac{1}{p}}.$$

Proposition 1. *For the function $\varphi : [\sigma, \varsigma] \to \mathbb{R}$, the following inequality holds for $\omega, y \in [\sigma, \varsigma]$ and $\omega < y$:*

$$\left| L_2^2(\sigma + \varsigma - y, \sigma + \varsigma - \omega) - (2A(\sigma, \varsigma) - A(\omega, y))\right|$$
$$\leq \frac{(y - \omega)^2}{12}.$$

Proof. The proof can be done for $\varphi(w) = w^2$ in Theorems 3 and 4. □

Proposition 2. *For the function $\varphi : [\sigma, \varsigma] \to \mathbb{R}$, the following inequality holds for $\omega, y \in [\sigma, \varsigma]$ and $\omega < y$:*

$$\left| L_2^2(\sigma + \varsigma - y, \sigma + \varsigma - \omega) - (2A(\sigma, \varsigma) - A(\omega, y))\right|$$
$$\leq \frac{4^{1-\frac{1}{q}}(y - \omega)^2}{16 \times 2^{p+1}}.$$

Proof. The proof can be done for $\varphi(w) = w^2$ in Theorem 5. □

Proposition 3. *For the function* $\varphi : [\sigma, \varsigma] \to \mathbb{R}$, *the following inequality holds for* $\omega, y \in [\sigma, \varsigma]$ *and* $\omega < y$:

$$\left| L^{-1}(\sigma + \varsigma - y, \sigma + \varsigma - \omega) - (2A(\sigma, \varsigma) - A(\omega, y))^{-1} \right|$$
$$\leq \frac{(y-\omega)^2}{48} \left[8H^{-1}\left(\sigma^3, \varsigma^3\right) - 4H^{-1}\left(\omega^3, y^3\right) \right].$$

Proof. The proof can be done for $\varphi(w) = \frac{1}{w}$, $w \neq 0$ in Theorem 3. □

4. Concluding Remarks

This study establishes novel Hermite–Hadamard–Mercer-type inequalities applicable to twice differentiable convex functions. Furthermore, it demonstrates that these newly derived inequalities serve as generalizations of certain previously established inequalities in [17]. Several applications involving specific properties of real numbers, utilizing recently established inequalities, are also presented. This presents an intriguing and innovative challenge for future researchers aiming to derive analogous inequalities for increased differentiability and various forms of convexity. It presents an intriguing challenge for upcoming researchers to derive analogous inequalities for various fractional integrals by employing convexity and non-fractal sets.

Author Contributions: Conceptualization, M.A.A., T.S., E.K. and A.H.; Funding acquisition, T.S. and E.K.; Investigation, M.A.A., T.S., E.K. and A.H.; Methodology, M.A.A., T.S. and E.K.; Supervision, T.S. and E.K.; Validation, M.A.A., T.S., E.K. and A.H.; Visualization, M.A.A., T.S., E.K. and A.H.; Writing original draft, M.A.A., T.S., E.K. and A.H.; Writing review & editing, M.A.A., T.S., E.K. and A.H. All authors have read and agreed to the published version of the manuscript.

Funding: This project is funded by National Research Council of Thailand (NRCT) and Suan Dusit University: N42A650384.

Institutional Review Board Statement: Not applicable

Informed Consent Statement: Not applicable.

Data Availability Statement: Not applicable.

Acknowledgments: We thanks the referees and the editor for their valuable comments.

Conflicts of Interest: The authors declare no conflict of interest.

References

1. Kirmaci, U.S. Inequalities for differentiable mappings and applications to special means of real numbers and to midpoint formula. *Appl. Math. Comput.*, **2004**, *147*, 137–146. [CrossRef]
2. Dragomir, S.S.; Agarwal, R.P. Two inequalities for differentiable mappings and applications to special means of real numbers and to trapezoidal formula. *Appl. Math. Lett.* **1998**, *11*, 91–95. [CrossRef]
3. Set, E.; Akdemir, A.O.; Ozdemir, E.M. Simpson type integral inequalities for convex functions via Riemann-Liouville integrals. *Filomat* **2017**, *31*, 4415–4420. [CrossRef]
4. Nie, D.; Rashid, S.; Akdemir, A.O.; Baleanu, D.; Liu, J.B. On some new weighted inequalities for differentiable exponentially convex and exponentially quasi-convex functions with applications. *Mathematics* **2019**, *7*, 727. [CrossRef]
5. Mercer, A.M. A Variant of Jensen's Inequality. *J. Inequalities Pure Appl. Math.* **2003**, *4*, 73.
6. Moradi, H.R.; Furuichi, S. Improvement and generalization of some Jensen–Mercer-type inequalities. *J. Math. Inequalities* **2007**, *14*, 377–383. [CrossRef]
7. Khan, M.A.; Husain, Z.; Chu, Y.M. New estimates for Csiszár divergence and Zipf–Mandelbrot entropy via Jensen–Mercer's inequality. *Complexity* **2022**, *2020*, 8928691.
8. Kian, M.; Moslehian, M.S. Refinements of the operator Jensen–Mercer inequality. *Electron. J. Linear Algebra* **2013**, *26*, 742–753. [CrossRef]
9. Öğülmxuxş, H.; Sarikaya, M.Z. Hermite-Hadamard-Mercer-type inequalities for fractional integrals. *Filomat* **2021**, *35*, 2425–2436. [CrossRef]
10. Wang, H.; Khan, J.; Khan, M.A.; Khalid, S.; Khan, R. The Hermite–Hadamard-Jensen–Mercer-type inequalities for Riemann–Liouville fractional integral. *J. Math.* **2021**, *2021*, 5516987. [CrossRef]

11. Abdeljawad, T.; Ali, M.A.; Mohammed, P.O.; Kashuri, A. On inequalities of Hermite–Hadamard-Mercer-type involving Riemann–Liouville fractional integrals. *AIMS Math.* **2021**, *6*, 712–725. [CrossRef]
12. Set, E.; Çelik, B.; Özdemir, M.E.; Aslan, M. Some New results on Hermite–Hadamard-Mercer-type inequalities using a general family of fractional integral operators. *Fractal Fract.* **2021**, *5*, 68. [CrossRef]
13. Chu, H.H.; Rashid, S.; Hammouch, Z.; Chu, Y.M. New fractional estimates for Hermite–Hadamard-Mercer's type inequalities. *Alex. Eng. J.* **2020**, *59*, 3079–3089. [CrossRef]
14. Sial, I.B.; Patanarapeelert, N.; Ali, M.A.; Budak, H.; Sitthiwirattham, T. On some new Ostrowski-Mercer-type inequalities for differentiable functions. *Axioms* **2022**, *11*, 132. [CrossRef]
15. Kara, H.; Ali, M.A.; Budak, H. Hermite–Hadamard–Mercer-type inclusions for interval-valued functions via Riemann–Liouville fractional integrals. *Turk. J. Math.* **2022**, *46*, 2193–2207. [CrossRef]
16. Butt, S.I.; Yousaf, S.; Asghar, A.; Khan, K.A.; Moradi, H.R. New Fractional Hermite–Hadamard–Mercer Inequalities for Harmonically Convex Function. *J. Funct. Spaces* **2021**, *2021*, 5868326. [CrossRef]
17. Sarikaya, M.Z.; Kiris, M.E. Some new inequalities of Hermite–Hadamard-type for s-convex functions. *Miskolc Math. Notes* **2015**, *16*, 491–501. [CrossRef]

Disclaimer/Publisher's Note: The statements, opinions and data contained in all publications are solely those of the individual author(s) and contributor(s) and not of MDPI and/or the editor(s). MDPI and/or the editor(s) disclaim responsibility for any injury to people or property resulting from any ideas, methods, instructions or products referred to in the content.

MDPI
St. Alban-Anlage 66
4052 Basel
Switzerland
www.mdpi.com

Axioms Editorial Office
E-mail: axioms@mdpi.com
www.mdpi.com/journal/axioms

Disclaimer/Publisher's Note: The statements, opinions and data contained in all publications are solely those of the individual author(s) and contributor(s) and not of MDPI and/or the editor(s). MDPI and/or the editor(s) disclaim responsibility for any injury to people or property resulting from any ideas, methods, instructions or products referred to in the content.

www.ingramcontent.com/pod-product-compliance
Lightning Source LLC
LaVergne TN
LVHW070152120526
838202LV00013BA/1005